I0024962

H. H. (Horace Hayman) Wilson

The Vishnu Purana a System of Hindu Mythology and Tradition

Translated from the Original Sanskrit, and Illustrated by Notes

Derived Chiefly from Other Puranas

H. H. (Horace Hayman) Wilson

The Vishnu Purana a System of Hindu Mythology and Tradition Translated from the Original Sanskrit, and Illustrated by Notes Derived Chiefly from Other Puranas

ISBN/EAN: 9783741151750

Manufactured in Europe, USA, Canada, Australia, Japa

Cover: Foto ©Thomas Meinert / pixelio.de

Manufactured and distributed by brebook publishing software
(www.brebook.com)

H. H. (Horace Hayman) Wilson

The Vishnu Purana a System of Hindu Mythology and Tradition

Translated from the Original Sanskrit, and Illustrated by Notes

Derived Chiefly from Other Puranas

THE

VISHŃU PURÁŃA:

A SYSTEM

OF

HINDU MYTHOLOGY AND TRADITION.

TRANSLATED

FROM THE ORIGINAL SANSKRIT,

AND

ILLUSTRATED BY NOTES

DERIVED CHIEFLY FROM OTHER PURÁŃAS,

BY THE LATE

H. H. WILSON, M.A., F.R.S.,

BODEN PROFESSOR OF SANSKRIT IN THE UNIVERSITY OF OXFORD,
ETC., ETC.

EDITED BY

FITZEDWARD HALL.

VOL. IV.

LONDON:

TRÜBNER & CO., 60, PATERNOSTER ROW.

1868.

VISHṆU PURÁṆA.

BOOK IV. (continued).

CHAPTER VI.

Kings of the lunar dynasty. Origin of Soma or the Moon: he carries off Tárá, the wife of Bṛihaspati: war between the gods and Asuras, in consequence: appeased by Brahmá. Birth of Budha: married to Ilá, daughter of Vaivaswata. Legend of his son Purúravas and the nymph Urvaśí: the former institutes offerings with fire: ascends to the sphere of the Gandharvas.

MAITREYA.—You have given me, reverend (preceptor), an account of (the kings of) the dynasty of the Sun. I am now desirous to hear a description of the princes who trace their lineage from the Moon, and whose race is still celebrated for glorious deeds. Thou art able to relate it to me, Brahman, if thou wilt so favour me.

PARÁŚARA.—You shall hear from me, Maitreya,* an account of the illustrious family of the Moon, which has produced (many celebrated) rulers of the earth,—a race adorned by (the regal qualities of) strength, valour, magnificence, prudence,† and activity, and enumerating, amongst its monarchs, Nahusha, Yayáti,

* Literally, "tiger of a sage," *muni-śárdúla*. See Vol. III., p. 118, note §.

† *Dyuti* and *śíla*.

Kártavíryárjuna,* and others equally renowned. That race will I describe to you. Do you attend.

Atri was the son of Brahmá, the creator of the universe, who sprang from the lotos that grew from the navel of Náráyańa. The son of Atri was Soma[1] (the moon), whom Brahmá† installed as the sovereign of plants, of Brahmans, and of the stars.‡ Soma celebrated the Rájasúya (sacrifice); and, from the glory thence acquired, and the extensive dominion with which he had been invested, he became arrogant (and licentious), and carried off Tárá, the wife of Bŕihaspati, the preceptor of the gods. In vain Bŕihaspati sought to recover his bride; in vain Brahmá commanded, and the holy sages remonstrated: Soma refused to relinquish her.§ Uśanas,‖ out of enmity to Bŕihaspati, took part with Soma.¶ Rudra, who had studied under Angiras,

---

[1] The Váyu says, the essence of Soma (Somatwa) issued from the eyes of Atri, and impregnated the ten quarters. The Bhágavata** says, merely, that Soma was born from the eyes of Atri. The Brahma Puráńa and Hari Vaḿśa give a grosser name to the effusion.

---

* That is to say, Arjuna, son of Kŕitavírya. See, for him, Chapter XI. of this Book.

† Called, in the original, by his epithet *abjayoni*.

‡ Compare Vol. II., p. 85.

§ बहुशश्च बृहस्पतिचोदितेन ब्रह्मणा चोद्यमानः सकलदेवर्षिभिर्याच्यमानोऽपि न मुमोच ।

‖ In the corresponding passage of the *Bhágavata-puráńa*,—IX., XIV., 6,—the name is Śukra. For the discordant accounts of the parentage of Uśanas, see Vol. II., p. 152, note 1: for Śukra, *ibid.*, pp. 117, 155.

¶ तस्य हि बृहस्पतिद्वेषादुशना पार्ष्णिग्राहोऽभवत् ।

** IX., XIV., 3.

(the father of Bríhaspati*), befriended his fellow-student. In consequence of Uśanas, their preceptor, joining Soma, Jambha, Kujambha, and all the Daityas, Dánavas, and other foes of the gods, came, also, to his assistance;† whilst Indra and all the gods were the allies of Bríhaspati.‡

Then there ensued a fierce contest, which, being on account of Táraká (or Tárá), was termed the Tárakámaya or Táraká war.§ In this, the gods, led by Rudra, hurled their missiles on the enemy; and the Daityas¶ (with equal determination assailed) the gods. Earth, shaken to her centre by the struggle between such foes, had recourse to Brahmá, for protection; on which he interposed, and, commanding Uśanas, with the demons, and Rudra** with the deities, to desist from strife, compelled Soma to restore Tárá to her husband.†† Finding that she was pregnant,‡‡ Bríhaspati desired her no longer to retain her burthen;§§ and, in obedience to his orders, she was delivered of a son,

* See Vol. I., p. 153, note 9.

† सहायमुशनं चक्रुः ।

‡ बृहस्पतेरपि सकलदेवसैन्यसहायः शक्रोऽभवत् ।

§ एवं च तयोरतीवोग्रः संग्रामस्तारकानिमित्तस्तारकामयो नामाभवत् । Nílakańtha, commenting on the *Mahábhárata*, *Sabhá-parvan*, *ll.* 939, explains the term *tárakámaya* as follows: तारका तारा बृहस्पतिभार्या । सैव कामयमानिनाशहेतुर्यस्मिन् । कामयो रोगः ।

|| *Asura.*

¶ Dánavas, in the original.

** Substituted for Śankara.

†† बृहस्पतेस्तारामदात् ।

‡‡ *Antahprasavá.*

§§ नैव मम क्षेत्रे भवत्यान्यसुतो धार्यस्समुत्सृजैनमलमतिधार्ष्ट्येनेति ।

whom she deposited in a clump of long Munja-grass.* The child, from the moment of its birth, was endued with a splendour that dimmed the radiance of every (other) divinity; and both Bṛihaspati and Soma,† fascinated by his beauty, claimed him as their child. The gods, in order to settle the dispute, appealed to Tárá; but she was ashamed, and would make no answer. As she still continued mute to their repeated applications, the child (became incensed, and) was about to curse her, saying: "Unless, vile woman, you immediately declare who is my father, I will sentence you to such a fate as shall deter every female, in future, from hesitating to speak the truth.": On this, Brahmá§ (again interfered, and) pacified|| the child, and then, addressing Tárá, said: "Tell me, daughter, is this the child of Bṛihaspati? or of Soma?" "Of Soma," said Tárá, blushing.¶ As soon as she had spoken, the lord of the constellations**—his countenance bright, and expanding with rapture,—embraced his son, and said: "Well done, my boy! Verily, thou art wise." And, hence, his name was Budha.[1]

---

[1] 'He who knows.' Much erroneous speculation has originated in confounding this Budha, the son of Soma, and regent of the planet Mercury,—'he who knows,' 'the intelligent,'—

---

* The Sanskrit has *ishíká*, which the scholiast explains to mean *munja*.

† Exchanged for Indu.

‡ दुष्टे कस्मान्मम तातं नाख्यासि । अद्यैव ते शास्तिमयमहं करोमि यथा नैवमन्याप्यतिमन्थरवचना भवतीति ।

§ Pitámaha, in the original.

|| *Saṁnivárya*, 'checking.'

¶ लज्जावत्याह सोमस्येति ।

** *Uḍupati*.

It has already been related how Budha begot Purúravas by Ilá.* Purúravas[1] was (a prince) renowned for liberality, devotion, magnificence, and love of truth, and for personal beauty. Urvaśí, having incurred the imprecation of Mitra and Varuńa, determined to take up her abode in the world of mortals, and (descending, accordingly,) beheld Purúravas. As soon as she saw him, she forgot all reserve, and, disregarding the delights of Swarga, became deeply enamoured of the prince. Beholding her infinitely superior to all other females, in grace, elegance, symmetry, delicacy, and

with Buddha, any deified mortal, or 'he by whom truth is known'; or, as individually applicable,† Gautama or Śákya, son of the Raja Śuddhodana,‡ by whom, the Buddhists themselves aver, their doctrines were first promulgated. The two characters have nothing in common; and the names are identical, only when one or other is misspelt.

[1] The story of Purúravas is told much in the same strain as follows, though with some variations, and in greater or less detail, in the Váyu, Matsya, Vámana, Padma, and Bhágavata Puráńas. It is, also, referred to in the Mahábhárata, Vol. I., p. 113. It is, likewise, the subject of the Vikrama and Urvaśí of Kálidása, in which drama the incidents offensive to good taste are not noticed. See Hindu Theatre, Vol. I., p. 187. The Matsya Puráńa, besides this story, which is translated in the introduction to the drama, has, in another part,—c. 94,—an account of a Purúravas who, in the Chákshusha Manwantara,§ was king of Madra, and who, by the worship of Vishńu, obtained a residence with the Gandharvas.

* See Vol. III., pp. 233—236.

† For a fanciful etymology of the name Buddha, as denoting the founder of Buddhism, see Vol. III., p. 210, note §.

‡ See Chapter XXII. of this Book.

§ See Vol. III., p. 2.

beauty, Purúravas was equally fascinated by Urvaśí. Both were inspired by similar sentiments, and, mutually feeling that each was everything to the other, thought no more of any other object.* Confiding in his merits, Purúravas addressed the nymph, and said:† "Fair creature, I love you. Have compassion on me, and return my affection." Urvaśí, half averting her face, through modesty, replied:‡ "I will do so, if you will observe the conditions I have to propose."§ "What are they?" inquired the prince. "Declare them." "I have two rams,"‖ said the nymph, "which I love as children. They must be kept near my bedside, and never suffered to be carried away.¶ You must, also, take care never to be seen, by me, undressed; and clarified butter alone must be my food." To these terms the king readily gave assent.

After this, Purúravas and Urvaśí dwelt together in Alaká, sporting amidst the groves and lotos-crowned lakes** of Chaitraratha†† and the other forests there situated, for sixty-one thousand years.[1] The love of

---

[1] One copy has sixty-one years; the Brahma Puráńa and

---

* उभयमपि तन्मनस्कमनन्यदृष्टि परित्यक्तसमस्तान्यप्रयोजनमासीत् ।

† राजा तु प्रागल्भ्यात्तामाह । Comment: प्रागल्भ्यात् । असंको-चात् ।

‡ लज्जावखण्डितमुखमुर्वशी प्राह ।

§ The love-making of Purúravas and Urvaśí was somewhat less delicate, as represented in the *Bhágavata-puráńa*, IX., XIV., 18—20.

‖ *Urańaka*, 'lambs'; and so below.

¶ शयनसमीपे ममोरणकद्वयं पुत्रभूतं नापनेयम् ।

** The original has "Mánasa and other lakes": मानसादिषु सरःसु । See Vol. II., p. 110, note *; and p. 117.

†† For this garden, see Vol. II., p. 110, note *; and p. 116.

Purúravas for his bride increased every day of its duration; and, the affection of Urvaśí augmenting equally in fervour, she never called to recollection* residence amongst the immortals. Not so with the attendant spirits at the court of Indra; and nymphs, genii, and quiristers† found heaven itself but dull, whilst Urvaśí was away.‡ Knowing the agreement that Urvaśí had made with the king, Viśwávasu§ was appointed, by the Gandharvas, to effect its violation; and he, coming, by night, to the chamber where they slept, carried off one of the rams. Urvaśí was awakened by its cries, and exclaimed: "Ah me! Who has stolen one of my children? Had I a husband, this would not have happened! To whom shall I apply for aid?" The Raja overheard her lamentation, but, recollecting that he was undressed, and that Urvaśí might see him in that state, did not move from the couch. Then the Gandharvas came and stole the other ram; and Urvaśí, hearing it bleat, cried out, that a woman had no protector, who was the bride of a prince so dastardly as to submit to this outrage. This incensed Purúravas

Hari Vaṃśa‖ have fifty-nine. One period is as likely as the other.

* न स्पृहां चकार ।

† *Apsaras*, *siddha*, and *gandharva*.

‡ विना चोर्वश्या सुरलोकोऽप्सरसां सिद्धगन्धर्वाणां च नातिरमणीयोऽभवत् । The Translator has not cared to reproduce the story of Purúravas and Urvaśí with very close literality.

§ See Vol. II., p. 285, note †; &c.

‖ Śl. 1367.

highly; and, trusting that the nymph would not see his person, as it was dark, he rose, and took his sword, and pursued the robbers, calling upon them to stop and receive their punishment. At that moment the Gandharvas caused a flash of brilliant lightning to play upon the chamber; and Urvaśí beheld the king undressed: the compact was violated; and the nymph immediately disappeared. The Gandharvas, abandoning the rams, departed to the region of the gods.

Having recovered the animals, the king returned, delighted, to his couch: but there he beheld no Urvaśí; and, not finding her anywhere, he wandered, naked, over the world, like one insane. At length, coming to Kurukshetra,* he saw Urvaśí sporting, with four other nymphs of heaven, in a lake beautified with lotoses; and he ran to her, and called her his wife, and wildly implored her to return. "Mighty monarch," said the nymph, "refrain from this extravagance. I am now pregnant.† Depart at present, and come hither, again, at the end of a year, when I will deliver to you a son, and remain with you for one night." Purúravas, thus comforted, returned to his capital. Urvaśí said to her companions: "This prince is a most excellent mortal. I lived with him long and affectionately united." "It was well done of you," they replied. "He is, indeed, of comely appearance, and one with whom we could live happily for ever."

When the year had expired, Urvaśí and the monarch met at Kurukshetra,‡ and she consigned to him his

---

* See Vol. II., p. 133, note 1.

† *Antarvatní.*

‡ This specification of place is supplied by the Translator.

first-born, Ayus; and these annual interviews were repeated, until she had borne to him five sons. She then said to Purúravas: "Through regard for me, all the Gandharvas have expressed their joint purpose to bestow upon my lord their benediction. Let him, therefore, demand a boon." The Raja replied: "My enemies are all destroyed; my faculties are all entire: I have friends and kindred, armies and treasures.* There is nothing which I may not obtain, except living in the same region with my Urvaśí. My only desire, therefore, is, to pass my life with her." When he had thus spoken, the Gandharvas brought to Purúravas a vessel with fire, and said to him: "Take this fire, and, according to the precepts of the Vedas,† divide it into three fires; then, fixing your mind upon the idea of living with Urvaśí, offer oblations; and you shall, assuredly, obtain your wishes." The Raja took the brasier, and departed, and came to a forest. Then he began to reflect, that he had committed a great folly, in bringing away the vessel of fire, instead of his bride; and, leaving the vessel in the wood, he went (disconsolate,) to his palace. In the middle of the night he awoke, and considered that the Gandharvas had given him the brasier to enable him to obtain the felicity of living with Urvaśí, and that it was absurd in him to have left it by the way. Resolving, therefore, to recover it, he rose, and went to the place where he had deposited the vessel; but it was gone. In its stead, he

---

* All my MSS. agree in reading बन्धुमानमितबलकोशः ।

† *Ámnáya*; and so below.

saw a young Aśwattha tree growing out of a Śamí-plant; and he reasoned with himself, and said: "I left, in this spot, a vessel of fire, and now behold a young Aśwattha tree growing out of a Śamí-plant. Verily, I will take these types of fire to my capital, and there, having engendered fire by their attrition, I will worship it."

Having thus determined, he took the plants to his city, and prepared their wood for attrition, with pieces of as many inches* long as there are syllables in the Gáyatrí. He recited that holy verse, and rubbed together sticks of as many inches as he recited syllables in the Gáyatrí.[1] Having thence elicited fire, he made it threefold,† according to the injunctions of the Vedas, and offered oblations with it; proposing, as the end of the ceremony, reunion with Urvaśí. In this way, celebrating many sacrifices, agreeably to the form in which offerings are presented with fire, Purúravas obtained a seat in the sphere of the Gandharvas, and

[1] It does not appear why this passage is repeated. The length of the sticks, conformably to the number of syllables in the usual form of the Gáyatrí, would be twenty-four inches. The Bhágavata attaches to the operation a piece of mysticism of a Tántrika origin. Purúravas, whilst performing the attrition, mentally identifies himself and Urvaśí with the two sticks, and repeats the Mantra उर्वश्यामायुरसि पुरूरवाः ।‡

* *Angula*, 'finger-breadths.'

† Professor Wilson thinks that there may be an allusion to this in the *Ṛigveda*, I., XXXI., 4. See his Translation, Vol. I., p. 80, note b.

‡ These words are not from the text of the *Bhágavata*, but from Śrídhara's comment on IX., XIV., 45, in that work.

was no more separated from his beloved.* Thus, fire, that was, at first, but one, was made threefold,† in the present Manwantara, by the son of Ilá.[1]‡

[1] The division of one fire into three is ascribed to Purúravas by the Mahábhárata and the rest. The commentator on the former specifies them as the Gárhapatya, Dakshiúa, and Áhavaníya,§ which Sir William Jones—Manu, II., 231,—renders nuptial, ceremonial, and sacrificial fires; or, rather, 1. household, that which is perpetually maintained by a householder; 2. a fire for sacrifices, placed to the south of the rest; and 3. a consecrated fire for oblations; forming the Tretágni, or triad of sacred fires, in opposition to the Laukika, or merely temporal ones. To Purúravas, it would appear, the triple arrangement was owing; but there are some other curious traditions regarding him, which indicate his being the author of some important innovations in the Hindu ritual. The Bhágavata|| says, that, before his time, there was but one Veda, one caste, one fire, and one god, Náráyaúa; and that, in the beginning of the Tretá age, Purúravas made them, all, 'three':

पुरूरवस एवासीत्त्रयी त्रेतामुखे नृप ।

That is, according to the commentator, the ritual was then instituted: कर्ममार्गः प्रकटो बभूव । The Matsya Puráúa has an account of this prince's going to the orbit of the sun and moon, at every conjunction, when oblations to progenitors are to be offered; as if obsequial rites had originated with Purúravas. The Mahábhárata¶ states some still more remarkable particulars. "The glorious Purúravas, endowed, although a mortal, with the properties of a deity, governing the thirteen islands of the ocean,

* For the legend of Purúravas and Urvaśí, see the *Śatapatha-bráhmaúa*, XI., V., I., 1.

† *Tretá.*

‡ Aila.

§ See Vol. III., p. 175, note §.

|| IX., XIV., 49.

¶ *Ádi-parvan*, *śl.* 3145—3147.

engaged in hostilities with the Brahmans, in the pride of his strength, and seized their jewels, as they exclaimed against his oppression. Sanatkumára came from the sphere of Brahmá, to teach him the rules of duty; but Purúravas did not accept his instructions; and the king, deprived of understanding by the pride of his power, and actuated by avarice, was, therefore, ever accursed by the offended great sages, and was destroyed."

विप्रैः स विग्रहं चक्रे वीर्योन्मत्तः पुरूरवाः ।
जहार च स विप्राणां रत्नान्युत्क्रोशतामपि ॥
सनत्कुमारस्तं राजन्ब्रह्मलोकादुपेत्य ह ।
अनुदर्शं ततश्चक्रे प्रत्यगृह्णान्न चाप्यसौ ॥
ततो महर्षिभिः क्रुद्धैः सद्यः शप्तो व्यनश्यत ।
लोभान्वितो बलमदान्नष्टसंज्ञो नराधिपः ॥

CHAPTER VII.

Sons of Purúravas. Descendants of Amávasu. Indra born as Gádhi. Legend of Ṛichíka and Satyavatí. Birth of Jamadagni and Viśwámitra. Paraśuráma, the son of the former. (Legend of Paraśuráma.) Śunaḥśepha and others, the sons of Viśwámitra, forming the Kauśika race.

PURÚRAVAS had six sons,—Áyus, Dhímat, Amávasu, Viśwávasu, Śatáyus, and Śrutáyus.[1] The son of

---

[1] Considerable variety prevails in these names; and the Matsya, Padma, Brahma, and Agni enumerate eight.* The lists are as follows:

Mahábhárata.†	Matsya.	Agni.	Kúrma.	Bhágavata.‡
Áyus	Áyus	Áyus	Áyus	Áyu
Dhímat	Dhṛitimat	Dhímat	Máyus	Śrutáyu
Amávasu	Vasu	Vasu	Amáyus	Satyáyu
Dṛiḍháyus	Dṛiḍháyus	Uśráyus	Viśwáyus	Raya
Vanáyus	Dhanáyus	Antáyus	Śatáyus	Vijaya
Śatáyus	Śatáyus	Śatáyus	Śrutáyus	Jaya
	Aśwáyus	Ṛitáyus		
	Divijáta §	Divijáta §		

The list of the Brahma is that of the Mahábhárata, with the addition of Śatáyus and Viśwáyus; and the Padma agrees with the Matsya.

---

* The *Harivaṁśa*, *ll.* 1372, 1373, and again in *ll.* 1413, 1414, gives seven, namely, Viśwáyus and Śrutáyus, besides the names of the *Mahábhárata*, Dhímat excepted; for the word *dhímán*, as is shown by the context, must be taken to qualify Amávasu.

† *Ádi-parvan*, *ll.* 3149.

‡ IX., XV., 1.

§ Reference to the originals of the passages referred to in note *, above, suggests grave doubts as to this name. But I have no access to the *Agni-puráṇa*.

Amávasu was Bhíma;[1] his son was Kánchana;[2] his son was Suhotra,[3] whose son was Jahnu.[*] This prince, whilst performing a sacrifice, saw the whole of the place† overflowed by the waters of the Ganges. Highly offended at this intrusion, his eyes red with anger, he united the spirit of sacrifice‡ with himself, by the power of his devotion, and drank up the river. The gods and sages, upon this, (came to him, and) appeased his indignation, and reobtained Gangá from him, in the capacity of his daughter; (whence she is called Jáhnaví).[4]

The son of Jahnu was Sumantu;[5] § his son was Ajaka;

---

[1] Son of Vijaya: Bhágavata. This line of princes is followed only in our text, the Váyu, Brahma, and Hari Vaḿśa, and the Bhágavata.

[2] Kánchanaprabha: Brahma. ||

[3] Hotraka: Bhágavata.

[4] The Brahma Puráńa and Hari Vaḿśa add, of this prince, that he was the husband of Káverí, the daughter of Yuvanáśwa, who, by the imprecation of her husband, became the Káverí river;—another indication of the Dakshińa origin of these works.¶ The Hari Vaḿśa has another Jahnu, to whom it gives the same spouse, as we shall hereafter see.**

[5] Sunuta: †† Brahma. Púru: Bhágavata.

---

* According to the *Váyu-puráńa*, his mother was Kediki. The *Harivaḿśa* calls her Keśiní.

† *Váta*.

‡ *Yajnapurusha*. See Vol. I., p. 61, note 1; p. 163, note *.

§ This name I find in only one MS.: one other has Sudhanu; and all the rest have Sujantu. Professor Wilson's Bengal translation has Sujahnu. The *Váyu-puráńa* reads Suhotra.

|| Both Kánchanaprabha and Kánchana: *Váyu-puráńa*, and *Harivaḿśa*.

¶ The *Váyu-puráńa* recounts the same legend.

** Where?

†† I find Sunaha, apparently.

his son was Balákáśwa;[1] his son was Kuśá,[2]* who had four sons,—Kuśámba,† Kuśanábha, Amúrtaraya,‡ and Amávasu.[3] Kuśámba, being desirous of a son,

---

[1] Valaka:§ Brahma. Ajaka: Bhágavata.||

[2] The Brahma Puráńa and Hari Vamśa add, that Kúśa was in alliance with the Pahlavas and foresters.

[3] Our authorities differ as to these names:

Váyu.	Brahma and Hari Vamśa.	Bhágavata.
Kuśáśwa or Kuśasthamba ¶	Kuśáśwa **	Kuśámbu ††
Kuśanábha	Kuśanábha	Kuśanábha
Amúrtarayaśa ‡‡	Amúrtimat	Múrtaya §§
Vasu	Kuśika	Vasu.

The Rámáyańa‖‖ has Kuśámba, Kuśanábha, Amúrtarajas,¶¶ and Vasu; and makes them, severally, the founders of Kauśámbi, of Mahodaya (which afterwards appears the same as Kanoj), Dharmárańya, and Girivraja; the latter being in the mountainous part of Magadha.

---

* The *Bhágavata-puráńa* has Jahnu, Púru, Baláka, Ajaka, Kuśa.

† Kuśika, here and below, in one MS. The Vaidik tradition assigns him to the family of Ishíratha.

‡ So read all my MSS. but one, which gives Amúrtiraya. See the *Mahábhárata*, *Śánti-parvan*, *śl.* 6184. I have displaced the Translator's "Amurttaya". His Hindu-made English version has Amúrta.

§ This seems very doubtful. Probably the reading is Baláka.

|| See note *, above.

¶ My MSS. give Kuśámba or Kuśastamba.

** In both the *Brahma-puráńa* and the *Harivamśa* I find Kuśámba. Indeed, I have nowhere met with "Kuśáśwa", as son of Kuśa.

†† Corrected from "Kuśámba". Kuśámbu is, of course, a gross error; but it is characteristic of the *Bhágavata-puráńa*.

‡‡ Judging from my MSS., I conjecture that the correct reading may be Amúrtárajasa.

§§ Corrected from "Amurttaraya".

‖‖ *Bála-káńd́a*, XXXII, 3—8. ¶¶ Corrected from "Amurttarajasa."

engaged in devout penance, to obtain one who should be equal to Indra. Observing the intensity of his devotions, Indra was alarmed, lest a prince of power like his own should be engendered, and determined, therefore, to take upon himself the character of Kuśámba's son.[1] He was, accordingly, born as Gádhi,* of the race of Kuśa (Kauśika). Gádhi had a daughter named Satyavatí. Ŕichíka, of the descendants of Bhŕigu, demanded her in marriage. The king was very unwilling to give his daughter to a peevish old Brahman, and demanded of him, as the nuptial present, a thousand fleet horses, whose colour should be white,† with one black ear. Ŕichíka, having propitiated Varuńa, the god of ocean, obtained from him, at (the holy place called) Aśwatírtha, a thousand such steeds, and, giving them to the king, espoused his daughter.[2]

---

[1] The Brahma and Hari Vamśa make Gádhi the son of Kuśika; the Váyu‡ and Bhágavata, of Kuśámba;§ the Rámáyańa,|| of Kuśanábha.

[2] The Rámáyańa notices the marriage, but has no legend. The Mahábhárata, Vana Parvan, has a rather more detailed narration, but much the same as in the text. According to the commentator, Aśwatírtha is in the district of Kanoj; perhaps, at the confluence of the Kálanadí with the Ganges. The agency of the god of Ocean, in procuring horses, is a rather curious additional coincidence between Varuńa and Neptune.

---

* Anciently, Gáthin. See Professor Wilson's Translation of the *Ŕigveda*, Vol. I., p. 27, note a.

† *Induvarchas.*

‡ But the Translator, according to note 3 in the preceding page, did not find Kuśámba in the *Váyu-puráńa*. It appears there, however, and as convertible with Kuśika. See Vol. III., p. 16, notes, ‡ ‡.

§ Correct by note †† in the last page. || *Bála-kánda*, XXXIV., 5.

In order to effect the birth of a son, Ṙichíka[1] prepared a dish of rice, barley, and pulse, with butter and milk, for his wife to eat; and, at her request, he consecrated a similar mixture for her mother, by partaking of which, she should give birth to a prince of martial prowess. Leaving both dishes with his wife, —after describing, particularly, which was intended for her, and which for her mother,—the sage went forth to the forests.* When the time arrived for the food to be eaten, the queen said to Satyavatí: "Daughter, all persons wish their children to be possessed of excellent qualities, and would be mortified to see them surpassed by the merits of their mother's brother. It will be desirable for you, therefore, to give me the mess your husband has set apart for you, and to eat of that intended for me; for the son which it is to procure me is destined to be the monarch of the whole world, whilst that which your dish would give you must be a Brahman, alike devoid of affluence, valour, and power." Satyavatí agreed to her mother's proposal; and they exchanged messes.

When Ṙichíka returned home, and beheld Satyavatí, he said to her: "Sinful woman, what hast thou done? I view thy body of a fearful appearance. Of a surety, thou hast eaten the consecrated food which was pre-

---

[1] In the Mahábhárata, Bhṙigu, the father of Ṙichíka, prepares the Charu.

---

* एष चरुर्भवत्यायमपरस्त्वन्मात्रा । सम्यगुपयोज्यः । इत्युक्त्वा वनं जगाम । The sequel of the story is considerably expanded in the English.

pared for thy mother: thou hast done wrong. In that food I had infused the properties of power, and strength, and heroism; in thine, the qualities suited to a Brahman,—gentleness, knowledge, and resignation. In consequence of having reversed my plans, thy son shall follow a warrior's propensities, and use weapons, and fight, and slay. Thy mother's son shall be born with the inclinations of a Brahman, and be addicted to peace and piety." Satyavatí, hearing this, fell at her husband's feet, and said: "My lord, I have done this thing through ignorance. Have compassion on me: let me not have a son such as thou hast foretold. If such there must be, let it be my grandson, not my son." The Muni, relenting at her distress, replied: "So let it be." Accordingly, in due season she gave birth to Jamadagni; and her mother brought forth Viśwámitra.* Satyavatí afterwards became the Kauśikí river.[1] Jamadagni married Reńuká, the daughter of Reńu, of the family of Ikshwáku, and had, by her, the destroyer of the Kshattriya race, Paraśuráma, who was a portion of Náráyańa, the spiritual guide of the universe.[2]

---

[1] So the Rámáyańa†—after stating that Satyavatí followed her husband in death,—adds, that she became the Kauśikí river; the Coosy,‡ which, rising in Nepal, flows through Purneah into the Ganges, opposite, nearly, to Rájmahal.

[2] The text omits the story of Paraśuráma; but, as the legend makes a great figure in the Vaishńava works in general, I have

---

* See *Original Sanskrit Texts*, Part I., p. 86.

† *Bála-káńda*, XXXIV., 8.

‡ See Vol. II., p. 146, note §.

LEGEND OF PARAŚURÁMA.

(From the Mahábhárata.*)

"JAMADAGNI (the son of Richíka,[1]) was a pious sage, who, by the fervour of his devotions, whilst engaged in holy study, obtained entire possession of the Vedas. Having gone to King Prasenajit, he demanded, in marriage, his daughter Reńuká; and the king gave her unto him. The descendant of Bhŕigu conducted the princess to his hermitage, and dwelt with her there; and she was contented to partake in his ascetic life. They had four sons, and then a fifth, who was Jámadagnya,† the last, but not the least, of the brethren. Once, when her sons were all absent to gather the fruits on which they fed, Reńuká, who was exact in the discharge of all her duties, went forth to bathe. On her way to the stream, she beheld Chitraratha, the Prince of Mŕittikávatí, with a garland of lotoses on his neck, sporting with his queen, in the water; and

---

inserted it from the Mahábhárata, where it is twice related; once, in the Vana Parvan, and once, in the Rájadharma section of the Śánti Parvan.‡ It is told, also, at length, in the Ninth Book of the Bhágavata,§ in the Padma and Agni Puráńas, &c.

[1] The circumstances of Ŕichíka's marriage, and the birth of Jamadagni and Viśwámitra, are told much in the same manner as in our text, both in the Mahábhárata and Bhágavata.

---

* *Vana-parvan*, *ll.* 11071—11110.

† Ráma, in the original; *i. e.*, Paraśuráma. See Vol. II., p. 23, notes 1 and **.

‡ Chapter XLIX.

§ Chapters XV. and XVI.

she felt envious of their felicity. Defiled by unworthy thoughts, wetted, but not purified, by the stream,* she returned, disquieted, to the hermitage; and her husband perceived her agitation. Beholding her fallen from perfection, and shorn of the lustre of her sanctity, Jamadagni reproved her, and was exceeding wroth. Upon this, there came her sons from the wood; first the eldest, Rumańwat, then Susheńa, then Vasu, and then Viśwávasu; and each, as he entered, was successively commanded, by his father, to put his mother to death; but, amazed, and influenced by natural affection, neither of them made any reply: therefore, Jamadagni was angry, and cursed them; and they became as idiots, and lost all understanding, and were like unto beasts or birds. Lastly, Ráma returned to the hermitage, when the mighty and holy Jamadagni said unto him: 'Kill thy mother, who has sinned; and do it, son, without repining.' Ráma, accordingly, took up his axe, and struck off his mother's head; whereupon the wrath of the illustrious and mighty Jamadagni was assuaged, and he was pleased with his son, and said: 'Since thou hast obeyed my commands, and done what was hard to be performed, demand from me whatever blessings thou wilt, and thy desires shall

---

* व्यभिचाराच्च तस्मात्सा क्लिन्नाम्भसि विचेतना ।

Nilakańtha, the commentator, quotes, hereupon, the following stanza, apparently from the *Mahábhárata*:

सुन्दरं पुरुषं दृष्ट्वा भ्रातरं पितरं सुतम् ।
योनिर्द्रवति नारीणां सत्यं सत्यं जनार्दन ॥

See the *Hitopadeśa* (ed. Lassen), Book I., *śl.* 110; and compare the ninth stanza of the extract given in the note to p. 141 of Vol. III.

be, all, fulfilled.' Then Ráma begged of his father these boons: the restoration of his mother to life, with forgetfulness of her having been slain, and purification from all defilement; the return of his brothers to their natural condition; and, for himself, invincibility in single combat, and length of days. And all these did his father bestow.

"It happened, on one occasion, that, during the absence of the Ŕishi's sons, the mighty monarch Kártavírya, (the sovereign of the Haihaya tribe, endowed, by the favour of Dattátreya, with a thousand arms, and a golden chariot that went wheresoever he willed it to go),* came to the hermitage[1] of Jamadagni, where the wife of the sage received him with all proper respect. The king, inflated with the pride of valour, made no return to her hospitality, but carried off with him, by violence, the calf of the milch-cow† of the sacred oblation,[2] and cast down the tall trees sur-

---

[1] In the beginning of the legend occurs the account of Kártavíryárjuna, with the addition, that he oppressed both men and gods. The latter applying to Vishńu for succour, he descended to earth, and was born as Paraśuráma, for the especial purpose of putting the Haihaya king to death.

[2] In the Rájadharma, the sons of the king carry off the calf. The Bhágavata ‡ makes the king seize upon the cow, by whose

---

* These descriptive epithets of Kártavírya are transferred hither, by the Translator, from *H.* 11035, 11036. Hence I have enclosed them in parentheses.

† Called, elsewhere, Surabhi.

‡ IX., XV., 26. The king's men, on the king's order, seize and carry off the cow.

rounding the hermitage. When Ráma returned, his father told him what had chanced; and he saw the cow in affliction; and he was filled with wrath. Taking up his splendid bow,[1] Bhárgava, the slayer of hostile heroes, assailed Kártavírya, who had, now, become subject to the power of death, and overthrew him in battle. With sharp arrows Ráma cut off his thousand arms; and the king perished. The sons of Kártavírya,* to revenge his death, attacked the hermitage of Jamadagni, when Ráma was away, and slew the pious and unresisting sage, who called, repeatedly, but fruitlessly, upon his valiant son. They then departed; and, when Ráma returned, bearing fuel from the thickets, he found his father lifeless, and thus bewailed his unmerited fate: 'Father, in resentment of my actions, have you been murdered by wretches as foolish as they are base. By the sons of Kártavírya are you struck down, as a deer, in the forest, by the huntsman's shafts. Ill have you deserved such a death,—you, who have ever trodden the path of virtue, and never offered wrong to any created thing. How great is the

---

aid Jamadagni had previously entertained Arjuna and all his train; borrowing, no doubt, these embellishments from the similar legend of Vasishtha and Viśwámitra, related in the Rámáyaṇa.

[1] The characteristic weapon of Ráma is, however, an axe (Paraśu), whence his name,—Ráma, 'with the axe.' It was given to him by Śiva, whom the hero propitiated on Mount Gandhamádana.† He, at the same time, received instruction in the use of weapons generally, and the art of war. Rájadharma.

---

* Arjuna, in the Sanskrit.

† *Mahábhárata*, *Śánti-parvan*, *ll.* 1748.

crime that they have committed, in slaying, with their deadly shafts, an old man, like you, wholly occupied with pious cares, and engaging not in strife! Much have they to boast of to their fellows and their friends,—that they have shamelessly slain a solitary hermit, incapable of contending in arms!' Thus lamenting, bitterly and repeatedly, Ráma performed his father's last obsequies, and lighted his funeral pile. He then made a vow, that he would extirpate the whole Kshattriya race. In fulfilment of this purpose, he took up his arms, and, with remorseless and fatal rage, singly destroyed, in fight, the sons of Kártavírya; and, after them, whatever Kshattriyas he encountered, Ráma, the first of warriors, likewise slew. Thrice seven times did he clear the earth of the Kshattriya caste;[1] and he filled, with their blood, the five large lakes of Samantapanchaka, from which he offered libations to the race of Bhrigu. There did he behold his sire again; and the son of Richíka beheld his son, and told him what to do. Offering a solemn sacrifice to the king of the gods, Jámadagnya presented the earth to the ministering priests. To Kaśyapa he gave the altar made of gold, ten fathoms in length, and nine in height.[2] With the permission of Kaśyapa, the Brahmans divided it in pieces amongst them; and they were, thence, called Khańdaváyana Brahmans. Having given the earth to Kaśyapa, the hero of immeasurable

[1] This more than 'thrice slaying of the slain' is explained, in the Rájadharma, to mean, that he killed the men of so many generations, as fast as they grew up to adolescence.

[2] It is sometimes read Narotsedha, 'as high as a man.'

prowess retired to the Mahendra mountain, where he still resides: and in this manner was there enmity between him and the race of Kshattriyas; and thus was the whole earth conquered by Ráma."[1] *

---

[1] The story, as told in the Rájadharma section, adds, that, when Ráma had given the earth to Kaśyapa, the latter desired him to depart, as there was no dwelling for him in it, and to repair to the seashore of the south, where Ocean made for him (or relinquished to him), the maritime district named Śúrpáraka. The traditions of the Peninsula ascribe the formation of the coast of Malabar to this origin, and relate that Paraśuráma compelled the ocean to retire, and introduced Brahmans and colonists, from the north, into Kerala, or Malabar. According to some accounts, he stood on the promontory of Dilli, and shot his arrows to the south, over the site of Kerala. It seems likely, that we have proof of the local legend being, at least, as old as the beginning of the Christian era, as the Mons Pyrrhus of Ptolemy is, probably, the mountain of Paraśu or Paraśuráma. See Catalogue of Mackenzie Collection, Vol. I., Introduction, p. xcv.; and Vol. II., p. 74. The Rájadharma also gives an account of the Kshattriyas who escaped even the thrice seven times repeated destruction of their race. Some of the Haihayas were concealed, by the earth, as women; the son of Vidúratha, of the race of Púru, was preserved in the Ṛiksha mountain, where he was nourished by the bears; Sarvakarman,† the son of Saudása, was saved by Paráśara, performing the offices of a Śúdra; Gopati, son of Śibi, was nourished by cows, in the forests; Vatsa, the son of Pratardana, was concealed amongst the calves in a cow-pen; the son of Deviratha was secreted, by Gautama, on the banks of the Ganges; Bṛihadratha was preserved in Gṛidhrakúṭa;

---

* It has not appeared worth while to point out the freedoms of translation which occur in this episode as here rendered.

† See Vol. III., p. 304, note 1.

The son of Viśwámitra was Śunahśepha,* the descendant of Bhŕigu,—given by the gods, and, thence, named Devaráta.[1] Viśwámitra had other sons, also,

---

and descendants of Marutta were saved by the ocean. From these the lines of kings were continued; but it does not appear, from the ordinary lists, that they were ever interrupted. This legend, however, as well as that of the Rámáyańa, Book I., Chapter LII., no doubt intimates a violent and protracted struggle, between the Brahmans and Kshattriyas, for supreme domination in India; as, indeed, the text of the Mahábhárata† more plainly denotes; as Earth is made to say to Kaśyapa: "The fathers and grandfathers of these Kshattriyas have been killed by the remorseless Ráma, in warfare on my account:"

एतेषां पितरश्चैव तथैव च पितामहाः ।
मदर्थं निहता युद्धे रामेणाक्लिष्टकर्मणा ॥

[1] The story of Śunahśepha is told by different authorities, with several variations. As the author of various Súktas in the Ŕich, he is called the son of Ajígarta. The Rámáyańa makes him the middle son of the sage Ŕichíka, sold to Ambarísha, king of Ayodhyá, by his parents, to be a victim in a human sacrifice offered by that prince. He is set at liberty by Viśwámitra; but it is not added that he was adopted. The Bhágavata‡ concurs in the adoption, but makes Śunahśepha the son of Viśwámitra's sister,§ by Ajígarta, of the line of Bhŕigu, and states his being purchased, as a victim, for the sacrifice of Hariśchandra. (See Vol. III., p. 287, note 1.) The Váyu makes him a son of Ŕichíka, but alludes to his being the victim at Hariśchandra's sacrifice. According to the Rámáyańa, Viśwámitra called upon his sons to take the place of Śunahśepha, and, on their refusing, degraded them to the condition of Cháńdálas. The Bhágavata says, that

---

* Here, and everywhere below, corrected from "Śunahśephas".

† *Śánti-parvan*, *ll.* 1800, 1801.

‡ IX., XVI., 30, 31.

§ ?

amongst whom the most celebrated were Madhuch-

---

fifty* only of the hundred sons of Viśwámitra were expelled their tribe, for refusing to acknowledge Śunaḥśepha or Devaráta as their elder brother. The others consented; and the Bhágavata† expresses this:

ज्येष्ठं मन्त्रदृशं चक्रुस्त्वामन्वञ्चो वयं स्म हि ।

"They said to the elder, profoundly versed in the Mantras, We are your followers:" as the commentator: अनुगन्तारः कनिष्ठाः स्म इत्यर्थः । The Rámáyańa also observes, that Śunaḥśepha, when bound, praised Indra with Richas, or hymns of the Rig-veda. The origin of the story, therefore,—whatever may be its correct version,—must be referred to the Vedas; and it, evidently, alludes to some innovation in the ritual, adopted by a part only of the Kauśika families of Brahmans.‡

---

* These fifty were the elder sons.

† IX., XVI., 35.

‡ On the subject treated of in this note Professor Wilson expressed himself, at a later date, as follows:

"The story of Śunaḥśepa, or, as usually written, Śunaḥśepha, has been, for some time, known to Sanskrit students, through the version of it presented in the Rámáyańa, Book I, Chapter LX., Schlegel; LXIII., Gorresio. He is, there, called the son of the Rishi Ŕichíka, and is sold for a hundred cows, by his father, to Ambarísha, king of Ayodhyá, as a victim for a human sacrifice. On the road, he comes to be lake Pushkara, where he sees Viśwámitra, and implores his succour, and learns, from him, a prayer, by the repetition of which, at the stake, Indra is induced to come and set him free. It is obvious that this story has been derived from the Veda; for Viśwámitra teaches him, according to Schlegel's text, two Gáthás,—according to Gorresio's, a Mantra: but the latter also states, that he propitiated Indra by Ŕichas,—Mantras of the Rig-veda (Ŕigbhis tushtáva devendram), Vol. I., p 249. Manu also alludes to the story (X., 105), where it is said that Ajígarta incurred no guilt by giving up his son to be sacrificed; as it was to preserve himself and family from perishing with hunger. Kullúka Bhaťťa names the son, Śunaḥśepha, and refers, for his authority, to the Bahwricha Bráhmańa. The story is

chhandas, Jaya, Kŕita,* Devadeva,† Ashťaka,‡ Kach-

---

told, in full detail, in the Aitareya Bráhmańa; but the Raja is named Hariśchandra. He has no sons, and worships Varuńa, in order to obtain a son, promising to sacrifice to him his first-born. He has a son, in consequence, named Rohita; but, when Varuńa claims his victim, the king delays the sacrifice, under various pretexts, from time to time, until Rohita attains adolescence, when his father communicates to him the fate for which he was destined. Rohita refuses submission, and spends several years in the forests, away from home. He, at last, meets, there, with Ajigarta, a Ŕishi, in great distress, and persuades him to part with his second son, Śunaśśepha, to be substituted for Rohita, as an offering to Varuńa. The bargain is concluded; and Śunaśśepha is about to be sacrificed, when, by the advice of Viśwámitra, one of the officiating priests, he appeals to the gods, and is, ultimately, liberated. The Aitareya Bráhmańa has supplied the commentator with the circumstances which he narrates, as illustrative of the series of hymns in this section. Dr. Rosen doubts if the hymns bear any reference to the intention of sacrificing Śunaśśepha: but the language of the Bráhmańa is not to be mistaken; as Ajigarta not only ties his son to the stake, but goes to provide himself with a knife with which to slay him. At the same time, it must be admitted, that the language of the Súktas is somewhat equivocal, and leaves the intention of an actual sacrifice open to question. The Bhágavata follows the Aitareya and Manu, in terming Śunaśśepha the son of Ajigarta, and names the Raja,[a] also, Hariśchandra. In the Vishńu Puráńa, he is called the son of Viśwámitra, and is termed, also, Devaráta, or god-given. But this relates to subsequent occurrences, noticed, in like manner, by the other authorities, in which he becomes the adopted son of Viśwámitra, and the eldest of all his sons; such of whom as refused to acknowledge his seniority being cursed to become the founders of various barbarian and outcaste races. Viśwámitra's share in the legend may, possibly, intimate his opposition, and that of some of his disciples, to human sacrifices." Translation of the *Rigveda*, Vol. I., p. 59, note a.

See, further, Professor Wilson's collective works, Vol. II., pp. 247—259; Professor Max Müller's *History of Ancient Sanskrit Literature*, pp. 408, *et seq.*

* I have substituted Jaya, Kŕita, for "Kŕitajaya". If we were to read only one name here, it would be, according to all my MSS., Jayakŕita. See note † in the next page.

† Two MSS. have Deva. See note ‡ in the next page. The *Harivanśa* has Devala.

‡ In several copies, Ashťa.

chhapa,* and Hárita.† These founded many families,‡ (all of whom were known by the name of) Kauśikas, and intermarried with the families of various Ŕishis.[1]

---

[1] The Bhágavata says one hundred sons, besides Devaráta and others, as Ashtaka, Hárita,§ &c. Much longer lists of names are given in the Váyu,|| Bhágavata,¶ Brahma, and Hari Vamśa. The two latter specify the mothers. Thus: Devaśravas, Kati (the founder of the Kátyáyanas), and Hiranyáksha were sons of Śálávati;** Reńuka, Gálava, Sánkŕiti, Mudgala, Madhuchchhandas, and Devala were sons of Reńu; and Ashtaka, Kachchhapa, and Hárita were the sons of Dŕishadwatí. The same works enumerate the Gotras, the families or tribes of the Kauśika Brahmans. These are: Párthivas, Devarátas, Yájnavalkyas, Sámarshańas, Udumbaras, Dumlánas, Tárakáyanas, Munchátas, Lohitas, Reńus, Kárishus, Babhrus, Páńinis,†† Dhyánajápyas,‡‡ Śyálantas, Hiranyákshas, Śankus, Gálavas, Yamadútas, Devalas, Śálankáyanas, Báshkalas, Dadátivádaras, Sauśrutas, Saindhaváyanas, Nishńátas,

---

* Corrected from "Kachchapa".

† So reads one of my MSS.; the rest having Háritaka.

These names form, in the original, one compound, with a plural case-ending for the whole. A consideration of the passage cited in note ||, below, has led me to make the alteration notified in note * in the preceding page. Devadeva, it may be suggested, originated, possibly, from a careless duplication of Deva, or from "Deva, Dhruva," by corruption.

‡ *Gotra.*

§ The Bhágavata specifies only Jaya and Kratumat, also.

|| Eight are there named: Madhuchchhandas, Jaya, Kŕita, Deva, Dhruva, Ashtaka, Kachchhapa, Púrańa. It will be satisfactory to the Sanskrit scholar to see the original:

मधुच्छन्दो जयश्चैव कृतदेवौ ध्रुवाष्टकौ ।
कच्छपः पूरणश्चैव विश्वामित्रसुतास्तु वै ॥

¶ This name should be omitted. See note §, above.

** Corrected from "Śilavati".

†† Corrected from "Pánini".

‡‡ Corrected from "Dhyánajyápyas".

Chunchulas, Śálankṛityas, Sánkṛityas, Bádaráṅyas,* and an infinity of others, multiplied by intermarriages with other tribes, and who, according to the Váyu, were, originally, of the regal caste, like Viśwámitra, but, like him, obtained Brahmanhood, through devotion. Now, these Gotras, or some of them, at least, no doubt existed, partaking more of the character of schools of doctrine, but in which teachers and scholars were very likely to have become of one family by intermarrying; and the whole, as well as their original founder, imply the interference of the Kshattriya caste with the Brahmanical monopoly of religious instruction and composition.

* The lists of the *Váyu-puráńa*, *Brahma-puráńa* and *Harivaṅśa* seem to be here amalgamated. I suspect numerous errors, but decline, generally, the task of emendation. A few accents have been supplied, where there was good warrant for them.

CHAPTER VIII.

Sons of Áyus. Line of Kshattravṛiddha, or kings of Káśí. Former birth of Dhanwantari. Various names of Pratardana. Greatness of Alarka.

ÁYUS, the eldest son of Purúravas, married the daughter of Ráhu (or Áráhu*), by whom he had five sons,—Nahusha, Kshattravṛiddha,[1] Rambha,[2] Raji, and Anenas.[3]

The son of Kshattravṛiddha was Suhotra,[4]† who had three sons,—Káśa,[5]‡ Leśa,[6]§ and Gṛitsama-

---

[1] Dharmavṛiddha: Váyu. Vṛiddhaśarman: Matsya. Yajnaśarman: Padma.

[2] Darbha: Agni. Dambha: Padma.

[3] Vipápman: Agni and Matsya. Vidáman: Padma. The two last authorities proceed no further with this line.

[4] Sunahotra: Váyu, Brahma.

[5] Káśya: Bhágavata.

[6] Sála:|| Váyu, Brahma, Hari Vaṁśa: whose son was Árshṭi-

---

* In the copies of the text accompanied by the commentary, the collocation of words, being आयुर्नामारराहोः, yields Aráhu or Áráhu. Two MSS., however, of the pure text have स राहोः, i. e., Ráhu.

The *Váyu-puráńa*, in the corresponding passage, gives, as wife of Purúravas, Prabhá, daughter of Swarbhánu. Swarbhánu, according to our Puráńa,—see Vol. II., p. 70,—had a daughter Prabhá. One of the Swarbhánus—for there is a second: see Vol. II., p. 71—is identified with Ráhu, *ibid.*, p. 304.

† Four MSS. have Sunahotra. This being corrected to Śunahotra, we have the genuine ancient reading. See note * in the next page.

‡ Káśya, in two MSS.

§ Two copies have Láśya.

|| I find Śala in the *Váyu-puráńa*.

da.* The son of the last was Śaunaka,[1] who first estab-

---

sheńa,† father of Charanta; Váyu: of Kaśyapa; Brahma and Hari Vamśa.‡

[1] Here is, probably, an error; for the Váyu, Bhágavata, and Brahma agree in making Śunaka the son of Gṛitsamada, and father of Śaunaka.

---

* Corrected, throughout this chapter, from "Ghritsamada".

"It is to be observed, that this Gṛitsamada, who is here described as belonging to the regal lineage of Purúravas, is the reputed Ṛishi of many hymns in the second *Maṅḍala* of the *Ṛigveda*. Regarding him the Commentator Sáyaṅa has the following remarks, in his introduction to that *Maṅḍala*:

* * * * * * * * * * * * * * * * * * *

"'The seer (*i. e.*, he who received the revelation) of this *Maṅḍala* was the Ṛishi Gṛitsamada. He, being formerly the son of Śunahotra in the family of the Ángirasas, was seized by the Asuras, at the time of sacrifice, and rescued by Indra. Afterwards, by the command of that god, he became the person named Gṛitsamada, son of Śunaka, in the family of Bhṛigu. Thus, the *Anukramaṅiká* (Index to the *Ṛigveda*) says of him: 'That Gṛitsamada, who, having been an Ángirasa, and son of Śunahotra, became a Bhárgava and son of Śunaka, saw the second *Maṅḍala*.' So, too, the same Śaunaka says, in his *Ṛishi-anukramaṅa*, regarding the *Maṅḍala* beginning with 'Thou, O Agni:'—Gṛitsamada, son of Śunaka, who is declared to have been, naturally, an Ángirasa, and the son of Śunahotra, became a Bhṛigu.' Hence, the seer of the *Maṅḍala* is the Ṛishi Gṛitsamada, son of Śunaka.'

"It will be noticed, that, (unless we are to suppose a different Gṛitsamada to be intended in each case,) there is a discrepancy between the Puráṅas on the one hand, and Sáyaṅa and the *Anukramaṅiká* on the other; as the Puráṅas make Gṛitsamada the son of Śunahotra or Suhotra, and the father of Śunaka; whilst the *Anukramaṅiká*, followed by Sáyaṅa, represents the same personage as having been, indeed, originally, the son of Śunahotra, of the race of Angiras, but as having afterwards become, by what process does not appear, the son of Śunaka, of the race of Bhṛigu." *Original Sanskrit Texts*, Part I., p. 228 (2nd ed.).

† Corrected from "Árshṭisena". My MSS. of the *Váyu-puráṅa* give Árshṭideśwa; and Árshṭisheṅa as son of Śaunaka.

‡ Kuśa: *Bhágavata-puráṅa*, IX., XVII., 3.

lished the distinctions of the four castes.[1] The son of Káśa was Káśirája;[2] his son was Dírghatamas;[3] his son was Dhanwantari, whose nature was exempt from human infirmities, and who, in every existence, had been master of universal knowledge.* In his past life, (or, when he was produced by the agitation of the milky sea†), Náráyańa had conferred upon him the boon, that he should subsequently be born in the family of

---

[1] The expression is चातुर्वर्ण्यप्रवर्तयिता, 'the originator (or causer) of the distinctions (or duties) of the four castes.' The commentator, however, understands the expression to signify, that his descendants were of the four castes. So, also, the Váyu:

पुत्रो गृत्समदस्य च शुनको यस्य शौनकः ।
ब्राह्मणाः क्षत्रियाश्चैव वैश्याः शूद्रास्तथैव च ।
एतस्य वंशे समुद्भूता विचित्रैः कर्मभिर्द्विजाः ॥

"The son of Gritsamada was Śunaka, whose son was Śaunaka. Brahmans, Kshattriyas, Vaiśyas, and Śúdras were born in his race; Brahmans by distinguished deeds." The existence of but one caste in the age of purity, however incompatible with the legend which ascribes the origin of the four tribes to Brahmá, is everywhere admitted. Their separation is assigned to different individuals;—whether accurately to any one may be doubted: but the notion indicates that the distinction was of a social or political character.

[2] Káśiya: Brahma.‡

[3] Dírghatapas: Váyu. Gritsatamas:§ Agni. The Bhágavata|| inserts a Ráshira before this prince; and the Váyu, a Dharma, after him.

---

* संसिद्धकार्यकरणः सर्वसंभूतिष्वशेषज्ञानवित् ।

† This explanation is borrowed from the commentary.

‡ Káśi: *Bhágavata-puráńa.* Káśaya (?): *Váyu-puráńa.* Káśeya: *Harivaíśa*, *śl.* 1734, in the best MSS. *Vide infra*, p. 40, note *.

§ Corrected from "Ghritsatamas".

|| And so the *Váyu-puráńa.*

Káśirája, should compose the eightfold system of medical science,[1] and should be, thereafter, entitled to a share of offerings (made to the gods). The son of Dhanwantari was Ketumat; his son was Bhímaratha; his son was Divodása;[2]* his son was Pratardana,† —

---

[1] The eight branches of medical science‡ are: 1. Śalya, extraction of extraneous bodies; 2. Śálákya, treatment of external organic affections: these two constitute surgery; 3. Chikitsá, administration of medicines, or medical treatment in general; 4. Bhútavidyá, treatment of maladies referred to demoniac possession; 5. Kaumárabhritya, midwifery and management of children; 6. Agada, alexipharmacy; 7. Rasáyana, alchemical therapeutics; 8. Vájikaraña, use of aphrodisiacs. Dhanwantari, according to the Brahma Vaivarta Puráńa, was preceded, in medical science, by Átreya, Bharadwája, and Charaka: his pupil Suśruta is the reputed author of a celebrated work still extant. It seems probable that Káśi or Benares was, at an early period, a celebrated school of medicine.§

[2] Some rather curious legends are connected with this prince, in the Váyu and Brahma Puráńas, and Hari Vaḿśa, and, especially, in the Káśi Khańda of the Skanda Puráńa. According to these authorities, Śiva and Párvatí, desirous of occupying Káśi, which

---

* See *Original Sanskrit Texts*, Part I., p. 230 (2nd ed.). Many of the personages named hereabouts are of Vaidik notoriety.

† Also called Dyumat. *Bhágavata-puráńa.*

‡ They are named as follows, in a couplet quoted by the scholiast:

कायबालग्रहोर्ध्वाङ्ग(?) शल्य दंष्ट्र जरा विषम् ।
वृषश्चाङ्गानि तस्याष्टौ चिकित्सा येषु संस्थिता ॥

A second classification is given, which differs less from that of Professor Wilson, but in which we find, as the third, fifth, and sixth branches, *káyaśuddhi*, *kumáratantra*, and *agadatantra*.

§ For further particulars, see a paper entitled *On the Medical and Surgical Sciences of the Hindus*, in Professor Wilson's *Essays, Analytical, &c.*, Vol. I., pp. 269—276.

so named from destroying the race of Bhadraśreńya. He had various other appellations, as: Śatrujit, the

---

Divodása possessed, sent Nikumbha, one of the Gańas of the former, to lead the prince to the adoption of Buddhist doctrines; in consequence of which, he was expelled from the sacred city, and, according to the Váyu, founded another on the banks of the Gomatí. We have, however, also some singular, though obscure, intimations of some of the political events of this and the succeeding reign. The passage of the Váyu is:

भद्रश्रेण्यस्य पुत्राणां शतमुत्तमधन्विनाम् ।
हत्वा निवेशयामास दिवोदासो नराधिपः ॥
भद्रश्रेण्यस्य राज्यं तु हृतं तेन बलीयसा ।
भद्रश्रेण्यस्य पुत्रस्तु दुर्दमो नाम नामतः ॥
दिवोदासेन बालेति घृणया स विवर्जितः ।
दिवोदासाद्दृषद्वत्यां वीरो जज्ञे प्रतर्दनः ॥
तेन पुत्रेण बालेन प्रहृतं तस्य वै पुनः ।
वैरस्यान्तं महाराज्ञा तदा तेन विधित्सता ॥

"The king Divodása, having slain the hundred sons of Bhadraśreńya, took possession of his kingdom, which was conquered by that hero. The son of Bhadraśreńya, celebrated by the name of Durdama, was spared, by Divodása, as being an infant. Pratardana was the son of Divodása, by Drishadwatí; and by that great prince, desirous of destroying all enmity, (was recovered) that (territory), which had been seized by that young boy, (Durdama)." This is not very explicit; and something is wanted to complete the sense. The Brahma Puráńa and Hari Vaḿśa* tell the story twice over, chiefly in the words of the Váyu, but with some additions. In Ch. 29 we have, first, the first three lines of the above extract; then comes the story of Benares being deserted; we then have the two next lines;† then follow:‡

---

* In Chapters XXIX. and XXXII.

† My MSS., and the printed and lithographed editions, of the *Harivaḿśa* do not bear out these unimportant statements.

‡ *Śl.* 1584, 1585; also, *Il.* 1742—1745.

victor over his foes,' from having vanquished all his enemies; Vatsa, or 'child', from his father's frequently

---

विषयस्य तु दायाद्यं हृतवान्स महीपतिः ।
बाह्यो पितृदायाद्यं दिवोदासहृतं बलात् ॥
भद्रश्रेण्यस्य पुत्रेण दुर्दमेन महात्मना ।
वैरस्यान्तो महाराज क्षत्रियेण विधित्सता ॥

"That prince (Durdama) invading his patrimonial possessions, the territory which Divodása had seized by force was recovered by the gallant son of Bhadraśreńya, Durdama, a warrior desirous, mighty king, to effect the destruction of his foes." Here the victory is ascribed to Durdama, in opposition to what appears to be the sense of the Váyu, and what is, undoubtedly, that of our text, which says, that he was called Pratardana, from destroying the race of Bhadraśreńya, and Śatrujit, from vanquishing all his foes: ततः प्रतर्दनः । स च भद्रश्रेण्यवंशविनाशादशेषाः शत्रवोऽनेन जिता इति शत्रुजिदभवत् । By Vairasya anta, 'the end of hostility or enmity,' is, obviously, not to be understood, here, as M. Langlois has intimated, a friendly pacification, but the end or destruction of all enemies. In the 32nd chapter of the Hari Vaḿśa, we have precisely the same lines, slightly varied as to their order; but they are preceded by this verse:*

भद्रश्रेण्यस्य पूर्वं तु पुरीं वाराणसीं भवात् ।
यदुवंशप्रसूतस्य तपस्वभिरतस्य च ॥

"The city, (that on the Gomati), before the existence of Benares, of Bhadraśreńya, a pious prince of the Yadu race." This verse is not in the Brahma Puráńa. After giving the rest of the above quotation, except the last line, the passage proceeds:†

अष्टारथो नाम नृपः सुतो भीमरथस्य वै ।
तेन पुत्रेषु बालेषु प्रहृतं तस्य भारत ।
वैरस्यान्तं महाराज क्षत्रियेण विधित्सता ॥

---

* Professor Wilson's authority seems to be peculiar here. See M. Langlois's Translation of the *Harivaḿśa*, Vol. I., p. 146, note 16.

† *Śl.* 1744, 1745.

calling him by that name; Ritadhwaja, 'he whose emblem was truth,' being a great observer of veracity; and Kuvalayáśwa, because he had a horse (aśwa) called Kuvalaya.[1] The son of this prince was Alarka, of whom this verse is sung, in the present day: "For sixty thousand and sixty hundred years, no other youthful monarch, except Alarka, reigned over the earth."[2]*

"The king called Ashtáratha was the son of Bhimaratha; and by him, great king, a warrior desirous of destroying his foes, was (the country) recovered, the children (of Durdama) being infants." तस्य दुर्दमस्य पुत्रेष्वसमर्थेषु । Commentary. According to the same authority, we are, here, to understand Bhimaratha and Ashtáratha as epithets of Divodása and Pratardana. From these scanty and ill-digested notices it appears, that Divodása, on being expelled from Benares, took some city and district on the Gomatí from the family of Bhadraśreńya; that Durdama recovered the country; and that Pratardana again conquered it from his descendants. The alternation concerned, apparently, only bordering districts; for the princes of Máhishmatí and of Káśí continue, in both an earlier and a later series, in undisturbed possession of their capitals and their power.

[1] The Váyu, Agni, Brahma Puráńas, and Hari Vaḿśa interpose two sons of Pratardana,—Garga† (or Bharga) and Vatsa; and they make Vatsa the father of Alarka; except the Brahma, which has Śatrujit and Ŕitadhwaja as two princes following Vatsa.

[2] The Váyu, Brahma, and Hari Vaḿśa repeat this stanza,‡ and add, that Alarka enjoyed such protracted existence, through the favour of Lopámudrá, and that, having lived till the period

* षष्टिं वर्षसहस्राणि षष्टिं वर्षशतानि च ।
अलर्कादपरो नान्यो बुभुजे मेदिनीं युवा ॥

† So reads the *Váyu-puráńa*.

‡ More or less literally. And so does the *Bhágavata-puráńa*, IX., XVII., 7.

The son of Alarka was Sannati;[1]* his son was Sunítha; his son was Suketu; his son was Dharma-

at which the curse upon Kásí terminated, he killed the Rákshasa Kshemaka,—by whom it had been occupied, after it was abandoned by Divodása,—and caused the city to be reinhabited:

शापस्यान्ते महाबाहुर्हत्वा क्षेमकराक्षसम् ।
रम्यां निवेशयामास पुरीं वाराणसीं पुनः ॥†

[1] Several varieties occur, in the series that follows, as the comparative lists will best show:

Bhágavata.‡	Brahma.	Váyu.	Agni.
Alarka	Alarka	Alarka	Alarka
Santati	Sannati	Sannati	Dharmaketu
Sunítha	Sunítha	Sunítha	Vibhu
Suketana	Kshema	Suketu §	Sukumára
Dharmaketu	Ketumat	Dhrishtaketu	Satyaketu
Satyaketu	Suketu	Veńuhotra	
Dhrishtaketu	Dharmaketu	Gárgya	
Sukumára	Satyaketu	Gargabhúmi	
Vítihotra	Vibhu	Vatsabhúmi‖	
Bharga	Ánarta		
Bhárgabhúmi	Sukumára		
	Dhrishtaketu		
	Veńuhotri¶		
	Bharga		
	Vatsabhúmi		

* I find only this reading. Professor Wilson's "Santati" I take to be a miscript of a very few MSS.

† *Harivaḿśa*, *śl.* 1591; and again, *śl.* 1748, 1749, with trifling deviations. The *Váyu-puráńa* has very nearly as above; the *Brahma-puráńa*, the very words there given.

‡ IX., XVII., 8, 9.

§ My MSS. of the *Váyu-puráńa* insert, between Suketu and Dhrishtaketu, Dharmaketu, Satyaketu, Vibhu, Suvibhu, and Sukumára.

‖ On the name here, in the *Váyu-puráńa*, see the Translator's next note.

¶ I find Veńuhotra both in the *Brahma-puráńa* and in the *Harivaḿśa*. See, too, note 1, in the next page.

ketu; his son was Satyaketu; his son was Vibhu; his son was Subvibhu; his son was Sukumára; his son was Dhŕishtaketu; his son was Vainahotra;* his son was Bhárga;† his son was Bhárgabhúmi,‡ from whom (also,) rules for the four castes were promulgated.[1]

The Hari Vamśa§ agrees, as usual, with the Brahma, except in the reading of one or two names. It is to be observed, however, that the Agni makes the Káśi princes the descendants of Vitatha, the successor of Bharata. The Brahma Puráńa and Hari Vamśa, determined, apparently, to be right, give the list twice over; deriving it, in one place, from Kshattravŕiddha, as in our text, the Váyu, and the Bhágavata; and, in another, with the Agni, from Vitatha. The series of the Brahma, however, stops with Lauhi, the son of Alarka, and does not warrant the repetition which the carelessness of the compiler of the Hari Vamśa has superfluously inserted.

[1] Our text is clear enough; and so is the Bhágavata: but the Váyu, Brahma, and Hari Vamśa contain additions of rather doubtful import. The former|| has:

वेणुहोत्रसुतश्चापि गार्ग्यो वै नाम विश्रुतः ।
गार्ग्यस्य गर्गभूमिस्तु वत्सो वत्सस्य धीमतः ।
ब्राह्मणाः क्षत्रियाश्चैव तयोः पुत्राः सुधार्मिकाः ॥

"The son of Veńuhotra was the celebrated Gárgya; Gargabhúmi was the son of Gárgya; and Vatsa, of the wise Vatsa: virtuous Brahmans and Kshattriyas were the sons of these two." By the second Vatsa is, perhaps, meant Vatsabhúmi; and the purport

---

* A single copy reads Vitahotra.

† One MS. has Bhárgava.

‡ Bhárgavabhúmi, in one copy.

§ *Śl.* 1586—1597; *Ál.* 1749—1753. The two lists there given vary from each other by a considerable number of items; and neither of them, in any copy of the *Harivaṁśa* that I have seen, harmonizes with the list in the *Brahma-puráńa*.

|| The *Váyu-puráńa* is intended.

These are the Kásí* princes, (or, descendants of

of the passage is, that Gárgya (or, possibly, rather, Bharga, one of the sons of Pratardana.) and Vatsa were the founders of two races (Bhúmi, 'earth', implying 'source' or 'founder'), who were Kshattriyas by birth, and Brahmans by profession. The Brahma† and Hari Vaṁśa, apparently misunderstanding this text, have increased the perplexity. According to them, the son of Veṅuhotra was Bharga; Vatsabhúmi was the son of Vatsa; and Bhargabhúmi (Bhṛigubhúmi: Brahma.) was from Bhárgava. "These sons of Angiras were born in the family of Bhṛigu, thousands of great might, Brahmans, Kshattriyas and Vaiśyas:"

वेणुहोत्रसुतश्चापि भर्गो नाम प्रजेश्वरः ।
वत्सस्य वत्सभूमिस्तु भर्गभूमिस्तु भार्गवात् (भृगुभूमिस्तु भार्गवात्) ॥
एते ह्यङ्गिरसः पुत्रा जाता वंशेऽथ भार्गवे ।
ब्राह्मणाः क्षत्रिया वैश्या वीर्ययुक्ताः सहस्रशः ॥‡

The commentator§ has: वत्सस्यालर्कपितुः पुत्रान्तरमाह । वत्सभूमिरिति । भार्गवात् । वत्सभ्रातुः । आङ्गिरसः । गालवस्याङ्गिरसत्वात् । भार्गवे । विश्वामित्रस्य भार्गवत्वात् । "Another son of Vatsa, the father of Alarka, is described: Vatsabhúmi, &c. From Bhárgava, the brother of Vatsa. (They were) Angirasas, from Gálava, belonging to that family, (and were born) in the family of Bhṛigu; from the descent of Viśwámitra." The interpretation is not very clear; but it authorizes the notion above expressed, that Vatsa and Bharga, the sons of Pratardana, are the founders of two races of Kshattriya-Brahmans.

* Altered, here and elsewhere, from "Káśya"; the original being काश्यपो भूपतयः or काश्यपो भूभुजः, 'the Káśi kings', or, as we should say, 'the Káśis'. These rulers take their name from Káśi, or Káśirája: *vide supra*, p. 33, note ‡. Śrídhara, commenting on the *Bhágavata-puráṅa*, IX., XVII., 10, says: काश्यः । काशेयाः । Compare Vol. II., p. 157, note †.

† This Puráṅa contains, almost literally, the stanzas cited just below.

‡ *Harivaṁśa*, *ll.* 1596—1598; with which compare *ll.* 1572—1574. See, on both passages, *Original Sanskrit Texts*, Part I., pp. 52, 53 (pp. 231, 232, 2nd ed.).

§ Nílakaṅṭha. Arjuna Miśra remarks to the like effect.

Káśa*).[1] We will now enumerate the descendants of Raji.

---

[1] On the subject of note 2, in p. 33, *supra*, some further illustration is derivable from the Mahábhárata, Śánti Parvan, Dánadharma.† Haryaśwa the king of the Káśis, reigning between the Ganges and the Yamuná, or in the Doab, was invaded and slain by the Haihayas,‡ a race descended, according to this authority, from Śaryáti, the son of Manu (see Vol. III., p. 255, note 1). Sadeva, the son of Haryaśwa, was, also, attacked and defeated by the same enemies. Divodása, his son, built and fortified Benares, as a defence against the Haihayas; but in vain; for they took it, and compelled him to fly. He sought refuge with Bharadwája, by whose favour he had a son born to him, Pratardana, who destroyed the Haihayas, under their king Vítahavya,§ and reestablished the kingdom of Káśi. Vítahavya, through the protection of Bhṙigu, became a Brahman.|| The Mahábhárata gives a list of his descendants, which contains several of the names of the Káśi dynasty of the text. Thus, Gṙitsamada is said to be his son; and the two last of the line are Śunaka and Śaunaka. *Vide supra*, p. 31, note 1.

---

* This parenthesis, which was not marked as such in the former edition, was supplied by the Translator. See note * in the preceding page. The patronym which occurs of Káśa is Káśeya. *Vide supra*, p. 32, note ‡.

† The passage referred to is found in the *Anuśásana-parvan*, Chap. XXX.

‡ The original so calls the hundred sons of Haihaya. He and Tálajangha were sons of Vatsa.

§ Corrected, here and below, from "Vítihavya".

|| For a legend touching this personage, see Professor Wilson's Translation of the *Ṙigveda*, Vol. II., pp. 207, 208; also, *Original Sanskrit Texts*, Part I., pp. 51, 52 (pp. 229, 230 of the 2nd ed.).

CHAPTER IX.

Descendants of Raji, son of Áyus: Indra resigns his throne to him: claimed, after his death, by his sons, who apostatize from the religion of the Vedas, and are destroyed by Indra. Descendants of Pratikshattra, son of Kshattravṛiddha.

RAJI had five hundred sons, all of unequalled daring and vigour. Upon the occurrence of a war between the demons* and the gods, both parties inquired of Brahmá which would be victorious. The deity replied: "That for which Raji shall take up arms." Accordingly, the Daityas immediately repaired to Raji, to secure his alliance; which he promised them, if they would make him their Indra, after defeating the gods. To this they answered, and said: "We cannot profess one thing, and mean another. Our Indra is Prahláda;† and it is for him that we wage war." Having thus spoken, they departed. And the gods then came to him, on the like errand. He proposed to them the said conditions; and they agreed that he should be their Indra. Raji, therefore, joined the heavenly host, and, by his numerous and formidable weapons, destroyed the army of their enemies.

When the demons were discomfited, Indra placed the feet of Raji upon his head, and said: "Thou hast preserved me from a great danger; and I acknowledge thee as my father.‡ Thou art the sovereign chief over

---

* *Asura.*

† For the history of Prahláda, see Vol. II., pp. 30—69.

‡ Hereupon the scholiast quotes the ensuing stanza:

all the regions; and I, the Indra of the three spheres, am thy son." The Raja smiled, and said, "Even be it so. The regard that is conciliated by many agreeable speeches is not to be resisted even when such language proceeds from a foe: (much less should the kind words of a friend fail to win our affection)."* He, accordingly, returned to his own city; and Indra† remained (as his deputy,) in the government of heaven.

When Raji ascended to the skies, his sons, at the instigation of Nárada, demanded the rank of Indra, as their hereditary right; and, as the deity refused to acknowledge their supremacy, they reduced him to submission, by force, and usurped his station. After some considerable time had elapsed, the god of a hundred sacrifices, (Indra), deprived of his share of offerings to the immortals, met with Bŕihaspati, in a retired place, and said to him: "Cannot you give me a little of the sacrificial butter,‡ even if it were no bigger than a jujube? For I am in want of sustenance." "If," replied Bŕihaspati, "I had been applied to, by you, before, I could have done anything for you that you wished: as it is, I will endeavour and restore you, in a few days, to your sovereignty." So saying, he commenced a sacrifice,§ for the purpose of increasing

अन्नदाता भयत्राता कन्यादाता तथैव च ।
जनिता चोपनेता च पञ्चैते पितरः स्मृताः ॥

This should seem to be a quotation, without reference to book, of the *Vŕiddha-chánakya*, IV., 19.

* अनतिक्रमणीया हि वैरिपक्षादप्यनेकविधचाटुवाक्यगर्भा प्रणतिः ।

† *Śatakratu*, one of his epithets, in the original.

‡ ? *Puroḍáśa-khaṅḍa.*

§ अभिचारिकं - - जुहाव ।

the might of Indra, and of leading the sons of Raji into error, (and so effecting their downfall).[1] Misled by their mental fascination, the princes became enemies of the Brahmans, regardless of their duties, and contemners of the precepts of the Vedas; and, thus devoid of morality and religion, they were slain by Indra, who, by the assistance of the priests (of the gods), resumed his place in heaven. Whoever hears this story shall retain, for ever, his proper place, and shall never be guilty of wicked acts.

Rambha (the third son of Áyus,) had no progeny.[2] Kshattravŕiddha had a son named Pratikshattra;[3] his

---

[1] The Matsya says, he taught the sons of Raji the Jinadharma, or Jaina religion:

जिनधर्मं समास्थाय वेदबाह्यं स वेदवित् ।

[2] The Bhágavata enumerates, however, as his descendants, Rabhasa, Gabhíra, and Akriya, whose posterity became Brahmans. The same authority gives, as the descendants of Anenas, the fifth* son of Áyus, Śuddha, Śuchi, Trikakud,† and Śántaraya.‡

[3] The Váyu agrees with our text, in making Pratipaksha (Pratikshattra) the son of Kshattravŕiddha;§ but the Brahma Puráńa and Hari Vaḿśa consider Anenas ‖ to be the head of this branch of the posterity of Áyus. The Bhágavata substitutes Kuśa (the Leśa of our text, the grandson of Kshattravŕiddha), for

---

* Corrected from "fourth".

† Here insert Dharmasárathi.

‡ Corrected from "Śántabhya".

§ I find Kshattradharma in the *Váyu-puráńa*. A little below, the same Puráńa calls him Kshattradharman. See note ††† in the following page.

‖ The descendants of Anenas are specified, in the *Brahma-puráńa*, as follows: Pratikshattra, Sŕinjaya, Jaya, Vijaya, Kŕiti, Haryaśwata, Sahadeva, Nadína, Jayatsena, Sankŕiti, Kshattradharman. And herewith tallies, punctually, the *Harivaḿśa*, ll. 1513—1517.

son was Sanjaya;* his son was† Vijaya;[1] his son was Yajnakŕita;[2]‡ his son was Harshavardhana;[3]§ his son was Sahadeva; his son was Adína;[4]|| his son was Jayasena;¶ his son was Sankŕiti;** his son was Kshattradharman.[5]†† These were the descendants of Kshattravŕiddha. I will now mention those of Nahusha.

---

the first name;‡‡ and this seems most likely to be correct. Although the different MSS. agree in reading क्षत्रवृद्धः, it should be, perhaps, क्षात्रवृद्धः, the patronymic Kshátravŕiddha; making, then, as the Bhágavata§§ does, Pratikshattra,|||| the son of the son of Kshattravŕiddha.

[1] Jaya: Bhágavata, Váyu.¶¶

[2] Vijaya: Váyu.¶¶ Kŕita: Bhágavata.

[3] Haryaśwa: Brahma, Hari Vaḿśa.*** Haryavana: Bhágavata.

[4] The last of the list: Váyu.††† Ahína: Bhágavata.

[5] Kshattravŕiddha: Brahma, Hari Vaḿśa.‡‡‡

---

* See note || in the preceding page.

† Sanjaya's son was Jaya, and Jaya's was Vijaya, according to all my MSS. Also see note †††, below.

‡ So read all my MSS. but one, which exhibits Kŕita. Professor Wilson had "Yajnakŕit".

§ A single copy has Haryaśwa. || In two MSS., Ahína.

¶ Only one of my MSS. gives this name; all the rest showing Jayatsena.

** Here the *Bhágavata-puráńa* interposes another Jaya.

†† In one MS. I find Kshattradharma; in another, Kshetradharman.

‡‡ *I. e.*, for Kshattravŕiddha.

§§ IX., XVII., 16. |||| Shortened to Prati. ¶¶ See note †††, below.

*** I find Haryaśwata in both works. See note || in the preceding page.

††† Here, again, Professor Wilson's MSS. of the *Váyu-puráńa* seem to be imperfect. Mine give the following series, to begin a little back: Kshattradharma, Pratipaksha, Sanjaya, Jaya, Vijaya, Jaya, Haryadwana, Sahadeva, Adína, Jayatsena, Sankŕiti, Kŕitadharman. At the end of the genealogy is this line:

इत्येते क्षत्रधर्माणो नहुषस्य निबोधत ।

‡‡‡ See note || in the preceding page.

CHAPTER X.

The sons of Nahusha. The sons of Yayáti: he is cursed by Śukra: wishes his sons to exchange their vigour for his infirmities. Púru alone consents. Yayáti restores him his youth: divides the earth amongst his sons, under the supremacy of Púru.

YATI, Yayáti,* Saṁyáti, Áyáti,† Viyati, and Kṛiti‡ were the six valiant sons of Nahusha.[1] Yati§ declined

---

[1] The Bhágavata refers, briefly, to the story of Nahusha, which is told in the Mahábhárata more than once,—in the Vana Parvan, Udyoga Parvan, Dánadharma Parvan, and others; also, in the Padma and other Puráńas. He had obtained the rank of Indra; but, in his pride, or at the suggestion of Śachí, compelling the Ṛishis to bear his litter, he was cursed, by them, to fall from his state, and reappear, upon earth, as a serpent. From this form he was set free by philosophical discussions with Yudhishṭhira, and received final liberation. Much speculation, wholly unfounded, has been started by Wilford's conjecture, that the name of this prince, with Deva, 'divine', prefixed, a combination which never occurs, was the same as Dionysius, or Bacchus.|| Authorities generally agree as to the names of the first three of his sons: in those of the others there is much variety; and the Matsya, Agni, and Padma have seven names, as follows, omitting the three first of the text:

---

* He, at least, of the sons of Nahusha, had Virajá for mother, according to the *Váyu-puráńa and Harivaṁśa*. See Vol. III., p. 164, notes § and ¶.

† This name, I find, is ordinarily corrupted into Ayáti or Áyati.

‡ In the *Mahábhárata*, *Ádi-parvan*, *ll.* 3155, they appear as Yati, Yayáti, Saṁyáti, Áyáti, Ayati, and Dhruva.

§ Yati married Go, daughter of Kákutstha, agreeably to the *Váyu-puráńa*, and the *Harivaṁśa*, *ll.* 1601.

|| See the *Asiatic Researches*, Vol. VI., p. 500; Vol. XIV., p. 376.

the sovereignty;[1] and Yayáti, therefore, succeeded to the throne. He had two wives, Devayání, the daughter of Uśanas, and Śarmishṭhá, the daughter of Vṛishaparvan; of whom this genealogical verse is recited: "Devayání bore two sons, Yadu and Turvasu.* Śarmishṭhá, the daughter of Vṛishaparvan,† had three sons, Druhyu,‡ Anu,§ and Púru."[2]|| Through the

Matsya.	Agni.	Padma.¶	Linga.**
Udbhava	Udbhava	Udbhava	Saṁyáti ††
Panśchi ‡‡	Panchaka	Pava	Champaka §§
Sanyáti |||	Pálaka	Viyáti	Andhaka
Meghayáti	Megha	Meghayáti	

[1] Or, as his name implies (यतिः), he became a devotee, a Yati: Bhágavata, &c.

[2] The story is told, in great detail, in the Ádi Parvan of the

* The Vaidik form is Turvaśa.

† A Dánava. See Vol. II., p. 70.

‡ In all my MSS. but one, the name, here, is Druhya.

§ So often do we meet with Áńu, that it may, perhaps, be regarded as the Pauráńik corruption of the original Anu.

|| Corrected from "Puru", here and elsewhere.

For apparent mention of the families sprung from the five sons of Yayáti, see the *Rigveda*, I., CVIII., 8, and Sáyańa's comment thereon.

¶ It is out of my power to verify the genealogical particulars referred to the *Padma-puráńa*, as no copy of that work is accessible to me.

** Prior Section, LXVI., 61, 62. I there find Yáti, Yayáti, Saṁyáti, Áyáti, Andhaka, and Vijáti. *Śl.* 61 ends with the words पञ्चमोऽभवत्, which Professor Wilson must have found corrupted into चम्पकोऽभवत्; for the next stanza begins:

विद्यातिचैति यविमे सर्वे मत्स्यातकीर्तयः ।

†† Corrected from "Śaryáti", in part a typographical error. Compare Vol. III., p. 13, note §§. Professor Wilson wrote *s* and *r* almost exactly alike.

‡‡ I find Panchi.

§§ See note **, above.

|||| Is this, in part, a printer's blunder, for Śaryáti, the name I find?

curse of Uśanas,* Yayáti became old and infirm before his time; but, having appeased his father-in-law,† he obtained permission to transfer his decrepitude to any one who would consent to take it. He first applied to his eldest son, Yadu, and said: "Your maternal grandfather has brought this premature decay upon me. By his permission, however, I may transfer it to you for a thousand years. I am not yet satiate with worldly enjoyments, and wish to partake of them through the

---

Mahábhárata; also, in the Bhágavata, with some additions, evidently of a recent taste. Śarmishthá, the daughter of Vrishaparvan, king of the Daityas,‡ having quarrelled with Devayání, the daughter of Śukra (the religious preceptor of the same race§), had her thrown into a well. Yayáti, hunting in the forest, found her, and, taking her to her father, with his consent, espoused her. Devayání, in resentment of Śarmishthá's treatment, demanded that she should become her handmaid; and Vrishaparvan, afraid of Śukra's displeasure, was compelled to comply. In the service of his queen, however, Yayáti beheld Śarmishthá, and secretly wedded her. Devayání complaining to her father of Yayáti's infidelity, Śukra inflicted on him premature decay, with permission to transfer it to any one willing to give him youth and strength in exchange, as is related in the text. The passage specifying the sons of Yayáti is precisely the same in the Mahábhárata|| as in our text, and is introduced in the same way: अत्रानुवंशश्लोको भवति ।

यदुं च तुर्वसुं चैव देवयानी व्यजायत ।
द्रुह्युं चानुं पूरुं च शर्मिष्ठा वार्षपर्वणी ॥

---

* Kávya, in the Sanskrit; from his father, Kavi. See Vol. I., p. 200, supplementary note on *ibid.*, p. 152.

† Śukra, in the original. *Vide supra*, p. 2, note ||.

‡ Read "Dánavas". See note † in the preceding page.

§ He was priest of the Daityas.

|| *Ádi-parvan*, *śl.* 3162. The correspondence is not of the closest.

means of your youth. Do not refuse compliance with my request." Yadu, however, was not willing to take upon him his father's decay; on which, his father denounced an imprecation upon him, and said: "Your posterity shall not possess dominion." He then applied, successively, to Druhyu, Turvasu, and Anu, and demanded of them their juvenile vigour. They all refused, and were, in consequence, cursed by the king.* Lastly, he made the same request of Śarmishṭhá's youngest son, Púru, who bowed to his father, and readily consented to give him his youth, and receive, in exchange, Yayáti's infirmities, saying that his father had conferred upon him a great favour.

The king Yayáti being, thus, endowed with renovated youth, conducted the affairs of state for the good of his people, enjoying such pleasures as were suited to his age and strength, and were not incompatible with virtue.† He formed a connexion with the celestial nymph Viśwáchí,‡ and was wholly attached to her, and conceived no end to his desires. The more they were gratified, the more ardent they became; as it is said in this verse:§ "Desire is not appeased by enjoyment: fire fed with sacrificial oil becomes but the more intense.|| No one has ever more than enough of rice,

---

* For an ancient allusion to the exclusion from sovereignty of Yadu and Turvaśa, see Professor Wilson's Translation of the *Ṛigveda*, Vol III., p. 179, text and note 3.

† सोऽपि च नवं यौवनमासाद्य धर्माविरोधेन यथाकामं यथाकालोपपन्नं यथोत्साहं विषयं चचार सम्यक्प्रजापालनमकरोत् ।

‡ See Vol. II., p. 76, note 3; p. 80, note; pp. 284, *et seq.*

§ The remainder of this chapter is metrical.

|| A quotation of the *Laws of the Mánavas*, II., 94.

or barley, or gold, or cattle, or women. Abandon, therefore, inordinate desire. When a mind finds neither good nor ill in all objects, but looks on all with an equal eye, then everything yields it pleasure. The wise man is filled with happiness, who escapes from desire, which the feeble-minded can with difficulty relinquish, and which grows not old with the aged.* The hair becomes grey, the teeth fall out, as man advances in years; but the love of wealth, the love of life, are not impaired by age." "A thousand years have passed," reflected Yayáti, "and my mind is still devoted to pleasure: every day my desires are awakened by new objects. I will, therefore, now renounce all sensual enjoyment, and fix my mind upon spiritual truth. Unaffected by the alternatives of pleasure and pain, and having nothing I may call my own, I will, henceforth, roam the forests with the deer."†

Having made this determination, Yayáti restored his youth to Púru, resumed his own decrepitude, installed his youngest son in the sovereignty, and departed to the wood of penance (Tapovana[1]). To Turvasu he consigned the south-east districts of his kingdom; the west, to Druhyu; the south, to Yadu; and

---

[1] Bhrigutunga, according to the Brahma.

---

* या दुस्त्यजा दुर्मतिभिर्या न जीर्यति जीर्यतः।
तां तृष्णां संत्यजन्प्राज्ञः सुखेनैवाभिपूर्यते॥

† पूर्णं वर्षसहस्रं मे विषयासक्तचेतसः।
तथाप्यनुदिनं तृष्णा ममैतेष्वेव जायते॥
तस्मादेतामहं त्यक्त्वा ब्रह्मण्याधाय मानसम्।
निर्द्वन्द्वो निर्ममो भूत्वा चरिष्यामि मृगैः सह॥

the north, to Anu; to govern, as viceroys,* under their younger brother Púru, whom he appointed supreme monarch of the earth.[1]

---

[1] The older brothers were made Mańd́ala-nŕipas,† kings of circles or districts: Bhágavata.‡ The situation of their governments is not exactly agreed upon.

	Váyu and Padma.	Brahma and Hari Vaḿśa. §	Bhágavata. ‖
Turvasu	South-east	South-east	West
Druhyu	West	West	South-east
Yadu	South-west	South	South
Anu	North	North	North

The Linga describes the ministers and people as expostulating with Yayáti, for illegally giving the supremacy to the youngest son; but he satisfies them by showing, that he was justified in setting the seniors aside, for want of filial duty. The Mahábhárata, Udyoga Parvan, Gálava Charita, has a legend of Yayáti's giving a daughter to the saint Gálava, who, through her means, obtains, from different princes, eight hundred horses, white with

---

* कृत्वा मण्डलिनो नृपान् । Comment: मण्डलेशाधिपान् ।

† And see the preceding note.

‡ Neither in the *Bhágavata-puráńa* nor even in the commentary on it do I find the term *mańd́ala-nŕipa*. *Íśwara* is the designation which that Puráńa gives to Turvasu and the rest.

§ So I find in the *Brahma-puráńa*, with which the *Linga-puráńa*, Prior Section, LXVII., 11—12, agrees. But the *Harivaḿśa*, *śl*. 1617—1619, has:

Turvasu,	South-east.
Druhyu	West.
Yadu,	North-east.
Anu,	North.
Púru,	Middle region.

‖ IX., XIX., 22.

one black ear, as a fee for his preceptor Viśwámitra. Yayáti, after his death and residence in Indra's heaven, is again descending to earth, when his daughter's sons give him the benefit of their devotions, and replace him in the celestial sphere. It has the air of an old story. A legend in some respects similar has been related in our text; p. 16, *supra*.

CHAPTER XI.

The Yádava race, or descendants of Yadu. Kártavírya obtains a boon from Dattátreya: takes Rávańa prisoner: is killed by Paraśuráma: his descendants.

I WILL first relate to you the family of Yadu, the eldest son of Yayáti, in which the eternal, immutable, Vishńu descended upon earth, in a portion of his essence;[1] of which the glory cannot be described, though for ever hymned, in order to confer the fruit of all their wishes—whether they desired virtue, wealth, pleasure, or liberation,—upon all created beings, upon men, saints, heavenly quiristers, spirits of evil,* nymphs, centaurs,† serpents, birds, demons,‡ gods, sages, Brahmans,§ and ascetics. Whoever hears the account of the race of Yadu shall be released from all sin; for the supreme spirit, that is without form,‖ and which is

---

[1] Or, 'in which Kríshńa was born.' It might have been expected, from the importance of this genealogy, that it would have been so carefully preserved, that the authorities would have closely concurred in its details. Although, however, the leading

---

* *Rákshasa*; which word, in the original, is preceded by *yaksha*, and followed by *guhyaka*,—terms left untranslated.

† *Kimpurusha*.

‡ To render *daitya* and *dánava* conjointly.

§ *Devarshi* and *dwijarshi*, in the original. For these two kinds of Rishis,—the second of which has the name of Brahmarshi, more usually,—see Vol. III., p. 68, note 1.

‖ *Nirákriti*. There is a variant, *narákriti*, 'in the form of a man.' It is noticed by the scholiast.

called Vishńu, was manifested in this family.*

Yadu had four sons,—Sahasrajit, Kroshtu,† Nala, and Raghu.[1] Śatajit was the son of the elder of these; and he had three sons, Haihaya, Veńu,[2]‡ and Haya.§ The

---

specifications coincide, yet, as we shall have occasion to notice, great and irreconcileable variations occur.

[1] The two first generally agree. There are differences in the rest; as:

Váyu.	Brahma.‖	Bhágavata.¶	Kúrma.
Nila	Nala	Nala	Nila
Ajita	Anjika	Ripu**	Jina
Raghu ††	Payoda		Raghu

The Brahma and Hari Vaḿśa‡‡ read Sahasrada for the first name; and the Linga has Balasani, in place of Nala.§§ The Agni makes Śatajit, also, a son of Yadu.

[2] Veńuhaya: Bhágavata, &c.‖‖ Uttánahaya: Padma. Veńu-

---

* This sentence renders a stanza.

† So read all my MSS.; and such is the lection of the *Váyu-puráńa*. The Translator's "Kroshti" I take to have been a typographical error for Kroshtri. See notes ‖ and ¶, below. Also *vide infra*, p. 61, note *.

‡ One MS. has Veńuhaya.

§ Maháhaya is the lection of one copy; and so reads the *Bhágavata-puráńa*. In the *Linga-puráńa*, Śatajit's sons are called Haihaya, Haya, and Veńuhaya; and so in the *Harivaḿśa* and the *Matsya-puráńa*.

‖ I find Sahasrajit, Payoda, Kroshtri, Nila, and Anjika.

¶ IX., XXIII., 20. For Kroshtu I there find Kroshtri.

** Corrected from "Aripu".

†† My MSS. have Laghu. And see note §§, below.

‡‡ In my MSS., Sahasrada, Payoda, Kroshtu, Nila, and Anjika.

§§ Yadu's five sons I find called, in the *Linga-puráńa*, Sahasrajit, Kroshtu, Nila, Ajaka, and Laghu. Only that it reads Ajika and Raghu, the *Matsya-puráńa* has the same names; and so has the *Kúrma-puráńa*, except that it gives Anjita and Raghu (or Laghu, in some MSS.).

‖‖ As the *Váyu-puráńa*, the *Kúrma-puráńa*, and the *Harivaḿśa*.

son of Haihaya was Dharmanetra;[1]* his son was Kunti;[2] his son was Sáhanji;[3]† his son was Mahishmat;[4] his son was Bhadrasena;[5]‡ his son was Durdama;§ his son was Dhanaka,[6] who had four sons,—Kritavírya,

haya: Matsya.|| They were the sons of Sahasrada: Brahma and Hari Vaḿśa.

[1] Dharmatantra: Váyu. Dharma:¶ Kúrma.**

[2] Kírtti: Váyu.††

[3] Sanjneya: Váyu. Śankhaṇa: Agni. Sáhanja, of Sáhanjaní-purí:‡‡ Brahma. Sanjnita: Linga.§§ Samhana: Matsya.|||| Sohanjí: Bhágavata.

[4] By whom the city of Máhishmatí (on the Narbudda) was founded:¶¶ Brahma Puráńa, Hari Vaḿśa.

[5] So the Bhágavata; but the Váyu,*** more correctly, has Bhadraśreńya.††† *Vide supra*, p. 33, note 2.

[6] Kanaka: Váyu, &c.‡‡‡ Varaka: Linga.§§§ Andhaka: Kúrma.||||||

* In a single MS., Dharma.

† Two of my MSS. have Sáhajit.

‡ My best MSS. have Bhadraśreńya. The *Váyu-puráńa* says he was Raja of Benares.

§ Durmada: *Váyu-puráńa* and *Bhágavata-puráńa*.

|| See note § in the preceding page.

¶ Haihaya's son was Dharma, and his was Dharmanetra, according to the *Linga-puráńa* and the *Kúrma-puráńa*.

** And *Bhágavata-puráńa*, which gives him a son Netra, father of Kunti.

†† And *Linga-puráńa*, *Kúrma-puráńa*, and *Brahma-puráńa*. Kárta and Kárti: *Harivaḿśa*.

‡‡ And so the *Harivaḿśa*, *sl.* 1848.

§§ I find Sanjeya. The *Kúrma-puráńa* has Sanjita.

|||| I find Sambata.

¶¶ One of my copies of the *Vishńu-puráńa* notices this fact.

*** And so the *Kúrma-puráńa*, *Linga-puráńa*, *Brahma-puráńa*, *Harivaḿśa*, &c.

††† See notes ‡ and ***, above.

‡‡‡ As the *Brahma-puráńa* and *Harivaḿśa*.

§§§ I find Dhanaka.

|||||| I find Dhenuka.

Kŕitágni,* Kŕitavarman,† and Kŕitaujas. Kŕitavírya's son was Arjuna, the sovereign of the seven Dwípas, the lord of a thousand arms. This prince propitiated the Sage Dattátreya, the descendant of Atri, who was a portion of Vishńu, and solicited, and obtained from him, these boons: a thousand arms; never acting unjustly; subjugation of the world by justice, and protecting it equitably; victory over his enemies; and death by the hands of a person renowned in the three regions of the universe. With these means he ruled over the whole earth with might and justice, and offered ten thousand sacrifices. Of him this verse‡ is still recited: "The kings of the earth will, assuredly, never pursue his steps in sacrifice, in munificence, in devotion, in courtesy, and in self-control."§ In his reign, nothing was lost, or injured;|| and so he governed

---

* Kŕitavírya: *Váyu-puráńa.*

† The *Kúrma-puráńa* has Kŕitadharma.

‡ It runs thus, in the *Bhágavata-puráńa*,—IX., XXIII., 24:

न नूनं कार्तवीर्यस्य गतिं यास्यन्ति पार्थिवाः ।
यज्ञदानतपोयोगश्रुतवीर्यदयादिभिः ॥

The *Váyu-puráńa* has:

न नूनं कार्तवीर्यस्य गतिं यास्यन्ति मानवाः ।
यज्ञैर्दानैस्तपोभिश्च विक्रमेण श्रुतेन च ॥

Compare the *Márkańd́eya-puráńa*, XIX., 20; also the *Brahma-puráńa*, &c.

§ न नूनं कार्तवीर्यस्य गतिं यास्यन्ति पार्थिवाः ।
यज्ञैर्दानैस्तपोभिर्वा प्रश्रयेण दमेन च ॥

See *Original Sanskrit Texts*, Part I., pp. 171, 172.

|| The scholiast quotes, from the *Kúrma-puráńa*, the following line, addressed to Arjuna:

अनष्टद्रव्यता चैव तव नामाभिकीर्तनात् ।

And I have found the ensuing stanza, of similar purport, in an extract from the *Brahmáńd́a-puráńa*:

the whole earth, with undiminished health, prosperity, power, and might, for eighty-five thousand years. Whilst sporting in the waters of the Narmadá, and elevated with wine, Rávańa came, on his tour of triumph, to (the city) Máhishmatí; and there he, who boasted of overthrowing the gods, the Daityas, the Gandharvas and their king, was taken prisoner by Kártavírya, and confined, like a (tame) beast, in a corner of his capital.[1]* At the expiration of his long reign, Kártavírya was killed by Paraśuráma, who was an embodied portion of the mighty Náráyańa.[2] Of the hundred sons of this king the five† principal were

---

[1] According to the Váyu, Kártavírya was the aggressor, invading Lanká, and there taking Rávańa prisoner. The circumstances are, more usually, narrated as in our text.

[2] *Vide supra*, p. 22. Kártavírya's fate was the consequence of an imprecation denounced by Ápava (or Vasishíha), the son of Varuńa, whose hermitage had been burnt, according to the Mahábhárata, Rájadharma,‡ by Chitrabhánu (or Fire), to whom the king had, in his bounty, presented the world. The Váyu makes the king himself the incendiary, with arrows given him, by Súrya, to dry up the ocean.

कार्तवीर्यार्जुनो नाम राजा बाहुसहस्रवान् ।
तस्य स्मरणमात्रेण हृतं नष्टं च लभ्यते ॥

"Arjuna, son of Kŕitavírya, *was* a king with a thousand arms. By simply calling him to mind, *a thing* lost or ruined is restored."

See, further, the *Harivaṁśa*, *l.* 1864.

* See *Original Sanskrit Texts*, Part II., p. 437, note 106.

† These, according to the *Bhágavata-puráńa*, IX., XXIII., 26, were all, out of a thousand, that survived the contest with Paraśuráma.

‡ *Anuśásana-parvan*, Chapter II.

Śúra,[1] Śúrasena, Vŕishańa,[2*] Madhu,[3†] and Jayadhwaja.[4] The son of the last was Tálajangha, who had a hundred sons, called, after him, Tálajanghas: the eldest of these was Vítihotra;‡ another was Bharata,[5] who had two sons, Vŕisha and Sujáti.[6§] The son of Vŕisha was Madhu:[7] he had a hundred sons, the chief

---

[1] Úrjita: Bhágavata.

[2] Vŕishabha: Bhágavata. Dhŕishńa: Matsya. Dhŕishńa: Kúrma.|| Pŕishokta:¶ Padma. Vŕishńi: Linga.** Kŕishńáksha: Brahma.††

[3] Kŕishńa, in all except the Bhágavata.‡‡

[4] King of Avanti: Brahma and Hari Vaḿśa.§§

[5] Ananta: Váyu and Agni;|||| elsewhere omitted.

[6] Durjaya¶¶ only: Váyu, Matsya.***

[7] This Madhu, according to the Bhágavata,††† was the son of Kártavírya. The Brahma and Hari Vaḿśa make him the son of Vŕisha, but do not say whose son Vŕisha was. The commentator on the latter asserts, that the name is a synonym of Payoda,— the son of Yadu, according to his authority, and to that alone.‡‡‡

---

* One MS. has Dhŕishańa.

† In three copies the reading is Madhudhwaja.

‡ In one MS., Vítahotra. In the *Váyu-puráńa*, Vírahotra.

§ Professor Wilson had "Sujáti", by typographical error, for Sujáti. But the original, in all my MSS., वृषसुजातौ, yields only Sujáta.

|| I find Vŕisha and Dhŕishńa.

¶ The *Harivaḿśa* has Dhŕishńokta or Dhŕishńokta.

** I find Dhŕishńa. †† I find Vŕishańa.

‡‡ The *Brahma-puráńa* has Madhupadhwaja.

§§ And so the *Linga-puráńa*. I have corrected Professor Wilson's "Avanti". A country, not a city, is intended.

|||| The *Linga-puráńa* has Anarta.

¶¶ He was son of Kŕishńa(?), according to the *Linga-puráńa*.

*** Vŕisha and others, unnamed, were sons of Vítihotra, according to the *Kúrma-puráńa* and *Linga-puráńa*.

††† By probable inference, but not explicitly: IX., XXIII., 28.

‡‡‡ But vide supra, p. 53, notes 1, ||, and ‡‡.

of whom was Vríshńi;* and from him the family† obtained the name of Vríshńi.[1] From the name of their father, Madhu, they were, also, called Madhu;‡ whilst, from the denomination of their common ancestor, Yadu, the whole were termed Yádavas.[2]§

---

[1] The Bhágavata agrees with our text; but the Brahma, Hari Vaṁśa, Linga, and Kúrma make Vríshańa|| the son of Madhu, and derive the family-name of Vríshńis, or Várshńeyas, from him.

[2] The text takes no notice of some collateral tribes which appear to merit remark. Most of the other authorities, in mentioning the sons of Jayadhwaja, observe, that, from them came the five great divisions of the Haihaya tribe. These, according to the Váyu,¶ were the Tálajanghas, Vítihotras, Avantis,**

---

* तस्यापि वृष्णिप्रमुखं पुत्रशतमासीत्। He had a hundred sons,—"Vríshńi and others."

† *Gotra*,

‡ The Translator had "Mádhavas", although the original runs: मधुसंज्ञाहेतुश्च मधुरभवत्।

§ In Professor Johnson's *Selections from the Mahábhárata*, p. 46, note 7, Professor Wilson seems to consider, but with little probability of correctness, as one race "the Yádavas, Jadavas, Jados, or Jats."

It has been speculated that "the Jartikas of the *Mahábhárata* and the Puráńas represent the Jaťs," and that the Jaťs "were * * transformed into the Jatano, or Gitano, the Gypsies of modern Europe." Sir H. M. Elliot's *Appendix to the Arabs in Sind*, pp. 148, 67. The same author remarks, as to writing Jat or Ját, that "the difference of the long and short *a* is a mere fashion of spelling, and shows no difference of origin, family, or habit." The two words, properly represented, are Jat and Jáť.

Also see Professor Lassen's *Indische Alterthumskunde*, Vol. II., p. 577, note 5. But the fullest extant dissertation on the Jáťs will be found in Sir H. M. Elliot's *Supplemental Glossary*, Vol. I., pp. 411—416.

|| In the best MSS. I find Vríshńi.

¶ My MSS. give: Vírahotras, Bhojas, Ávartis (or Avantis), Tuńdikeras, and Tálajanghas. The *Linga-puráńa* has: Vítihotras, Haryátas, Bhojas, Avantis, and Śúrasenas.

** Corrected, here and below, from "Ávantyas"; the original, in some MSS.,—see the last note,—being आवन्त्यः.

Tuńdikeras,* and Játas.† The Matsya and Agni omit the first, and substitute Bhojas; and the latter are included in the list in the Brahma, Padma, Linga, and Hari Vaḿśa. For Játas the reading is Saujátas or Sujátas.‡ The Brahma Puráńa§ has, also, Bharatas, who, as well as the Sujátas, are not commonly specified, it is said, 'from their great number.' They are, in all probability, invented, by the compiler, out of the names of the text, Bharata and Sujáti.|| The situation of these tribes is Central India; for the capital of the Tálajanghas was Máhishmatí,¶ or Chuli-Maheśwar,**—still called, according to Colonel Tod, Sahasra báhu kí basti, 'the village of the Thousand-armed,' that is, of Kártavírya. Annals and Antiquities of Rajasthan, Vol. I., p. 39, note. The Tuńdikeras and Vítihotras are placed, in the geographical lists, behind the Vindhyan Mountains; and the termination -kaira †† is common in the valley of the Narmadá, as Bairkaira, &c.; or we may have Tuńdikera abbreviated, as Tuńduri, on the Tapteo. The Avantis were in Ujjayini;‡‡ and the Bhojas were in the neighbourhood, probably, of Dhár, in Malwa.§§ These tribes must have preceded, then, the Rájput tribes by whom these countries are now occupied, or: Rahtors, Chauháns, Pawárs, Gehlots, and the rest. There are still some vestiges of them; and a tribe of Haihayas still exists "near the

* Tauńḍikeras, according to the *Brahma-puráńa* and *Harivaḿśa*.

† Nowhere do I find this name.

‡ As in the *Harivaḿśa*, *sl.* 1895.

§ And so the *Harivaḿśa*.

|| *Vide supra*, p. 57, note §.

¶ What ground is there for this assertion?

** See Vol. II., p. 106, note 6.

†† The correct form is खेड़ा, which is, doubtless, corrupted from खेट, 'village'.

‡‡ Has this statement any foundation beyond the fact that Ujjayini was called Avanti? See Vol. III., p. 246, note 3.

§§ At least, a Bhoja—one of some half dozen kings of that name, known to India,—reigned at Dhárá in the eleventh century. See Vol. II., p. 159.

M. Vivien de Saint-Martin would identify the Bhojas with the Bhotias, *Géographie du Véda*, p. 136.

very top of the valley of Sohagpoor, in Bhagel-khund, aware of their ancient lineage, and, though few in number, are still celebrated for their valour." Tod's Annals, &c. of Rajasthan, Vol. I., p. 39. The scope of the traditions regarding them—especially, of their overrunning the country, along with Śakas and other foreign tribes, in the reign preceding that of Sagara (see Vol. III., p. 289),—indicates their foreign origin, also; and, if we might trust to verbal resemblances, we might suspect, that the Hayas and Haihayas of the Hindus had some connexion with the Hia, Hoiei-ke, Hoiei-hu, and similarly denominated Hun or Turk tribes who make a figure in Chinese history.* Deguignes, Histoire Générale des Huns, Vol. I., Part I., pp. 7, 55, 231; Vol, I., Part II., pp. 253, &c. At the same time, it is to be observed, that these tribes do not make their appearance until some centuries after the Christian era, and the scene of their first exploits is far from the frontiers of India: the coincidence of appellation may be, therefore, merely accidental.† In the word Haya, which, properly, means 'a horse,' it is not impossible, however, that we have a confirmatory evidence of the Scythian origin of the Haihayas, as Colonel Tod supposed; although we cannot, with him, imagine the word 'horse' itself is derived from Haya.‡ Annals, &c. of Rajasthan, Vol. I., p. 76.

* Colonel Tod speculates that "The Ulhya [Haihaya] race, of the line of Boodha, may claim affinity with the Chinese race which first gave monarchs to China." *Annals and Antiquities of Rajasthan*, Vol. I., p. 39, note †.

† See Vol. II., p. 134, note †.

‡ It is not at all clear that Colonel Tod proposes such a derivation.

CHAPTER XII.

Descendants of Kroshṭu. Jyámagha's connubial affection for his wife Śaibyá: their descendants kings of Vidarbha and Chedi.

KROSHṬU,* the son of Yadu,[1] had a son named Vṛijinívat;[2]† his son was Swáhi;[3]‡ his son was Rushadgu;[4]§ his son was Chitraratha; his son was Śaśabindu,|| who was lord¶ of the fourteen great gems;[5] he had a hundred thousand wives and a

---

[1] In the Brahma Puráńa and Hari Vaḿśa, we have two families from Kroshṭri; one, which is much the same as that of the text; the other makes short work of a long story, as we shall again notice.

[2] Vajravat: Kúrma.**

[3] Śánti:†† Kúrma. Swáha: Matsya. Triśanku:‡‡ Linga.§§

[4] Vishaḿśu: Agni. Ŕishabha:|||| Linga. Kuśika: Kúrma.¶¶ Ruśeku: Bhágavata.***

[5] Or articles the best of their kind;††† seven animate, and

---

* So read all my MSS., instead of the "Kroshṭri" of the former edition. *Vide supra*, p. 53, note †.

† And so the *Váyu-puráńa*, *Linga-puráńa*, *Kúrma-puráńa*, &c. Variants of our text are Vṛijinivat, Vṛijinivat, and Bṛihaddhwaja.

‡ Variants: Śáhi and Áhi.

§ The Translator misread this name as "Rushadru". Two of my MSS. have Urośanku. The reading of the best MSS. of the *Harivaḿśa* is Rushadgu.

|| In the *Rámáyańa*, *Bála-káńḍa*, LXX., 28, the Śaśabindus are named in connexion with the Haihayas, Tálajanghas, and Śúras.

¶ *Chakravartin.*

** See note †, above. Vṛijinavat: *Bhágavata-puráńa*. †† I find Khyáti.

‡‡ In the *Linga-puráńa* I find Swátin(?), and Kuśanku as his son.

§§ The *Váyu-puráńa* and *Brahma-puráńa* have Swáhi.

|||| I do not find that the *Linga-puráńa* gives this name, or any at all, between Kuśanku and Chitraratha. ¶¶ I find Kuśanku.

*** Raśádu seems to be the reading of the *Váyu-puráńa*; Ushadgu, that of the *Brahma-puráńa*.

††† The commentary on the *Vishńu-puráńa* gives one set of these "gems",

million of sons.[1] The most renowned of them were Přithuyaśas, Přithukarman,* Přithujaya,† Přithu-

seven inanimate: a wife, a priest,‡ a general, a charioteer,§ a body of foot-soldiers,|| a horse, and an elephant, (or, instead of the last three, an executioner, an encomiast, a reader of the Vedas); and, a chariot, an umbrella,¶ a jewel, a sword, a shield, a banner, and a treasure.

[1] The text states this in plain prose; but the Váyu quotes a verse which makes out but a hundred hundred or 10.000 sons:

तत्रानुवंशश्लोकोऽयं विप्रैर्गीतः पुराविदैः ।
शशबिन्दोस्तु पुत्राणां शतानामभवच्छतम् ।
धीमतामनुरूपाणां भूरिद्रविणतेजसाम् ॥

from the *Dharma-saṁhitá*, a metrical work; and Śrídhara, in his scholia on the *Bhágavata-puráńa*, IX., XXIII., 31, gives another set, from the *Márkańdeya-puráńa*. The first-named set is that represented by Professor Wilson; but his parenthetical substitutes are derived from some source unknown to me.

The extract from the *Dharma-saṁhitá* is as follows:

चक्रं रथो मणिः खड्गश्चर्म रत्नं च पञ्चमम् ।
केतुर्निधिश्च सप्तैव प्राणहीनानि चक्षते ॥
भार्या पुरोहितश्चैव सेनानी रथकृच्च यः ।
पत्त्यश्वौ कलभश्चेति प्राणिनः सप्त कीर्तिताः ।
चतुर्दशेति रत्नानि सर्वेषां चक्रवर्तिनाम् ॥

Śrídhara's quotation from the *Márkańdeya-puráńa* I have not succeeded in verifying:

गजवाजिरथस्त्रीषुनिधिमाल्याम्बरद्रुमाः ।
शक्तिपाशमणिच्छत्रविमानानि चतुर्दश ॥

* Přithudharman: *Váyu-puráńa*.

† In the *Váyu-puráńa* I find Přithunjaya.

‡ *Purohita*.

§ *Rathakřit*; 'a car-maker'(?).

|| *Patti*.

¶ I find no reading but *chakra*, a word of various meanings, 'army' being one of them.

kírtti, Prithudána,* and Prithuśravas.† The son of the last of these six[1] was Tamas;[2] his son was Uśanas,[3]‡ who celebrated a hundred sacrifices of the horse; his son was Śiteyus;[4]§ his son was Rukmakavacha;[5] his son was Parávrit,|| who had five sons,

---

[1] The Matsya has the first, third, and fifth of our text, and Prithudharma, Prithukírtti, and Prithumat. The Kúrma has, also, six names,¶ but makes as many successions.

[2] Suyajna: Agni, Brahma, Matsya.** Dharma: Bhágavata.††

[3] Ushat: Brahma. Hari Vaṁśa.

[4] Śitikshu: Agni. Śineyus: Brahma.‡‡ Ruchaka§§: Bhágavata. The Váyu has Marutta and Kambalabarhis, brothers, instead.

[5] Considerable variety prevails here. The Brahma and Hari Vaṁśa have Marutta,|||| the Rájarshi (a gross blunder: see Vol. III., p. 243), Kambalabarhis, Śataprasúti, Rukmakavacha; the Agni, Marutta, Kambalabarhis, Rukmeshu; whilst the Bhágavata makes Ruchaka son of Uśanas, and father to the five princes who, in

---

* Prithudátri: *Váyu-puráńa*.

† He alone is named in the *Brahma-puráńa* and *Harivaṁśa*.

‡ The *Linga-puráńa* has Śaśabindu, Ananteka, Yajna, Dhriti, Uśanas.

§ Thus read two MSS., while Śatáyus and Śatavapus are found in others. But the ordinary lection is Siteshu; and so read the *Kúrma-puráńa* and *Linga-puráńa*.

|| In the *Kúrma-puráńa*, he has only one son, Jyámagha.

¶ Prithuyaśas, Prithukarman, Prithunjaya, Prithuśravas, and Prithusattama. Uśanas is son of the last.

** And the *Harivaṁśa*.

†† The *Váyu-puráńa* has something different; but I am unable to decipher what it is.

‡‡ And the *Harivaṁśa*.

§§ Corrected from "Purujit". See note 5 in this page, and note ‡ in the next.

|||| Also read Maruta, in several MSS. See, further, note ‡ in the following page.

Rukmeshu, Príthurukma,* Jyámagha, Pálita, and Harita.[1]† To this day the following verse relating to Jyámagha is repeated: "Of all the husbands submissive to their wives, who have been, or who will be, the most eminent is the king Jyámagha,[2] who was the

---

the text, are the grandsons of Rukmakavacha.‡

[1] The Bhágavata has Purujit, Rukma,§ Rukmeshu, Príthu, and Jyámagha. The Váyu reads the two last names Parigha and Hari.‖ The Brahma and Hari Vaḿśa insert Parájit¶ as the father of the five named as in the text.**

[2] Most of the other authorities mention, that the elder of the five brothers, Rukmeshu, succeeded his father in the sovereignty; and that the second, Príthurukma, remained in his brother's service. Pálita and Harita were set over Videha (विदेहेषु पिता वसत् । Linga††) or Tirhoot; and Jyámagha went forth to settle where he might: according to the Váyu, he conquered Madhyadeśa (the country along the Narmadá), Mekalá, and the Śuktimat mountains.‡‡ So the Brahma Puráńa states, that he established himself along the Ŕikshavat mountain, and dwelt in Śuktimatí. He names his son, as we shall see, Vidarbha. The country so

---

* Corrected, here and below, from "Prithurukman". The word occurs in the midst of a compound. For its form as given above, see the *Harivaḿśa*, *sl.* 1980, with which the *Váyu-puráńa*, &c. agree.

† One of my MSS. gives Parávrit but one son, Rukmeshu, and makes him father of Príthurukma and the rest.

‡ This is not exact, as appears from note 1 in this page. The *Linga-puráńa* has Śiteshu, Maruta, Kambalabarhis, Rukmakavacha.

§ Corrected from "Rukman".

‖ And so reads the *Linga-puráńa*.

¶ Instead of Parávrit.

** Only they have Hari, not Harita; and, in some MSS., Palita, for Pálita.

†† Prior Section, LXVIII., 33.

‡‡ It does not appear, from my MSS. of the *Váyu-puráńa*, that mention is made of Madhyadeśa. The names occur of Narmadá, Mekalá, Mŕittikávatí, Śuktimatí, and the Ŕikshavat mountains.

husband of Śaibyá." Śaibyá was barren; but Jyámagha* was so much afraid of her, that he did not take any other wife. On one occasion, the king, after a desperate conflict, with elephants and horse, defeated a powerful foe, who, abandoning wife, children, kin, army, treasure, and dominion, fled. When the enemy was put to flight, Jyámagha beheld a lovely princess left alone and exclaiming "Save me, father! Save me, brother!" as her (large) eyes rolled wildly with affright. The king was struck by her beauty, and penetrated with affection for her, and said to himself: "This is fortunate. I have no children, and am the husband of a sterile bride. This maiden has fallen into my hands, to rear up to me posterity. I will espouse her. But, first, I will take her in my car, and convey her to my palace, where I must request the concurrence

---

called is Berar; and, amongst his descendants, we have the Chaidyas, or princes of Baghelkhańd and Chandail,† and Daśárha (more correctly, perhaps, Daśárńa, Chhattisgarh‡); so that this story of Jyámagha's adventures appears to allude to the first settlement of the Yádava tribes along the Narmadá, more to the south and west than before.

अयवर्ती निरिं मत्वा पुत्रिमत्वामचाविचत् ।

Something very similar is read in the *Linga-puráńa* and also in the *Brahma-puráńa*.

* "Though desirous of progeny": अपत्यकामोऽपि ।

† That the ancient Chedi is not represented by Baghelkhańd and Chandail, is now settled beyond all doubt. See Vol. II., p. 157, note §§.

The Pandits of Central India, beguiled by distant verbal similarity, maintain that Chedi is one with the modern District of Chandeyree (Chanderi); and this groundless identification has even found its way into popular literature. See the Hindi *Premasâgara*, Chapter LIII.

‡ I have questioned this position. See Vol. II., p. 160, note †.

of the queen in these nuptials." Accordingly, he took the princess into his chariot, and returned to his own capital.

When Jyámagha's approach was announced, Śaibyá came to the palace-gate, attended by the ministers, the courtiers, and the citizens, to welcome the victorious monarch. But, when she beheld the maiden standing on the left hand of* the king, her lips swelled and slightly quivered with resentment, and she said to Jyámagha: "Who is this light-hearted damsel that is with you in the chariot?" The king, unprepared with a reply, made answer precipitately, through fear of his queen: "This is my daughter-in-law." "I have never had a son," rejoined Śaibyá; "and you have no other children. Of what son of yours, then, is this girl the wife?"† The king, disconcerted by the jealousy and anger which the words of Śaibyá displayed, made this reply to her, in order to prevent further contention: "She is the young bride of the future son whom thou shalt bring forth." Hearing this, Śaibyá smiled gently, and said "So be it;" and the king entered into his great palace.

In consequence of this conversation regarding the birth of a son having taken place in an auspicious conjunction, aspect, and season,‡ the queen, although passed the time of women, became, shortly afterwards, pregnant, and bore a son. His father named him Vi-

---

* According to some MSS., simply "at the side of".

† स्नुषासंबन्धता ह्येषा कतमेन सुतेन ते ।

‡ *Lagna*, *horá*, *aṁśaka*, and *avayava*. The scholiast defines *horá* to be half a *ráśi*; *aṁśaka*, a ninth of one; and *avayava*, a twelfth of one.

darbha, and married him to the damsel he had brought home.* They had three sons,—Kratha, Kaiśika,[1]† and Romapáda.[2] The son of Romapáda was Babhru;[3] and his son was Dhŕiti.[4] The son of Kaiśika was Chedi,‡ whose descendants were called the Chaidya kings.[5] The son of Kratha was Kunti;[6]§ his son was

---

[1] The Bhágavata has Kuśa; the Matsya, Kauśika.|| All the authorities agree in specifying three sons.

[2] Lomapáda: Agni.¶

[3] Vastu: Váyu. Kŕiti: Agni.

[4] Áhuti: Váyu. Iti: Padma. Dyuti: Matsya. Bhŕiti: Kúrma.** This latter is singular, in carrying on the line of Romápada for twelve generations further.††

[5] The Bhágavata, however, makes the princes of Chedi continuous from Romapáda; as, Babhru, Dhŕiti,‡‡ Uśika, Chedi—the Chaidyas, amongst whom were Damaghosha and Śiśupála.

[6] Kombhi: Padma.

---

* The original runs: सत्रा च विदर्भ इति पिता नाम चक्रे । स च तां स्नुषामुपयेमे । The scholiast says, in explanation: स च । विदर्भः । कथं स्नुषामुपयेमे । आगमवचः पूर्वमतिक्रान्तत्वादित्याशयम् । This obedient youth, then, because of his father's prediction, married a woman who, it seems, may have been of nubile age before he was born.

† Two of my best MSS. have Kanśika.

‡ Chidi (?): *Váyu-puráńa.*

§ क्रथस्य स्नुषापुत्रस्य कुन्तिरभवत् । "Kunti was offspring of Kratha, son of the *so-called* daughter-in-law." Comment: स्नुषायाः । आगमवचः स्नुषायाः सत्याः पुत्रस्य ।

|| And so the *Váyu-puráńa*, the *Kúrma-puráńa*, the *Linga-puráńa*, &c.

¶ Add the *Váyu-puráńa*, the *Harivaḿśa*, &c. The *Linga-puráńa* reads Romapáda.

** I find Dhŕiti. The *Linga-puráńa* has Sudhŕiti.

†† There seem to be names of only seven descendants of Dhŕiti. Some of Kaniska's descendants, also, are particularised. But the state of my MSS. does not warrant further detail with certainty.

‡‡ Kŕiti is the ordinary reading.

Vŕishńi;[1] his son was Nirvŕiti;[2]* his son was Daśárha; his son was Vyoman;† his son was Jímúta; his son was Vikŕiti;[3]‡ his son was Bhímaratha;§ his son was Navaratha;[4] his son was Daśaratha;[5] his son was Śakuni; his son was Karambhi;|| his son was Deva-ráta;¶ his son was Devakshattra;[6] his son was Ma-

---

[1] Dhŕishńa: Váyu. Dhŕishńi: Matsya.**

[2] Nivŕitti: Váyu.†† Nidhŕiti: Agni. The Brahma makes three sons,—Avanta, Daśárha, and Balivŕishahan. In the Linga, it is said, of Daśárha, that he was ताम्रारिगणसूदनः,‡‡ 'destroyer of the host of copper (faced; European?) foes.'

[3] Vikala: Matsya.

[4] Nararatha: Brahma, Hari Vaḿśa.§§

[5] Dŕidharatha: Agni. Devaráta: Linga.||||

[6] Soma: Linga.¶¶ Devanakshattra: Padma.

---

* One MS. has Nirdhŕiti; another, Nivŕitti. The *Linga-puráńa* has Nidhŕiti, preceded by Bahudhŕishńa. The *Kúrma-puráńa* gives Nivŕitti.

† Two MSS. give, like the *Bhágavata-puráńa*, Vyoma. The *Váyu-puráńa* has Vyoman; the *Linga-puráńa*, Vyápta.

One of my best MSS. of the *Vishńu-puráńa* inserts Abhijit after Vyoman.

‡ In three copies, Vankŕiti.

§ The *Váyu-puráńa* interposes Rathavara between Bhímaratha and Navaratha.

|| Karambhaka: *Váyu-puráńa*. Karambha, in the *Linga-puráńa*; also, in the *Kúrma-puráńa*, which has, hereabouts, numerous names, &c. which I am unable to make out in my MSS.

¶ And so the *Linga-puráńa*, &c. Devaráj: *Kúrma-puráńa*.

** Vŕita: *Linga-puráńa*.

†† My MSS. have Nirvŕitti, also.

‡‡ In my MSS. there is a very different reading:

दशार्हो निधृतो नाम्ना महारिगणसूदनः ।

§§ This work—and so the *Brahma-puráńa*—has, in the present chapter, many other peculiarities, here unnoticed, as to proper names.

|||| Dŕidharatha, in my MSS.

¶¶ I find Devakshattra there.

dhu;[1] his son was Anavaratha;* his son was Kuruvatsa; his son was Anuratha;† his son was Puruhotra; his son was Aḿśu;‡ his son was Satwata,§ from whom

[1] There is great variety in the succeeding appellations:

Bhágavata.	Váyu.	Brahma.‖
Madhu	Madhu ¶	Madhu
Kuruvaśa	Manu **	Manavadas
Anu	Puruvatsa ††	Purudwat
Puruhotra	Purudwat	Madhu and Satwa
Áyu	Satwa	
Sátwata	Satwata	Satwata

Matsya.	Padma.	Kúrma.
Madhu	Madhu	Madhu
Uruvas	Puru	Kuru ‡‡
Purudwat	Punarvasu	Anu §§
Jantu	Jantu	Aḿśa ‖‖
Satwata	Satwata	Andhaka ¶¶
		Satwata

* Two of my best MSS. omit this name.

† One MS. has Anurata; another, Anu, with a son Anuta, father of Puruhotra.

‡ All my MSS. but two give Aḿśa.

§ Some MSS. have Sátwata.

‖ Perhaps my MS. is defective; but it names only Madhu, Purudwat, Satwa, and Sátwata.

¶ The *Váyu-puráńa* seems to place Devana between Devakshattra and Madhu.

** I think the *Váyu-puráńa* has Mahátejas, Manu, and Manuvasa, and as brothers.

†† Puruvaśa, in my MSS.,—and as son of Mahátejas, perhaps.

‡‡ I find Kuruvaśa; and, apparently, Purudwat follows, before Anu.

§§ After Anu I find Purukutsa. ‖‖ Aḿśu, in my MSS.

¶¶ This name is not mentioned in my MSS.; nor is there room for it. For Andhaka, *vide infra*, p. 71, note ‖.

the princes of this house were termed Sátwatas. This was the progeny of Jyámagha; by listening to the account of whom, a man is purified from his sins.

The Linga* has Purushaprabhu, Manwat, Pratardana, Satwata; and the Agni, Dravavasu, Purubuta, Jantu, and Sátwata. Some of these originate, no doubt, in the blunders of copyists; but they cannot, all, be referred to that source.

---

* My best MSS. have: Madhu, Kuruvamśa or Kuruvamśaka, Anu, Amśu and Purudwat, Satwa (son of Amśu), Sátwata.

CHAPTER XIII.

Sons of Satwata. Bhoja princes of Mrittikávati. Súrya the friend of Sattrájita: appears to him in a bodily form: gives him the Syamantaka gem: its brilliance and marvellous properties. Sattrájita gives it to Prasena, who is killed by a lion: the lion killed by the bear Jámbavat. Kríshńa, suspected of killing Prasena, goes to look for him in the forests: traces the bear to his cave: fights with him for the jewel: the contest prolonged: supposed, by his companions, to be slain: he overthrows Jámbavat, and marries his daughter, Jámbavatí: returns, with her and the jewel, to Dwáraká: restores the jewel to Sattrájita, and marries his daughter, Satyabhámá. Sattrájita murdered by Śatadhanwan: avenged by Kríshńa. Quarrel between Kríshńa and Balaráma. Akrúra possessed of the jewel: leaves Dwáraká. Public calamities. Meeting of the Yádavas. Story of Akrúra's birth: he is invited to return: accused, by Kríshńa, of having the Syamantaka jewel: produces it in full assembly: it remains in his charge: Kríshńa acquitted of having purloined it.

THE sons of Satwata* were Bhajin,† Bhajamána, Divya, Andhaka,‡ Devávŕidha,§ Mahábhoja, and Vŕishńi.[1]‖ Bhajamána¶ had three sons, Nimi,[2] Kri-

---

[1] The Agni acknowledges but four sons; but all the rest

---

* Variant: Sátwata; and so throughout this chapter. Satwata's wife was Kauśalyá, according to the *Váyu-puráńa*, *Brahma-puráńa*, and *Harivaṁśa*.

† Corrected from "Bhajina".

‡ For the conflicting accounts of his parentage, see Goldstücker's *Sanskrit Dictionary*, *sub voce*.

§ Corrected, in this chapter, from "Devávriddha".

‖ Sátwata's sons, according to the *Bhágavata-puráńa*, IX., XXIV., 6, 7, were Bhajamána, Bhaji, Divya, Vŕishńi, Devávŕidha, Andhaka, and Mahábhoja.

¶ He was skilled in the *Dhanurveda*, the *Kúrma-puráńa* alleges.

kańa,[1]* and Vŕishńi,[2] by one wife, and as many † by another, ‡—Śatájit, Sahasrájit, and Ayutájit.[3] § The son of Devávŕidha was Babhru, of whom this verse is recited: "We hear, when afar, and we behold, when

---

agree in the number, || and, mostly, in the names. Mahábhoja is sometimes read Mahábhága. ¶

[1] Kŕimi: Brahma,** Agni, Kúrma. ††

[2] Pańava: Váyu. Kramańa: Brahma. ‡‡ Kŕipańa: Padma. Kinkińa: Bhágavata. §§

[3] Dhŕishńhi: Bhágavata, |||| Brahma. ¶¶

[3] The Brahma and Hari Vamśa add, to the first three, Śúra and Puranjaya,*** and, to the second, Dáśaka. †††

---

* Corrupted, in some of my MSS., into Kŕikwańa and Kŕiuwańa.

† This second family is unrecognized by the *Kúrma-puráńa*.

‡ Both wives bore the name of Śŕinjayá, agreeably to the *Váyu-puráńa* and *Harivamśa*.

§ Professor Wilson had "Śatajit, Sahasrajit, and Ayutajit"; but, in all my MSS. but one, I find as above. All the names are, apparently, different in the *Váyu-puráńa*, my copies of which are, here, very illegible. The *Linga-puráńa* has Ayutáyus, Śatáyus, and Harshakŕit, with Śŕinjayá as their mother, and does not name the first set of sons at all.

|| Not so. See the end of the next note.

¶ As in the *Linga-puráńa*; Mahábáhu, in the *Brahma-puráńa* and *Harivamśa*. Add: for Bhajin, Bhajana, *Linga-puráńa*; Bhogin, *Brahma-puráńa* and *Harivamśa*. Also see note |' in the preceding page.

The *Linga-puráńa* reads, instead of Bhajamána, *bhrájamána*, and makes it an epithet of Bhajana.

** And *Harivamśa*.

†† I find Nisi(?) there. Nimlochi: *Bhágavata-puráńa*.

‡‡ And so reads the *Harivamśa*.

§§ Kŕitaka: *Kúrma-puráńa*.

|||| Vŕishńi is the accepted lection.

¶¶ Vŕisha, in my MSS. The *Harivamśa* has Dhŕishńu. There is no third son in the *Kúrma-puráńa*.

*** And so adds the *Váyu-puráńa*.

††† This is the reading of my best MSS. Professor Wilson had "Dásaka". The *Váyu-puráńa*, in my MSS., has Vámaka.

nigh, that Babhru is the first of men, and Deváv́ridha is equal to the gods. Sixty-six persons, following the precepts of one, and six thousand and eight, who were disciples* of the other, obtained immortality." † Mahábhoja was a pious prince: his descendants were the Bhojas, the princes of Mŕittikávatí,[1]‡ thence called Márttikávatas.[2]§ Vŕishńi had two sons, Sumitra and Yudhájit:[3] from the former, Anamitra|| and Śini were

---

[1] By the Parńáśá river:¶ Brahma Puráńa: a river in Malwa.

[2] These are made, incorrectly, the descendants of Babhru, in the Hari Vaḿśa.**

[3] The Bhágavata, Matsya, and Váyu agree, in the main, as to the genealogy that follows, with our text. The Váyu states that Vŕishńi had two wives, Mádrí and Gándhárí: by the former he had Yudhájit and Anamitra, and, by the latter, Sumitra and Devamíd́husha.†† The Matsya also names the ladies, but gives Su-

---

* So the scholiast explains the word *purusha* here.

† यथैव शृणुमो दूरात्संपश्यामस्तथान्तिकात् ।
बभ्रुः श्रेष्ठो मनुष्याणां देवैर्देवावृधः समः ॥
पुरुषाः षड् षष्टिश्च सहस्राणि चाष्ट च ।
येऽमृतत्वमनुप्राप्ता बभ्रोर्देवावृधादपि ॥

These stanzas occur in the *Linga-puráńa*, Prior Section, LXVIII., 6—8, and in the *Bhágavata-puráńa*, IX., XXIV., 9, 10, with the sole difference, in both works, of 'sixty-five' for 'sixty-six'. Also compare the *Harivaḿśa*, *śl.* 2011—2013. The *Váyu-puráńa* &c. have very different numbers.

‡ The commentator alleges that the city was called Mŕittikávarta: मृत्तिकावर्तं नाम पुरम् । तत्र स्थिता नृपा मार्त्तिकावताः । In the text, no city at all is named, as appears from the next note.

§ The original has only तस्यान्वये भोजा मार्त्तिकावता बभूवुः ।

|| A single MS. has Anamitra.

¶ See Vol. II., p. 152, notes 2 and §.

** *Śl.* 2014.

†† There seems to be something wrong here; for my MSS. of the *Váyu-puráńa* agree in reading:

born.'* The son of Anamitra was Nighna,† who had two sons, Prasena and Sattrájita.‡ The divine Áditya (the Sun) was the friend of the latter.

On one occasion, Sattrájita, whilst walking along the

---

mitra to Gándhárí, and makes Mádrí the mother of Yudhájit, Devamidhusha, Anamitra, and Śini. The Agni has a similar arrangement, but substitutes Dhríshía for Vríshńi, and makes him the fifteenth in descent from Satwata. The Linga,§ Padma, Brahma Puráńas, and Hari Vaḿśa|| have made great confusion, by altering, apparently without any warrant, the name of Vríshńi to Kroshtri.

' The Bhágavata¶ makes them sons of Yudhájit; the Matsya and Agni, as observed in the preceding note, his brothers, as well as Sumitra's.

गांधारी जनयामास सुमित्रं मित्रनन्दनम् ।
माद्री युधाजितं पुत्रं सा तु वै देवमीढुषम् ।
अनमित्रं शिनिं चैव तावुभौ पुरुषोत्तमौ ॥

Here, Gándhárí is represented as having only one son, Sumitra; and Mádrí has Yudhájit, Devamidhusha, Anamitra, and Śini.

Instead of Devamidhusha, Professor Wilson gave, by inadvertence, "Devamidhush", as the name in the *Váyu-puráńa*. At the same time, he found, in the *Matsya-puráńa*, "Devamidhusha".

* The Sanskrit runs: वृष्णेः सुमित्रो युधाजिच्च पुत्रोऽभवत् । अन-
मित्रशिनी तथा । Anamitra and Śini are, thus, other sons of Vríshńi. The *Kúrma-puráńa* says, expressly:

वृष्णेस्तु पुत्रो बलवाननमित्रः शिनिस्तथा ।

† Nimna: *Bhágavata-puráńa*.

‡ Corrected, everywhere, from "Satrájit". The *Bhágavata-puráńa* has both Sattrájita and Sattrájit; the *Linga-puráńa*, the latter. In the *Váyu-puráńa*, the reading seems to be Śakrajit.

§ This Puráńa, in my MSS., has Vríshńi, not Kroshtri. It states, too, that he had Sumitra by Gándhárí, and, by Mádrí, Devamidhusha, Anamitra, and Śini.

|| According to my best MSS., Gándhárí is mother of Sumitra, and of him only: Mádrí, of Yudhájit, Devamidhusha, and Anamitra.

¶ IX., XXIV., 12.

sea-shore, addressed his mind to Súrya, and hymned his praises; on which, the divinity appeared and stood before him. Beholding him in an indistinct shape, Sattrájita said to the Sun: "I have beheld thee, lord, in the Heavens, as a globe of fire. Now do thou show favour unto me, that I may see thee in thy proper form."* On this, the Sun, taking the jewel called Syamantaka from off his neck, placed it apart; and Sattrájita beheld him of a dwarfish stature, with a body like burnished copper, and with slightly reddish eyes.† Having offered his adorations, the Sun desired him to demand a boon; and he requested that the jewel might become his. The Sun presented it to him, and then resumed his place in the sky. Having obtained the spotless gem of gems, Sattrájita wore it on his neck; and, becoming as brilliant, thereby, as the Sun himself, irradiating all the regions with his splendour, he returned to Dwáraká. The inhabitants of that city, beholding him approach, repaired to the eternal male, Purushottama,—who, to sustain the burthen of the earth, had assumed a mortal form (as Kríshńa),—and said to him: "Lord, assuredly the (divine) Sun is coming to visit you." But Kríshńa‡ smiled, and said: "It is not the divine Sun, but Sattrájita, to whom Áditya has presented the Syamantaka gem; and he now wears it. Go and behold him without apprehension." Accordingly, they departed. Sattrájita, having

* यथैव व्योम्नि वह्निपिण्डोपमं त्वामहमपश्यं तथैवाद्याग्रतो गतमप्यत्र भ· किंचिन्न भगवता प्रसादीकृतं विशेषमुपलक्षयामि ।

† ततस्तमाताम्रोज्ज्वलह्रस्ववपुषमीषदापिङ्गलनयनमादित्यमद्राक्षीत्।

‡ Here, as just before, the Translator has supplied the name of Kríshńa.

gone to his house, there deposited the jewel, which yielded, daily, eight loads* of gold, and, through its marvellous virtue, dispelled all fear of portents, wild beasts, fire, robbers, and famine.†

Achyuta was of opinion‡ that this wonderful gem should be in the possession of Ugrasena;§ but, although he had the power of taking it from Sattrájita, he did not deprive him of it, that he might not occasion any disagreement amongst the family. Sattrájita, on the other hand, fearing that Kŕishńa|| would ask him for the jewel, transferred it to his brother Prasena. Now, it was the peculiar property of this jewel, that, although it was an inexhaustible source of good to a virtuous person, yet, when worn by a man of bad character, it was the cause of his death. Prasena, having taken the gem and hung it round his neck, mounted his horse, and went to the woods to hunt. In the chase, he was killed¶ by a lion. The lion, taking the jewel in his mouth, was about to depart, when he was observed and killed by Jámbavat, the king of the bears, who, carrying off the gem, retired into his cave, and gave it to his son Sukumáraka** to play with.

---

* *Bhára*, which here, more probably, imports a weight of gold equal to twenty *tulás*. So the commentator understands the term; and the same view is taken by Śrídhara, commenting on the *Bhágavata-puráńa*, X., LVI., 11.

† तत्प्रभावाच्च सकलस्यैव राष्ट्रस्योपसर्गावृष्टिव्यालाग्निचौरदुर्भिक्षादिभयं न भवति ।

‡ Read 'wished', लिप्सां चक्रे ।

§ Called, in the original, *bhúpati*, or 'king'. He is spoken of further on.

|| Exchanged, by the Translator, for Achyuta.

¶ And so was his horse, according to the original.

** Corrected from "Sukumára", here and everywhere below.

When some time had elapsed, and Prasena did not appear, the Yádavas* began to whisper, one to another, and to say:† "This is Kŕishńa's doing. Desirous of the jewel, and not obtaining it, he has perpetrated the murder of Prasena, in order to get it into his possession."

When these calumnious rumours came to the knowledge of Kŕishńa,‡ he collected a number of the Yádavas, and, accompanied by them, pursued the course of Prasena by the impressions of his horse's hoofs.§ Ascertaining, by this means, that he and his horse had been killed by a lion, he was acquitted, by all the people, of any share in his death. Desirous of recovering the gem, he thence followed the steps of the lion, and, at no great distance, came to the place where the lion had been killed by the bear. Following the footmarks of the latter, he arrived at the foot of a mountain, where he desired the Yádavas to await him, whilst he continued the track. Still guided by the marks of the feet, he discovered a cavern, and had scarcely entered it, when he heard the nurse of Sukumáraka saying to him: "The lion killed Prasena; the lion has been killed by Jámbavat. Weep not, Sukumáraka. The Syamantaka is your own." Thus assured of his object,‖ Kŕishńa advanced into the cavern, and saw the brilliant jewel in the hands of the nurse, who

---

* *Yadulokah.*

† कर्णाकर्ण्यकथयत् ।

‡ Bhagavat, in the original.

§ The scene of this hunt of Kŕishńa's was, according to the *Váyu-puráńa*, the Ŕikshavat and Vindhya mountains.

‖ [illegible] ।

was giving it, as a plaything, to Sukumáraka. The nurse soon descried his approach, and, marking his eyes fixed upon the gem with eager desire, called loudly for help. Hearing her cries, Jámbavat, full of anger, came to the cave; and a conflict ensued between him and Achyuta, which lasted twenty-one days. The Yádavas who had accompanied the latter waited seven or eight days, in expectation of his return; but, as the foe of Madhu still came not forth, they concluded that he must have met his death in the cavern. "It could not have required so many days," they thought, "to overcome an enemy;" and, accordingly, they departed, and returned to Dwáraká, and announced that Kŕishńa had been killed.

When the relations of Achyuta heard this intelligence, they performed all the obsequial rites suited to the occasion. The food and water thus offered to Kŕishńa, in the celebration of his Śráddha, served to support his life and invigorate his strength in the combat in which he was engaged; whilst his adversary, wearied by daily conflict with a powerful foe, bruised and battered, in every limb, by heavy blows, and enfeebled by want of food, became unable longer to resist him. Overcome by his mighty antagonist, Jámbavat cast himself before him, and said: "Thou, mighty being, art, surely, invincible by all the demons, and by the spirits of heaven, earth, or hell; much less art thou to be vanquished by mean and powerless creatures in a human shape, and, still less, by such as we are, who are born of brute origin.* Undoubtedly,

* असुरसुरयक्षगन्धर्वराक्षसादिभिरप्यखिलैर्भवान्न जेतुं शक्यः कि-

thou art a portion of my sovereign lord, Náráyańa, the defender of the universe." Thus addressed by Jámbavat, Kŕishńa explained to him, fully, that he had descended to take upon himself the burthen of the earth, and kindly alleviated the bodily pain which the bear suffered from the fight, by touching him with his hand. Jámbavat again prostrated himself before Kŕishńa, and presented to him his daughter, Jámbavatí, as an offering suitable to a guest.* He also delivered to his visitor the Syamantaka jewel. Although a gift from such an individual was not fit for his acceptance, yet Kŕishńa† took the gem, for the purpose of clearing his reputation. He then returned, along with (his bride) Jámbavatí, to Dwáraká.

When the people of Dwáraká beheld Kŕishńa alive and returned, they were filled with delight, so that those who were bowed down with years recovered youthful vigour; and all the Yádavas, men and women, assembled round Ánakadundubhi, (the father of the hero), and congratulated him. Kŕishńa‡ related to the whole assembly of the Yádavas all that had happened, exactly as it had befallen, and, restoring the Syamantaka jewel to Sattrájita, was exonerated from the crime of which he had been falsely accused. He then led Jámbavatí into the inner apartments.

When Sattrájita reflected that he had been the cause

सुतापि मनोभिरल्पवीर्यैर्नराधमभूतैश्च तिर्यग्योन्यनुसृतिभिः किं पुनरस्मद्विधैः ।

* जाम्बवतीं नाम कन्यां गृहागमनार्घभूतां ग्राहयामास ।

† Achyuta, in the Sanskrit.

‡ The original has Bhagavat.

of the aspersions upon Kŕishńa's character, he felt alarmed; and, to conciliate the prince, he gave him to wife his daughter, Satyabhámá. The maiden had been, previously, sought in marriage by several of the most distinguished Yádavas, as Akrúra, Kŕitavarman, and Śatadhanwan,* who were highly incensed at her being wedded to another, and leagued in enmity against Sattrájita. The chief amongst them, with Akrúra and Kŕitavarman, said to Śatadhanwan:† "This caitiff Sattrájita has offered a gross insult to you, as well as to us, who solicited his daughter, by giving her to Kŕishńa. Let him not live. Why do you not kill him, and take the jewel? Should Achyuta therefore enter into feud with you, we will take your part." Upon this promise, Śatadhanwan undertook to slay Sattrájita.‡

When news arrived that the sons of Páńdu had been burned in the house of wax,[1]§ Kŕishńa,‖ who knew the real truth, set off for Váráńávata, to allay the ani-

---

[1] This alludes to events detailed in the Mahábhárata.¶

---

* तां चाक्रूरकृतवर्मशतधन्वप्रमुखा यादवाः पूर्वं वरयामासुः ।

† अक्रूरकृतवर्मप्रमुखाश्च शतधन्वानमूचुः । In the passage quoted in the last note, *pramukha* is rendered "most distinguished"; here, "chief". Read: "Akrúra, Kŕitavarman, Śatadhanwan, and other Yádavas"; and "Akrúra, Kŕitavarman, and others."

‡ एवमुक्तस्तथेत्यसावप्याह ।

§ *Jatu*, 'lac'. The house referred to was smeared and stocked with lac and other combustibles, with the intention of burning Kuntí and her sons in it. The design fell through, so far as they were concerned.

‖ Bhagavat, in the original.

¶ *Ádi-parvan*, CXLI.—CLI. These chapters comprise a section bearing the title of *Jatugŕiha-parvan*.

mosity of Duryodhana, and to perform the duties his relationship required. Śatadhanwan, taking advantage of his absence, killed Sattrájita in his sleep, and took possession of the gem. Upon this coming to the knowledge of Satyabhámá, she immediately mounted her chariot, and, filled with fury at her father's murder, repaired to Váraṅávata, and told her husband how Sattrájita had been killed by Śatadhanwan, in resentment of her having been married to another, and how he had carried off the jewel; and she implored him to take prompt measures to avenge such heinous wrong. Kṛishṅa, who is ever internally placid, being informed of these transactions, said to Satyabhámá, as his eyes flashed with indignation: "These are, indeed, audacious injuries: but I will not submit to them from so vile a wretch.* They must assail the tree, who would kill the birds that there have built their nests.† Dismiss excessive sorrow: it needs not your lamentations to excite any wrath."‡ Returning, forthwith, to Dwáraká, Kṛishṅa§ took Baladeva apart, and said to him: "A lion slew Prasena, hunting in the forests; and now Sattrájita has been murdered by Śatadhanwan. As both these are removed, the jewel which belonged to them is our common right. Up, then; ascend your car; and put Śatadhanwan to death!"

Being thus excited by his brother, Balaráma engaged resolutely in the enterprise. But Śatadhanwan,

* सत्ये ममैषावहासना । नाहमेतां तस्य दुरात्मनः सहिष्ये ।

† न ह्यनुल्लङ्घ्य वरपादपं तत्कृतनीडाश्रयिणो विहंगा वध्यन्ते ।

‡ तदलमत्यर्थममुनास्मत्पुरतः शोकप्रेरितवाक्यपरिकरेण ।

§ Vásudeva, in the Sanskrit.

being aware of their hostile designs, repaired to Kŕitavarman, and required his assistance. Kŕitavarman, however, declined to assist him; pleading his inability to engage in a conflict with both Baladeva and Kŕishńa.* Śatadhanwan, thus disappointed, applied to Akrúra. But he said: "You must have recourse to some other protector. How should I be able to defend you? There is no one, even amongst the immortals,—whose praises are celebrated throughout the universe,—who is capable of contending with the wielder of the discus; at the stamp of whose foot the three worlds tremble; whose hand makes the wives of the Asuras widows; whose weapons no host, however mighty, can resist. No one is capable of encountering the wielder of the ploughshare, who annihilates the prowess of his enemies by the glances of his eyes, that roll with the joys of wine; and whose vast ploughshare manifests his might, by seizing and exterminating the most formidable foes."† "Since this is the case," replied Śatadhanwan,‡ "and you are unable to assist me, at least accept and take care of this jewel." "I will do so," answered Akrúra, "if you promise, that, even in the last extremity, you will not divulge its being in my possession." To this Śatadhanwan agreed; and Akrúra took the jewel. And the former, mounting a very swift mare,—one that could travel a hundred leagues a day,—fled (from Dwáraká).

* Here again the original has Vásudeva; and so frequently below.

† Akrúra's speech is rendered very freely. Kŕishńa and Baladeva are eulogized, in it, under the names, respectively, of Chakrin and Sírin.

‡ Śatadhanus is the name, in the original, here and several times below.

When Kŕishńa heard of Śatadhanwan's flight, he harnessed his four horses,—Śaibya, Sugríva, Meghapushpa, and Baláhaka,—to his car, and, accompanied by Balaráma,* set off in pursuit. The mare (held her speed, and) accomplished her hundred leagues; but, when she reached the country of Mithilá, (her strength was exhausted, and) she (dropped down and) died. Śatadhanwan,[1] dismounting, continued his flight on foot. (When his pursuers came to the place where the mare had perished,) Kŕishńa said to Balaráma:† "Do you remain in the car, whilst I follow the villain on foot, and put him to death. The ground here is bad; and the horses will not be able to drag the chariot across it." Balaráma, accordingly, stayed with the car; and Kŕishńa followed Śatadhanwan on foot. When he had chased him for two kos, he discharged his discus; and, although Śatadhanwan was at a considerable distance, the weapon struck off his head. Kŕishńa, then coming up, searched his body and his dress for the Syamantaka jewel, but found it not. He then returned to Balabhadra, and told him that they had effected the death of Śatadhanwan to no purpose; for the precious gem, the quintessence of all worlds, was not upon his person. When Balabhadra heard this, he flew into a violent rage, and said to Vásudeva: "Shame light upon you, to be thus greedy of wealth! I acknowledge no

[1] The Váyu calls Sudhanwan, or Śatadhanwan, king of Mithilá.

* Substituted, by the Translator, for Baladeva.
† The Sanskrit has Balabhadra, here and just below.

brotherhood with you. Here lies my path. Go whither you please. I have done with Dwáraká, with you, with all our house. It is of no use to seek to impose upon me with thy perjuries."* Thus reviling his brother, who fruitlessly endeavoured to appease him, Balabhadra went to the city of Videha,† where Janaka[1] received him hospitably; and there he remained. Vásudeva returned to Dwáraká. It was during his stay in the dwelling of Janaka, that Duryodhana, the son of Dhŕitaráshŕra, learned from Balabhadra the art of fighting with the mace. At the expiration of three years, Ugrasena and other chiefs of the Yádavas,‡ being satisfied that Kŕishńa had not the jewel, went to Videha,§ and removed Balabhadra's‖ suspicions, and brought him home.

Akrúra, carefully considering the treasures¶ which the precious jewel secured to him, constantly celebrated

---

[1] A rather violent anachronism, to make Janaka contemporary with Balaráma.

---

* अलमेभिर्ममाग्रतोऽलीकशपथैः ।

† Videha is a country. The name of its capital, here intended, is not mentioned. See Vol. II., p. 165.

‡ I find बभ्रूग्रसेनप्रभृतिभिर्यादवैः, "Babhru, Ugrasena, and other Yádavas."

Who is the Babhru here mentioned? There would be an anachronism in identifying him with the Babhru, son of Deváv́ridha, named in p. 72, *supra*.

§ *Videhapuri*, "the capital of Videha." See note †, above.

‖ My MSS. yield 'Baladeva's'.

¶ The original has 'gold', *suvarńa*.

religious rites,* and, purified with holy prayers,[1] lived in affluence for fifty-two years;† and, through the virtue of that gem, there was no dearth or pestilence‡ in the whole country.[2] At the end of that period, Śa-

---

[1] The text gives the commencement of the prayer;§ but the commentator does not say whence it is taken: सवनगतौ क्षत्रियवैश्यौ निघ्नन्ब्रह्महा भगवति । "O goddess, the murderer of a Kshattriya or Vaiśya engaged in religious duties is the slayer of a Brahman;" i. e., the crime is equally heinous. Perhaps the last word should be भवति|| 'is'.

[2] Some of the circumstances of this marvellous gem¶ seem to identify it with a stone of widely diffused celebrity in the East, and which, according to the Mohammedan writers, was given, originally, by Noah to Japheth; the Hajarul matar of the

---

* *Yajna*, 'sacrifices.'

† सवनगतो हि क्षत्रियवैश्यौ निघ्नन्ब्रह्महा भवतीत्यतो दीक्षाकवचं प्रविष्ट एव तस्थौ द्विषष्टिवर्षाणि । "For he that kills a Kshattriya or a Vaiśya engaged in sacrifice is *on a par, for sinfulness, with* the slayer of a Brahman: therefore he kept himself invested with the mail of religious observances for sixty-two years."

‡ Read "portent, famine, epidemic, or the like," तथोपसर्गदुर्भिक्षमरकादिकं नाभूत् ।

§ I am at a loss to account for Professor Wilson's supposition that a prayer is here given. All that the scholiast says is: सवनगतौ । दीक्षितौ ।

|| So read almost all my MSS. See note †, above.

¶ M. Langlois, in his translation of the *Harivanśa*, Vol. I., p. 170, note 4, observes: "Qu'était-ce que cette pierre poétique du *Syamantaca*? On pourrait, d'après ce récit, supposer que c'était quelque mine de diamants, qui avait répandu la richesse et l'abondance dans les états du prince qui la possédait. On pourrait croire aussi que le *Syamantaca* était la même chose que cette pierre merveilleuse appelée par les Indiens *soûryacânta*, et que nous prenons quelquefois pour le cristal; ou bien un ornement royal, marque distinctive de l'autorité, que tous ces princes se disputaient."

trughna, the great-grandson of Satwata,* was killed by the Bhojas; and, as they were in bonds of alliance with Akrúra, he accompanied them in their flight from

---

Arabs, Sang yeddah of the Persians, and Jeddah tásh of the Turks, the possession of which secures rain and fertility. The author of the Habíbus Siyar gravely asserts, that this stone was in the hands of the Mongols, in his day, or in the tenth † century.‡

---

* This does not harmonize with the descent of Śatrughna given in the next chapter, if the same person is intended in both places. Moreover, the Śatrughna of the next chapter is brother of Akrúra. *Vide infra*, pp. 94, 95.

† This should be "sixteenth". See the end of the next note.

‡ "When, after escaping the tremendous catastrophe of the Deluge, the ark rested on Mount Júd, and the great patriarch, either by the direct inspiration of the Divine Being, or from the impulse of his own discretion, proceeded to allot to his children the different quarters of the earth, he assigned to Yapheth the countries of the north and east. And we are further informed, that, when the latter was about to depart for the regions allotted to him, he requested that his father would instruct him in some form of prayer, or invocation, that should, whenever he required it, procure for his people the blessing of rain. In compliance with this request, Noah imparted to his son one of the mysterious names of God, inscribing it on a stone; which, as an everlasting memorial, he delivered, at the same time, into his possession. Yapheth now proceeded, with the whole of his family, to the north-east, according to appointment; devoting himself, as is the manner of those who inhabit the boundless plains in that quarter, to a wandering and pastoral life; and, having instituted, for his followers, the most just and virtuous regulations for their conduct, never failed to procure for them, through the influence of the sacred deposit consigned to him by his father, rain and moisture for their lands, whenever occasion made it necessary. This stone has been denominated, by the Arabs, the *Hidjer-ul-mattyr*, lapis imbifer, or rain-stone; by the Persians, *Sang-yeddah*, aid-stone, or stone of power; and, by the Turks, *Jeddah-tausk*. And it is affirmed, that the same stone was preserved among the Moghúls and Ousbeks, possessing the same mysterious property, to the days of the author, in the beginning of the sixteenth century." Major David Price's *Chronological Retrospect, &c.*, Vol. II., pp. 457, 458.

Dwáraká. From the moment of his departure, various calamities, portents, snakes, dearth,* plague,† and the like began to prevail; so that he whose emblem is Garuda‡ called together the Yádavas, with Balabhadra and Ugrasena, and recommended them to consider how it was that so many prodigies should have occurred at the same time. On this, Andhaka, one of the elders of the Yadu race, thus spake: "Wherever Śwaphalka,§ the father of Akrúra, dwelt, there famine, plague, dearth, and other visitations were unknown. Once, when there was want of rain in the kingdom of Káśirája,|| Śwaphalka was brought there, and immediately there fell rain from the heavens.¶ It happened, also, that the queen of Káśirája conceived, and was quick with a daughter;** but, when the time of delivery arrived, the child issued not from the womb. Twelve years passed away, and still the girl was unborn. Then Káśirája spake to the child, and said: 'Daughter, why is your birth thus delayed? Come forth. I desire to behold you. Why do you inflict this protracted suffering upon your mother?' Thus addressed, the infant answered: 'If, father, you will present a cow, every day, to the Brahmans, I shall, at the end of three years more, be born.' The king, accordingly, presented, daily, a cow to the Brahmans; and, at the end of three years, the damsel came into

* *Anávṛishṭi.* † *Maraka.*

‡ Uragári, in the original; significatively, 'the enemy of snakes.'

§ For his origin, *vide infra*, p. 94.

|| Corrected, throughout, from "Káśirájá".

¶ "God rained", देवो ववर्ष.

** Ascertained, says the scholiast, for such, by means of astrology, &c.

the world. Her father called her Gándiní;* and he subsequently gave her to Śwaphalka, when he came to his palace for his benefit. Gándiní, as long as she lived, gave a cow to the Brahmans every day. Akrúra was her son by Śwaphalka; and his birth, therefore, proceeds from a combination of uncommon excellence.† When a person such as he is is absent from us, is it likely that famine, pestilence, and prodigies‡ should fail to occur? Let him, then, be invited to return. The faults of men of exalted worth must not be too severely scrutinized."§

Agreeably to the advice of Andhaka the elder,‖ the Yádavas sent a mission, headed by Keśava, Ugrasena, and Balabhadra, to assure Akrúra¶ that no notice would be taken of any irregularity committed by him; and, having satisfied him that he was in no danger, they brought him back to Dwáraká. Immediately on his arrival, in consequence of the properties of the jewel, the plague, dearth, famine, and every other calamity and portent ceased. Kŕishńa, observing this, reflected,[1] that the descent of Akrúra from Gándiní

[1] Kŕishńa's reflecting, the commentator observes, is to be understood of him only as consistent with the account here given of him, as if he were a mere man; for, as he was omniscient,

* So called because of the 'cow' given away 'daily' by her father.

† तदियं गुणमिथुनादुत्पत्तिः ।

‡ मरकदुर्भिक्षाद्युपद्रवाः ।

§ अलमतिगुणवतामपराधान्वेषणेन ।

‖ The original calls him "elder of the Yadus", यदुवृद्धस्यान्धकस्य तद्वचनमाकर्ण्य ।

¶ Called, in the Sanskrit, Śwáphalki, from the father, Śwaphalka.

and Śwaphalka was a cause wholly disproportionate to such an effect, and that some more powerful influence must be exerted, to arrest pestilence and famine. "Of a surety", said he to himself, "the great Syamantaka jewel is in his keeping; for such, I have heard, are amongst its properties. This Akrúra, too, has been lately celebrating sacrifice after sacrifice: his own means are insufficient for such expenses: it is beyond a doubt, that he has the jewel." Having come to this conclusion, he called a meeting of all the Yádavas at his house, under the pretext of some festive celebration.* When they were all seated, and the purport of their assembling had been explained, and the business accomplished, Kŕishńa† entered into conversation with Akrúra, and, after laughing and joking, said to him: "Kinsman, you are a very prince in your liberality; but we know very well, that the precious jewel which was stolen by Śatadhanwan‡ was delivered, by him, to you, and is now in your possession, to the great benefit of this kingdom.§ So let it remain.

there was no occasion for him to reflect or reason. Kŕishńa, however, appears, in this story, in a very different light from that in which he is usually represented; and the adventure, it may be remarked, is detached from the place in which we might have expected to find it,—the narrative of his life,—which forms the subject of the next Book.

* अन्यत्प्रयोजनमुद्दिश्य सकलयादवसमाजमात्मगेहे एवाचीकरत् ।

† Janárdana, in the Sanskrit.

‡ Corrected from "Sudhanwan",—a mere slip of the pen, presumably. But *vide supra*, p. 83, note 1.

§ दानपते जानीम एव वयं यथा शतधन्वना तदिदमखिलजगत्सा-

We all derive advantage from its virtues. But Balabhadra suspects that I have it; and, therefore, out of kindness to me, show it (to the assembly)." When Akrúra, who had the jewel with him, was thus taxed, he hesitated what he should do. "If I deny that I have the jewel," thought he, "they will search my person, and find the gem hidden amongst my clothes. I cannot submit to a search." So reflecting, Akrúra said to Náráyańa, the cause of the whole world: "It is true that the Syamantaka jewel was entrusted to me by Śatadhanwan.* When he went from hence, I expected, every day, that you would ask me for it; and with much inconvenience, therefore, I have kept it until now.† The charge of it has subjected me to so much anxiety, that I have been incapable of enjoying any pleasure, and have never known a moment's ease. Afraid that you would think me unfit to retain possession of a jewel so essential to the welfare of the kingdom, I forbore to mention to you its being in my hands. But now take it, yourself, and give the care of it to whom you please." Having thus spoken, Akrúra drew forth, from his garments, a small gold box,‡ and took from it the jewel. On displaying it to the assembly of the Yádavas, the whole chamber where they sat was illuminated by its radiance. "This", said

---

एभूतं स्यमन्तकरत्नं भवतः समर्पितं तद्देशद्वारकोपकारकं भवतः सकाशे तिष्ठति।

* Here we find Śatadhanus again, in the Sanskrit.

† अपगते च तस्मिन्नद्य श्वः परश्वो वा भगवान्मां याचिष्यतीति कृतमतिरतिकृच्छ्रेणैतावन्तं कालमधारयम्।

‡ *Samudgaka.*

Akrúra, "is the (Syamantaka) gem, which was consigned to me by Śatadhanwan. Let him to whom it belongs now take it."

When the Yádavas beheld the jewel, they were filled with astonishment, and loudly expressed their delight. Balabhadra immediately claimed the jewel, as his property jointly with Achyuta, as formerly agreed upon;* whilst Satyabhámá demanded it, as her right, as it had, originally, belonged to her father. Between these two, Kṛishńa considered himself as an ox between the two wheels of a cart,† and thus spake to Akrúra, in the presence of all the Yádavas: "This jewel has been exhibited to the assembly, in order to clear my reputation. It is the joint right of Balabhadra and myself, and is the patrimonial inheritance of Satyabhámá. But this jewel, to be of advantage to the whole kingdom, should be taken charge of by a person who leads a life of perpetual continence. If worn by an impure individual, it will be the cause of his death. Now, as I have sixteen thousand wives, I am not qualified to have the care of it. It is not likely that Satyabhámá will agree to the conditions that would entitle her to the possession of the jewel;‡ and, as to Balabhadra, he is too much addicted to wine and the pleasures of sense to lead a life of self-denial. We are, therefore, out of the question; and all the Yáda-

---

* तमालोक्य ममायमच्युतेनैव सामान्यः समन्विच्छित इति बलभद्रः सस्पृहोऽभवत्।

† बलसत्यावलोकनात्कृष्णो ऽप्यात्मानं चक्रान्तरावस्थितमिव मेने। Bala and Satyá are the proper names that here occur.

‡ कथं चैतत्सत्यभामा। The original has nothing more.

vas, Balabhadra, Satyabhámá,* and myself request you, most bountiful Akrúra, to retain the care of the jewel, as you have done hitherto, for the general good: for you are qualified to have the keeping of it; and, in your hands, it has been productive of benefit to the country. You must not decline compliance with our request." Akrúra, thus urged, accepted the jewel, and, thenceforth, wore it, publicly, round his neck, where it shone with dazzling brightness; and Akrúra moved about like the sun, wearing a garland of light.

He who calls to mind the vindication† of (the character of) Kŕishńa‡ from false aspersions shall never become the subject of unfounded accusation in the least degree, and, living in the full exercise of his senses, shall be cleansed from every sin.[1]

[1] The story of the Syamantaka gem occurs in the Bhágavata,§ Váyu, Matsya, Brahma, and Hari Vaḿśa,|| and is alluded to in other Puráńas.¶ It may be considered as one common to the whole series. Independently of the part borne, in it, by Kŕishńa, it presents a curious and, no doubt, a faithful, picture of ancient manners,—in the loose self-government of a kindred clan, in the acts of personal violence which are committed, in the feuds which ensue, in the public meetings which are held, and the part that is taken, by the elders and by the women, in all the proceedings of the community.

* Here again called Satyá, in the original.

† *Kshálana*, literally, 'washing'.

‡ Substituted, by the Translator, for Bhagavat.

§ X., LVI. and LVII.

|| Chapters XXXVIII. and XXXIX.

¶ The version of the story given in the preceding pages is much fuller than that of any other Puráńa I have examined.

CHAPTER XIV.

Descendants of Śini, of Anamitra, of Śwaphalka and Chitraka, of Andhaka. The children of Devaka and Ugrasena. The descendants of Bhajamána. Children of Śúra: his son Vasudeva: his daughter Prithá married to Páńdu: her children, Yudhishthira and his brothers; also Karńa, by Áditya. The sons of Páńdu by Mádrí. Husbands and children of Śúra's other daughters. Previous births of Śiśupála.

THE younger brother* of Anamitra† was Śini;‡ his son was Satyaka; his son was Yuyudhána, also known by the name of Sátyaki; his son was Asanga;§ his son was Túńi;[1]|| his son was Yugandhara.[2] These princes were termed Śaineyas.¶

[1] Bhúti: Váyu. Kuńi: Bhágavata.** Dyumni: Matsya.††

[2] The Agni makes these, all, brother's sons of Satyaka, and adds another, Ŕishabha, the father of Śwaphalka.

* 'Son', according to two MSS. † *Vide supra*, p. 73.

‡ This Śini, according to the *Bhágavata-puráńa*, IX., XXIV., 13, was son of Anamitra. The same work, in the stanza immediately preceding that just referred to, recognizes the Śini of our text,—a brother of Anamitra. The *Kúrma-p.*, also,—*vide supra*, p. 74, note *,—speaks of two Śinis:

अनमित्राच्छिनिर्जज्ञे कनिष्ठो वृष्णिनन्दनात् ।

Here, Śini is youngest son of Anamitra, son of Vŕishńi.

From this the *Váyu-puráńa* differs slightly:

अनमित्राच्छिनिर्जज्ञे कनिष्ठाद्वृष्णिनन्दनात् ।

According to this, Śini was son of Anamitra, youngest son of Vŕishńi. The *Linga-puráńa*, Prior Section, LXIX., 16, knows only one Śini, the youngest son of Vŕishńi. (?)

§ Variants: Sanga, Sanjaya, and Asima. Jaya: *Bhágavata-puráńa*.

|| Kuńi, in one MS.; Śrińi, in another.

¶ The *Váyu-puráńa* calls them Bhautyas, as being descendants of Bhúti.

** And so in the *Linga-puráńa*.

†† Bhúmi, in the *Harivanśa*, which here wants a stanza, in the Calcutta edition.

In the family of Anamitra, Př́iśni* was born; his son was Śwaphalka,[1] the sanctity of whose character† has been described: the younger brother of Śwaphalka was named Chitraka.‡ Śwaphalka had, by Gándiní, besides Akrúra, Upamadgu,§ Mŕidura,|| Arime-

[1] The authorities are not agreed here. Śwaphalka,¶ according to the Agni, as just remarked, comes from Śini, the son of Anamitra. The Bhágavata, instead of Př́iśni, has Vŕishńi, son of Anamitra;** the Brahma†† and Hari Vaḿśa‡‡ have Vŕishńi; and the Agni, Př́ishńi, son of Yudhájit.§§ The Matsya also makes Yudhájit the ancestor of Akrúra, through Ŕishabha and Jayanta. Yudhájit, in the Brahma, &c., is the son of Kroshṭri.||||

* Vŕishńi, in four MSS. † "Sanctity of character" is for *prabháva*.
‡ Chitraratha: *Bhágavata-puráńa*. According to the *Linga-puráńa*, Chitraka was son of Sumitra.
§ Two MSS. give Upamangu, as in, for instance, the *Váyu-puráńa*; which then has Mangu, as has the *Brahma-puráńa*.
Several of the notes that follow should be compared together, and with note ¶ in p. 96, *infra*.
|| Also read Mŕidara and Mŕidu. The *Brahma-puráńa* has Medura.
¶ According to the *Linga-puráńa*, Śwaphalka was son of Yudhájit, son of a son of Mádrí. This unnamed son, the commentator says, was Devamídhusha; and he explains the term Várshńi, applied to Śwaphalka, as signifying "founder of the Vŕishńi family". The text is as follows:

माद्र्याः सुतस्य संजज्ञे सुतो वार्ष्णिर्युधाजितः ।
श्वफल्क इति विख्यातस्त्वंशोऽस्यहितकारकः ॥

Comment: माद्र्याः सुतस्य देवमीढुषसंज्ञकस्यप्रथमपुत्रस्य युधाजितः सुतः । वार्ष्णिर्वृष्णिकुलोद्भवः । श्वफल्क इति विख्यातः संजज्ञे इत्यन्वयः ।
** Vŕishńi was Anamitra's third son, according to the Puráńa referred to: IX., XXIV., 14.
†† My MS. gives Př́ishńi, son of Yudhájita. ‡‡ *Śl.* 1908.
§§ The *Váyu-puráńa* has:

माद्र्याः सुतस्य जज्ञे तु सुतः पृश्निर्युधाजितः ।

Compare the first verse of the stanza quoted in note ¶, above; and see the *Harivaḿśa*, *śl.* 2080. |||| *Vide supra*, p. 73, note 3, *ad finem*.

jaya,* Giri, Kshattropakshattra,† Śatrughna,‡ Arimardana,§ Dharmadhṛik,|| Dṛishṭaśarman,¶ Gandhamocha, Áváha,** and Prativáha.[1]†† He had, also, a daughter, Sutárá.‡‡

---

[1] The different authorities vary in the reading of these names,

---

* Professor Wilson had "Śárimejaya"; his Hindu-made English version, "Ravi, Sárinjaya," preceded by "Mṛida". The original, -मृदुरविशारिमेजय-, might be resolved into "Mṛidu, Raviśa, Arimejaya": but that this is corrupt appears from the high authority of the *Váyu-puráńa*, which reads:

उपमद्गुस्तथा मद्गुर्मृदुरश्चारिमेजयः ।

† These names are written, in the original, as one long compound; and it is more likely than not that we should here read "Kshattra, Upakshattra". Professor Wilson's Bengal translation has "Girikshetra, Upakshetra". One MS. gives Kshattropeta. The *Váyu-puráńa* gives, plainly, Girirakshas and Yaksha.

‡ Śatruhan: *Brahma-puráńa*.

§ Three MSS. have Avimardana. The *Váyu-puráńa* seems to give Párimardana.

|| Dharmabhṛit: *Váyu-puráńa* and *Brahma-puráńa*.

¶ Corrected from "Dhrishṭasarman". One MS. has Dṛishṭadharma.

** Professor Wilson had, instead of two names, "Gandhamojaváha"; and all my MSS. but one—which has Gandhamobaváha,—might be read to yield Gandhamojáváha. There is little risk in the alteration which I have ventured; as the *Váyu-puráńa* has

* * * * * * गन्धमोचस्तथापरः ।
आवाहप्रतिवाहौ च वसुदेवा वराङ्गना ॥

†† In the *Brahma-puráńa* there are, hereabouts, in my single MS., many partly undecipherable, and yet indubitable, variations from the *Vishńu-puráńa*. The *Harivaṁśa* adds to our Puráńa, with reference to the chapter under annotation, not a few particulars which it has seemed scarcely worth while to swell the notes by transcribing, particularly as that work is so easily accessible.

‡‡ The *Váyu-puráńa* calls her Vasudevá. See the Sanskrit quotation in note **, above. In the *Linga-puráńa*, her name is Sudhárá, according to my MSS.; in the *Harivaṁśa*, Sundarí.

Devavat and Upadeva* were the sons of Akrúra.† The sons of Chitraka‡ were Pŕithu and Vipŕithu,§ and many others.[1] Andhaka|| had four sons, Ku-

though they generally concur in the number.¶

[1] The Matsya and Padma call them sons of Akrúra, but, no doubt, incorrectly.**

* Instead of these two names, one MS. has Deva and Anupadeva, as has Professor Wilson's Bengal translation. The *Brahma-puráńa* gives Vasudeva and Upadeva; the *Harivaḿśa*, Prasena and Upadeva.

† His wife, according to the *Linga-puráńa*, *Brahma-puráńa*, and *Harivaḿśa*, is Ugraseni.

‡ Corrected from "Chitrika".

§ Corrected from "Vipritha". Vidúratha: *Bhágavata-puráńa*.

|| The *Váyu-puráńa* has Satyaka.

¶ The *Linga-puráńa* has, in my MSS.: Akrúra, Upamangu, Mangu, Vŕita, Janamejaya, Girirakshas, Upaksha, Śatrughna, Arimardana, Dharmabhŕit, Vŕishńadharma, Godhana, Vara, Áváha, and Prativáha. The *Harivaḿśa*, *ll.* 1916—1918, has, in my best MSS.: Akrúra, Upamangu, Mangu, Mŕidara, Arimejaya, Arikshipa, Upeksha, Śatrughna, Arimardana, Dharmadhŕik, Yatidharman, Gŕidhramojándhaka, Áváha, Prativáha. In *ll.* 2083—2085, we find Madura for Mŕidara, Girikshipa for Arikshipa, Ákshepa for Upeksha, Śatruhan for Śatrughna, Dharmabhŕit for Dharmadhŕik, and Dharmin for Yatidharman. The *Bhágavata-puráńa* has: Akrúra, Ásanga, Sárameya, Mŕidura, Mŕiduvid (or Mŕiduri), Giri, Dharmavŕiddha, Sukarman, Kshetropeksha, Arimardana, Śatrughna, Gandhamáda, Pratibáhu. The *Brahma-puráńa* has, with other names, Arimejaya, Áváha, and Prativáha. The readings of the *Váyu-puráńa*, scattered through the preceding notes, are especially deserving of attention.

There is little doubt, that, of all the Puráńas, the *Váyu-puráńa* generally presents, in their oldest extant Pauráńik form, the particulars that make up the works of the class to which it belongs.

** In the *Váyu-puráńa* they are called Pŕithu, Vipŕithu, Aświagríva, Aświabáhu, Supárśwaka, Gaveshańa, Arishtanemi, Aświa, Suvarman, Dharmabhŕit, Abhúmi, and Bahubhúmi. In the *Linga-puráńa* we read: Vipŕithu, Pŕithu, Aświagríva, Subáhu, Sudhásúka, Gaveshańa, Arishtanemi, Aświa, Dharma, Dharmabhŕit, Subhúmi, and Bahubhúmi. Much the same persons are named in the *Brahma-puráńa*, where they are called sons of Sumitra. The list slightly differs, again, in the *Harivaḿśa*, *ll.* 1920, 1921; 2087—2089.

kura,* Bhajamána, Śuchi.[1] Kambalábarhisha.† The son of Kukura was Vŕishńa;[2]‡ his son was Kapotaroman; his son was Viloman;[3]§ his son was Bhava,[4] who was also called Chandanodakadundubhi;[5]‖—he was a

---

[1] Śamin:¶ Váyu. Śaśi: Matsya. Śini: Agni.** This last makes them the sons of Babhru, and calls the first Sundara.

[2] Vŕishńi: Bhágavata,†† Váyu, Matsya, &c.‡‡ Dhŕishńa: Agni. Dhŕishńu: Brahma,§§ Hari Vaḿśa.

[3] The Bhágavata puts Viloman first. The Linga makes it an epithet of Kapotaroman; saying he was Vilomaja, 'irregularly begotten.' In place of Viloman, we have Raivata, Váyu;‖‖ Taittiri, Matsya; Tittiri, Agni.¶¶

[4] Nava: Agni. Bala: Linga.*** Nala: Matsya. Tamas: Kúrma. Anu: Bhágavata.

[5] The Matsya, Váyu, and Agni agree with our text. The

---

* Corrected, here and below, from "Kokkura", which I find nowhere. The *Váyu-puráńa* has Kakuda.

† Corrected from "Kambalavarbish".

‡ In one MS. is Dhŕishńi; in another, Vŕishńi.

§ One MS. here inserts Taittiri; another, Taitiri.

‖ The ordinary reading, that followed by the Translator, is: कुकुर-सुता भवसंज्ञचन्दनोदकदुन्दुभिः; and the scholiast has: भवसंज्ञस्यै-वोपनाम चन्दनोदकदुन्दुभिः। But I find, in one MS., कुम्बसुता भवसंज्ञः। तस्माच्चन्दनानकदुन्दुभिः, which makes Chandanánakadundubhi son of Bhava; and another MS. has, by corruption, चन्दनो नाम-कदुन्दुभिः। The *Váyu-puráńa* exhibits Chandanodakadundubhi, making him son of Revata; and the *Linga-puráńa* gives Chandanánakadundubhi.

¶ Corrected from "Śami".

** Śama, in my MS. of the *Brahma-puráńa*. The *Harivaḿśa* has, in different MSS., Śama and Śami.

†† Vahni is the name I there find.

‡‡ As the *Linga-puráńa*.

§§ I find Vŕishńi.

‖‖ Revata, in my MSS. Vilomaka: *Linga-puráńa*.

¶¶ Also the *Brahma-puráńa*.

*** Nala is the name, in all my MSS.

friend of the Gandharva Tumburu;*—his son was Abhijit;† his son was Punarvasu;‡ his son was Áhuka;§ and he had, also, a daughter, named Áhukí. The sons of Áhuka were Devaka and Ugrasena.‖ The former had four sons, Devavat, Upadeva,¶ Sudeva, and Devarakshita;** and seven daughters, Vŕikadevá,†† Upadevá,‡‡ Devarakshitá, Śrídevá, Śántidevá, Sahadevá,§§ and Devakí:‖‖ all the daughters were married to Vasudeva.¶¶ The sons of Ugrasena were Kaḿsa, Nyagrodha, Sunáman,*** Kanka, Śanku,†††

Linga, Padma, and Kúrma read Ánakadundubhi as a synonym of Balu. The Brahma and Hari Vaḿśa have no such name, but here insert Punarvasu, son of Taittiri.‡‡‡ The Bhágavata has a

* Variant: Tumbaru. See Vol. II., pp. 264—293.

† The *Váyu-puráńa* has Abhijita.

‡ One of my MSS. inverts the order of Abhijit and Punarvasu; and so do the *Brahma-puráńa* and the *Harivaḿśa*.

§ The *Váyu-puráńa* gives him two brothers, Báhuvat and Ajita.

‖ In the *Váyu-puráńa*, Áhuka has a third son, Dhŕiti.

¶ One MS. has Deva and Anupadeva.

** Devavardhana: *Bhágavata-puráńa*.

†† Vŕishadevá: *Linga-puráńa*.

‡‡ One of my MSS. has Upadeví; also, for some of the names that follow, Śrídeví, Śántideví, and Sahadeví.

§§ Mahádevá, in one copy.

‖‖ In the *Bhágavata-puráńa* they are Dhŕitadevá, Śántidevá, Upadevá, Śrídevá, Devarakshitá, Sahadevá, Devakí. See, further, the *Harivaḿśa*, *ll.* 2090, 2097.

¶¶ Here ends the genealogical portion of the *Linga-puráńa*,—Prior Section, LXIX, 42,—with these words:

नवोग्रसेनस्य सुतास्तेषां कंसस्तु पूर्वजः ।
तेषां पुत्राश्च पौत्राश्च शतशोऽथ सहस्रशः ॥

*** Variant: Sunábha.

††† Four MSS. have Sanku; one, Sanka. The *Brahma-puráńa* has Subhúshańa.

‡‡‡ See note ‡, above.

Subhúmi,* Ráshṭrapála,† Yuddhamushṭi,‡ and Tushṭimat;§ and his daughters|| were Kaṁsá, Kaṁsavatí, Sutanu,¶ Ráshṭrapálí, and Kankí.**

The son of Bhajamána[1] was Vidúratha;†† his son was Śúra;‡‡ his son was Śamin;[2]§§ his son was Pratikshattra;[3] his son was Swayaṁbhoja;[4] his son was Hŕidika,|||| who had Kŕitavarman, Śatadhanus,¶¶ Deva-

---

different series, or: Anu, Andhaka, Dundubhi, Arijit,*** Punarvasu, Áhuka.

[1] This Bhajamána is the son of Andhaka, according to all the best authorities: so the Padma calls this branch the Ándhakas. The Agni makes him the son of Babhru.

[2] Váta, Nivála, Śamin: Váyu.†††

[3] Sonáśwa: Matsya. Sonáksha: Padma. Śini: Bhágavata.

[4] Bhojaka: Agni. Bhoja: Padma.

---

* Swabhúmi, the reading of Professor Wilson's Bengal translation, occurs in three MSS.; Kusumi, in one. Subhú: *Bhágavata-puráńa*.

† Here the *Váyu-puráńa* inserts Sutanu.

‡ Corrected from "Yuddhamushṭhi". One MS. has Yuddhasŕishṭi. Sŕishṭi: *Bhágavata-puráńa*.

§ Instead of these last two names, the *Váyu-puráńa* has Yuddha, Tushṭa, and Pushṭimat.

|| They are called, in the *Váyu-puráńa*, Karmavatí, Dharmavatí, Śatánkrú(?), Ráshṭrapálá, and Kahlá(?).

¶ Śúrabhú: *Bhágavata-puráńa*.

** Kanká, in two MSS., as in the *Bhágavata-puráńa*.

For these sons and daughters, see the *Harivaṁśa*, *ll.* 2028, 2029.

†† See Vol. III., p. 268, note *; also, *infra*, Chapter XX., near the beginning.

‡‡ The *Váyu-puráńa* gives him a brother, Ráshṭrádhideva or Rájyádhideva.

§§ Bhajamána: *Bhágavata-puráńa*.

|||| Hŕidika: *Bhágavata-puráńa*. ¶¶ Śatadhanwan: *Váyu-puráńa*.

*** I find Arídyota.

††† I there find six other brothers: Śoṇi, Śwetaváhana, Gadavarman, Nidána, Śakru, and Śakrajit.

míḍhusha,* and others.[1] Śúra, the son of Devamíḍhusha,[2] was married to Márishá,† and had, by her,

[1] Ten sons: Matsya, &c.‡

[2] Devárha: § Váyu, Padma, Agni, and Matsya;‖ and a different series follows, or: Kambalabarhisha,¶ Asamaujas, Samaujas, Sudaṁshira,** Suvaśa, Dhrishṭa, Anamitra,†† Nighna, Sattrájit.‡‡ They all make Vasudeva the son of Śúra, however; but the three first leave it doubtful whether that Śúra was the son of Bhajamána, or not. The Bhágavata and Brahma agree with the text, which is, probably, correct. The Brahma has Śúra, son of Devamíḍhusha;§§ although it does not specify the latter amongst the sons of Hridika.

* In one MS., Devárhaṅa, and with Devamíḍha just below: the latter is the name in the *Bhágavata-puráńa*. Another MS. has Devamíḍha, and then Devamíḍhaka.

† In the *Váyu-puráńa* we read, according to my MSS.:

माष्यां तु जनयामास शूरो वै देवमीढुषम् ।

It is, thus, stated, that Devamíḍhusha was son of Śúra and Máshí. This Śúra seems to be the one named a little above.

By Aśmakí, Śúra had Devamíḍhushá, it is stated just before the line quoted.

‡ As the *Váyu-puráńa*, my MSS. of which are, here, so incorrect, that I scruple to conjecture their readings. Ten sons are named in the *Harivaṁśa*, *ll.* 2036, 2037.

§ Mention is made of this reading, as a variant, by the commentator on the *Vishńu-puráńa*.

‖ See note *, above.

¶ Corrected from "Kambalavarhish".

** Corrected from "Sudanśira".

†† I find Anumitra.

‡‡ In the *Váyu-puráńa*, at least according to my MSS., there are undeniable traces, through a haze of miscription, of several names quite different from those here given. Also see the *Harivaṁśa*, *ll.* 2038, *et seq.*

For the name Sattrájit, *vide supra*, p. 74, note ‡.

§§ Corrected from "Devamíḍhush". In the *Harivaṁśa*, *ll.* 1922, 1923, Śúra is son of Devamíḍhusha and Aśmakí, and Vasudeva is son of Śúra and Bhojyá.

ten sons. On the birth of Vasudeva, who was one of these sons, the gods, to whom the future is manifest,* foresaw that the divine being† would take a human form in his family; and, thereupon, they sounded, with joy, the drums of heaven: from this circumstance, Vasudeva was also called Ánakadundubhi.[1] His‡ brothers were Devabhága, Devaśravas,§ Anádhrishti,|| Karundhaka, Vatsabálaka,¶ Srinjaya,** Śyáma,†† Śamíka,‡‡ and Gańdúsha;§§ and his|||| sisters were Prithá, Śrutadevá, Śrutakírtti, Śrutaśravas, and Rájádhidevî.

Śúra had a friend named Kuntibhoja,¶¶ to whom, as he had no children, he presented, in due form, his daughter Prithá.*** She was married to Páńdu, and

[1] Ánaka, a larger, and Dundubhi, a smaller, drum.

---

* अव्याहतदृष्टिभिः ।

† Bhagavat.

‡ Insert 'nine', following the original.

§ Devaśrava, in one copy.

|| One MS. has Anávrishti; another, Adhrishti. Anádrishi(?): Váyu-purána.

¶ In one MS. the name is Vatsandhamaka; in another, Yámśavánaka.

** The last three names are, in the Váyu-purána, Keda, Nandana, and Bhrinjila, as best I can read them.

†† Equivalent variant: Śyámaka.

‡‡ The Váyu-purána seems to give Sanika.

§§ Devabhága, Devaśravas, Ánaka, Srinjaya, Śyámaka, Kanka, Śamíka, Vatsaka, Vrika: Bhágavata-purána. See, forther, the Harivamśa, śl. 1926—1926.

|||| Insert 'five'; for the Sanskrit has: वसुदेवादीनां पञ्च भगिन्यो ऽभवन् ।

¶¶ Kunti, in two MSS.: and this is the name in the Bhágavata-purána, &c.

*** The following is taken from the Bhágavata-purána, IX., XXIV., 31—35:

bore him Yudhishṫhira, Bhíma,* and Arjuna, who were, in fact, the sons of the deities Dharma, Váyu (Air), and Indra.† Whilst she was yet unmarried, also, she had a son‡ named Karńa, begotten by the divine Áditya§ (the Sun). Páńdu had another wife, named

---

साथ दुर्वाससो विद्यां देवहूतीं प्रतीप्सितात् ।
तस्या वीर्यपरीक्षार्थमाजुहाव रविं शुचिम् ॥
तद्देवोपागतं देवं वीक्ष्य विस्मितमानसा ।
मन्त्रार्थं प्रयुक्ता मे याहि देव क्षमस्व मे ॥
अमोघं दर्शनं देवि आधत्से त्वयि आत्मजम् ।
योनिर्यथा न दुष्येत कर्ताहं ते सुमध्यमे ॥
इति तस्यां स आधाय गर्भं सूर्यो दिवं गतः ।
ततः कुमारः संजज्ञे द्वितीय इव भास्करः ॥
तं सा त्यक्तवती तोये लज्जालोकस्य बिभ्यती ।
अपितामहमाशुपाह पाण्डुर्वै सत्यविक्रमः ॥

Burnouf's translation of this passage is subjoined:

"Pṛithâ avait reçu de Durvâsas satisfait un charme capable de faire apparaître les Dieux à sa voix; un jour Pṛithâ voulant essayer la force de ce charme, appela le brillant soleil.

"Le Dieu lui apparut aussitôt; mais frappée d'étonnement à sa vue, Pṛithâ lui dit: C'est uniquement pour essayer ce charme que je t'ai appelé, ô Dieu; va, et pardonne-moi ma curiosité.

"Ma présence ne peut être stérile, ô femme; c'est pourquoi je désire te rendre mère; mais je ferai en sorte, ô belle fille, que ta virginité n'en souffre pas.

"Ayant ainsi parlé, le Dieu du soleil eut commerce avec Pṛithâ; et après l'avoir rendue mère, il remonta au ciel; la jeune fille mit aussitôt au monde un enfant mâle qui resplendissait comme un second soleil.

"Pṛithâ abandonna cet enfant dans les eaux du fleuve, parce qu'elle craignait les mauvais discours du peuple; Pâṇḍu ton aïeul, ce monarque plein d'un vertueux héroïsme, prit ensuite la jeune fille pour femme."

* Variant: Bhímasena.

† The two last names are Anila and Śakra, in the Sanskrit.

‡ कानीनः पुत्रः the original calls him. In the *Laws of the Mánavas*, IX., 172, the term *kánína* is applied to the son of an unmarried woman who subsequently becomes the wife of her lover.

§ Substituted, by the Translator, for Bháswat or Bháskara; for the MSS. allow an option.

Mádrí, who had, by the twin sons of Áditya, Násatya and Dasra, two sons, Nakula and Sahadeva.[1]

Śrutadevá was married to the Kárúsha (prince) Vŕiddhaśarman, and bore him the fierce Asura[*] Dantavaktra.[†] Dhŕishťaketu,[‡] Raja of Kaikeya,[2][§] married Śrutakírtti, and had, by her, Santardana and four other sons,[||] known as the five Kaikeyas. Jayasena,[¶] king of Avantí,[**] married Rájádhideví, and had Vinda and Anuvinda.[††] Śrutaśravas was wedded to

---

[1] The Mahábhárata[‡‡] is the best authority for these circumstances.

[2] The Padma calls him king of Kashmir.

---

[*] *Mahásura.*

[†] The *Váyu-puráńa* does not call him an Asura, but king of the Karúshas:

करूषाधिपतिर्वीरो दन्तवक्रो महाबलः ।

[‡] Unnamed alike in the text and in the commentary. The Translator seems to have taken his appellation from the *Bhágavata-puráńa*, IX., XXIV., 37.

[§] Kekaya, in two MSS. The *Bhágavata-puráńa* has Kaikaya; also, "five Kaikayas", just below.

[||] In the *Váyu-puráńa*, they are called Chekitána, Bŕihatkshattra, Vinda, and Anuvinda; the last two being entitled आवत्यौ (आवन्त्यौ?). That Puráńa, in my MSS.,—which, perhaps, have omitted something,—make no mention of the husband or children of Rájádhideví.

[¶] Here, again, Professor Wilson has supplemented the original,—probably by the aid of the *Bhágavata-puráńa*, IX., XXIV., 38. It is observable that the names of Jayasena's two sons are not specified there.

[**] The original has आवन्त्यो, "of Avanti", the country; and the term applies to Vinda and Anuvinda. Some MSS. have आवन्त्यौ. Compare note ||, above.

[††] Corrected from "Anavinda".

[‡‡] Particularly in the *Ádi-parvan*: see the references in Messrs. Böhtlingk and Roth's *Sanskrit-Wörterbuch*.

Our text above is, in part, substantially repeated in Chapter XX. of this Book.

Damaghosha,* Raja of Chedi, and bore him Śiśupála.[1] This prince was, in a former existence, the unrighteous but valiant monarch† of the Daityas, Hirańyakaśipu,‡ who was killed by the divine guardian of creation, (in the man-lion Avatára). He was, next, the ten-headed§ (sovereign, Rávańa), whose unequalled|| prowess, strength, and power were overcome by the lord of the three worlds, (Ráma). Having been killed by the deity in the form of Rághava, he had long enjoyed the reward of his virtues, in exemption from an embodied state, but had now received birth, once more, as Śiśupálá, the son of Damaghosha, king of Chedi.¶ In this character,** he renewed, with greater inveteracy than ever, his hostile hatred towards the god surnamed Puńdaríkáksha,†† a portion of the

---

[1] The Brahma Puráńa and Hari Vaḿśa‡‡ make Śrutadevá mother of Śiśupála; and Přithukírtti, of Dantavaktra.

---

* Called, in the *Váyu-puráńa*, a *rájarshi*.

† *Purusha*.

‡ See Vol. II., pp. 34, *et seq.*

§ Daśánana, in the Sanskrit: see the next chapter. I have supplied the parentheses that follow.

Daśagríva is, in a corresponding passage, the epithetical name of Rávańa, in the *Váyu-puráńa*.

|| *Akshata*.

¶ बहुकालोपभुक्तविविधभोगो भगवत्सकाशाच्छरीरपातोद्भवपुण्यफलोऽथ भगवतैव राघवरूपिणा सोऽपि निधनमुपनीतश्चेदिराजदमघोषपुत्रः शिशुपालनामाभवत् ।

** शिशुपालत्वे ।

†† The original has Puńdaríkanayana, a synonym of Puńdaríkáksha; on the signification of which, see Vol. I., p. 2, note 1.

‡‡ *Śl.* 1930—1932.

supreme being, who had descended to lighten the burthens of the earth, and was, in consequence, slain by him. But, from the circumstance of his thoughts being constantly engrossed by the supreme being, Śiśupála was united with him, after death:* for the lord giveth to those to whom he is favourable whatever they desire; and he bestows a heavenly and exalted station even upon those whom he slays in his displeasure.

---

* तथैव सायुज्यमवाप ।

CHAPTER XV.

Explanation of the reason why Śiśupála, in his previous births as Hirańyakaśipu and Rávańa, was not identified with Vishńu, on being slain by him, and was so identified, when killed as Śiśupála. The wives of Vasudeva: his children: Balaráma and Krishńa his sons by Devakí: born, apparently, of Rohińí and Yaśodá. The wives and children of Krishńa. Multitude of the descendants of Yadu.

MAITREYA.—Most eminent of all who cultivate piety, I am curious to hear from you, and you are able to explain to me, how it happened, that the same being who, when killed, by Vishńu, as Hirańyakaśipu and Rávańa, obtained enjoyments which, though scarcely attainable by the immortals, were but temporary, should have been absorbed into the eternal Hari, when slain, by him, in the person of Śiśupála.*

PARÁŚARA.—When the divine author of the creation, preservation, and destruction of the universe accomplished the death of Hirańyakaśipu, he assumed a body composed of the figures of a lion and a man;† so that Hirańyakaśipu was not aware that his destroyer was

---

* This chapter opens with three stanzas:

मैत्रेय उवाच ।
हिरण्यकशिपुत्वे च रावणत्वे च विष्णुना ।
अवाप निहतो भोगानप्राप्यानमरैरपि ॥
न लयं तत्र तेनैव निहतः स कथं पुनः ।
संप्राप्तः शिशुपालत्वे सायुज्यं शाश्वते हरौ ॥
एतदिच्छाम्यहं श्रोतुं सर्वधर्मभृतां वर ।
कौतूहलपरेणैतत्पृष्टो मे [illegible]मर्हसि ॥

† *Nri-sinha.*

Vishńu. Although, therefore, the quality of purity, derived from exceeding merit, had been attained, yet his mind was perplexed by the predominance of the property of passion; and the consequence of that intermixture was, that he reaped, as the result of his death by the hands of Vishńu, only unlimited power and enjoyment upon earth, as Daśánana,* the sovereign of the three spheres: he did not obtain absorption into the supreme spirit,† that is without beginning or end, because his mind was not wholly dedicated to that sole object. So, also, Daśánana, being entirely subject to the passion of love,‡ and engrossed completely by the thoughts of Jánakí, could not comprehend that the son of Daśaratha§ whom he beheld was, in reality, (the divine) Achyuta. At the moment of his death, he was impressed with the notion, that his adversary was a mortal; and, therefore, the fruit he derived from being slain by Vishńu was confined to his birth in the illustrious family of the kings of Chedi, and the exercise of extensive dominion. In this situation, many circumstances brought the names of Vishńu to his notice: and, on all these occasions, the enmity that had accumulated through successive births influenced his mind; and, in speaking constantly with disrespect of Achyuta, he was ever repeating his different appellations. Whether walking, eating, sitting, or sleeping, his animosity was never at rest; and Kríshńa was ever present to his thoughts, in his ordinary semblance,

---

* दशाननत्वे। Rávańa is meant. For Daśánana, *vide supra*, p. 104, text and note §.

† *Para-brahman.*

‡ Ananga, in the original.

§ Dáśarathi.

having eyes as beautiful as the leaf of the lotos, clad in bright yellow raiment, decorated with a garland, with bracelets on his arms and wrists, and a diadem on his head; having four robust arms, bearing the conch, the discus, the mace, and the lotos. Thus uttering his names, even though in malediction, and dwelling upon his image, though in enmity, he beheld Kŕishńa, when inflicting his death, radiant with resplendent weapons, bright with ineffable splendour in his own essence as the supreme being; and all his passion and hatred ceased, and he was purified from every defect. Being killed by the discus of Vishńu, at the instant he thus meditated, all his sins were consumed by his divine adversary, and he was blended with him by whose might he had been slain. I have, thus, replied to your inquiries. He by whom the divine Vishńu is named, or called to recollection, even in enmity, obtains a reward that is difficult of attainment to the demons and the gods. How much greater shall be his recompense, who glorifies the deity in fervour and in faith!*

Vasudeva, also called Ánakadundubhi, had Pauraví,[1]

---

[1] Pauraví is, rather, a title attached to a second Rohińí, to distinguish her from the first, the mother of Balaráma.† She is also said, by the Váyu,‡ to be the daughter of Báhlíka.

---

* The whole of this paragraph is very freely rendered.

† The commentator says: पौरवी। पुरुवंशोद्भवेति रोहिण्या विशेषणम्। अत एव पौरव्या न पृथक्संकीर्तनम्।

‡ The MSS. at present accessible to me state:

रोहिणी पौरवी चैव बाह्लीकस्यात्मजाभवत्।

Rohińí, Madirá, Bhadrá, Devakí, and several other wives. His sons, by Rohińí, were Balabhadra, Sárańa,* Śat́ha,† Durmada, and others.‡ Balabhadra§ espoused Revatí, and had, by her, Niśat́ha|| and Ulmuka. The sons of Sárańa were Márshi, Márshimat,¶ Śiśu, Satyadhŕiti,** and others. Bhadráśwa, Bhadrabáhu, Durgama, Bhúta,†† and others‡‡ were born in the family of Rohińí,§§ (of the race of Púru||||). The sons (of Vasudeva), by Madirá, were Nanda, Upananda, Kŕitaka,¶¶ and others. Bhadrá*** bore him

---

According to this, Pauravi was daughter of Válmika.

In my copies of the *Linga-puráńa*, however, Pauravi is called daughter of Báhlika. Some MSS. of the *Harivamśa* here have Báhlika; others, Báhlika.

* More than half my copies have Śárańa.

† So read, like Professor Wilson's Bengal translation, all my MSS. but one, which gives Śala. In the MS. which the Professor followed all but exclusively, I find the ठ of this name so written as to look exceedingly like ब. Hence his "Śara", now corrected.

‡ The *Bhágavata-puráńa* names Bala, Gada, Sárańa, Durmada, Vipula, Dhruva, and Kŕita.

§ In two copies, Baladeva. || One MS. gives Nishadha.

¶ Altered from "Márshfi, Márshfimat", a reading which I find in only a single MS., and that not a good one. The variants of these names are numerous, but of no appreciable importance.

** In one MS. I find Satya and Dhŕiti.

†† Instead of these two names, one of my MS. has Damabhúta; another, Madabhúta.

‡‡ The commentator says that the others are Pińd́áraka and Uśínara.

§§ My best and oldest MSS. unaccompanied by the commentary yield Pauravi, on which reading the scholiast remarks: पौरव्या इति पाठेऽपि रौहिणी भार्या इत्यर्थः। एवमेव रोहिण्याश्चनया इयोति हरिवंशे पञ्चात्मजया वंशः।

|||| According to all my MSS., Puru. See note † in the preceding page.

¶¶ In addition to these, the *Bhágavata-puráńa* mentions Śúra, and speaks of others unnamed.

*** According to the *Bhágavata-puráńa*, Kauśalyá—whom the commentator identifies with Bhadrá,—had but one son, Keśin.

Upanidhi, Gada,* and others. By his wife Vaiśálí,† he had one son, named Kauśika. Devakí bore him six sons,‡—Kírttimat, Sushena,§ Udáyin,|| Bhadrasena, Ŕijudása,¶ and Bhadradeha;** all of whom Kamsa put to death.[1]

---

[1] The enumeration of our text is rather imperfect. The Váyu†† names the wives of Vasudeva, Pauraví, Rohiní, Madirá, Rudrá, Vaiśákhí, Devakí; and adds two bondmaids,‡‡ Sugandhí and Vanarájí. The Brahma Puráńa and Hari Vamśa§§ name twelve wives and two slaves: Rohiní, Madirá, Vaiśákhí, Bhadrá, Sunámní, Sahadevá, Śántidevá, Śrídevá, Devarakshitá, Vŕikadeví, Upadeví, Devakí; and Śantanu|||| and Vadavá.¶¶ The children of the two slaves, according to the Váyu, were Puńdra, who became a king, and Kapila, who retired to the woods. In the Bhágavata, we have thirteen wives: Pauraví, Rohiní, Bhadrá, Madirá, Rochaná, Ilá, Devakí,*** Dhŕitadeví, Śántidevá, Upadeví,†††

---

* For two Gadas in the *Bhágavata-puráńa*, see note ‡ in the preceding page, and note || in the page following.

† Variants: Vaiśáli and Kauśali.

‡ The *Bhágavata-puráńa*, IX., XXIV., 53, 54, names eight: Kírttimat, Sushena, Bhadrasena, Ŕiju, Sammardana, Bhadra, Sankarshańa (lord of serpents), and Hari; with a daughter, Subhadrá. In commenting on the same Puráńa, X., I., 8, Śrídhara, according to my best MSS., substitutes Mŕidu and Santardana for Ŕiju and Sammardana.

§ Nearly all my MSS. give Sushena.

|| Udadhi, in one copy.

¶ Corrected from "Ŕijudása".

** One MS. has Bhadradeva; and another reads Bhadra and Vidhideva.

†† This work says, that Ánakadundubhi had, in all, thirteen wives.

‡‡ *Parichárika*.

§§ *Śl.* 1947—1949.

|||| Sutanu, in my MSS., &c.

¶¶ Corrected from "Baravá".

*** IX., XXIV., 44.

††† I find Dhŕitadevá and Upadevá.

When Devakí was pregnant the seventh time, Yoganidrá (the sleep of devotion),* sent by Vishńu, extricated the embryo from its maternal womb, at midnight, and transferred it to that of Rohińí; and, from having been thus taken away, the child (who was Balaráma,) received the name of Sankarshańa. Next, (the divine Vishńu himself,) the root of the vast universal tree, inscrutable by the understandings of all gods, demons, sages, and men, past, present, or to come, adored by Brahmá† and all the deities,‡ he who is without beginning, middle, (or end), being moved to relieve the earth of her load, descended into the womb of Devakí, and was born as her son Vásudeva. Yoganidrá, proud to execute his orders, removed the embryo to Yaśodá, the wife of Nanda the cowherd. At his birth, the earth was relieved from all iniquity; the sun, moon, and planets shone with unclouded splendour; all fear of calamitous portents was dispelled; and universal

---

Śrídevá, Devarakshitá, and Sahadevá.§ The last seven, in this and the preceding list, are the daughters of Devaka.||

---

* See Book V., Chapters I.—III.

† Designated, in the original, by the epithet *abjabhava*.

‡ The original adds "also Anala and others".

§ IX., XXIV., 49—51.

|| So says the commentator on the *Bhágavata-puráńa*, not the text itself.

The children of these daughters are named as follows, in the *Bhágavata-puráńa*: of Dhritadevá, Viprishńa; of Śántidevá, Praśama, Prasrita, and others; of Upadevá, Kalpavarsha and others, all kings; of Śrídevá, Vasu, Hamsa, Suvamśa, and three others; of Devarakshitá, Gada and eight others; of Sahadevá, Púru and Viśruta (incarnations of Dharma and of the Vasus), and six others.

happiness prevailed.* From the moment he appeared, all mankind were led into the righteous path, in him.

Whilst this powerful being resided in this world of mortals, he had sixteen thousand and one hundred wives: of these the principal were Rukmińí,† Satyabhámá,‡ Jámbavatí,§ Chárubhásiní,|| and four others. By these the universal form, who is without beginning, begot a hundred and eighty thousand sons, of whom thirteen are most renowned,—Pradyumna,¶ Chárudeshńa, Sámba, and others.** Pradyumna married Kakudmatí,†† the daughter of Rukmin, and had, by her, Aniruddha.‡‡ Aniruddha married Subhadrá,§§ the granddaughter of the same Rukmin; and she bore him

---

* सुप्रसन्नादित्यचन्द्रादिग्रहमत्यातङ्कादिभयं सुस्वमानसमखिलमेवैतज्जगदपास्ताधर्ममभवत्तस्मिंश्च पुण्डरीकनयने जायमाने ।

For Puńdaríkanayana, *vide supra*, p. 104, note ††.

† Daughter of Bhíshmaka, king of Vidarbha. The story of Kŕishńa's abducting her is told in Book V., Chapter XXVI.

‡ Daughter of Satrájit. *Vide supra*, p. 80.

§ Daughter of Jámbavat. *Vide supra*, p. 79.

|| Professor Wilson had "Játahásiní", a misprint for Jálahásiní, the reading of all my copies but one. This one, my Ajmere MS., has Chárubhásiní, which is much more likely to be correct. In early mediæval times, च and ज were hardly distinguishable, and there was something of resemblance between रु and ल. It is, therefore, very likely that Jálahásiní originated in a graphical corruption of Chárubhásiní.

¶ See Book V., Chapter XXVI.

** The *Linga-puráńa* names Chárudeshńa, Sucháru, Cháruvesha, Yaśodhara, Cháruśravas, Cháruyaśas, Pradyumna, and Sámba, as sons by Rukmińí.

†† Corrected from "Kakudwatí", with the suffrage of my two best MSS. and the Translator's Hindu-made English version. Kakudmatí is the only form authorised by the grammarians: see the *gańa* on Páńini, VIII., II., 9. Compare Vol. II., p. 184, text and note ‡.

‡‡ See Book V., Chapter XXVIII.

§§ One MS. has Suchandrá.

a son named Vajra. The son of Vajra was Pratibáhu;* and his son was Sucháru.[1]

---

[1] The wives and children of Kŕishńa are more particularly described in the next book. The Brahma Puráńa and Hari Vaḿśa† add some details of the descendants of Vasudeva's brothers. Thus, Devabhága is said to be the father of Uddhava; Anádhŕishti,‡ of Devaśravas, a great scholar or Pandit. Devaśravas, another brother of Vasudeva, had Śatrughna and another son, called Ekalavya, who, for some cause being exposed when an infant, was found and brought up by the Nishádas, and was, thence, termed Nishádin. Vatsavat (Vatsabálaka§) and Gańdúsha being childless, Vasudeva gave his son Kauśika,|| to be adopted by the former; and Kŕishńa gave Chárudeshńa and three others to the latter. Kanavaka¶ (Karundhaka) had two sons,—Tantrija** and Tantripála.†† Avákeŕinjima‡‡ (Śŕinjaya) had, also, two,—Víra and Aśwahanu. The gracious Śamíka became as the son (although the brother) of Śyáma,§§ and, disdaining the joint rule which the princes of the house of Bhoja exercised, made himself paramount. Yudhishthira was his friend. The extravagant numbers of the Yádavas merely indicate that they were (as they undoubtedly were) a powerful and numerous tribe, of whom many traces exist in various parts of India.||||

---

* Professor Wilson had "Báhu"; but his Bengal translation and all my MSS. give as above.

† *Śl.* 1935.

‡ He is called father of Nivŕittiśatru. It is Uddhava that is characterized as a great scholar.

§ For the names parenthesized in this note, *vide supra*, p. 101.

|| Read Káśika, also.

¶ Corrected from "Kanaka".

** I find the two forms Tandrija and Tantija.

†† In my MSS., &c., Tandripála and Tantipála. Professor Wilson reads the two brothers' names like M. Langlois.

‡‡ The correct name seems to be Gŕinjima.

§§ See the *Harivaḿśa*, *śl.* 1938. The MSS. here differ.

|||| *Vide supra*, p. 68, note §.

In this manner the descendants of Yadu multiplied; and there were many hundreds of thousands of them, so that it would be impossible to repeat their names in hundreds of years. Two verses relating to them are current:* "The domestic instructors of the boys in the use of arms amounted to three crores and eighty† lacs (or thirty-eight millions‡). Who shall enumerate the whole of the mighty men of the Yádava race, who were tens of ten thousands and hundreds of hundred thousands in number?"§ Those powerful Daityas|| who were killed in the conflicts between them and the gods were born again, (upon earth,) as men, as tyrants and oppressors; and, in order to check their violence, the gods, also, descended to the world of mortals, and became members of the hundred and one branches of the family of Yadu.¶

---

* तिस्रः कोट्यः सहस्राणामष्टाशीति शतानि च ।
कुमाराणां गृहाचार्याश्चापयोग्यासु ये रताः ॥
संख्यानं यादवानां कः करिष्यति महात्मनाम् ।
यत्रायुतानामयुतं लक्षेणास्ते शताधिकम् ॥

The commentator observes that the last line is also read:

यत्रायुतानामयुतलक्षेणास्ते सदाहुकः ।

The Áhuka here referred to is, he says, father of Ugrasena. *Vide supra*, p. 76.

† Read "eighty-eight". See the Sanskrit, as quoted in the preceding note.

‡ To be corrected to "thirty-eight millions and eight hundred thousand".

§ What follows of this chapter is, also, in verse.

|| The original has Daiteyas.

¶ तेषामुत्सादनार्थाय भुवि देवो यदोः कुले ।
अवतीर्णः कुलशतं यत्रैकाभ्यधिकं द्विज ॥

Only one god is here spoken of; and he, as the context shows, is Vishńu. Compare the beginning of Chapter XI.,—pp. 52, 53, *supra*.

Vishńu was, to them, a teacher and a ruler; and all the Yádavas were obedient to his commands.

Whoever listens frequently to this account of the origin of the heroes of the race of Vríshńi shall be purified from all sin, and obtain the sphere of Vishńu.

CHAPTER XVI.

Descendants of Turvasu.

PARÁŚARA.—I shall now summarily give you an account of the descendants of Turvasu.*

The son of Turvasu was Vahni;[1] his son was Gobhánu;[2] his son was Traiśámba;[3] his son was Karandhama;† his son was Marutta. Marutta had no children; and he, therefore, adopted Dushyanta,‡ of the family of Púru;§ by which the line of Turvasu

[1] Varga: Agni.

[2] Bhánumat: Bhágavata,|| which also inserts Bhaga before him.

[3] Tribhánu: Váyu.¶ Trisánu: Brahma.** Traiśáli: Agni. Triśári: Matsya.

* I find a variant, Turvaśu,—a temper between the Vaidik Turvaśa and the ordinary Pauráńik form. For the personage in question, see p. 46 of this volume. Three of my MSS. yield Yadu, instead of Turvasu.

† My Arrah MS. gives Turvasu, Vahni, Bhárgava, Bhánu, Traiśánu, Karandhama; my Ajmere MS., Turvasu, Vahni, Bharga, Bhánu, Chitrabhánu, Karandhama.

These two copies, preserved in remotely separate districts of India, contain only the text of the *Vishńu-puráńa*; and the peculiarities which they offer suggest that the commentator—whose readings Professor Wilson unhesitatingly follows,—may have taken very considerable liberties with the lections of manuscripts current in his day. For other peculiarities of the kind here adverted to, see Vol. III., p. 334, note ††; and p. 335, note †: also, p. 112, note ||, *supra*, and p. 125, note ‡, *infra*.

‡ One MS. has Dushmanta.

§ Paurava, for "of the family of Púru", here and just after.

|| I find there,—IX., XXIII., 16,—Vahni, Bharga, Bhánumat.

¶ I find Trisánu. The *Bhágavata-puráńa*, however, has Tribhánu.

** And the *Harivaṁśa*. From this point I am unable to verify the Translator's references to the *Brahma-puráńa*.

merged into that of Púru.[1] This took place in consequence of the malediction denounced (on his son) by Yayáti.[2]

---

[1] Besides Bharata,—who, as will be hereafter seen, was the son of Dushyanta,—the Váyu, Matsya, Agni, and Brahma Puráńas enumerate several descendants in this line, for the purpose, evidently, of introducing, as the posterity of Turvasu, the nations of the south of India. The series is Varuttha,* (Karútthámа,† Brahma), Ándira‡ (Ákrira, Brahma); whose sons are Páńdya, Karńáta, Chola, Kerala.§ The Hari Vaḿśa|| adds Kola; and the Agni, very incorrectly, Gándhára.

[2] The curse alluded to is the failure of his line (Prajá-samuchchheda), denounced upon Turvasu, as the punishment of refusing to take his father's infirmities upon him (*vide supra*, p. 48). He was, also, sentenced to rule over savages and barbarians,—Mlechchhas, or people not Hindus. The Mahábhárata adds, that the Yavanas sprang from Turvasu. As sovereign of the south-east,¶ he should be the ancestor of the people of Arracan, Ava, &c.; but the authorities cited in the preceding note refer the nations of the Peninsula to him, and, consequently, consider them as Mlechchhas. Manu also places the Dravidas (or Tamuls) amongst Mlechchhas;** and these and similar passages indicate a period prior to the introduction of Hinduism into the south of India.

---

* In the *Váyu-puráńa* I find Śarútha(?).

† The *Harivaḿśa*, in my best MSS., agrees with the *Brahma-puráńa*.

‡ The *Harivaḿśa* has Ándíra; the *Váyu-puráńa*, Ádíra (or Adira?).

§ The *Váyu-puráńa* has Páńdya, Kerala, Chola, and Kulya (??).

|| *Śl.* 1836. Karńáta is omitted there.

¶ *Vide supra*, p. 49, and p. 50, notes 1 and §.

** See Vol. II., p. 184, note †; and Vol. III., p. 296, note ‡.

CHAPTER XVII.

Descendants of Druhyu.

THE son of Druhyu* was Babhru;† his son was Setu;‡ his son was Áradwat;[1] his son was Gándhára;[2]

---

[1] Also Áraddha,§ in MSS.; and Áraíía, Matsya, which last seems to be the preferable reading. The Váyu has Áruddha;|| the Brahma, Angárasetu.¶ But Áraíía is a northern country, contiguous to, or synonymous with, Gándhára.

[2] Of Gándhára it is said, in the Váyu, that it is a large country, named after him, and is famous for its breed of horses:

ख्यायते यस्य नाम्ना तु गान्धारविषयो महान् ।
गान्धारदेशजाश्चापि तुरगा वाजिनां वराः ॥**

The Matsya reads the beginning of the second line, आरट्टदेशजा-स्तु: showing that Áraíía †† and Gándhára are much the same. See Vol. II., p. 174, note 2.

---

* So read all my MSS. here. Compare note ‡ in p. 40. *supra*.

† Babhrusetu, in my best MSS. of the *Harivaṁśa*; in others, Babhrusena. Druhyu had two sons, Babhru and Setu: *Váyu-puráńa*.

‡ Angárasetu: *Harivaṁśa*. And his son was Gándhára.

§ I have not met with this variant. One MS. has Arada.

|| I find Aruddha, son of Setu; and the son of Babhru is said to have been Ripu.

¶ The *Bhágavata-puráńa* has Árabdha.

** Compare the *Harivaṁśa*, *ll.* 1839, 1840.

†† Professor Wilson has elsewhere identified the people of this country with the Aratri of Arrian. Their locality is indicated in the following lines from the *Mahábhárata*,—*Karńa-parvan*, *ll.* 2055, 2056:

शतद्रुश्च विपाशा च तृतीयैरावती तथा ।
चन्द्रभागा वितस्ता च सिन्धुषष्ठा बहिर्गिरेः ॥
आरट्टा नाम ते देशा नष्टधर्मा न तान्व्रजेत् ।

See the *Asiatic Researches*, Vol. XV., pp. 106, 107; also, Professor Lassen's *De Pentapotamia Indica*, pp. 23, 24, and his *Indische Alterthumskunde*, Vol. I., pp. 821, 822.

his son was Dharma;[1]* his son was Dhṛita;[2]† his son was Duryáman;[3]‡ his son was Prachetas,§ who had a hundred sons; and they were the princes of the lawless Mlechchhas (or barbarians) of the north.[4]

---

[1] The Brahma Puráńa and Hari Vaḿśa, in opposition to all the rest, make Dharma|| and his successors the descendants of Anu.

[2] Ghṛita: Agni.¶

[3] Durdama: Váyu and Bhágavata.** The Matsya, Brahma, and Agni insert a Vidupa (Dudduha,†† or Vidula) before Prachetas.

[4] So the Bhágavata and Matsya. The Mahábhárata says, the descendants of Druhya are the Vaibhojas, a people unacquainted with the use of cars or beasts of burthen, and who travel on rafts: they have no kings.

---

* All my MSS. but two have Gharma; but the *Váyu-puráńa* reads Dharma.

† In one MS., Vṛita.

‡ Most of my MSS. give Durgama; two, Durdama. I nowhere find "Duryáman".

§ He had a son Suchetas, according to the *Harivaḿśa*, *sl.* 1841.

|| Good MSS of the *Harivaḿśa* have Gharma.

¶ Some MSS. of the *Váyu-puráńa* give this; others, Dhṛita. The same variety of reading is found in MSS of the *Harivaḿśa*.

** I find, in it, Durmada.

†† This is the name in the *Harivaḿśa*.

CHAPTER XVIII.

Descendants of Anu. Countries and towns named after some of them, as Anga, Banga, and others.

ANU,[1] the fourth son of Yayáti, had three sons, Sabhánara, Chákshusha,* and Parameksh u.[2] The son of the first was Kálánara;[3]† his son was Sŕinjaya;‡ his son was Puranjaya;§ his son was Janamejaya; his son was Mahámańi;[4]|| his son was Mahámanas, who had two sons, Uśínara and Titikshu. Uśínara¶ had five

---

[1] By some unaccountable caprice, the Brahma Puráńa and Hari Vamśa, unsupported by any other authority, here substitute, for Anu, the name of Kaksheyu, a descendant of Púru, and transfer the whole series of his posterity to the house of Púru.

[2] Paksha and Parapaksha: Váyu. Parameshu: Matsya. Paroksha, Bhágavata.

[3] Kálánala:** Váyu. Koláhala: Matsya.††

[4] Mahásála: Agni.‡‡ Mahásíla: Bhágavata.

---

* Two MSS. have Chakshu, the reading of the *Bhágavata-puráńa*

† One MS. has Kálanara; another, Kálánala.

‡ Corrected, here and elsewhere, from "Śrinjaya."

§ Omitted in the *Bhágavata-puráńa*.

|| In three copies I find Mahásála.

¶ For a people bearing this name, see the *Kaushítaki-bráhmańa Upanishad*, IV., 1.

** And so in the *Harivaḿśa*. Kálánala's son, according to my MSS. of the *Váyu-puráńa*, was Mahámanas: in other words, the Śŕinjaya, &c. of our text are not mentioned. Nor, from the integrity of the metre, does it seem that anything is wanting.

†† Kálanara: *Bhágavata-puráńa*. Paramanyu, in my best MSS. of the *Harivaḿśa*.

‡‡ And so reads the *Harivaḿśa*.

sons*: Śibi, Nṛiga,[1] Nara,[2]† Kṛimi,‡ Darva.[3]§ Śibi had four sons:|| Vṛishadarbha,¶ Suvíra, Kaikeya,**

---

[1] Nṛiga:†† Agni.‡‡ Vana: Bhágavata.

[2] Nava: Matsya.§§ Śama:|||| Bhágavata.

[3] Vrata: Agni. Suvrata: Matsya.¶¶ Daksha: Bhágavata.*** According to the Brahma Puráńa and Hari Vaḿśa,††† the five sons of Uśínara were the ancestors of different tribes. Śibi was the progenitor of the Śaibas; Nṛiga, of the Yaudheyas; Nava, of the Navaráshṭras;‡‡‡ Vrata,§§§ of the Ambashṭhas; and Kṛimi founded the city Kṛimilá.||||

---

* Their mothers, according to the *Váyu-puráńa*, were, severally, Dṛishadwatí, Nṛigá, Navá, Kṛimí, and Darvá. Compare the *Harivaḿśa*, *śl.* 1675.

† Nṛiga and Nara are in all my MSS. but one. This, Professor Wilson's all but exclusive favourite, has -नृगनर°. Read the first symbol as तृ,—which, in that place, it very much resembles,—and suppose an error in न, and we get Professor Wilson's "Tṛińa, Gara," now discarded. Transpose, in -नृगनर°, the ग and न, and the true lection is restored.

‡ One MS. has Mṛishi.

§ Corrected from "Dárvan", for which I find no warrant, and which is scarcely possible. A very much commoner reading than Darva is Darvi; and one MS gives Darbha.

|| According to the *Váyu-puráńa*, they originated the Vṛishadarbhas, Suvídarbhas, Kekayas, and Madrakas.

¶ In one MS. I find Pṛishadarbha. The *Váyu-puráńa* has Vṛishadarbha; and so have the *Bhágavata-puráńa* and the *Harivaḿśa*.

** Kekaya, in the *Váyu-puráńa*; Kaikeya, in the *Harivaḿśa*.

†† See notes * and †, above, and ‡‡, below.

‡‡ And in the *Harivaḿśa*.

§§ Add the *Váyu-puráńa* and the *Harivaḿśa*.

|||| See note ***, below.

¶¶ Add the *Váyu-puráńa* and the *Harivaḿśa*.

*** The *Bhágavata-puráńa* gives Uśínara four sons: Śibi, Vana, Śami, and Daksha.

††† *Śl.* 1678, 1679.

‡‡‡ The *Harivaḿśa* speaks of Navaráshṭra as the kingdom of Nava.

§§§ This reading is very questionable. See note ¶¶, above.

|||| The *Váyu-puráńa* alleges that Śibi and the rest possessed Śibapura,

and Madraka.[1]* Titikshu† had one son, Ushadratha;[2]‡ his son was Hema;[3] his son was Sutapas; his son was Bali, on whose wife five sons§ were begotten by Dírghatamas, or Anga,|| Banga,¶ Kalinga,** Suhma,†† and Puńdra;[4]‡‡ and their descendants, and

---

[1] Bhadra and Bhadraka: Matsya, Agni. These sons of Śibi give name to different provinces and tribes in the west and north-west of India.

[2] Rushadratha: Agni.§§ Tushadratha: Matsya.

[3] Pheńa: Agni.|||| Sena: Matsya.

[4] Odra,¶¶ or, in some copies, Andhra:*** Bhágavata.

Yaudheya, Navaráshṭra, Kṛimilápurí, and Ambashṭhá. The passage runs, in the *Váyu-puráńa*:

शिबेः शिबपुरं ख्यातं यौधेयं तु नृगस्य तु ।
नवस्य नवराष्ट्रं तु कृमेस्तु कृमिलापुरी ॥
सुव्रतस्य तथाम्बष्ठा ।

* Corrected from "Madra".

† He was a renowned king in the east, the *Váyu-puráńa* states.

‡ A single MS. gives Rushadratha, the reading of the *Váyu-puráńa*, in my MSS. The *Harivaṁśa* has Ushadratha.

§ The original has वालेयं क्षत्रं, "Kshatriyas of the race of Bali".

|| See Vol. II., p. 166, notes 3 and §.

¶ See Vol. II., p. 166, note 4; Vol. III., p. 293, note §§.

** See Vol. II., p. 156, notes 3 and §.

†† Only one of my MSS. has Suhma; the rest yielding Sumbha. In Professor Wilson's Bengal translation, the name is Sumadra. But Suhma is the correct reading, according to the *Mahábhárata* (*Ádi-parvan*, *śl.* 4219), the *Váyu-puráńa*, the *Harivaṁśa*, &c. For the Suhmas, see Vol. II., p. 165, note 11.

‡‡ One of my MSS. has Pauńdra; another, Pauńdraka. See Vol. II., p. 170, notes 5 and **.

§§ Ruśadratha: *Bhágavata-puráńa*. |||| Add the *Harivaṁśa*.

¶¶ This is additional to the five names in the text; for the *Bhágavata-puráńa* distinctly says,—IX., XXIII., 4, 5,—that Dírghatamas begot six sons.

For Ońdra, see Vol. II., p. 177, notes 3 and **.

*** See Vol. II., p. 170, notes 1 and ‡; also, p. 164, note †.

the five countries they inhabited, were known by the same names.[1]*

The son of Anga was Pára;[2]† his son was Divi-

---

[1] Of Suhma:‡ it may be remarked, that it is specified, in the Siddhánta Kaumudi,§ as an example of Páńini's rule प्राचां नगरान्ते (VII., III., 24), by which Nagara, compounded with names of countries in the east, becomes Nágara, as Sauhmanágara (सौह्मनागरः), 'produced, &c. in a city of Suhma.' The descendants of Anu, according to the Mahábhárata, were, all, Mlechchhas. The last-named work,|| as well as the Váyu and Matsya Puráńas, have an absurd story of the circumstances of the birth of Dírghatamas, who was the son of Ujási¶ or Utathya, the elder brother of Bŕihaspati by Mamatá, and of his begetting Anga and the rest. They agree in assigning descendants of all four castes to them; the Váyu stating that Bali had पुत्रांश्चातुर्वर्ण्यकरान्;** and the Matsya ascribing it to a boon given by Brahmá to Bali: चतुरो नियतान्वर्णांस्त्वं स्थापयेति, 'Do thou establish the four perpetual castes.' Of these, the Brahmans are known as Báleyas; बालेयाः ब्राह्मणाश्च ह. The Matsya calls Bali the son of Virochana, and चायुष्कल्पमवस्थितः, 'existing for a whole Kalpa;' identifying him, therefore,—only in a different period and form,—with the Bali of the Vámana Avatára.††

[2] Anápána:‡‡ Váyu. Khanápána:§§ Bhágavata. Adhivá-

---

* The original of this clause runs: ममायसंततिवंशाय पञ्च विषया बभूवुः ।

† One MS. has Anapána; another, Anapánga.

‡ See Vol. II., p. 165, note 11; and p. 177, note §.

§ Vol. I., p. 579, Calcutta edition of Samvat 1920.

|| *Ádi-parvan*, Chapter CIV.

¶ Almost certainly, Utathya has no such second name.

** The entire verse is:

पुत्रानुत्पादयामास चातुर्वर्ण्यकरान्भुवि ।

†† See Vol. II., p. 69, and p. 210, note 1; also, Vol. III., p. 18, note 1, and p. 93.

‡‡ Aunapána, in my MSS.

§§ I find Khanapána.

ratha;* his son was Dharmaratha;[1]† his son was Chitraratha; his son was Romapáda,‡:—also called Daśaratha,§—to whom, being childless, Daśaratha, the son of Aja,|| gave his daughter Śántá, to be adopted.[3] After

hana: Agni. Dadhiváhana:¶ Matsya.**

[1] This prince is said, in the Váyu, to have drunk the Soma juice, along with Indra:

येन विष्णुपदे गिरौ सोमः शक्रेण सह वै ।
पीतो महात्मना ॥

[2] The Matsya and Agni insert a Satyaratha.

[3] This is noticed in the Rámáyańa, in the story of the hermit Ŕishyaśringa, to whom Śántá was given in marriage. Her adoptive father is called, in the Rámáyańa,—as he is in the Agni and Matsya,—Lomapáda:†† the meaning is the same, 'hairy foot.' Rámáyańa, I., IX. and X.‡‡ See, also, Prelude to the Uttara Ráma Charitra, Hindu Theatre, Vol. I., p. 289.

* Corrected from "Divaratha",—a mere oversight, unquestionably. All my MSS., and the *Mahábhárata*, &c. have Diviratha.

† In a single copy I find Hirańyaratha.

Hereabouts there are very deplorable omissions in all my MSS. of the *Váyu-puráńa*. With the exception of one, and that very indifferent, there is a hiatus from this point to the closing stanza of Chapter XXII. As is stated in the proper place, I have the help of some extracts from a point in Chapter XXI.

‡ Lomapáda, in the *Harivańśa*.

§ Read: "his son *was* Chitraratha, *also* called Romapáda; his son *was* Daśaratha." So, at least, it is natural to render; the original being ततश्चित्ररथो रोमपादसंज्ञो यस्य पुत्रो दशरथो ऽभवत् । But the Translator has the authority of the commentator.

In the *Bhágavata-puráńa*, IX., XXIII., 6—10, it is Chitraratha that is called Romapáda; he has only one son, Chaturanga; and there is no mention of any Daśaratha but the father of Śántá. With this compare the *Harivańśa*.

|| See Vol. III., p. 313.

¶ In Lakshmívallabha's *Kalpadrumakaliká*, mention is made of Dadhiváhana, Rája of Champá, who fought with Śatáníka, Rájá of Kauśámbí.

** Add the *Harivańśa*.

†† The true *Rámáyańa* has Romapáda.

‡‡ *Bála-káńda*, I., X. and XI., in the genuine *Rámáyańa*.

this,* Romapáda had a son named Chaturanga; his son was Prithulákshа;† his son was Champa, who founded (the city of) Champá.[1] The son of Champa was Haryanga; his son was Bhadraratha, who had two sons, Bṛihatkarman and Bṛihadratha.‡ The son of the first was Bṛihadbhánu;[2] his son was Bṛihanmanas;§ his son was Jayadratha, who, by a wife who was the daughter of a Kshattriya father and Brahmani mother, had a son named Vijaya.[3]‖ His son was Dhṛiti; his

---

[1] The Bhágavata differs, here, from all the other authorities, in omitting Champa, the founder of Champápurí,¶— a city of which traces still remain in the vicinity of Bhagulpoor;—having inserted him, previously, amongst the descendants of Ikshwáku (see Vol. III., p. 289, note 1). Champá is everywhere recognized as the capital of Anga; and the translators** of the Rámáyaṅa were very wide of the truth, when they conjectured that it might be Angwa, or Ava.

[2] Bṛihaddarbha: Brahma. The Bhágavata omits the two successors of Champa, and makes Bṛihadratha, Bṛihatkarman, and Bṛihadbhánu sons of Pṛithulákshа.

[3] The Váyu, Matsya, and Hari Vaṁśa make Vijaya the brother†† of Jayadratha. The Bhágavata agrees with our text.‡‡

---

* I find no Sanskrit for this. † Pṛithula is the reading of one MS.

‡ Two of my best MSS.—those from Arrah and Ajmere,—have Bhadraratha, father of Bṛihadratha, father of Bṛihatkarman; another has, instead of Haryanga, Harshaṅa, father of Bṛihadratha, father of Bṛihatkarman.

§ The *Harivaṁśa*, *śl.* 1702, has Bhadraratha, Bṛihatkarman, Bṛihaddarbha, Bṛihanmanas.

‖ According to the *Harivaṁśa*, Bṛihanmanas had, for sons, Jayadratha, by Yaśodeví, and Vijaya, by Satyá.

¶ Champá,—formerly Máliní: *Harivaṁśa*, *śl.* 1699. We now see, probably, the source of the error "Champamálíní", in Vol. III., p. 289, note 1.

** Messrs. Carey and Marshman: Vol. I., p. 119, note.

†† Read "half-brother".

‡‡ The *Bhágavata-puráṅa* has: Bṛihadratha, father of Bṛihanmanas, father of Jayadratha, father (by Sambhúti) of Vijaya.

son was Dhŕitavrata; his son was Satyakarman;* his son was Adhiratha,[1] who found Karńa† in a basket,‡ on the banks of the Ganges, where he had been exposed by his mother, Príthá.§ The son of Karńa was Vŕishasena.[2]|| These were the Anga kings. You shall next hear who were the descendants of Púru.

The mother of Vijaya, from her origin, was of the Súta caste,—the genealogist and charioteer. Manu, X., 47. Her son was of the same caste; children taking the caste of the mother: consequently, the descendants of Vijaya, kings of Anga, were Sútas. And this explains the contemptuous application of the term Súta to Karńa, the half-brother of the Páńdus; for he, as will presently be mentioned, was adopted into the Anga family, and succeeded to the crown.

[1] Some variety prevails in the series of princes here; but this arises from not distinguishing the collateral lines,—the descendants of Jayadratha from those of Vijaya. The Váyu and Matsya give the latter as in our text; but they agree, also, with the Agni and Brahma,¶ in the successors of Jayadratha, as Dŕidharatha (or Bŕihadratha) and Janamejaya (or Viśwajit).**

[2] Śúrasena: Váyu. Vikarńa: Brahma.††

---

* Satkarman: *Bhágavata-puráńa.*

† "The half-brother of the Páńdavas, by their mother Príthá, who, before her marriage to Páńdu, had borne Karńa to Súrya, the god of the sun. The affair was kept secret. The infant was exposed on the banks of the Jumna, where he was found, and brought up, as his own, by Adhiratha—the Súta, or charioteer, of king Śúra,—and his wife Rádhá; whence Karńa is called, also, a Súta, and Rádheya, or son of Rádhá." So runs one legend, in the words of Professor Wilson, in Professor Johnson's *Selections from the Mahábhárata*, p. 16, note 3.

‡ *Mañjúshá*, which the commentator explains by *káshtha-panjara.* Perhaps the receptacle was a wooden crib.

§ The original is: अधिरथो योऽसौ • • • कर्णं पुत्रमवाप ।

|| Father of Vŕisha, says the *Harivaḿśa.*

¶ Add the *Harivaḿśa.*

** According to the *Harivaḿśa*, *śl.* 1704, Viśwajit was father of Karńa.

†† And so the *Harivaḿśa.*

CHAPTER XIX.

Descendants of Púru. Birth of Bharata, the son of Dushyanta: his sons killed: adopts Bharadwája or Vitatha. Hastin, founder of Hastinápura. Sons of Ajamídha, and the races derived from them, as Pánchálas, &c. Kripa and Kripí found by Śántanu. Descendants of Ṛiksha, the son of Ajamídha. Kurukshetra named from Kuru. Jarásandha and others, kings of Magadha.

THE son of Púru was Janamejaya; his son was Prachinwat;* his son was Pravíra;† his son was Manasyu;‡ his son was Abhayada;[1]§ his son was Su-

[1] Abhayada: Váyu. Vítamaya: Agni. Vátáyudha: Matsya. Chárupada:|| Bhágavata. The Mahábhárata, Ádi Parvan, pp. 136, 138, has two accounts of the descendants of Púru, differing, materially, in the beginning, from each other, and from the lists of the Puráńas. In the first,¶ Pravíra** is made the son of Púru; his son is Manasyu, who has three sons, Śakta, Samhanana, and Vágmin; and there the line stops. Another son of Púru is Raudráśwa, whose sons are Ṛicheyu and the rest, as in our text;†† making them the second in descent, instead of the eleventh.

* Corrected from "Práchinvat", for which I find no warrant in MSS.

† One MS. has Suvíra.

‡ The reading of the *Bhágavata-puráńa* is Namasyu.

§ Professor Wilson had "Bhayada". This, however, I find in no MSS. save his favourite,—so often alluded to, which is, frequently, most incorrect,—and in his Hindu-made English version.

|| Corrected from "Chárupáda".

¶ *Śl.* 3695—3701.

** With Íśwara and Raudráśwa for brothers.

†† I find their names to be: Ṛicheyu, Kaksheyu, Kṛikańeyu, Sthańḍileyu, Vaneyu, Jaleyu, Tejeyu, Satyeyu, Dharmeyu, Sannateyu.

Anwagbhánu is named first of all, where it is said that Raudráśwa's sons were ten. With which of them is he to be identified?

dyumna;[1]* his son was Bahugava;[2] his son was Saṁyáti;[3]† his son was Ahaṁyáti;[4] his son was Raudráśwa[5], who had ten sons:‡ Ŕiteyu,[6] Kaksheyu,§ Sthańdileyu,

In the second list,|| the son of Púru is Janamejaya, whose successors are Práchinwat,¶ Saṁyáti, Ahaṁyáti, Sárvabhauma, Jayatsena, Aváchína, Ariha, Maháhhauma, Ayutanáyin, Akrodhana, Devátithi, Ariha, Ŕiksha, Matinára,—who is, therefore, the fifteenth from Púru, instead of the fourth, as in the first account, or the twelfth, as in the text.

[1] Dhundu: Váyu. Śaṁbhu: Agni. Sudhanwan: Brahma.**

[2] Bahuvidha: Agni and Matsya.††

[3] Saṁpáti: Agni.

[4] Omitted: Váyu. Bahuvádin: Matsya.

[5] Bhadráśwa: Matsya.

[6] Ŕájeyu: Váyu. Ŕicheyu: Agni. They were the sons of

* In one MS., Sudyu.

† Four MSS. have Saṁpáti.

‡ One of my MSS. gives, instead of Ghŕiteyu, &c., Kŕiteyu, Gańeyu, Dharmeyu, Santateyu, Varpeyu, Pramaneyu; another gives, after Sthaleyu, only Dharmeyu, Satyeyu, Dhaneyu: another,—the sole one that names ten,—Ŕiteyu, Kaksheyu, Sthańdileyu, Ghŕiteyu, Kŕiteyu, Sthaleyu, Jaleyu, Dharmeyu, Dhaneyu, Prasannateyu. No two of all my MSS. agree as to this family. Professor Wilson's Bengal translation has names (in a different order,) as in the text, except that Kŕiteyu stands in place of Vrateyu. Vrateyu is the ninth son, in the *Bhágavata-puráńa*, IX., XX., 4; he and Vaneyu being transposed.

The *Harivaṁśa*, *śl.* 1659, 1660, has, according to my best MSS.: Ŕicheyu, Kŕiśańeyu, Kaksheyu, Sthańdileyu, Sannateyu, Kŕiteyu, Jaleyu, Sthaleyu, Dhaneyu, Vaneyu. The variants of different copies are numerous. The mother of these ten sons, according to some MSS., was Ghŕitáchi, the Apsaras.

§ Kaksheyu: *Bhágavata-puráńa*.

|| *Śl.* 3763—3776.

¶ Thus the name is spelled, on etymological grounds, in the *Mahábhárata*, *Ádi-parvan*, *śl.* 3765, *et seq.*

** And in the *Harivaṁśa*. Sudyu: *Bhágavata-puráńa*.

†† Most of my MSS. of the *Harivaṁśa* give Subáhu, and then Raudráśwa; thus omitting Saṁyáti and Ahaṁyáti.

Ghṛiteyu,* Jaleyu, Sthaleyu, Santateyu, Dhaneyu,† Vaneyu,‡ and Vrateyu.[1]§ The son of Ṛiteyu was Rantinára,[2]‖ whose sons were Taṁsu,¶ Apratiratha,**

---

the Apsaras Ghṛitáchí:†† or of Miśrakeśí: Mahábhárata.‡‡ The Brahma Puráṇa and Hari Vaṁśa have, very unaccountably, and in opposition to all other authorities, transferred the whole of the descendants of Anu to this family; substituting, for Anu, the second name in our text, Kaksheyu (p. 120, *supra*).

[1] The Váyu names, also, ten daughters,§§ Rudrá, Śúdrá, Madrá, Subhágá, Amalajá, Talá, Khalá, Gopajálá, Támrarasá, and Ratnakúṭí;‖‖ and adds, that they were married to Prabhákara, a Ṛishi, of the race of Atri. The Brahma Puráṇa and Hari Vaṁśa¶¶ have a legend of the birth of Soma (the Moon) from him and one of these ten; who succeeded to the power and prerogatives of Atri. The sons of the other wives were less distinguished; but they formed families eminent amongst holy Brahmans, called Swastyátreyas.

[2] Atimára or Atibhára:*** Bhágavata. Antinára: Matsya. Ma-

---

* One copy has Vṛiteyu. The *Bhágavata-puráṇa* reads Kṛiteyu.

† Dharmeyu: *Bhágavata-puráṇa*. ‡ Satyeyu: *Bhágavata-puráṇa*.

§ This name is in no MS. accessible to me. See note ‡ in the foregoing page.

‖ My Ajmere and Arrah MSS. have Aginára; another MS., Atitára; another, Atirátra; another, Matinára.

¶ Two MSS. have Sumati; another, Trasu. One of the two copies that read Sumati adds Asumati; the Ajmere MS., Pramati: and they, thus, recognise four sons. ** My Ajmere MS. has Apratihata.

†† So says the *Bhágavata-puráṇa*. Also see the end of note ‡ in the page preceding. ‡‡ *Ádi-parvan*, *śl.* 3698.

§§ In the *Harivaṁśa*, *śl.* 1661, they are called, in my MSS. of best note: Bhadrá, Śúdrá, Madrá, Śaladá, Maladá, Khalá, Balá, Haladá, Surasá, Gochapalá. Here, again, there are very many various readings.

‖‖ I suspect a mistake here; but my single MS. of the *Váyu-puráṇa* does not enable me to ascertain the true reading. In the *Harivaṁśa*, the epithet स्त्रीरत्नकूटाः is applied to all the ten sisters.

¶¶ *Śl.* 1663—1688. *** I find Rantibhára.

and Dhruva.[1]* The son of the second† of these was Kańwa; and his son was Medhátithi, from whom the Káńwáyanas‡ Brahmans[2]§ descended. Anila[3]|| was

tinára: Mahábhárata,¶ Agni, and Brahma.** According to the Matsya and Hari Vaḿśa (not in the Brahma Puráńa), Gaurí, the daughter of this prince, was the mother of Mándhátri, of the family of Ikshwáku.††

[1] In place of these, the Matsya has Amúrtirajas and Nrichandra; and there are several varieties in the nomenclature. In place of the first, we have Vasu (or Trasu), Váyu; Taḿsurogha, Agni; Taḿsurodha, Brahma;‡‡ and Sumati, Bhágavata. Pratiratha is read, for the second, in the Agni and Brahma;§§ and, for the third, Suratha, Agni; Subáhu, Hari Vaḿśa.

[2] Medhátithi is the author of many hymns in the Ŕig-veda; and we have, therefore, Brahmans and religious teachers descended from Kshatriyas.

[3] Malina: Váyu. Raibhya:|||| Bhágavata. Dharmanetra: Brahma

* According to the *Mahábhárata*, *Ádi-parvan*, *ll.* 3702–3704, Malinára, likewise called Anádhrishti, had four sons: Taḿsu, Mahat, Atiratha, and Druhyu.

† The son of Atiratha, the Ajmere MS. says explicitly.

‡ Variant: Kaińwáyana. Also *vide infra*, p. 140, note †.

§ According to the *Bhágavata-puráńa*, Praskańwa and others, all Bráhmanas.

|| This reading is in only one of my MSS., most of which read Ainila. Two have Elina, son of Medhátithi. The Ajmere MS., too, has Elina; but it calls him son of Púru. In the Arrah MS., the reading is Ailina, son of Trasu.

¶ *Vide supra*, p. 137, note 1, *ad finem*.

** Add the *Harivaḿśa*.

†† Compare Vol. III., p. 265, note 1, near the end.

‡‡ The *Harivaḿśa* has, in different MSS., Taḿsurodha, Taḿsurodya, Taḿsurogha, &c.

§§ Also in the *Harivaḿśa*, which has Apratiratha, likewise,- the preferable reading.

|||| Son of Sumati, and father of Dushyanta.

the son of Tamsu; and he had four sons, of whom

Puráńa. The Hari Vaḿśa* omits him; making sad blundering work of the whole passage. Thus, the construction is such as to intimate that Taḿsu (or Taḿsurodha) had a wife named Ilá,† the daughter of Medhátithi,—that is, his brother's great-grand-daughter:

मेधातिथिः सुतस्तस्य यस्मात्काण्वायना द्विजाः ।
इला नाम तु यस्यासीत्कन्या वै जनमेजय ।
ब्रह्मवादिन्यधिस्त्री च तंसुस्तामभ्यगच्छत ॥

But this, as the commentator observes, is contrary to common sense (सर्वथात्वादयुक्तं); and he would read it, therefore, इलिनो नाम तु यस्यासीत्कन्या, 'the daughter of him who was named Ilin;' a Raja so called. But, in the Váyu and Matsya, we have Ilini, the daughter of Yama, married to Taḿsu, and mother of Malina or Anila; more correctly, perhaps, Allina:

इलिना तु यमस्यासीत्कन्या साजनयत्सुतम् ।
तसौ (तंसो) सुदयितं पुत्रं मलिनं ब्रह्मवादिनम् ॥
उपदानवी ततो लेभे चतुरस्त्वैलिनात्मजात् ।
दुष्मन्तमिति ॥‡

The blunder of the Hari Vaḿśa, therefore, arises from the compiler's reading Yasya, 'of whom,' instead of Yamasya, 'of Yama.' It is not an error of transcription; for the metre requires Yasya: and the remark of the commentator proves the correctness of the reading. The name occurs Ílina (ईलिन), the son of Taḿsu, in the Mahábhárata,§ agreeably to the Anuvaḿśa-śloka which is there quoted. 'Saraswatí bore Taḿsu to Matinára; and Taḿsu begot a son, Ílina, by Kálingí:'

तंसुं सरस्वती पुत्रं मतिनारादजीजनत् ।
ईलिनं जनयामास कालिङ्ग्यां तंसुरात्मजम् ॥

---

* *Śl.* 1718, 1719.

† Ilini is the accepted reading.

‡ In but one of my copies of the *Váyu-puráńa* do I find any portion of this passage; and there only two lines of it occur, and in a miserably depraved form.

§ *Ádi-parvan*, *śl.* 3780.

Dushyanta* was the elder.[1]† The son of Dushyanta was the emperor Bharata. A verse‡ explanatory of

[1] The Váyu, Matsya, and Bhágavata agree with our text, in making these the grandsons of Tamsu; even the Brahma Puráńa concurs: but the Hari Vamsa§ makes them his sons; having, apparently, transformed Tamso sutah (तंसो सुतः), 'the son of Tamsu,' into a synonym of Tamsu, or Tamsurodha; as in these parallel passages:

तंसो सुतोऽथ राजर्षिर्धर्मनेत्रः प्रतापवान् ।
उपदानवी ततो पुत्रांश्चतुरोऽजनयच्छुभान् ॥

"The son of Tamsu was the illustrious sage Dharmanetra: Upadánavi had, from him, four excellent sons." Brahma Puráńa.

तंसुरोधोऽथ राजर्षिर्धर्मनेत्रः प्रतापवान् ।
* * * * * * * * * * * * * *
उपदानवी सुतांल्लेभे चतुरस्तंसुरोधतः ॥||

Tamsurodha was a royal sage, the illustrious institutor of laws. Upadánavi had four sons from Tamsurodha." Hari Vamsa. The commentator explains Dharmanetra (धर्मनेत्र) to be 'institutor of laws' (धर्मप्रवर्तक). We have Upadánavi before,**—as the daughter of Vrishaparvan, the Daitya,—married to Hiranyáksha. Hamilton (Buchanan)¶ calls her the wife of Sughora. The four sons are named, in other authorities, with some variations: Dushyanta, Sushyanta (or Rishyanta, or Sumanta), Pravíra, and Anagha (or Naya). The Mahábhárata†† enumerates five,—Dushyanta, Śúra, Bhíma, Pravasu, and Vasu,—but makes them the sons of Ilina, and grandsons of Tamsu.

* Variant: Dushmanta.

† The original has दुष्मन्ताद्याश्चत्वारः पुत्राः, "four sons, *namely*, Dushyanta and others."

‡ So says the original, though, as is seen, two stanzas are quoted.

§ *Śl.* 1720, 1721.

|| These lines are not read much alike in any two of my copies. The MSS. are, evidently, very corrupt just here.

¶ *Genealogies of the Hindus*, p. 122.

** Vol II., p. 70, text and note 5.

†† *Ádi-parvan*, *ll.* 3708

his name is chanted by the gods: "The mother is only the receptacle; it is the father by whom a son is begotten. Cherish thy son, Dushyanta; treat not Śakuntalá with disrespect. Sons, who are born from the paternal loins, rescue their progenitors from the infernal regions. Thou art the parent of this boy: Śakuntalá has spoken truth."[*] From the expression 'cherish' (bharaswa) the prince was called Bharata.[1]†

[1] These two ślokas are taken from the Mahábhárata, Ádi Parvan, p. 112,‡ and are part of the testimony borne, by a heavenly messenger, to the birth of Bharata. They are repeated in the same book, in the account of the family of Púru, p. 139.§ They occur, with a slight variation of the order, in other Puráńas, as the Váyu &c.,|| and show the greater antiquity of the story of Śakuntalá, although they do not narrate it. The meaning of the name Bharata is differently explained in the Śakuntalá.¶ He is said

[*] माता भस्त्रा पितुः पुत्रो येन जातः स एव सः ।
भरस्व पुत्रं दुष्यन्त मावमंस्थाः शकुन्तलाम् ॥
रेतोधाः पुत्र उन्नयति नरदेव यमक्षयात् ।
त्वं चास्य धाता गर्भस्य सत्यमाह शकुन्तला ॥

In the *Bhágavata-puráńa*, IX., XX., 21, 22, we find these identical words, with the change—mending the metre,—of पुत्र उन्नयति into पुत्रो नयति. Burnouf translates the passage as follows:

"La mère est le réceptacle; c'est au père qui l'a engendré qu'appartient le fils: protége ton fils, ô Duchyanta; ne méprise pas Çakuntalâ.

"Un fils qui donne à son père de la postérité, ô roi, le fait remonter de la demeure de Yama; tu es le père de cet enfant: Çakuntalâ a dit la vérité."

† This sentence is added by the Translator.

‡ *Śl.* 3102, 3103.

§ *Śl.* 3783, 3784.

|| Add the *Harivaḿśa*, *ll.* 1724—1726.

¶ The two explanations that follow occur near the end of Act VII. of the *Śákuntala*.

Bharata had, by different* wives, nine sons; but they were put to death by their own mothers, because Bharata remarked, that they bore no resemblance to him, and the women were afraid that he would, therefore, desert them. The birth of his sons being thus unavailing, Bharata sacrificed to the Maruts; and they gave him Bharadwája,—the son of Bŕihaspati, by Mamatá, the wife of Utathya,†—expelled by the kick of Dírghatamas, (his half-brother, before his time). This verse explains the purport of his appellation: "'Silly woman,' said Bŕihaspati, 'cherish this child of two fathers' (bhara dwá-jam‡). 'No, Bŕihaspati,' replied Mamatá: 'do you take care of him.' So saying, they both abandoned him; but, from their expressions, the boy was called Bharadwája."§ He was, also, termed Vitatha, in allusion to the unprofitable (vitatha) birth

---

to be so called from 'supporting' the world: he is, also, there named Sarvadamana, 'the conqueror of all.'

---

* My Ajmere and Arrah MSS. read 'three'. Herewith the *Bhágavata-puráńa* agrees, and, further, calls them natives of Vidarbha.

† See Vol. III., p. 16, note §.

‡ The rational etymology of Bharadwája is *bharat + vája*.

§ मूढे भर द्वाजमिमं भर द्वाजं बृहस्पते ।
याती यदुक्त्वा पितरौ भरद्वाजस्ततस्त्वयम् ॥

This stanza, which occurs in the *Bhágavata-puráńa*, IX., XX., 38, also, is thus rendered by Burnouf:

"Femme ignorante, nourris ce fils de deux pères, (disait Bŕihaspati). Nourris-le toi-même, ô Bŕihaspati, (répondit Mamatá). Et parce que le père et la mère, après avoir ainsi parlé, s'en allèrent, (laissant l'enfant,) il fut nommé Bharadvádja."

of the sons of Bharata.[1] The son of Vitatha was Bha-

[1] The Brahma Puráńa and Hari Vaḿśa (the latter, especially,) appear to have modified this legend, with the view, perhaps, of reconciling those circumstances which are related of Bharadwája, as a sage, with his history as a king. Whilst, therefore, they state that Bharadwája was brought, by the winds, to Bharata, they state that he was so brought to perform a sacrifice, by which a son was born, whom Bharadwája also inaugurated:

धर्मसंक्रमणे चापि मरुद्भिर्भरताय वै ।
अयाजयद्भरद्वाजो महद्भिः क्रतुभिर्हि तम् ॥
पूर्वं तु वितथे तस्य कृते पुत्रजन्मनि ।
ततोऽथ वितथो नाम भरद्वाजात्सुतोऽभवत् ॥ *

In the Váyu, Matsya, and Agni, however, the story is much more consistently narrated; and Bharadwája, being abandoned by his natural parent, is brought by the winds, as a child, not as a sage; and, being adopted by Bharata, is one and the same with Vitatha, as our text relates. Thus, in the Váyu, the Maruts bring to Bharata, already sacrificing for progeny, (भरद्वाजं ततः पुत्रं बार्हस्पत्यं) "Bharadwája, the son of Bṛihaspati;" and Bharata, receiving him, says: "This Bharadwája shall be Vitatha:"

ततः स वितथो नाम भरद्वाजवदात्स्वयम् ।

The Matsya, also, says, the Maruts, in compassion, took the child, and, being pleased with Bharata's worship, gave it to him, and he was named Vitatha:

अनुजग्मुर्भरद्वाजं मरुतः कृपयान्विताः ।
. . . .
तेन ते मरुतस्तस्य मरुत्स्तोमेन तुष्टुवुः ॥
उपनिन्युर्भरद्वाजं पुत्रार्थं भरताय वै ।
. . . .
पूर्वं तु वितथे तस्मिन्कृते वै पुत्रजन्मनि ।
ततस्तु वितथो नाम भरद्वाजो नृपो भवान् ॥

And the Agni tells the whole story in one verse:

ततो मरुद्भिरानीय पुत्रः स तु बृहस्पतेः ।
संक्रामितो भरद्वाजः क्रतुभिर्वितथोऽभवत् ।

"Then, the son of Bṛihaspati being taken by the winds, Bhara-

* *Harivaḿśa*, *ll.* 1729, 1730.

vanmanyu:[1]* his sons were many;† and, amongst them, the chief were Bṛihatkshattra, Mahávírya, Nara,

dwája was transferred with sacrifice, and was Vitatha." The account given in the Bhágavata is to the same purpose. The commentator on the text also makes the matter clear enough: भरद्वाजस्यैव भरतपुत्त्वदशायां वितथेति नाम ।‡ "The name of Bharadwája, in the condition of son of Bharata, was Vitatha." It is clear that a new-born infant could not be the officiating priest at a sacrifice for his own adoption, whatever the compiler of the Hari Vaṁśa may please to assert. From Bharadwája, a Brahman by birth, and king by adoption, descended Brahmans and Kshattriyas, the children of two fathers:

तस्मादैव भरद्वाजाद्ब्राह्मणाः क्षत्रिया भुवि ।
द्व्यामुष्यायणकौलीनाः स्मृता द्विपितरस्तु वै ॥§

The Mahábhárata, in the Ádi Parvan, tells the story very simply. In one place,—p. 136, v. 3710,—it says, that Bharata, on the birth of his children proving vain, obtained, from Bharadwája, by great sacrifices, a son, Bhumanyu; and, in another passage, it makes Bhumanyu the son of Bharata by Sunandá, daughter of Sarvasena, king of Káśi:|| p. 139, v. 3785. The two are not incompatible.

[1] Manyu: Bhágavata. Suketu: Agni.¶ But the Brahma and Hari Vaṁśa omit this and the next generation, and make Suhotra, Anuhotra,** Gaya, Garga, and Kapila the sons of Vitatha. They then assign to Suhotra two sons, Káśika and Gṛitsamati,†† and

* Two MSS. have Bhumanyu.

† The *Bhágavata-puráńa* says there were five: Bṛihatkshattra, Jaya, Mahávírya, Nara, and Garga.

‡ My MSS. have a different reading from this, which is ungrammatical. The gloss, as I find it, ends with the words वितथजातां वितथमाह ।

§ This is from the *Váyu-puráńa*; but I am unable to correct it by my copy; for I have only one here, and that most indifferent, generally: *vide supra*, p. 124, note †.

|| In the original, Sunandá is termed Káśeyí, and by the patronym of Sárvaseni.

¶ Bhuvanmanyu: *Váyu-puráńa*.

** I find Suhotṛi.

†† Corrected from "Ghṛitsamati".

and Garga.[1] The son of Nara was Sankriti;* his sons were Ruchiradhí† and Rantideva.[2]‡ The son of Garga was Śini;[3] and their descendants, called Gárgyas§ and Śainyas,|| although Kshattriyas by birth, became Brahmans.[4] The son of Maháviŕya was Urukshaya,[5]¶

identify them and their descendants with the progeny of Áyus, who were kings of Káśi"** (*vide supra*, p. 37, note 1): a piece of confusion unwarranted by any other authority except the Agni.

[1] Bŕihat, Ahárya, Nara, Garga: Matsya.

[2] Guruvírya and Trideva: Váyu. The first is called Gurudhi, Matsya; and Guru, Bhágavata: they agree in Rantideva. The Bhágavata describes the great liberality of this prince, and his practice of Yoga. According to a legend preserved in the Megha Dúta,†† his sacrifices of kine were so numerous, that their blood formed the river Charmańwatí,‡‡ the modern Chumbul.

[3] Śibi: Matsya.

[4] The other authorities concur in this statement; thus furnishing an additional instance of one caste proceeding from another. No reason is assigned: the commentator says it was from some cause: केनचित्कारणेन ब्राह्मणाश्च बभूवुः।§§

[5] Durbhakshaya:|||| Váyu. Urukshat: Matsya. Duritakshaya: Bhágavata.

* In four MSS. the name is Saḿskriti.

† My Ajmere MS. has Suradhi; the Arrah MS., Gurudhi.

‡ One Rantideva, we read in the *Harshacharita*, was killed by Rangavati, one of his wives. See my *Vásavadattá*, Preface, p. 53.

§ Three MSS. yield Gargas.

|| Saineyas, according to one MS.

¶ In one MS., Urunjaya. The *Váyu-puráńa* has, in my MS., Bhíma.

** Read "Káśi kings". They were so called as being descendants of Káśirája, i. e., King Káśi. *Vide supra*, p. 33, note *. Káśi is a patronym of Káśa.

†† Stanza XLVII., edition of Professor Wilson.

‡‡ The name of the river is not in the poem itself, but is supplied by the commentators.

§§ Compare note * in p. 145, *infra*.

|||| My MS. has an illegible name; but it is not this, certainly.

who had three sons, Trayyáruńa,* Pushkarin, and Kapi,[1]† the last of whom became a Brahman.‡ The son of Bŕihatkshattra was Suhotra,[2]§ whose son was

---

[1] Trayyáruńi, Pushkaráruńi, Kavi;|| all became Brahmans:

उरुक्षतः सुता ह्येते सर्वे ब्राह्मणतां गताः ।

Matsya. And there were three chief branches of the Kávyas, or descendants of Kavi:

काव्यानां तु वरा ह्येते त्रयः प्रोक्ता महर्षयः ।
गर्गाः संकृतयः काव्याः क्षत्रोपेता द्विजातयः ॥

Gargas, Sankŕitis, and Kávyas. Ibid.

[2] In the Mahábhárata,¶ Suhotra is the son of Bhumanyu;** and, in one place,†† the father of Ajamídha, &c., and, in another,‡‡ of Hastin. The Brahma Puráńa, in some degree, and the Hari Vańsa, in a still greater, have made most extraordinary confusion in the instance of this name. In our text, and in all the best authorities, we have three Suhotras, perfectly distinct: 1. Suhotra, great-grandson of Amávasu, father of Jahnu, and ancestor of Viśwámitra and the Kauśikas (*vide supra*, p. 14); 2. Suhotra, son of Kshattrávŕiddha, and grandson of Áyus, and progenitor of the race of Káśi kings§§ (*vide supra*, pp. 30, *et seq.*); and, 3. Su-

---

* Two MSS. give Trayyáruńi.

† Nearly all my MSS. have Kapila; but, in some of them, Kapila is written over Kapi.

‡ The original says that they all three became Bráhmans: पुत्रत्रयम-भूत् । तच्च त्रितयमपि पश्चाद्विप्रतामुपजगाम । Professor Wilson's Bengal version is here correct. Compare Vol. III, p. 48, note ‡.

§ Omitted in the *Bhágavata-puráńa*, which makes Hastin son of Bŕihatkshattra.

|| The same names are found in the *Bhágavata-puráńa*. The *Váyu-puráńa* seems to read Trayyáruńi, Pushkaráruńi, and Kapi.

¶ *Ádi-parvan*, *ll.* 3714.

** And of Pushkariṅí.

†† *Ádi-parvan*, *ll.* 3720.

‡‡ *Ibid.*, *ll.* 3786, 3787.

§§ See the preceding page, note **.

Hastin, who founded the city of Hastinápura.[1*] The

hotra, the son of Bṛihatkshattra, grandson of Vitatha, and parent of Hastin. In the two blundering compilations mentioned, we have, first (Hari Vaṁśa, ch. 20), a Suhotra, son of Bṛihatkshattra, of the race of Púru: his descent is not given; but, from the names which follow Suhotra, the dynasty is that of our present text: secondly (Hari Vaṁśa, ch. 27), Suhotra, son of Kánchana, of the line of Amávasu, and father of Jahnu, &c.: thirdly (Hari Vaṁśa, ch. 29), Suhotra, the son of Kshattravṛiddha, and progenitor of the Káśi kings: fourthly (Hari Vaṁśa, ch. 32), we have the first and third of these personages confounded; Suhotra is made the son of Vitatha, and progenitor of the Káśi kings, the dynasty of whom is repeated; thus connecting them with the line of Púru, instead of Áyus, in opposition to all authority. Again, we have a notable piece of confusion; and Suhotra, the son of Vitatha, is made the father of Bṛihat, the father of the three princes who, in our text, and in the Hari Vaṁśa, ch. 20, are the sons of Hastin; and amongst whom Ajamídha is made the father of Jahnu, and ancestor of the Kauśikas, instead of being, as in ch. 27, and as everywhere else, of the family of Amávasu. The source of all this confusion is obvious. The compilers extracted all the authentic traditions accurately enough; but, puzzled by the identity of name, they have, also, mixed the different accounts together, and caused very absurd and needless perplexity. It is quite clear, also, that the Hari Vaṁśa does not deserve the pains taken, and taken fruitlessly, by Mr. Hamilton and M. Langlois, to reduce it to consistency. It is of no weight whatever, as an authority for the dynasties of kings,† although it furnishes some particular details, which it has picked up, possibly, from authentic sources not now available.

[1] It was finally ruined by the encroachments of the Ganges; but vestiges of it were, at least until lately, to be traced along the river, nearly in a line with Delhi, about sixty miles to the east.

* Two of my best MSS. have Hástinapura. With reference to the name of this place, see the *Mahábhárata*, *Ádi-parvan*, *ll.* 1786, *et seq.*

† Nevertheless, it is but little inferior to the *Vishńu-puráńa*.

sons of Hastin were Ajamídha,[1] Dwimídha, and Purumídha.* One son of Ajamídha was Kańwa, whose son was Medhátithi.[2]† His‡ other son was Bríhadishu,§ whose son was Bríhadvasu:[3]|| his son was Bríhatkarman;[4] his son was Jayadratha;[5]¶ his son was Viśwajit;[6] his son was Senajit, whose sons were Ru-

[1] In one place, son of Suhotra;** in another, grandson of Hastin:†† Mahábhárata.

[2] The copies agree in this reading; yet it can scarcely be correct. Kańwa has already been noticed, as the son of Apratiratha.‡‡ According to the Bhágavata, the elder§§ son of Ajamídha was Priyamedha,|||| from whom a tribe of Brahmans descended. The Matsya has Bríhaddhanus, and names the wife of Ajamídha, Dhúminí. It also, however, along with the Váyu, makes Kańwa the son of Ajamídha, by his wife Kesiní.

[3] Bríhaddhanus: Bhágavata. Also called Bríhaddharman: Hari Vaḿśa.¶¶

[4] Bríhatkáya: Bhágavata.

[5] Satyajit: Hari Vaḿśa.

[6] Aśwajit: Matsya. Viśada: Bhágavata.

* One MS. gives Suramídha. That Purumídha left no offspring, we learn from the *Bhágavata-puráńa*, IX., XXI., 30.

† The original adds, as has the *Váyu-puráńa*: यतः काण्वायना द्विजाः; thus verbally repeating what is stated in p. 130, *supra*. Here, as before, some MSS. yield Káńwáyana.

‡ *I. e.*, Ajamídha's, as the Sanskrit states distinctly.

§ Bríhaddhanus: *Váyu-puráńa*.

|| Two of my best MSS. have Bríhaddhanus.

¶ Bríhadratha, in one MS. And so reads the *Váyu-puráńa*.

** *Ádi-parvan*, *śl.* 3720.

†† *Ibid.*, *śl.* 3769.

‡‡ *Vide supra*, pp. 129, 130.

§§ The *Bhágavata-puráńa* does not say "elder".

|||| Corrected from "Priyamedhas".

¶¶ Bríhadvishńu(?): *Váyu-puráńa*.

chiráśwa, Káśya, Dṛidhadhanus, and Vatsabhanu.[1]* The son of Ruchiráśwa was Pṛithusena;† his son was Pára;‡ his son was Nípa: he had a hundred sons, of whom Samara, the principal, was the ruler of Kámpilya.[2] Samara had three sons, Pára, Sampára,§ Sadaśwa.|| The son of Pára was Pṛithu; his son was Sukṛiti; his son was Vibhrája;[3]¶ his son was Anuha,**

Bhágavata.††	Matsya.	Hari Vaṁśa.‡‡
[1] Ruchiráśwa	Ruchiráśwa	Ruchira
Káśya	Káśya	Śwetaketu
Dṛidhabanu	Dṛidháśwa	Mahiumára
Vatsa.	Vatsa, king of Avanti.	Vatsa, king of Avanti.

[2] Kámpilya appears to be the Kampil of the Mohammedans, situated in the Doab.§§ It was included in Southern Panchála.||| The Matsya makes Samara the son of Káśya.

[3] Vibhrája¶¶ in MSS.; also in the Váyu.

* The "Vasabanu" of the former edition was an inadvertence: it occurs in Professor Wilson's Hindu-made English version. Two of my MSS. have Vatsa.

† Pṛithusheṇa: *Váyu-puráṇa.*

‡ It seems, from the *Bhágavata-puráṇa*, that Pára and Pṛithusena were, both, sons of Ruchiráśwa.

§ One MS. has Sanghára.

|| Sadáśwa is the more ordinary reading.

¶ Corrected from "Vibhrátra", which, unquestionably, is no word. It is enough to remind the Sanskrit scholar, that ज is often so written as to be easily mistakeable for त. "Bidhátra" is the name in Professor Wilson's Bengal translation. See Vol. III., p. 336, note §§.

** Anuha is a common variant. It is noted, in the Translator's rough copy, that a certain MS. here reads Chaturbhuja.

†† IX., XXI., 23.

‡‡ Ruchiráśwa, Kávya (?), Dṛidhadhanus, Vatsa: *Váyu-puráṇa.*

§§ See Vol. II., p. 160, note 6.

||| See the *Mahábhárata*, *Ádi-parvan*, *ll.* 5512.

¶¶ See note ¶, above.

who married Kŕitwí,* the daughter of Śuka (the son of Vyása), and had, by her, Brahmadatta;[1] his son† was Viśwaksena; his son was Udaksena;[2] and his son was Bhalláṭa.[3]

The son of Dwimíḍha[4] was Yavínara; his son was Dhŕitimat;[5] his son was Satyadhŕiti; his son was Dŕi-

---

[1] The Bhágavata omits the descents subsequent to Nípa, and makes Brahmadatta the son of Nípa by Sukŕiti.‡ In the Hari Vaḿśa§ is a curious legend of the different transmigrations of Brahmadatta and his six companions, who were, successively, as many Brahmans, then foresters, then deer, then water-fowl, then swans, and, finally, Brahmans again; when, with the king, they obtained liberation. According to the Bhágavata, Brahmadatta composed a treatise on the Yoga, a Yoga-tantra.

[2] Daṅḍasena: Hari Vaḿśa.

[3] Bhalláka: Váyu.|| Bhalláda: Bhágavata. The Váyu makes him the last of the race.¶ The Hari Vaḿśa** adds, that he was killed by Karńa.†† The Matsya names his successor Janamejaya, when the race of the Nípas was exterminated by Ugráyudha; as noticed below.‡‡

[4] So the Váyu and Bhágavata. The Matsya and Hari Vaḿśa, with less consistency, derive this family, also, from Ajamíḍha.§§

[5] Kŕitimat: Bhágavata.

---

* Kŕipí, in one MS. But the reading is scarcely of any account.

† By Go, according to the *Bhágavata-puráńa*.

‡ I find Kŕitwí, daughter of Śuka.

§ Chapter XXI.

|| I find Bhallára(?) in my one MS.

¶ This statement seems to be an error. See note ‡‡, below.

** *Śl.* 1070.

†† Rádheya, in the original. Karńa was so called from his foster-mother, Rádhá, wife of Dhŕitaráshṭra. *Vide supra*, p. 126, note †.

‡‡ And so says the *Váyu-puráńa*, at least in my MS.

§§ And with these our Puráńa agrees. For, after naming Bhalláṭa, it proceeds: भल्लाटात्मजो ह्रिमीकः । ह्रिमीकस्य यवीनरस्सुतः ।

dhanemi; his son was Supárśwa;[1] his son was Sumati; his son was Sannatimat;* his son was Kṛita,† to whom Hiraṇyanábha taught (the philosophy of) the Yoga; and he[2] compiled twenty-four Saṁhitás (or compendia), for the use of the eastern Brahmans who study the Sáma-veda. The son of Kṛita was Ugráyudha,‡ by whose prowess§ the Nípa race of Kshattriyas was destroyed.[3]|| His son was Kshemya;¶ his son was

---

[1] Between these two the Váyu** inserts Mahat and Rukmaratha; the Matsya, Sudhanwan, Sárvabhauma, Mahápaurava, and Rukmadhara; the Brahma Puráṇa, Sudharman, Sárvabhauma, Mahat, and Rukmaratha.

[2] The Bhágavata†† says, he was the author of six Saṁhitás of the Sáma-veda.

[3] The Hari Vaṁśa‡‡ says, he killed Nípa, the grandfather of Pṛishata; but it had, previously, stated, that it was the son of Bhalláṭa—several descents after Nípa,—who was killed by Ugráyudha;§§ and, again (ch. 32||||), Pṛishata, conformably to other

---

* Two of my best MSS. have, respectively, Santimat and Samnati.

† The *Bhágavata-puráṇa* has Kṛitin. But neither this nor Kṛiti seems to be the right name. See Vol. III., p. 60, notes § and ||. There is, here, in the *Váyu-puráṇa*, something that I am unable to read in my MS.

‡ Son of Nípa, who was, apparently, son of Kṛitin, according to the *Bhágavata-puráṇa*.

§ येन प्राचुर्येण, "by whom, to a great extent."

|| The original has only नीपक्षयः कृतः। Professor Wilson has inserted, in his text, the commentator's gloss: नीपाः। पार्थिवविशेषाः। तेषां क्षयः कृतः।

¶ Kshema, in one MS. This is the reading I find in the *Váyu-puráṇa*.

** In my MS., it gives, as son of Dṛidhanemi, Suvarman; then, Sárvabhauma, several illegible names, and Rukmaratha, father of Supárśwa.

†† IX., XXI., 28, 29. See note †, above.

‡‡ *Śl.* 1083.

§§ *Śl.* 1072.

|||| *Śl.* 1793.

Suvíra; his son was Nŕipanjaya;[1]* his son was Bahuratha.† These were, all, called Pauravas.

Ajamídha had a wife called Nílinî;‡ and, by her, he had a son named Níla: his son was Śánti;§ his son was Suśánti; his son was Purujánu;[2]|| his son was Chakshus;[3]¶ his son was Haryaśwa,[4]** who had five sons, Mudgala, Śŕinjaya,[5]†† Bŕihadishu, Pravíra,[6]‡‡ and

authorities, appears as the father of Drupada, in the family of Śŕinjaya. The Hari Vaḿśa§§ relates the destruction of Ugráyudha by Bhíshma, in consequence of his demanding, in marriage, the widow of Śántanu;||| after which, Pŕishata, it is said, recovered possession of Kámpilya.

[1] Puranjaya:¶¶ Bhágavata.

[2] Purujáti: Váyu.*** Puruja: Bhágavata. The Brahma Puráńa and Hari Vaḿśa omit Níla and Śánti.

[3] Ríksha: Váyu. Pŕithu: Matsya. Arka: Bhágavata. Omitted: Brahma.

[4] Báhyáśwa: Agni.††† Bhadráśwa: Matsya. Bharmyáśwa: Bhágavata.

[5] Jaya: Matsya. Sanjaya: Bhágavata.

[6] Yavínara: Agni and Bhágavata. Javínara: Matsya.

* Two MSS. give Ripunjaya; one, Puranjaya.

† Víraratha: *Váyu-puráńa.*

‡ In one MS., Nalinî; the lection of the *Bhágavata-puráńa.*

§ The *Váyu-puráńa* omits this name.

|| A single copy exhibits Purajánu. And see note ***, below.

¶ Corrected from "Chakshu". One copy has Arka.

** There is no name here, in my copy of the *Váyu-puráńa.*

†† Two MSS. have Sanjaya. Referring to this place, and to Vol. II., p. 180, Professor Wilson seems to connect Śŕinjaya with the people of the same name, dwelling "towards the Punjab". Translation of the *Rigveda*, Vol. III., p. 438, note 4.

‡‡ Two MSS. have Yavínara.

§§ Chapter XX.

||| Called Bhíshma's father.

¶¶ I find Ripunjaya.

*** Purajánu, in my MS.

††† Add the *Harivaḿśa*, *ll.* 1777.

Kámpilya.[1] Their father said: "These my five (pancha) sons are able (alam) to protect the countries;" and, hence, they were termed the Panchálas.[2] From Mudgala descended the Maudgalya Brahmans:[3]* he had (also,) a son named Badhryaśwa,[4]† who had (two

---

[1] Kapila: Matsya. Krimiláśwa: Brahma.

[2] Panchála was, at first, the country north and west of Delhi, between the foot of the Himálaya and the Chumbul. It was afterwards divided into Northern and Southern Panchála, separated by the Ganges. Mákandi (on the Ganges,) and Kámpilya‡ were the chief cities of the latter; Ahikshatra,§ in the former. The Panchálas, according to the Mahábhárata, expelled Saṁvaraṅa from Hastinápura; but it was recovered by Kuru. The purport of the term Panchála is similarly explained in other Puráńas. In the Mahábhárata, they are the grandsons of Ajamídha.

[3] The Matsya says, that they, as well as the Káńwas, were, all, followers or partizans of Angiras:

मुद्गलस्यापि मौद्गल्याः क्षत्रोपेता द्विजातयः ।
एते ह्याङ्गिरसः पक्षे संस्थिताः कण्वमुद्गलाः ॥

The Hari Vaṁśa‖ has nearly the same words.¶

[4] Badhryaśwa:** Váyu. Panchâśwa: Agni. Bandhyáśwa:

---

* The original says that they were, at first, Kshattriyas: क्षत्रोपेता द्विजातयो बभूवुः । On this the commentator observes, as before: क्षत्रिया एव सन्तः केनचित्कारणेन ब्राह्मणा बभूवुरित्यर्थः । *Vide supra*, p. 137, note 4.

† This name, or some corruption of it, is found in all my MSS. The Translator's "Bahwaśwa" I have here displaced, as having, at least so far as I am aware, no authority except that of Professor Wilson's Bengal translation.

Badhryaśwa is the genuine name—in the oldest Hindu book,—of the father of Divodása. See the *Rigveda*, VI., LXI., 1.

‡ See the *Mahábhárata*, *Ádi-parvan*, *śl.* 5512.

§ See Vol. II., p. 160, note 9, and the annotations thereon.

‖ *Śl.* 1781, 1782. ¶ And the same may be said of the *Váyu-puráńa*.

** Corrected from "Badhryáśwa" by Professor Wilson himself, in his Translation of the *Rigveda*, Vol. III., p. 504, note 1.

children,) twins, (a son and daughter), Divodása and Ahalyá. The son of Śaradwat (or Gautama*), by Ahalyá,† was Śatánanda;[1] his son was Satyadhŕiti,‡ who was a proficient in military science. Being enamoured of the nymph Urvaśí, Satyadhŕiti was the parent of two children, a boy and a girl. Śántanu,§ a Raja, whilst hunting, found these children exposed in a clump of long Śara grass, and, compassionating their

Matsya. Bhármya:|| Bhágavata. But there is some indistinctness as to his descent. The Matsya and Hari Vaḿśa¶ give the son of Mudgala only his patronymic, Maudgalya. According to the first, his son was Indrasena, and his son, Bandhyáśwa. The second** makes Badhryaśwa the son of Maudgalya, by Indrasená. The Bhágavata†† makes Bhármya the patronymic of Mudgala, the son of Bharmyáśwa, and who is the father of Divodása‡‡ and Ahalyá:

मिथुनं मुद्गलाद्भार्म्याद्दिवोदासः पुमानभूत् ।

The commentator has: भार्म्यात् । भर्म्याश्वपुत्रात् ।

[1] In the Rámáyańa, Śatánanda appears as the family priest of Janaka, the father of Sítá.

* Parenthesized by me, because supplied by the Translator. Two of my MSS. have Gautama, not Śaradwat. Compare Vol. III., p. 16, note ‡.

† For a story regarding Ahalyá and Gautama, translated from the *Rámáyańa*, by Dr. Muir, see his *Original Sanskrit Texts*, Part I., pp. 121, 122 (2nd ed.).

‡ It was, agreeably to the *Bhágavata-puráńa*, his son Śaradwat that was father of Kŕipa and Kŕipí, named just below.

§ *Vide supra*, p. 143, note 3, *ad finem*.

|| The *Bhágavata-puráńa* does not substitute Bhármya for "Babhwaśwa," but makes Mudgala, the Bhármya,—*i. e.*, son of Bharmyáśwa,—father of Divodása and Ahalyá. The Pańchálakas, collectively, are called Bhármyas in the same Puráńa, IX., XXII., 3.

¶ *Śl.* 1780. ** *Harivaḿśa*, *śl.* 1782, 1783. †† IX., XXI., 34.

‡‡ For another Divodása, presumably of later date than he of the *Ŕigveda*,—which work, as we have seen in note † to the preceding page, knows the son of Badhryaśwa,—*vide supra*, p. 33.

condition, took them, and brought them up. As they were nurtured through pity (kṛipá), they were called Kṛipa and Kṛipí.* The latter became the wife of Droṇa, and the mother of Aśwatthámán.†

The son of Divodása was Mitráyu;[1]‡ his son was Chyavana,§ his son was Sudása;|| his son was Sau-

[1] From whom the Maitreya Brahmans were descended: Hari Vaṁśa.¶ In the Matsya and Agni,** the son of Mitráyu is called Maitreya (see Vol. I., p. 6). The Brahma Puráṇa and Hari Vaṁśa here close the lineage of Divodása: the Agni adds but one name, Somápi. They then proceed with the descendants of Sṛinjaya, one of the Panchálas,—or, Panchadhanus, Somadatta, Sahadeva,—and then, as in our text. The Váyu and Bhágavata agree with the latter, in making the line continuous from Divodása. According to the Matsya and Brahma Puráṇas,†† the race of Ajamíḍha became extinct in the person of Sahadeva; but Ajamíḍha himself was reborn, as Somaka, in order to continue his lineage, which was, thence, called the Somaka family. It was in the reign of Drupada that the possessions of the Panchálas were divided; Droṇa, assisted by the Páṇḍavas, conquering the country, and ceding the southern portion again to Drupada, as related in the Mahábhárata. The two princes last named in the list figure in the Great War.

* The translation here both compresses and expands the original.

† He bears the patronym of Drauṇáyani. See the *Mahábhárata*, *Ádi-parvan*, *ll.* 7019, &c.

‡ I find Mitrayu everywhere but in one MS., which has Mitraghna. For Mitráyu, see the *Bhágavata-puráṇa*, IX., XXII., 1; also, Vol. III., p. 64, note *. Mitrayu occurs in some MSS. of the *Bhágavata-puráṇa*. The *Váyu-puráṇa* has Mitrayu.

§ The original calls him a king.

|| The *Váyu-puráṇa*, I think, gives him a brother, Pratiratha.

¶ *Śl.* 1789, 1790. The Maitreyas are there said to be Kshattriyas.

** Also in the *Váyu-puráṇa*.

†† Compare the *Váyu-puráṇa*, my copy of which is, just here, such as to forbid my entering into details with any security from error.

dása, also called Sahadeva;* his son was Somaka; he had a hundred sons, of whom Jantu was the eldest, and Príshata the youngest. The son of Príshata was Drupada; his son was Dhríshtadyumna; his son was Dhríshtaketu.†

Another son of Ajamídha was named Ŕiksha;[1] his son was Saḿvarańa; his son‡ was Kuru, who gave his name to the holy district Kurukshetra;§ his sons were Sudhanus,|| Jahnu, Parikshit,¶ and (many) others.[2] The son of Sudhanus was Suhotra; his son

[1] The Hari Vaḿśa** gives him two brothers, Dhúmravarńa†† and Sudarśana. In the Mahábhárata, one list‡‡ agrees with the text; the other§§ calls Saḿvarańa the son of Ajamídha, by his wife Ŕikshá.

[2] One other is named in the Bhágavata,|||| Matsya, Brahma, and Agni,—Animejaya, Arimardana,¶¶ and Nishadháśwa. The Hari Vaḿśa has Sudhanwan,*** in place of Jahnu; having, also, Sudhanus.

* According to two MSS. and the Translator's Bengal version, Sahadeva was son of Sudása.

† Corrected from "Dríshtaketu".

‡ By Tapatí: *Bhágavata-puráńa.*

§ The original runs: य इदं धर्मक्षेत्रं कुरुक्षेत्रं चकार । For Kurukshetra, see Vol. II., p. 133, note 1; p. 142, note 4.

|| Sudhanwan: *Váyu-puráńa.*

¶ Here, and everywhere, Professor Wilson put "Paríkshit", a late form of Parikshit which my MSS. very rarely present.

** *Śl.* 1799.

†† The *Váyu-puráńa* mentions him.

‡‡ *Ádi-parvan, ll.* 3724.

§§ *Ibid., ll.* 3790, *et seq.*

|||| This has Nishadháśwa.

¶¶ Him the *Váyu-puráńa* names.

*** Corrected from "Sudhanwat".

was Chyavana; his son was Kŕitaka;[1] his son was Uparichara,* the Vasu,[2]† who had seven‡ children, Bŕihadratha,§ Pratyagraha,|| Kuśámba,¶ Mávella,

---

[1] Kŕita: Váyu.** Kŕitayajna: Brahma. Kŕimi: Matsya. Kŕitin:†† Bhágavata.

[2] The story of Uparichara, or a Vasu‡‡ who, by command of Indra, became king of Chedi, is told in the Mahábhárata, Ádi Parvan§§ (Vol. I., p. 85). He is there said to have, at first, five sons, Bŕihadratha (king of Magadha), Pratyagraha,|||| Kuśámba (also called Mańivábana), Mávella, and Yadu, by his wife Giriká; afterwards he has, by Adriká, an Apsaras (condemned to the form

---

* There may be a question whether this is the name in the *Váyu-puráńa*.

† Read "Vasu, *surnamed* Uparichara." A Vasu—see Vol. II., p. 22,—is a sort of demigod; and it does not appear that Uparichara was turned into one. He has the longer epithet of Chaidyoparichara, in the *Harivaḿśa*, *śl.* 1806.

‡ The *Váyu-puráńa* names all seven; but I can read only the first four, in my very incorrect MS.

§ Mahávatha, king of Magadha: *Váyu-puráńa*.

|| Corrected from "Pratyagra", and notwithstanding that this is the name in all my MSS. except one, which has Pratyagratha. For all the MSS. are wrong; the name being as I have given it. Proof of this is to be found in the *Mahábhárata*, *Ádi-parvan*, *śl.* 2363, quoted in note ||||, below.

We read, in the *Váyu-puráńa*, further:

प्रत्यग्रः कुशश्चैव यमाहुर्मणिवाहनम् ।

The *Vishńu-puráńa*, hereabouts, is in prose. Did the *Bhágavata-puráńa*—which is metrical,—copy therefrom, in its Pratyagra?

¶ Kuśa: *Váyu-puráńa*. See the verse of Sanskrit in the preceding note.

** I find Kŕitaka.

†† Corrected from "Kŕiti".

‡‡ See note †, above.

§§ *Śl.* 2334, *et seq.*

|||| Corrected from "Pratyagra". The original runs:

प्रत्यग्रहः कुशाम्बश्च यमाहुर्मणिवाहनम् ।

The same verse occurs in the *Harivaḿśa*, *śl.* 1806.

Matsya, and others.* The son of Bŕihadratha was Kuśágra;† his son was Ŕishabha;[1]‡ his son was Pushpavat;§ his son was Satyadhŕita;[2]|| his son was Sudhanwan;¶ and his son was Jantu.** Bŕihadratha had†† another son, who, being born in two parts, which were put together (sandhita) by (a female fiend named) Jará, he was denominated Jarásandha.[3] His son was Saha-

of a fish), Matsya (a son), and Satyavatí (or Kálí, a daughter): the latter was the mother of Vyása. The same legend is referred to in the accounts of Uparichara and his family, in the Bhágavata, Matsya, Hari Vaḿśa, &c.

[1] Vŕishabha: Matsya.

[2] Satyajita: Váyu. Satyahita:‡‡ Bhágavata.§§ Satyadhŕita or Pushya: Matsya.

[3] This story is told in the 16th section of the Sabhá Parvan of the Mahábhárata, where, also, he is called the son of Bŕihadratha. In the Váyu, he is the son of Satyajita.|||| The Agni has Satyahita, Úrja, Sambhava, Jarásandha; and the Matsya, Satyadhŕita, Dhanusha, Śarva, Sambhava, Jarásandha.

* The *Bhágavata-puráńa* names Bŕihadratha, Kuśámba, Matsya, Pratyagra, and Chedipa, and calls them kings of Chedi.

† In the *Váyu-puráńa*, the name, in my copy, is Kuśágrya.

‡ In one MS., Vŕishabha.

§ Putravat, in one copy.

|| Two MSS. exhibit Satyahita.

¶ A single copy gives Sumanas.

** Úrjha, in my careless MS. of the *Váyu-puráńa*; and his son was Nabhasa; and his, Jarásandha.

†† By another wife, says the *Bhágavata-puráńa*.

‡‡ So in the *Váyu-puráńa*, too.

§§ IX., XXII., 7. And it places Pushpavat after, not before, Satyahita. It then makes Jahu son of Pushpavat, and does not speak of Sudhanwan and Jantu.

|||| Not so, according to my single MS., which is, often, very incorrect. See note **, above.

deva; his son was Somápi;[1]* his son was Śrutaśravas.[2]† These were kings of Magadha.‡

---

[1] Somádhi: Váyu.§ Udápi: Agni. Udáyus: Brahma. Somavit: Matsya.||

[2] Śrutakarman: Agni. Śrutaśarman: Brahma.

---

* Somádhi, in one MS.

† Omitted in my copy of the *Váyu-purána*.

‡ Corrected, throughout this work, from "Magadhá".

For a continuation of the kings of Magadha, see Chapter XXIII. of this Book.

§ Regarding Somádhi, it says, agreeably to the reading of my one MS.:

यतश्च षाडुसोमाधिर्मागधः परिकीर्तितः ।

|| Márjári: *Bhágavata-purána*, IX., XXII., 44; but, in the seventh stanza, Somápi.

CHAPTER XX.

Descendants of Kuru. Devápi abdicates the throne: assumed by Śántanu: he is confirmed by the Brahmans: Bhíshma his son by Gangá: his other sons. Birth of Dhŕitaráshtra, Páńdu, and Vidura. The hundred sons of Dhŕitaráshtra. The five sons of Páńdu: married to Draupadí: their posterity. Parikshit, the grandson of Arjuna, the reigning king.

PARIKSHIT (the son of Kuru,)* had four sons, Janamejaya, Śrutasena, Ugrasena, and Bhímasena.[1] The

[1] This, although it occurs in other authorities, appears to be an error; for these are the sons of a subsequent Parikshit (see the next chapter, p. 162). The Matsya omits Parikshit here; and the Bhágavata † states that he had no children. In most of the Puráńas, however, the line of Parikshit is continued; but there is very great confusion in the lineage. According to the Váyu, ‡ Janamejaya was the son of Parikshit, whose son was Śrutasena, whose son was Bhímasena. Janamejaya had, also, a son named Suratha; but Suratha was, also, the name of the son of Jahnu, from whom the line continues as in the text. The Brahma Puráńa and Hari Vaḿśa also make Suratha the son both of Janamejaya and of Jahnu; and they observe, that there are two Ŕikshas, two Parikshits, three Bhímasenas, and two Janamejayas, in the Lunar race. § Some of the confusion probably originates with the Mahábhárata, which, as before noticed, ‖ gives two lists from Púru to Śántanu, differing from one another, and from all the lists of the Puráńas. In the first of these lists, each collateral

* I have supplied the parentheses. But *vide supra*, p. 148.

† IX., XXII., 9.

‡ In the single MS. to which I am here reduced, it is said that Janamejaya was son of Parikshа (*sic*), and that Bhímasena was son of Śrutasena. Janamejaya and Śrutasena are not connected there.

§ *Harivaḿśa*, *ll.* 1815—1818. ‖ *Vide supra*, p. 137, note 1.

son of Jahnu* was Suratha; his son was Vidúratha;† his son was Sárvabhauma; his son was Jayasena;‡ his son was Árávin;§ his son was Ayutáyus; his son was Akrodhana; one of his sons was Devátithi,|| and another was called Ŕiksha;¶ his son was Dilípa;** his son was Pratípa, who had three sons, Devápi††,

---

names have been retained as appear to have furnished our text and that of other Puráńas with distinct persons; thus making the members of one fraternity so many descents. Of the two lists, however, the second is, probably, to be regarded as the more recent, if not more correct; for Vaiśampáyana repeats it at Janamejaya's request, because the latter is not satisfied with the summary account which the former had first communicated to him. Mahábhárata, Vol. I., p. 136 and p. 138.

---

* *Vide supra*, p. 148.

† *Vide supra*, p. 99, text and note ††. Bindumati, who slew a Vidúratha, was his queen, as we learn from Varáhamihira's *Bŕihat-sańhitá*, LXXVIII., 1. See Vol. III., p. 268, note *.

‡ In one MS., Jayatsena, the name I find in the *Váyu-puráńa*.

§ Anádhita, in the Ajmere and Arrah MSS. In the *Váyu-puráńa* I find Árádhin.

|| One MS. gives Devápi. The *Bhágavata-puráńa* has Jayasena, Rádhika, Ayuta, Krodhana, Devátithi.

¶ Ŕishya: *Bhágavata-puráńa*.

** The ordinary reading, and that known to Professor Wilson, is as follows: तस्माद्देवातिथिः । तत ऋक्षोऽन्यः । ऋक्षाद्भीमसेनः । ततश्च दिलीपः । "From him (Akrodhana), Devátithi; from him, another Ŕiksha; from Ŕiksha, Bhímasena; and, from him, Dilípa." The commentator remarks, touching Ŕiksha: पूर्वोक्तादजमीढपुत्रादृक्षादन्यः । The word अन्यः, 'other', connected with Ŕiksha, is, thus, to distinguish him from Ŕiksha, son of Ajamídha, mentioned in p. 148, *supra*.

Every one of my MSS. inserts Bhímasena; and so does Professor Wilson's Hindu-made English version. The *Bhágavata-puráńa* omits him.

†† Devápi was son of Ŕishṭishena, according to the *Ŕigveda*, X., XCVIII., 5.

Śántanu,* and Váhlíka. The first adopted, in childhood, a forest-life; and Śántanu became king. Of him this verse is spread through the earth: "Śántanu is his name; because, if he lays his hands upon an old man, he restores him to youth, and, by him, men obtain tranquillity (śánti)."†

In the kingdom over which Śántanu ruled there was no rain for twelve years. Apprehensive that the country would become a desert, the king assembled the Brahmans, and asked them why no rain fell, and what fault he had committed. They told him, that he was, as it were, a younger brother married before an elder;‡ for he was in the enjoyment of the earth, which was the right of his elder brother, Devápi.§

* One MS. has, throughout this chapter, Śantanu; the reading of the *Bhágavata-puráńa*, and that which I find in the *Váyu-puráńa*.

† यं यं कराभ्यां स्पृशति जीर्णं यौवनमेति सः ।
शान्तिं चाप्नोति येनाग्र्यां कर्मणा तेन शान्तनुः ॥

Compare the *Bhágavata-puráńa*, IX., XXII., 13; the *Mahábhárata*, *Ádi-parvan*, *ll.* 3799; &c.

‡ We read, in the *Mánava-dharmaśástra*, III., 171, 172:

दाराग्निहोत्रसंयोगं कुरुते योऽग्रजे स्थिते ।
परिवेत्ता स विज्ञेयः परिवित्तिस्तु पूर्वजः ॥
परिवित्तिः परिवेत्ता यया च परिविद्यते ।
सर्वे ते नरकं यान्ति दातृयाजकपञ्चमाः ॥

"He who, while his elder brother is unwedded, marries a wife with the nuptial fires, is to be known as a *parivettri*; and his elder brother, as a *parivitti*. The *parivitti*, the *parivettri*, the female by whom the offence is committed, he who gives her away, and, fifthly, the officiating priest, all go to hell."

This is Dr. Muir's translation of the preceding verses, on which he observes: "The Indian writers regard the relation of a king to his realm as analogous to that of a husband to his wife. The earth is the king's bride." *Original Sanskrit Texts*, Part I., p. 275, foot-note (2nd ed.).

§ ते तमूचुः । अयमयज ते ऽग्रजेयमवनिस्त्वया भुज्यते परिवेत्ता त्वम् ।

"What, then, am I to do?" said the Raja. To which they replied: "Until the gods shall be displeased with Devápi, by his declining from the path of righteousness,* the kingdom is his; and to him, therefore, you should resign it." When the minister of the king, Aśmasárin,† heard this, he collected a number of ascetics who taught doctrines opposed to those of the Vedas, and sent them into the forest, where, meeting with Devápi, they perverted the understanding of the simple-minded prince, and led him to adopt heretical notions. In the meantime, Śántanu, being much distressed to think that he had been guilty of the offence intimated by the Brahmans, sent them, before him, into the woods, and then proceeded thither, himself, to restore the kingdom to his elder brother. When the Brahmans arrived at the hermitage of Devápi, they informed him, that, according to the doctrines of the Vedas, succession to a kingdom was the right of the elder brother. But he entered into discussion with them, and in various ways advanced arguments which had the defect of being contrary to the precepts of the Vedas. When the Brahmans heard this, they turned to Śántanu, and said: "Come hither, Raja. You need give yourself no further trouble in this matter: the dearth is at an end. This man is fallen from his state; for he has uttered words of disrespect to the authority of the eternal, uncreated Veda; and, when the elder brother is degraded, there is no sin in the prior espou-

* यावद्देवापिर्न पतनादिभिर्दोषैरभिभूयते ।

† Corrected from "Asmarisárin." Two of my MSS., those of Ajmere and Arrah, do not name the minister.

sals of his junior." Śántanu, thereupon, returned to his capital, and administered the government (as before); and his elder brother, Devápi, being degraded from his caste by repeating doctrines contrary to the Vedas, Indra* poured down abundant rain, which was followed by plentiful harvests[1].†

[1] The Mahábhárata merely states that Devápi retired to a

* Parjanya, in the Sanskrit.

† The subjoined close translation of this legend concerning Śántanu is taken from Dr. Muir's *Original Sanskrit Texts*, Part I., pp. 274—276 (2nd ed.):

"Devápi, while yet a boy, retired to the forest; and Śántanu became king. Regarding him this verse is current in the world: 'Every decrepit man whom he touches with his hands becomes young. He is called Śántanu from that work whereby he obtains supreme tranquillity (*śánti*). The god did not rain on the country of this Śántanu for twelve years. Beholding, then, the ruin of his entire realm, the king inquired of the Bráhmans: 'Why does not the god rain on this country? What is my offence?' The Bráhmans replied: 'This earth, which is the right of thy elder brother, is now enjoyed by thee; thou art a *parivettri* (one married before his elder brother).' Receiving this reply, he again asked them: 'What must I do?' They then answered: 'So long as Devápi does not succumb to declension from orthodoxy, and other offences, the royal authority is his, by right; to him, therefore, let it be given, without further question.' When they had so said, the king's principal minister, Aśmasárin, employed certain ascetics propounding doctrines contrary to the declarations of the Vedas to proceed into the forest, by whom the understanding of the very simple-minded prince (Devápi) was led to adopt a system at variance with those sacred books. King Śántanu, being distressed for his offence, in consequence of what the Bráhmans had said to him, went, preceded by those Bráhmans, to the forest, in order to deliver over the kingdom to his elder brother. Arriving at the hermitage, they came to prince Devápi. The Bráhmans addressed to him statements founded on the declarations of the Veda, to the effect that the royal authority should be exercised by the elder brother. He, on his part, expressed to them many things that were vitiated by reasonings contrary to the tenour of the Veda. The Bráhmans then said to Śántanu: 'Come hither, O king. There is no occasion for any excessive hesitation in this affair. The offence which led to the drought is

The son of Váhlíka* was Somadatta, who had three sons, Bhúri, Bhúriśravas, and Śala.[1]

The son of Śántanu was the illustrious and learned Bhíshma, who was born to him by the holy river-goddess,† Gangá;‡ and he had, by his wife, Satyavatí,§ two sons, Chitrángada and Vichitravírya. Chitrángada, whilst yet a youth, was killed in a conflict with a Gan-

religious life.|| The story of his heresy is narrated, much as in the text, in the Bhágavata, Váyu, &c. The Matsya adds, that he was, also, leprous; on which account his subjects contemned him. He was, probably, set aside in favour of his younger brother, either on that account, or on that of his heresy; such a disposition being conformable to Hindu law. According to the Bhágavata and Matsya, he is still alive, at a place called Kalápagráma,¶ where, in the Kṛita age of the next Mahâyuga, he will be the restorer of the Kshattriya race.

[1] The Matsya says that Váhlíka** had a hundred sons, or lords of the Váhlíkas.

now removed. Your brother has fallen by uttering a contradiction of the words of the Veda, which have been revered from time without beginning; and, when the elder brother has fallen, the younger is no longer chargeable with the offence of *párivettrya* (i. e., of marrying before his elder brother).' When he had been so addressed, Śántanu returned to his capital, and exercised the royal authority. And, although his eldest brother, Devápi, continued to be degraded by having uttered words opposed to the doctrines of the Veda, the god Parjanya rained, in order to produce a harvest of all sorts of grain."

* Váhlíka, in one MS., as in my one MS. of the *Váyu-puráńa*.

† *Amara-nadí*.

‡ One of my MSS. has the synonymous Jáhnaví.

§ *Vide supra*, p. 149, note 2.

|| *Ádi-parvan*, *ll.* 3750 and 3798. In the *Udyoga-parvan*, *ll.* 5056, it is said that he was a leper.

¶ See Vol. III., p. 197, note ||; and p. 325, text and note *.

** The *Matsya-puráńa* states that his sons were the seven Váhlíśwara kings. See *Original Sanskrit Texts*, Part I., p. 277 (2nd ed.).

dharva, also called Chitrángada. Vichitravírya* married Ambiká† and Ambáliká, the daughters of the king of Kási,‡ and, indulging too freely in connubial rites, fell into a consumption, of which he died. By command of Satyavatí, my son Kŕishńa-dwaipáyana, ever obedient to his mother's wishes,[1]|| begot, upon the widows of his brother,§ the princes Dhŕitaráshtra and Páńdu, and, upon a female servant, Vidura. Dhŕitaráshtra had Duryodhana,¶ Duhśásana, and other sons, to the number of a hundred.** Páńdu, having incurred the curse of a deer, (whose mate he had killed in the chase), was deterred from procreating children; and his wife

[1] Before her marriage to Śántanu, Satyavatí had a son, Kŕishńa-dwaipáyana,†† or Vyása, by Paráśara. He was, therefore, the half-brother of Vichitravírya, and legally qualified to raise up offspring to him by his widow. This law is abrogated in the present age. The whole story of the sons of Śántanu is told at length in the Mahábhárata.‡‡

* From this point to near the end of the present Book there is, unfortunately, a break in my valuable Ajmere MS.

† Corrected from "Ambá". This was the eldest sister of Ambiká and Ambáliká, and married a king of Śálwa. See the *Mahábhárata*, *Udyoga-parvan*, *ll.* 5950, *et seq.*

‡ I have corrected the Translator's "Káśi".

§ The original says, more distinctly, "of Vichitravírya." For the ground of Professor Wilson's substitution, see note 1, above.

|| मातुर्हितमनुविधायिना ।

¶ By Gándhárí, according to two MSS.; and so says the *Bhágavata-puráńa*.

** The *Bhágavata-puráńa* adds a daughter, Duhśalá.

†† So called "from his dark complexion (*kŕishńa*), and his having been born upon an island (*dwípa*) in the Ganges." Professor Wilson, in Professor Johnson's *Selections from the Mahábhárata*, p. 8, note 2.

‡‡ *Ádi-parvan*, *ll.* 3800, *et seq.*

Kuntí bare to him, in consequence, three sons,—who were begotten by the deities Dharma, Váyu, and Indra,*—namely, Yudhishthira, Bhímasena,† and Arjuna; and his wife Mádrí had two sons, Nakula and Sahadeva, by the celestial sons of Aświní.‡ These had, each, a son, by Draupadí.§ The son of Yudhishthira was Prativindhya; of Bhímasena, Śrutasoma;|| of Arjuna, Śrutakírtti; of Nakula, Śatáníka; and, of Sahadeva, Śrutakarman. The Páńdavas had, also, other sons.[1] By his wife Yaudheyí,¶ Yudhishthira had Devaka. The son of Bhímasena, by Hidimbá, was Ghatotkacha; and he had, also, Sarvatraga,** by his wife Káśí.†† The son of Sahadeva, by Vijayá, was Suhotra;

---

[1] The Mahábhárata‡‡ names some of them rather differently, and adds some particulars. Thus, Yaudheya was the son of Yudhishthira, by his wife Deviká, daughter of Govásana, of the Śaibya tribe. The son of Bhímasena was Sarvaga, by Balandhará, princess of Káśi: he had, also, Ghatotkacha,§§ by Hidimbá. Abhimanyu was the son of Arjuna, by Subhadrá. The wives and sons of the other two are the same; but Kareńumatí is termed a princess of Chedi; and Vijayá, of Madra.

---

* Śakra, in the Sanskrit.

† Corrected from "Bhíma", here and below.

‡ Compare pp. 102, 103, *supra*.

§ तेषां द्रौपद्यां पञ्च पुत्रा बभूवुः ।

|| Two MSS. have Śrutasena.

¶ Pauravi: *Bhágavata-puráńa*.

** In one MS., Sarvaga.

†† One MS. has Káśeyí. This, like the corresponding Kásyá of the *Mahábhárata*, is a derivative of Káśi. "Sarvagata, by Kálí", according to the *Bhágavata-puráńa*.

‡‡ *Ádi-parvan*, *ll.* 3828—3833.

§§ Corrected from "Ghatotkacha".

and Niramitra was the son of Nakula, by Kareńumatí. Arjuna had Irávat, by the serpent-nymph Ulúpí;* Babhruváhana, who was adopted as the son of his maternal grandfather,† by the daughter of the king of Mańipúra;‡ and, by his wife Subhadrá, Abhimanyu, who, even in extreme youth, was renowned for his valour and his strength, and crushed the chariots of his foes in fight. The son of Abhimanyu, by his wife Uttará, was Parikshit, who, after the Kurus were all destroyed,§ was killed,|| in his mother's womb, by the magic Bráhma weapon,¶ hurled by Aśwatthámán. He was, however, restored to life by the clemency of that being whose feet receive the homage of all the demons and the gods, and who, for his own pleasure, had assumed a human shape, (Křishńa). This prince,[1]

---

[1] In the details immediately preceding, the Puráńas generally concur; deriving them, probably, from the same source,—the Ádi Parvan of the Mahábhárata,—and employing, very frequently, the same words. The period at which the chapter closes is supposed

---

* Corrected from "Ulopi". Ulúpí was daughter of the *nága* Kauravya, according to the authority of the *Mahábhárata*, *Ádi-parvan*, *ll.* 7788, 7789. The *Bhágavata-puráńa*, IX., XX., 31,—at least, as the passage is explained by the commentator, Śrídhara,—makes Ulúpí daughter of the king of Mańipúra.

† The original has: मणिपुरपतिपुत्र्यां च पुत्रिकाधर्मेण बभ्रुवाहनं नाम पुत्रमजीजनत् । See Śrídhara on the *Bhágavata-puráńa*, IX., XX., 31.

‡ Corrected from "Manipura", on the warrant of all my MSS. Mańipúra was a city on the sea-coast of Kalinga. See the *Mahábhárata*, *Ádi-parvan*, *ll.* 7824.

§ The commentator hereupon etymologizes the name Parikshit, परि-क्षीणेषु कुरुष्विति । भगवतश्चाद्भुतवधे परिक्षिन्नामाभिधानो च हेतुः ।

|| *Bhasmí-křita*, "reduced to ashes."

¶ *Brahmástra*. See Vol. III., p. 81, note •.

Parikshit, now reigns over the whole world, with undivided sway.

---

to be that at which the Vyása who arranged or compiled the Puráńas is believed to have flourished. Parikshit died of the bite of a snake, according to the Mahábhárata, Ádi Parvan. The Bhágavata is supposed to have been narrated to him in the interval between the bite and its fatal effect.

CHAPTER XXI.

Future kings. Descendants of Parikshit, ending with Kshemaka.

I WILL now enumerate the kings who will reign in future periods.[1] The present monarch, Parikshit,[2]* will have four sons, Janamejaya, Śrutasena, Ugrasena, and Bhímasena.[3]† The son of Janamejaya‡ will be Śatáníka,[4] who will study the Vedas under Yájnavalkya, and military science with Kṛipa; but, becoming dissatisfied with sensual enjoyments, he will

---

[1] The style now adopted is that of prophecy; as Vyása could not, consistently, have recorded the events which were posterior to his time.

[2] Also read Parikshita, Pariksha, and Parikshi.

[3] *Vide supra*, p. 152. The Váyu and Matsya relate, rather obscurely, a dispute between Janamejaya and Vaiśampáyana, in consequence of the former's patronage of the Brahmans of the Vájasaneyi branch of the Yajurveda, in opposition to the latter, who was the author of the black, or original, Yajus (see Vol. III., p. 52). Janamejaya twice performed the Aśwamedha, according to the Vájasaneyi ritual, and established the Trisarvi,§—or use of certain texts, by Aśmaka and others,—by the Brahmans of Anga and by those of the middle country. He perished, however, in consequence; being cursed by Vaiśampáyana. Before their disagreement, Vaiśampáyana related the Mahábhárata to Janamejaya. Mahábhárata, Ádi Parvan.

[4] The reading of the text is, rather, "his (Parikshit's) other

---

* Nearly all my MSS. omit this name.

† See the opening of the last Chapter, and the Translator's note on it.

‡ One of my MSS. names him here. See note 4 in this page.

§ In my single copy of the *Váyu-puráṇa*,—of which I can decipher very little just here,—the reading is *Triswachi*.

acquire spiritual knowledge, from the instructions of Śaunaka, and ultimately obtain salvation.* His son will be Aśwamedhadatta (a son given by the gods, in reward for the sacrifice of a horse[1]); his son will be Adhisímakríshńa;[2]† his son will be Nichakru,[3]‡ who

son will be Śatáníka;" तस्यापरः शतानीको भविष्यति।§ But the commentator refers 'his' to Janamejaya: तस्य। जनमेजयस्य। The Váyu, Matsya, and Bhágavata also make Śatáníka the son of Janamejaya. The Brahma Puráńa has a totally different series, or: Parikshit, Súryápída, Chandrápída, Janamejaya, Satyakarńa, Śwetakarńa, Sukumára, and Ajaśyáma.

[1] The Bhágavata interposes Sahasráníka. The Bŕihatkathá|| has the same descent,¶ but calls the son of Sahasráníka, Udayana or Vatsa.** The Bhágavata has Aśwamedhaja.

[2] Adhisámakríshńa††: Váyu. Adhisomakríshńa: Matsya. The

* परं निर्वाणमाप्स्यति।

† Corrected from "Asimakrishńa".

‡ Corrected from "Nichakra", which I find nowhere but in the Bengal translation. One MS. gives Vichakshus. In the *Váyu-puráńa* I find Nŕibandhu, (or Nirvaktra?), and then, Ushńa(?), Chitraratha, Śuchidratha, Dhŕitimat, Susheńa. The *Brahmáńda-puráńa* has Nŕibandhu, Chitraratha, Śuchidratha, Dhŕitimat, Susheńa.

In a Sanskrit collection of Pauráńik extracts, prepared for Colonel Wilford, to which I have access, there is part of a chapter from the *Váyu-puráńa*, and a similar draft from the *Brahmáńda-puráńa*,—beginning with mention of Adhisímakríshńa,—covering nearly all the rest of this Book. The present and the two ensuing Chapters of the *Vishńu-puráńa* likewise occur there.

For the present I am reduced to a single MS. of the *Váyu-puráńa*: *vide supra*, p. 124, note †.

§ This means: "Another Śatáníka will be his *son*". The word अपरः, 'another', is here used with allusion to Śatáníka, son of Nakula, spoken of in p. 159, *supra*. Two of my MSS. have जनमेजयस्य तस्य; and one omits अपरः. The identical words अपरः शतानीकः are rendered, near the end of this chapter, "another Śatáníka".

|| Read *Kathásaritságara*. See the opening of its second *Lambaka*.

¶ The succession—Arjuna being called the founder of the family,—runs thus: Abhimanyu, Parikshit, Janamejaya, Śatáníka, Sahasráníka, Udayana.

** Read Vatsaràja. For its meaning, see Vol. II., p. 158, note †

†† I find Adhisímakríshńa. The *Bhágavata-puráńa* has Asímakríshńa.

will remove the capital to Kauśámbí,* in consequence of Hastinápura† being washed away by the Ganges; his son will be Ushńa;[1] his son will be Chitraratha;‡ his son will be Vŕishńimat;[2]§ his son will be Susheńa; his son will be Sunítha;[3] his son will be Ŕicha;[4] his son will be Nŕichakshus;[5]|| his son will be Sukhá-

former states, that the Váyu Puráńa was narrated in this king's reign, in the second year of a three years' sacrifice at Kurukshetra.

[1] Nemichakra: Bhágavata. Vichakshus: Matsya. They agree with the text, as to the removal of the capital, and the cause.

[1] Ukta: Bhágavata. Bhúrijyeshtha: Matsya.

[2] Suchidratna.¶ Váyu; Śuchidrava, Matsya; Kaviratha, Bhágavata; is interposed between Chitraratha and Vŕishńimat.**

[3] Sutirtha: Váyu.††

[4] Ruchi: Váyu.‡‡ Omitted: Matsya and Bhágavata.

[5] Chitráksha:§§ Váyu.

* कौशाम्ब्यां निवत्स्यति । † Two MSS. have Hástinapura.

‡ Śuchiratha, supplying an additional descent, was here inadvertently passed by. He is not named in Professor Wilson's Hindu-made English version.

§ Four MSS. have Vŕishńimat. This and similar corruptions may have originated in the all but undistinguishable way in which [illegible] and [illegible] are written in many MSS. Or they may have arisen from local peculiarity of pronunciation: thus, in Bengal, the *shń* of Kŕishńa has the sound of *shť*.

|| Corrected from "Nrichakshu". One MS. has Vakshu.

¶ An error for Śuchidratha? See note ‡ in the preceding page.

** I find Vŕishńimat.

†† Sunitha, in my MS.: see note §§, below. The *Brahmáńda-puráńa* has the same reading.

‡‡ I find Trivakshya: see the next note. Instead of the Ŕicha, &c. of our text, the *Brahmáńda-puráńa* has Nŕibandhu, Suratha, Medhávin, Nŕipanjaya, &c.

§§ Colonel Wilford's manuscript extracts from the *Váyu-puráńa* give no name here; and the reading there found leaves no room for one:

bala:[1]* his son will be Pariplava;† his son will be Sunaya;[2] his son will be Medhávin; his son will be Nŕipanjaya;[3] his son will be Mŕidu;[4]‡ his son will be Tigma;[5] his son will be Bŕihadratha; his son will be Vasudána;[6]§ and his son will be another Śatáníka;|| his son will be Udayana;[7] his son will be Ahínara;[8] his son will be Khańdapáńi;[9] his son will be Nirami-

---

[1] Sukhínala: Bhágavata.¶

[2] Sutapas: Matsya.

[3] Puranjaya: Matsya.

[4] Úrva: Matsya. Dúrva: Bhágavata.

[5] Tigmátman:** Matsya. Timi: Bhágavata.

[6] Sudása: Bhágavata. Vasudáman: Matsya.

[7] The Matsya concurs with the text (*vide supra*, p. 163, note 1)[1] the Bhágavata has Durdamana.

[8] Vahínara: Bhágavata.††

[9] Dańdapáńi:‡‡ Bhágavata, Váyu, Matsya.

स वै सुनीथात्प्रभविता निचक्षो भविता ततः ।
निचक्षस्य तु दायादो भविता वै सुखावलः ।

My other MS. of the *Váyu-puráńa* is here very corrupt.

* Corrected from "Subhibala". Professor Wilson's Bengal translation has "Subhávala (in another MS., Subhivala)".

† Pariśraya, in the *Váyu-puráńa*; and then follow Sunaya (or Suratha?), Medhávin, Dańdapáńi, Niramitra, &c. This list is meagre as compared with that of the *Vishńu-puráńa*.

‡ Durbala, in one MS. Durvi: *Brahmáńda-puráńa*.

§ One copy has Vasunáda.

|| Besides the three persons of this name mentioned in the present chapter and the last, the *Aitareya-bráhmańa*, VIII., XXI., speaks of a Śatáníka, son of Satrájit. For still another Śatáníka, *vide supra*, p. 124, note ¶.

¶ Sukhábala: *Váyu-puráńa*.

** See Professor Aufrecht's *Catalog. Cod. Manuscript.*, &c., p. 40.

†† So the *Brahmáńda-puráńa*, too; and the *Matsya-puráńa* has the same name, with the variant Mahirata.

‡‡ And thus reads the *Brahmáńda-puráńa*.

tra;[1] his son will be Kshemaka.[2]* Of him this verse is recited: "The race which gave origin to Brahmans and Kshattriyas, and which was purified by regal sages, terminated† with Kshemaka, in the Kali age."[3]‡

[1] Nimi: Bhágavata.

[2] Kshepaka: Váyu.§

[3] The same memorial verse is quoted in the Matsya and Váyu Puráńas, preceded by one which states the number of princes twenty-five. The specification, however, commencing with Śatánika, is twenty-six or twenty-seven. The passage is:

पञ्चविंश नृपा ह्येते भविष्याः पुरुवंशजाः ।
अनुवंशिकः श्लोकोऽयं गीतो विप्रैः पुराविदैः ॥
ब्रह्मक्षत्रस्य यो योनिर्वंशो देवर्षिसत्कृतः ।
क्षेमकं प्राप्य राजानं संस्थां प्राप्स्यति वै कलौ ॥||

* In three MSS., Kshema. My Arrah MS. gives Ahinara, Niramitra, Naravábana, Brahmadańda, Kshemaka.

In MSS. of various Puráńas, Nirámitra is a frequent reading, instead of Niramitra. *Vide infra*, p. 174, note *.

† Read 'shall terminate', *prápsyate*.

‡ ब्रह्मक्षत्रस्य यो योनिर्वंशो राजर्षिसत्कृतः ।
क्षेमकं प्राप्य राजानं स संस्थां प्राप्स्यते कलौ ॥

Compare the *Bhágavata-puráńa*, IX., XXII., 43.

§ Kshemaka, in my MS.

|| These verses are taken from the *Váyu-puráńa*. The *Matsya-puráńa* does not give the first, and exhibits slight differences in its readings of the rest.

Stanzas very similar occur in the *Brahmáńda-puráńa*; only, in reading पञ्चत्रिंशत्, they make, in my MS., the kings to be thirty-five in number.

CHAPTER XXII.

Future kings of the family of Ikshwáku, ending with Sumitra.

I WILL now repeat to you the future princes of the family of Ikshwáku.[1] *

The son of Bŕihadbala[2] will be Bŕihatkshańa;[3] † his son will be Urukshepa;[4] ‡ his son will be Vatsa;[5] his son will be Vatsavyúha;[6] his son will be Prativyoma;[7] §

---

[1] See Vol. III., p. 259.

[2] Bŕihadratha: Váyu. ||

[3] Bŕihatkshaya: ¶ Váyu. Bŕihadrańa: Bhágavata. Omitted: Matsya.

[4] Omitted: Váyu. ** Urukshaya: †† Matsya. Urukriya: Bhágavata.

[5] Omitted by all three.

[6] Vatsavŕiddha: Bhágavata.

[7] Prativyúha: ‡‡ Váyu.

---

* Here the genealogy is continued which breaks off in Vol. III., p. 336. For the continuation, compare the *Bhágavata-puráńa*, IX., XII., 9–15.

† Bŕihatkshetra is the reading of several MSS.

‡ This reading I find nowhere except in the Translator's Bengal translation. Most of my MSS. have Gurukshepa; two, Urukshaya; one, Urunjaya.

§ Corrected from "Prativyoman". The *Matsya-puráńa*, too, has Prativyoma.

|| The *Brahmáńda-puráńa* has Bŕihadbala. Three of my copies of the *Matsya-puráńa* have Bŕihadratha; but the oldest and best has Bŕihadbala. See, with reference to the *Matsya-puráńa*, note ¶ in p. 173, *infra*.

¶ This is the name in the *Brahmáńda-puráńa*.

** I find Kshaya; and so in the *Brahmáńda-puráńa*.

†† One of my MSS. seems to give Surakshaya; another is, here, very illegible; and the third has Urukshaya.

‡‡ So reads the *Brahmáńda-puráńa*, also.

his son will be Divákara;[1] his son will be Sahadeva;[*] his son will be Bŕihadaśwa;[2] his son will be Bhánuratha;[3] † his son will be Supratíka;[4] ‡ his son will be Marudeva;[5] his son will be Sunakshatra; his son will be Kiṁnara;[6] his son will be Antariksha; his son will be

---

[1] The Bhágavata inserts Bhánu. § The Matsya || says, that Ayodhyá was the capital of Divákara.¶ The Váyu omits the next twelve names; probably, a defect in the copies.**

[2] Dhruváśwa: Matsya.

[3] Bhánumat: Bhágavata. Bhávyaratha or Bhávya: Matsya.

[4] Pratikáśwa: Bhágavata. Pratipáśwa: †† Matsya.

[5] The Bhágavata and Matsya ‡‡ prefix a Supratípa§§ or Supratíka. ||||

[6] Pushkara: Bhágavata.

---

* Hereupon the commentator remarks: यत्र यत्र भाव्यां वैवस्वतं इत्यादि तत्र कल्पयुगादिभेदेन व्यवस्थापनीयम् ।

† My Arrah MS. inserts Pratitáśwa, as son of Bhánuratha and father of Supratíka. The *Váyu-puráńa* and the *Brahmáńda-puráńa* insert Pratita.

‡ Corrected from "Supratítha", which occurs in none of my MSS., and looks very like an inadvertence.

In the Hindu-made English translation, Supratíka is so written, that, unless scrutinized a little closely, it might be mistaken for Supratítha.

I may here refer, as there is frequent occasion for doing in the course of my annotations, to the remark made in Vol. III., p. 335, note §§.

§ And it reads Diváka, not Divákara.

|| Its words are:

तस्यैषा मध्यदेशे तु अयोध्या नगरी शुभा ।

¶ And so say the *Váyu-puráńa* and the *Brahmáńda-puráńa*.

यस्य साम्प्रतमध्यास्ते अयोध्यां नगरीं नृपः ।

But compare note 2 in p. 163, *supra*.

** My MSS. of the *Váyu-puráńa* have the twelve names. Eight are as in the *Vishńu-puráńa*: for the the rest, see my annotations.

†† So reads one of my copies, as against Pratitáśwa in the other two. The *Brahmáńda-puráńa* has Supratíta.

‡‡ The reading in my MS. of the *Brahmáńda-puráńa* is Sahadeva.

§§ This is the only reading that I find. |||| See note ‡, above.

be Suvarńa;[1] his son will be Amitrajit;[2] his son will be Bŕihadrája;[3] his son will be Dharmin;[4]* his son will be Kŕitanjaya;† his son will be Rańanjaya; his son will be Sanjaya; his son will be Śákya;[5] his son will be Śuddhodana;[6] his son will be Rátula;[7]‡ his son

---

[1] Suparvan or Sumantra: Matsya.§ Sutapas: Bhágavata.||

[2] Amantravit: Matsya.¶

[3] Bŕihadbhrája:** Bhágavata.

[4] Omitted: Matsya.†† Barhis: Bhágavata.

[5] The Bhágavata and Váyu have Śákya. My copy of the Matsya‡‡ has Śádhya; but the Radcliffe MS., more correctly, no doubt, Śakya (शक्यः).

[6] In some copies, Krodhodana;§§ but it is, also, Śuddhodana, Matsya and Váyu; Śuddhoda, Bhágavata.

[7] Ráhula: Váyu.|||| Siddhártha or Pushkala: Matsya.¶¶

---

* Corrected from "Dharman",—the reading of the Translator's Bengal version, also,—on the warrant of all my MSS. The *Váyu-puráńa* and the *Brahmáńda-puráńa*, too, have Dharmin.

† The *Brahmáńda-puráńa* has Suvrata between Kŕitanjaya and Rańanjaya.

‡ Two MSS. have Bábula; one, Bhánula.

§ Two of my MSS.—like the *Brahmáńda-puráńa*,—give Suparńa; the remaining one, Suvarńa.

|| Suparńa: *Váyu-puráńa*.

¶ In my copies, Sumitra and Amitrajit. Bŕihadrája is distinctly called son of the former.

** Instead of this meaningless name, I find, as in our text, Bŕihadrája. The *Váyu-puráńa* and the *Brahmáńda-puráńa* have Bharadwája.

†† A single MS. has Viryavat; but, probably, it is corrupt.

‡‡ One of my MSS. has Sájya: another, Śakya; the oldest and best, both, as if the person intended had two names.

§§ "Krodyodana" is the name in the Hindu-made English version, which swarms with blunders quite as bad.

|||| The *Váyu-puráńa* and the *Brahmáńda-puráńa* here read, in my MSS.:

शुद्धोदनस्य भविता शक्यार्थे (?) राहुलः स्मृतः ।

Compare the extract in the next note.

¶¶ Two of my copies are extremely incorrect just here. The third and

will be Prasenajit; his son will be Kshudraka;* his

Lángala: Bhágavata. This and the two preceding names are of considerable chronological interest; for Śákya is the name of the author, or reviver, of Buddhism, whose birth† appears to have occurred in the seventh, and death in the sixth, century before Christ (B. C. 621—543). There can be no doubt of the individual here intended, although he is out of his place; for he was the son—not the father—of Śuddhodana, and the father of Ráhula; as he is termed, in the Amara‡ and Haima Kośas,§ Śauddhodani‖ or Śuddhodanasuta, 'the son of Suddhodana,' and Ráhulasú, 'the parent of Ráhula.' So, also, in the Maháwanso, Siddhártha or Śákya is the son of Suddhodano,¶ and father of Ráhulo. Turnour's translation, p. 9. Whether they are rightly included amongst the princes of the race of Ikshwáku is more questionable; for Śuddhodana is, usually, described as a petty prince, whose capital was not Ayodhyá, but Kapila or Kapilavastu.** At the same time, it appears that the provinces of the Doab had passed into the possession of princes of the Lunar line; and the children of the Sun may have been reduced to the country north of the Ganges, or the modern Goruckpoor, in which Kapila was situated. The Buddhists do, usually, consider their teacher Śákya to be descended from Ikshwáku. The chronology is less easily adjusted; but it is not altogether incompatible. According to the lists of the text, Śákya, as the twenty-second of the line of Ikshwáku, is contemporary with Ripunjaya, the

oldest reads:

शुद्धोदनस्य भविता सिद्धार्थः पुष्कलः सुतः ।

* Kshudrahaka, in one copy.

† There are some recent well-known speculations as to the age of Buddha; but it does not seem advisable to cumber these pages with them. These speculations would place the death of Buddha in B. C 477.

‡ I., I., I., 10. § II., 151. ‖ Corrected from "Saudhodani".

¶ See Burnouf's *Introduction à l'Histoire du Buddhisme Indien*, Vol. I., p. 141; also, *Le Lotus de la Bonne Loi*, p. 388.

** On the river Rohiní, an affluent to the Raptee. Burnouf's *Introduction*, &c., Vol. I., p. 143, note 2.

son will be Kuńdaka;[1] his son will be Suratha;[2] his

---

twenty-second* and last of the kings of Magadha, of the family of Jarásandha; but, agreeably to the Buddhist authorities, he was the friend of Bimbasára, a king who, in the Pauráńik list,† appears to be fifth of the Śaiśunága dynasty, and tenth from Ripunjaya. The same number of princes does not necessarily imply equal duration of dynasty; and Ikshwáku's descendants may have outlasted those of Jarásandha; or, as is more likely,—for the dynasty was obscure, and is, evidently, imperfectly preserved,—several descents may have been omitted, the insertion of which would reconcile the Pauráńik lists with those of the Buddhists, and bring Śákya down to the age of Bimbasára. It is evident, from what occurs in other authorities, that the Aikshwáka‡ princes are regarded as contemporaries even of the Śaiśunága dynasty: *vide infra*, p. 182, note 4.

[1] Kaholika:§ Váyu. Kulaka‖ or Kahullaka: Matsya. Omitted:¶ Bhágavata. In the Mahávíra Charitra, a work written by the celebrated Hemachandra, in the twelfth century, we have a Prasenajit,** king of Magadha, residing at Rajagŕiha, succeeded by Śreńika,†† and he, by Kúlika. The Bauddhas have a Prasenajit contemporary with Śákya,‡‡ son of Mahápadma, king of Magadha. There is some confusion of persons, either in the Pauráńik genealogies, or in the Buddhist and Jaina traditions; but they agree in bringing the same names together about the same period.

[2] Omitted:§§ Bhágavata.

---

* *Vide infra*, p. 177, notes 1, &c. † *Vide infra*, p. 180.

‡ Corrected, here and several times further on, from "Aikshwákava."

§ I find Kulika. And so reads the *Brahmáńda-puráńa*.

‖ This is the preponderant reading, in my MSS.

¶ Not so. The *Bhágavata-puráńa*, IX., XII., 14, has Rańaka.

** Lakshmívallabha, in his *Kalpadrumakaliká*, speaks of him. Different is the Prasenajit mentioned *infra*, p. 186, note *.

†† A surname of Bimbisára: *Asiatic Researches*, Vol. XX., p. 46.

‡‡ This Prasenajit was king of Kośala; and Bimbisára, king of Magadha, was contemporary with him. See Burnouf's *Introduction à l'Histoire du Buddhisme Indien*, Vol. I., p. 145.

§§ The *Bhágavata-puráńa* has, like our text, Suratha.

son will be* Sumitra.† These are the kings of the family of Ikshwáku, descended from Bŕihadbala. This commemorative verse is current concerning them: "The race of the descendants of Ikshwáku will terminate with Sumitra: it will end, in the Kali age, with him."[1]‡

[1] The Váyu and Bhágavata§ have the same stanza.|| We have, here, twenty-nine or thirty princes of the later Solar line, contemporary with the preceding twenty-six or twenty-seven of the later dynasty of the Moon.

* The original qualifies him as 'another', अन्यः. The allusion is not clear.

† Besides this Sumitra and that named at p. 73, *supra*, the *Harsha-charita* speaks of one,—son of Agnimitra,—who was slain by Múladeva. See the *Vásavadattá*, Preface, p. 53.

‡ इक्ष्वाकूणामयं वंशः सुमित्रान्तो भविष्यति ।
यतस्तं प्राप्य राजानं च संस्थां प्राप्स्यते कलौ ॥

The *Matsya-puráńa* and the *Brahmáńda-puráńa* have, essentially, the same stanza.

§ IX., XII., 16.

|| The stanza in the *Váyu-puráńa* differs, in the latter line, from the stanza in the *Vishńu-puráńa*; but the sense of the two is the same.

CHAPTER XXIII.

Future kings of Magadha, descendants of Bŕihadratha.

I WILL now relate to you the descendants of Bŕihadratha, who will be (the kings) of Magadha. There have been several powerful princes of this dynasty, of whom the most celebrated was Jarásandha.* His son was Sahadeva; his son is Somápi;[1]† his son will be Śrutavat;[2]‡ his son will be Ayutáyus;[3]§ his son

---

[1] Somádhi;|| Váyu, Matsya:¶ and they now affect greater precision, giving the years of the reigns. Somádhi, 58, Váyu; 50,** Matsya.

[2] Śrutaśravas,†† 67 years, Váyu; 64, Matsya.

[3] 36 years, Váyu;‡‡ Apratípa, 26,§§ Matsya.

---

* *Vide supra*, pp. 160, 161.

† Also Márjári, in the *Bhágavata-puráńa*. *Vide supra*, p. 161, note ||.

‡ Śrutaśravas, at p. 161, *supra*. § In one copy, Śrutáyus.

|| And so reads the *Brahmáńda-puráńa*.

¶ My manuscripts of the *Matsya-puráńa* are so carelessly executed, that I have seldom thought it worth while to consult them. As, however, we are now approaching the historical period, I use them, though to little satisfactory purpose, as will be manifest. These manuscripts are five in number; but only four of them contain the section relating to future kings and peoples. Of these *four*, one, as compared with the others, is noticeably meagre, and omits at least a third of the kings named in the present chapter. At the same time, it exhibits a large number of variants. But these peculiarities seem to be merely a result of carelessness.

** I find 58 years; the original being:

पञ्चाशतं तथाष्टौ च समा राज्यमकारयत् ।

The *Brahmáńda-puráńa*, too, has 58 years.

†† So read the *Bhágavata-puráńa* and the *Brahmáńda-puráńa*, too; and the latter assigns him 67 years.

‡‡ Ayutáyus, and 34 years: *Brahmáńda-puráńa*.

§§ In my MSS., Apratápin, and 36 years:

अप्रतापी च षट्त्रिंशत्समा राज्यमकारयत् ।

will be Niramitra;[1]* his son will be Sukshattra;[2]† his son will be Brihatkarman;[3] his son will be Senajit;[4] his son will be Śrutanjaya;[5]‡ his son will be Vipra;[6]§ his son will be Śuchi;[7] his son will be Kshemya;[8]||

[1] 100¶ years, Váyu; 40, Matsya.**

[2] 58 years, Váyu; 56, Matsya;†† Sunakshatra, Bhágavata.

[3] 23 years, Váyu and Matsya;‡‡ Brihatsena, Bhágavata.

[4] 23§§ years, Váyu; 50, Matsya; Karmajit, Bhágavata.||||

[5] 40 years, Váyu and Matsya.¶¶

[6] Mahábala, 35*** years, Váyu; Vidhu,††† 28, Matsya.

[7] 58 years, Váyu; 64,‡‡‡ Matsya.

[8] 28 years, Váyu§§§ and Matsya.||||||

* Niramitra is a variant in our Puráńa and others. *Vide supra*, p. 168, note *.

† Sukshetra, in one MS.

‡ Śritanjaya: *Bhágavata-puráńa*.

§ Two copies give Ripunjaya.

|| Kshema: *Bhágavata-puráńa*. Also see notes §§§ and ||||||, below.

¶ Colonel Wilford's MS. has 60. And so has the *Brahmáńda-puráńa*.

** One copy has Mitra.

†† A single MS. has Sumitra. The *Brahmáńda-puráńa* gives Sukshattra 50 years.

‡‡ And so the *Brahmáńda-puráńa*.

§§ 100, in Colonel Wilford's manuscript extracts.

|||| Munishita, and 50 years: *Brahmáńda-puráńa*.

¶¶ One of my MSS. of the *Matsya-puráńa* gives 35 years. The *Brahmáńda-puráńa* gives as many years to Śatayajus.

*** Corrected from "25"; for I find 35 in every one of my MSS.

††† In two of my MSS. the name is Prabhu; but the oldest of all has Víryavat. Vibhu, and 28 years: *Brahmáńda-puráńa*.

‡‡‡ I find 58 years; and so has the *Brahmáńda-puráńa*.

§§§ In this Puráńa I find Kshema. And so reads the *Brahmáńda-puráńa*, with 26 years.

|||||| Two copies have Kshema, 38 years; the other, Pahsha, 28 years.

his son will be Suvrata;[1] his son will be Dharma;[2] his son will be Suśrama;[3*] his son will be Dṙidhasena;[4]

---

[1] 60 years,† Váyu; 64, Matsya.‡

[2] 5 years, Váyu;§ Sunetra, 35,|| Matsya; Dharmanetra,¶ Bhágavata.

[3] 38 years, Váyu;** Nivṙitti,†† 58, Matsya; Śama, Bhágavata.‡‡

[4] 48 years, Váyu;§§ Trinetra,|||| 28, Matsya; Dyumatsena,¶¶ Bhágavata.

---

* Suśrata, in a single MS. Professor Wilson's unmeaning "Suśama", now displaced,—for which I find no authority but his Bengal translation,—evidently originated in a misreading of सुश्रम: carelessly written.

† In my MSS. of the *Váyu-puráńa*, 64 years. And therewith agrees the *Brahmáńda-puráńa*.

‡ Anuvrata (or Anuvratasuta??), in two copies; in one, "Kshema's son," unnamed. All three agree in assigning him 60 years.

§ This Puráńa has, in my MSS., Dharmanetra, who will accede to the throne at five, and will reign for 58 years (??). Dharmakshetra, and 5 years: *Brahmáńda-puráńa*.

|| So in one copy; and another has 28; but the oldest of all has 50.

¶ I find Dharmasútra.

** This Puráńa, in my MSS., has 58 years, and gives them to Suvrata. In one copy, this name is altered to Sunetra.

†† I find Nirvṙiti.

‡‡ Nṙibhṙita, and 58 years: *Brahmáńda-puráńa*. And then follows, there, Suvrata, with 38 years.

§§ Two of my copies give 58 years to Dṙidhasena:

चत्वारिंशद्वर्षाणि च दृढसेनो भविष्यति ।

One assigns him 48 years, by writing चत्वा over पञ्च; another has 58 years, but gives them to Bṙihatsena; and the remaining copy here has a hiatus.

The *Brahmáńda-puráńa* has Bṙihatsena, and 48 years.

|||| One MS. has Sunetra.

¶¶ I find, as in our text, Dṙidhasena.

his son will be Sumati;[1] his son will be Subala;[2]* his son will be Sunita;[3]† his son will be Satyajit;[4] his son will be Viśwajit;[5] his son will be Ripunjaya.[6] These

---

[1] 33 years, Váyu;‡ Mahatsena,§ 48, Matsya.

[2] 22 years, Váyu;‖ Netra, 33, Matsya.¶

[3] 40 years, Váyu;** Abala,†† 32, Matsya.

[4] 80 years,‡‡ Váyu; omitted,§§ Matsya.‖‖

[5] 35 years,¶¶ Váyu; omitted,*** Matsya.†††

[6] 50 years, Váyu‡‡‡ and Matsya;§§§ Puranjaya and Ripunjaya‖‖‖ are identified, Bhágavata.

---

* Corrected from "Suvala".

† One copy has Sunitha, the name in the *Bhágavata-puráńa.*

‡ Herewith, both as to name and period, the *Brahmáńḍa-puráńa* coincides.

§ Dŕiḍhasena, in one copy of the *Matsya-puráńa*; Bŕihatsena, in another.

‖ In one copy I find Subala, and 32 years; in another, Subala, and 22 years; in another, Subala, and 32 years; and two MSS. here omit a line.

¶ Sudhanwán, and 33 years: *Brahmáńḍa-puráńa.*

** But I find the name, in four MSS. out of five, to be Sunetra. The *Brahmáńḍa-puráńa* has the same name and the same number of years.

†† Two copies have Achala.

‡‡ I find 83 in four MSS.: the fifth, which has 50, is by far the most incorrect, generally, of all.

§§ My oldest MS. has Sunetra, 40 years; then, Sarvajit, 80 years: a second has Sunetra, 40 years; then, Satyajit, 80 years: the third, and worst of all, has only, instead of the two, Sarvajit, 80 years.

‖‖ The *Brahmáńḍa-puráńa* gives Satyajit a reign of only 30 years.

¶¶ My two best MSS. have 25; the third and fourth, 36; and the worst of all, 63.

*** Viśwajit is named in all my three copies. The oldest of them gives him 35 years; the others, 53 and 25 years, respectively.

††† According to the *Brahmáńḍa-puráńa,* Viśwajit will reign for a period of 35 years.

‡‡‡ Three of my MSS. exhibit Arinjaya; the fourth, and equally the most inferior of the five, Ripunjaya.

§§§ The *Brahmáńḍa-puráńa* has Ripunjaya, and 50 years.

‖‖‖ Corrected from "Viśwajit",—a mere slip of the pen, certainly. The *Bhágavata-puráńa,* IX., XXII., 47, names Viśwajit and his son Ripunjaya; and, in XII., I., 2, it speaks of the Bárhadratha Puranjaya, slain by his minister Śunaka. See the beginning of p. 178, *infra,* and note 1 thereon.

are the Bárhadrathas, who will reign for a thousand years.[1]

---

[1] Our list and that of the Váyu* specifies twenty-one kings† after Sahadeva: the Bhágavata specifies twenty,‡ and, in another passage,§ states that to be the number. My copy of the Matsya names but nineteen; and the Radcliffe,|| but twelve: but both agree in making the total thirty-two. They all concur with the text, also, in stating, that 1000 years had elapsed from the Great War, at the death of the last Bárhadratha prince;¶ and this is more worthy of credit than the details, which are, obviously, imperfect.

---

* The *Váyu-puráńa* says that thirty-two kings will spring from Bŕihadratha, and that their kingdom will endure for a thousand years:

द्वात्रिंशच्च नृपा ह्येते भवितारो बृहद्रथात् ।
पूर्णं वर्षसहस्रं वै तेषां राज्यं भविष्यति ॥

† It names twenty-three.

‡ It names twenty-one.

§ Not the text, but Śridhara, where commenting on XII., I., I.

|| Those copies are defective, doubtless. See notes ḑḑ and *** in the preceding page.

¶ The words of the *Matsya-puráńa*, as given in two of my MSS., are:

द्वात्रिंशच्च नृपा ह्येते भवितारो बृहद्रथाः ।
पूर्णं वर्षसहस्रं तु तेषां राज्यं भविष्यति ॥

We find, in the *Brahmáńd́a-puráńa*,—unless the reading is corrupt,—only twenty-two kings spoken of:

द्वाविंशत्येते हि नृपा भवितारो बृहद्रथाः ।
पूर्णं वर्षसहस्रं वै तेषां राज्यं भविष्यति ॥

CHAPTER XXIV.

Future kings of Magadha. Five princes of the line of Pradyota. Ten Śaiśunágas. Nine Nandas. Ten Mauryas. Ten Śungas. Four Kańwáyanas.* Thirty Andhrabhrityas. Kings of various tribes and castes, and periods of their rule. Ascendancy of barbarians. Different races in different regions. Period of universal iniquity and decay. Coming of Vishńu as Kalki. Destruction of the wicked, and restoration of the practices of the Vedas. End of the Kali, and return of the Krita, age. Duration of the Kali. Verses chanted by Earth, and communicated by Asita to Janaka. End of the Fourth Book.

THE last of the Bŕihadratha dynasty,† Ripunjaya,‡ will have a minister named Sunika,[1]§ who, having killed his sovereign, will place his son Pradyotana upon the throne:[2] his son will be Pálaka;[3]¶ his son

[1] Munika,** Váyu; Pulika, Matsya; Śunaka, Bhágavata.

[2] For 23 years, Váyu and Matsya.††

[3] 24 years, Váyu;‡‡ Tilaka or Bálaka,§§ 28, Matsya.

---

* Corrected from "Kańwas". *Vide infra*, p. 193, note ‡.

† The *Váyu-puráńa*, the *Matsya-puráńa*, and the *Brahmáńd́a-puráńa* premise the extinction of the Bŕihadrathas and Vítahotras, and do not here name the last of the Bŕihadrathas. But *vide supra*, p. 176, notes 6 and ‡‡.

‡ *Vide supra*, p. 176, note . § A single MS. has Śunaka

‖ Corrected from "Pradyota", which I find in only one MS. Pradyota is the reading of the *Váyu-puráńa* and of the *Bhágavata-puráńa*. The *Brahmáńd́a-puráńa* has Sudyota, and 23 years.

Mention is found of a Pradyota who had a son Jagbanjaya. See my Preface to the *Vásavadattá*, p. 53. ¶ Gopálaka, in one copy.

** Sunika is the reading in all my four copies of the *Váyu-puráńa*, and in Colonel Wilford's manuscript extracts. The *Brahmáńd́a-puráńa* has the same name.

†† The *Matsya-puráńa*, in my copies, gives to Pulika's son the name of Bálaka. Nowhere does it speak of Pradyota or of the Pradyotas.

‡‡ Add the *Brahmáńd́a-puráńa*. §§ The only reading I find is Pálaka.

will be Viśákhayúpa;[1][*] his son will be Janaka;[2] and his son will be Nandivardhana.[3] These five kings of the house of Pradyota† will reign over the earth for a hundred and thirty-eight‡ years.[4]

---

[1] 50 years, Váyu;§ 53, Matsya.||

[2] Ajaka, 21 years, Váyu;¶ Súryaka, 21, Matsya; Rájaka,** Bhágavata.

[3] 20 years, Váyu†† and Matsya.‡‡

[4] This number is also specified by the Váyu and Bhágavata;§§ and the several years of the reigns of the former agree with the total. The particulars of the Matsya compose 145||| years; but there is, no doubt, some mistake in them.

---

* Almost as ordinary a reading, in my MSS., is Viśákharúpa; and two of them have Viśákhapúpa.

† The original is पञ्च प्रद्योताः, "the five Pradyotas;" the reading recognized by the commentator. One MS. yields, however, "the five Pradyotanas." The *Bhágavata-puráńa* has पञ्च प्रद्योतनाः, the gloss on which is प्रद्योतनाः । प्रद्योतवंश्याः । The *Váyu-puráńa* has Pradyotas.

‡ "Twenty-eight", according to four copies.

§ Three of my MSS., including the two oldest and best, have Viśákhadhúpa; another, Viśákhayópa; the remaining one, Viśákhasúpa.

|| Two MSS. have Viśákharúpa; one, Viśákhayúpa, the reading of the *Bhágavata-puráńa.*

The *Brahmáńda-puráńa* has Viśákhayúpa, and 100 years.

¶ One MS. of the *Váyu-puráńa* — very inferior, — has 31 years. In the *Brahmáńda-puráńa,* Ajaka is assigned 21 years.

** Corrected from "Rajaka".

†† The name that I find everywhere in the *Váyu-puráńa* is Vartivardhana.

‡‡ 30 years are assigned to Nandivardhana in all my copies of the *Matsya-puráńa.* The *Brahmáńda-puráńa* gives him 20 years.

§§ XII., I., 4.

||| By note ‡‡, above, we are enabled to alter this number to one nearer correctness, — namely, 155 There is, however, still a mistake of 3 in excess, — owing, doubtless, to corruptness of the MSS.; for all mine agree in stating the total to be 152.

The next prince will be Śiśunága;[1] his son will be Kákavarńa;[2]* his son will be Kshemadharman;[3] his son will be Kshattraujas;[4] his son will be Vidmisára;[5]†

---

[1] Śiśunáka—who, according to the Váyu‡ and Matsya,§ relinquished Benares to his son, and established himself at Girivraja (or Rájagriha), in Behar,—reigns 40 years. Váyu and Matsya.

[2] 36 years, Váyu|| and Matsya.

[3] Kshemakarman,¶ 20 years, Váyu; Kshemadharman, 36, Matsya.

[4] 40 years, Váyu;** Kshemajit or Kshemárchis, 36, Matsya;†† Kshetrajna, Bhágavata.

[5] Bimbisára,‡‡ 28 years, Váyu; Bindusena or Vindhyasena, 28, Matsya;§§ Vidhisára, Bhágavata.

---

* A Kákavarńa, Raja of Chańdi, is spoken of in the *Harsha-charita*. See my *Vásavadattá*, Preface, p. 53.

† Two MSS. have Vidbisára; another, Vidisára. But all three are corruptions. See note ¶ in the next page.

‡ हत्वा तेषां यशः कृत्स्नं शिशुनाको भविष्यति ।
वाराणस्यां सुतं स्थाप्य सो यास्यति गिरिव्रजम् ॥

Two copies have Giripraja; one, Girivrata. Equally gross mistakes, it is to be presumed, disfigure all my MSS. of the *Váyu-puráńa*.

§ The first verse of a stanza there given is the same as in the preceding note. The second verse runs:

वाराणस्यां सुतं स्थाप्य प्रयास्यति गिरिव्रजम् ।

|| Śakavarńa or Śákavarńa is the name in all my copies of the *Váyu-puráńa*.

¶ Kshemavarman, in three MSS. of the *Váyu-puráńa*, those of best note; while the rest have Kshemadharman.

The *Brahmáńda-puráńa* has Kshemadharman, and 20 years.

There is a break in Colonel Wilford's manuscript extract from the *Brahmáńda-puráńa*, where there should be mention of the two kings preceding Kshemadharman.

** Therewith agrees the *Brahmáńda-puráńa*.

†† Three of my copies have Kshemavit, 24 years; the other, Kshemárchis, 40 years.

‡‡ This reading says much for the comparative correctness of the *Váyu-puráńa*.

§§ Viddhisára(?), and 28 years: *Brahmáńda-puráńa*.

his son will be Ajátaśatru;[1]* his son will be Dar-

[1] 25 years, Váyu;† 27, Matsya:‡ but the latter inserts a Kańwáyana,§ 9 years, and Bhúmimitra (or Bhúmiputra), 14 years, before him. In this and the preceding name we have appellations of considerable celebrity in the traditions of the Bauddhas. Vidmisára—read, also, Vindhasára,‖ Vilwisára, &c.,—is, most probably, their Bimbasára,¶ who was born at the same time with Śákya, and was reigning at Rájagriha, when he began his religious career. The Mahávamso says that Siddhatto and Bimbisáro were attached friends, as their fathers had been before them. P. 10. Śákya is said to have died in the reign of Ajátaśatru, the son of Bimbasára, in the eighth year of his reign. The Váyu transposes these names; and the Matsya still more alters the order of Ajátaśatru; but the Bhágavata concurs with our text. The Buddhist authority differs from the Puráńas, materially, as to the duration of the reigns; giving to Bimbisáro, 52 years, and to Ajátasattu, 32. The latter, according to the same, murdered his father. Mahávamso, p. 10. We may, therefore, with some confidence, claim for these princes a date of about six centuries B. C. They are considered contemporary with Śuddhodana, &c., in the list of the Aikshwákas** (*vide supra*, p. 169, note 7).

* An Ajátaśatru, king of the Káśis, is commemorated in the *Kaushítaki-bráhmańa Upanishad*, IV., 1, and elsewhere.

† In all my MSS. of the *Váyu-puráńa*, the order is: Ajátaśatru, Kshattraujas, Bimbisára.

‡ The *Brahmáńda-puráńa*, at least in my single MS., gives 35 years to Ajátaśatru.

§ The name here intended is very doubtful in all my three MSS. of the *Matsya-puráńa*.

‖ This—and so the Bindusena mentioned in the Translator's last note,—looks like a corruption of Bindusára; and Bindusára was a remote descendant of Bimbisára. *Vide infra*, p. 186, note *.

¶ Vidmisára, &c. are, all, misspellings of Bimbisára. *Vide infra*, p. 186, note *.

On the correct form of the name of the king intended, see Burnouf's *Introduction à l'Histoire du Buddhisme Indien*, Vol. I., p. 145, note 1.

** *Vide supra*, p. 171, note ‡.

bhaka;[1]* his son will be Udayáśwa;[2]† his son will, also, be Nandivardhana; and his son will be Mahánandin.[3]‡ These ten Śaiśunágas will be kings of the earth for three hundred and sixty-two years.[4]

---

[1] Harshaka,§ 25 years, Váyu; Vaṁśaka, 24,|| Matsya.¶

[2] 33 years, Váyu;** Udibhi or Udásin,†† 33, Matsya. According to the Váyu, Udaya or Udayáśwa founded Kusumapura (or Páṫaliputra), on the southern angle‡‡ of the Ganges:

स वै पुरवरं राजा पृथिव्यां कुसुमाह्वयम् ।
गंगाया दक्षिणे कोणे चतुर्थेऽब्दे§§ करिष्यति ॥

The legends of Śákya, consistently with this tradition, take no notice of this city, in his peregrinations on either bank of the Ganges. The Maháwaṁso calls the son and successor of Ajátaśatru, Udayibhaddako (Udayibhadraka). P. 15.

[3] 42 and 43 years, Váyu; 40 and 43, Matsya.¶¶ The Maháwaṁso has, in place of these, Anuruddhako, Muṅdo, and Nágadásako; all, in succession, parricides: the last, deposed by an insurrection of the people. P. 15.

[4] The several authorities agree in the number of ten Śaiśu-

---

* Corrected from "Dharbaka". The *Bhágavata-puráńa* agrees with our text.

† Udayana is almost as common a reading. Ajaya is the name in the *Bhágavata-puráńa*.

‡ Corrected from "Mahánandi", the reading of the *Bhágavata-puráńa*.

§ I find Darśaka.

|| Two of my MSS. have 24; the other two, 40.

¶ The *Brahmáńda-puráńa*, at least in my MS., has Daśaka, and a reign of 35 years.

** The name that I find there is Udayin; but, in two MSS., Udaya.

†† Three of my MSS. have Udámbhin; one, Udásin. The *Brahmáńda-puráńa* has the latter, and 23 years.

‡‡ I find कूले, 'bank'.

§§ Two MSS. read चतुरस्त्रं; and so does the *Brahmáńda-puráńa*.

|| || Corrected from "Udayinbhadraka".

¶¶ More clearly: Nandivardhana, 42 years, *Váyu-puráńa*; 40 years, *Matsya-puráńa*: Mahánandin, 43 years, in both those Puráńas. The *Brahmáńda-puráńa* agrees, as to these two kings, with the *Váyu-puráńa*.

The son of Mahánandin* will be born of a woman of the Śúdra (or servile) class: his name will be Nanda,

---

nágas, and in the aggregate years of their reigns, which the Matsya and the Bhágavata call 360. The Váyu has 362,† with which the several periods correspond:‡ the details of the Matsya give 363.§ The Váyu‖ and Matsya¶ call the Śaiśunágas Kshattrabandhus, which may designate an inferior order of Kshattri-

---

* Corrected from "Mahánanda". † And so has the *Brahmáńda-puráńa*.

‡ I make only 332.

§ Even taking account of the reigns mentioned near the beginning of note 1 in p. 161, *supra*, I make out but 354.

‖ The nominal and numerical details given below are there expressed as follows:

एतैः सार्धं भविष्यन्ति तावत्कालं नृपाः परे ।
ऐक्ष्वाकवश्चतुर्विंशत्पञ्चालाः पञ्चविंशतिः ॥
काश्यकास्तु चतुर्विंशच्चतुर्विंशत्तु हैहयाः ।
द्वात्रिंशद्वै कलिङ्गास्तु पञ्चविंशत्तथा शकाः ॥
कुरवश्चापि षट्त्रिंशदष्टाविंशत्तु मैथिलाः ।
शूरसेनास्त्रयोविंशद्वीतिहोत्राश्च विंशतिः ।
तुल्यकालं भविष्यन्ति सर्व एव महीक्षितः ॥

¶ The following particulars answer to those contained in the last note:

एतैः सार्धं भविष्यन्ति तावत्कालं नृपाः परे ।
तुल्यकालं भविष्यन्ति सर्वे ह्येते महीक्षितः ॥
चतुर्विंशत्तथैक्ष्वाकाः पञ्चालाः सप्तविंशतिः ।
काशेयास्तु चतुर्विंशदष्टाविंशत्तु हैहयाः ॥
कलिङ्गाश्चैव द्वात्रिंशदश्मकाः पञ्चविंशतिः ।
कुरवश्चापि षट्त्रिंशदष्टाविंशत्तु मैथिलाः ॥
शूरसेनास्त्रयोविंशद्वीतिहोत्राश्च विंशतिः ।
एते सर्वे भविष्यन्ति एककालं महीक्षितः ॥

There are similar verses in the *Brahmáńda-puráńa*; but they are copied, in Colonel Wilford's volume of Pauráńik extracts,—where alone I have access to them,—with such deplorable carelessness, and with so many omissions, that I can do no more than refer to them. They seem to resemble the corresponding stanzas in the *Matsya-puráńa* rather more closely than those in the *Váyu-puráńa*.

(called) Mahápadma; for he will be exceedingly avaricious.[1] Like another Paraśuráma,* he will be the annihilator of the Kshattriya race; for, after him, the

---

yas. They also observe, that, contemporary with the dynasties already specified,—the Pauravas, the Bárhadrathas, and Mágadhas,—there were other races of royal descent, as: Aikshwáka princes, 24:† Panchálas, 25, Váyu; 27, Matsya: Kálakas‡, or Kásakas, or Káśeyas, § 24: Haihayas, 24, Váyu; 28, Matsya: Kalingas, 32, Váyu; 40, Matsya: Śakas, Váyu; Aśmakas, Matsya, 25:¶ Kurus,** 26:†† Maithilas, 28: Śúrasenas, 23: and Vitihotras, 20.

[1] The Bhágavata calls him Mahápadmapati, 'the lord of Mahápadma;' which the commentator interprets 'sovereign of an infinite host' or 'of immense wealth;'‡‡ Mahápadma signifying 100,000 millions. The Váyu and Matsya,§§ however, consider Mahápadma as another name of Nanda.‖‖

---

* *Vide supra*, p. 23.

† It is to be understood, in this and similar cases, that the two Puráńas agree.

‡ This is the name that I find in the *Váyu-puráńa*.

§ Two of my MSS. of the *Matsya-puráńa* have this reading; another, Kásheyas; another, Káleyas.

‖ One of my MSS. of the *Matsya-puráńa* gives 29: the other three, 32.

¶ That is to say, where the *Váyu-puráńa* names the Śakas, the *Matsya-puráńa* names the Aśmakas.

** Corrected from "Kuravas".

†† I find 36 in both Puráńas.

‡‡ See the commentator's words, at the end of note ‖‖, below.

§§ They say nothing of Nanda, naming Mahápadma only. The same is the case with the *Brahmáńda-puráńa*.

‖‖ So considers the *Bhágavata-puráńa*, where we read—XII., 1., 8 and 9:

महापद्मपतिः कश्चिन्नन्दः क्षत्रविनाशकृत् ।

* * * * * * * * * * * * *

शासिष्यति महापद्मो द्वितीय इव भार्गवः ।

On the first of these verses the commentator, Śridhara, remarks: नन्दो नाम कश्चिन्महापद्मसंख्यायाः सेनायाः धनस्य वा पतिर्भविष्यति । अत एव महापद्म इत्यपि तस्य नाम ।

kings of the earth will be Śúdras. He will bring the whole earth under one umbrella: he will have eight sons, Sumálya* and others, who will reign after Mahápadma; and he and his sons[1] will govern for a hun-

[1] So the Bhágavata, also; but it would be more compatible with chronology to consider the nine Nandas as so many descents. The Váyu and Matsya† give eighty-eight years to Mahápadma, and only the remaining twelve to Sumálya and the rest of the remaining eight; these twelve years being occupied with the efforts of Kauṭilya to expel the Nandas. The Mahávaṁso, evidently intending the same events, gives names and circumstances differently; it may be doubted, if with more accuracy. On the deposal of Nágadásako, the people raised to the throne the minister Susanágo, who reigned eighteen years. This prince is, evidently, confounded with the Śiśunága of the Puráṇas. He was succeeded by his son, Kálásoko, who reigned twenty years; and he was succeeded by his sons, ten of whom reigned together for twenty-two years: subsequently there were nine, who, according to their seniority, reigned for twenty-two years. The Brahman Chánako put the ninth surviving brother, named Dhananando (Rich Nanda), to death, and installed Chandagutto. Mahávaṁso, pp. 15 and 21. These particulars, notwithstanding the alteration of some of the names, belong, clearly, to one story; and that of the Buddhists looks as if it was borrowed and modified from that of the Brahmans. The commentary on the Mahávaṁso, translated by Mr. Turnour (Introduction, p. xxxviii.), calls the sons of Kálásoko "the nine Nandos;" but another Buddhist authority, the Dípawaṁso, omits Kálásoko, and says that Susanágo had ten brothers, who, after his demise, reigned, collectively, twenty-two years. Journal of the Asiatic Society of Bengal, November, 1838 (p. 930).

* Several of my MSS. have Sumálya; and so has Professor Wilson's Bengal translation. The *Matsya-puráṇa*, in my copies, has Sukalya, with Kuśala as a variant. Sahalya: *Brahmáṇḍa-puráṇa*.

† Add the *Brahmáṇḍa-puráṇa*.

dred years.* The Brahman Kautilya will root out the nine Nandas.[1]

Upon the cessation of the race of Nanda, the Mauryas will possess the earth; for Kautilya will place Chandragupta[2] on the throne. His son will

[1] For the particulars of the story here alluded to, see the Mudrá Rákshasa, Hindu Theatre, Vol. II. Kautilya is also called, according to the commentator on our text, Vátsyáyana, Vishńugupta, and Cháńakya. According to the Matsya Puráńa, Kautilya retained the regal authority for a century; but there is some inaccuracy in the copies.†

[2] This is the most important name in all the lists; as it can scarcely be doubted that he is the Sandrocottus, or,—as Athenæus writes, more correctly,—the Sandrocoptus, of the Greeks, as I have endeavoured to prove in the Introduction to the Mudrá Rákshasa.‡ The relative positions of Chandragupta, Vidmisára (or Bimbisára), and Ajátaśatru serve to confirm the identification. Śákya was contemporary with both the latter, dying in the eighth year of Ajátaśatru's reign. The Maháwanso says he reigned twenty-four years afterwards; but the Váyu makes his whole reign but twenty-five years,§ which would place the close of it B. C. 526. The rest of the Śaiśunága dynasty, according to the Váyu and Matsya, reigned 143 or 140 years; bringing their close to B. C. 383. Another century being deducted for the duration

* Burnouf, citing a high Buddhist authority, a Sanskrit work, gives the following genealogy: Bimbisára (king of Rájagŕiha), Ajátaśatru, Udayibhadra, Muńda, Kákavarńin, Sahálin, Tulakuchi, Mahámańdala, Prasenajit, Nanda, Bindusára (king of Pátaliputra), Susíma. *Introduction à l'Histoire du Buddhisme Indien*, Vol. I., pp. 358, 359.

A Mongol authority interposes a king between Nanda and Chandragupta. See the *Foĕ Koué Ki*, p. 230.

† There is something to the same effect in the *Váyu-puráńa* and in the *Brahmáńda-puráńa*.

‡ The identification of Chandragupta with Sandrocyptus is the property of Sir William Jones. See the *Asiatic Researches*, Vol. IV., p. 11.

§ I find twenty-four years, and so in the *Brahmáńda-puráńa*.

be Bindusára;[1] his son will be Aśokavardha-

of the Nandas would place the accession of Chandragupta B. C. 283. Chandragupta was the contemporary of Seleucus Nicator, who began his reign B. C. 310, and concluded a treaty with him B. C. 305. Although, therefore, his date may not be made out quite correctly from the Pauráńik premises, yet the error cannot be more than twenty or thirty years. The result is much nearer the truth than that furnished by Buddhist authorities. According to the Mahâwamso, a hundred years had elapsed from the death of Buddha to the tenth year of the reign of Kálásoko (p. 15). He reigned other ten years, and his sons, forty-four, making a total of 154 years between the death of Śákya and the accession of Chandragupta, which is, consequently, placed B. C. 389, or above seventy years too early. According to the Buddhist authorities, Chan-ta-kut-ta (or Chandragupta) commenced his reign 396 B. C. Burmese Table; Prinsep's Useful Tables. Mr. Turnour, in his Introduction, giving to Kálásoko eighteen years subsequent to the century after Buddha, places Chandragupta's accession B. C. 381, which, he observes, is sixty years too soon; dating, however, the accession of Chandragupta from 328 B. C., or immediately upon Alexander's death,—a period too early by eight or ten years, at least. The discrepancy of dates, Mr. Turnour is disposed to think, "proceeds from some *intentional perversion* of the Buddhistical chronology." Introduction, p. L. The commentator on our text says that Chandragupta was the son of Nanda, by a wife named Murá, whence he and his descendants were called Mauryas: चन्द्रगुप्तं नन्दस्यैव पत्न्यन्तरस्य मुरासंज्ञस्य पुत्रं मौर्याणां प्रथमम्। Colonel Tod considers Maurya a corruption of Mori, the name of a Rajput tribe. The Tíká on the Mahâwamso builds a story on the fancied resemblance of the word to Mayúra (Sanskrit), Mori (Prakrit), 'a peacock.' There being abundance of pea-fowl in the place where the Śákya tribe built a town, they called it Mori; and their princes were, thence, called Mauryas. Turnour, Introduction to the Mahâwamso, p. XXXIX. Chandragupta reigned, according to the Váyu Puráńa, 24 years; according to the Mahâwamso, 34; to the Dípawamso, 24.

[1] So the Mahâwamso, Bindusáro. Burmese Table, Bin-tu-sa-

na:[1] his son will be Suyaśas;* his son will be Da-

---

ra. The Váyu has Bhadrasára, 25 years;† the Bhágavata, Várisára. The Matsya names but four princes of this race, although it concurs with the others, in stating the series to consist of ten. The names are, also, differently arranged; and one is peculiar.‡ They are Śatadhanwan, Bŕihadratha,§ Śuka, and Daśaratha.¶

[1] Aśoka, 36 years, Váyu;** Śuka,†† 26,‡‡ Matsya; Aśokavardhana, Bhágavata; Asoko and Dhammásoko, Maháwaḿso. This king is the most celebrated of any in the annals of the Buddhists.§§ In the commencement of his reign, he followed the Brahmanical faith, but became a convert to that of Buddha, and a zealous encourager of it. He is said to have maintained, in his palace, 64,000 Buddhist priests, and to have erected 84,000 columns (or topes) throughout India. A great convocation of Buddhist priests was held in the eighteenth year of his reign, which was followed by missions to Ceylon and other places. According to Buddhist chronology, he ascended the throne 218 years after the death of Buddha, B. C. 325. As the grandson of Chandragupta, however, he must have been some time subsequent to this, or,—agreeably to the joint duration of the reigns of Chandragupta and Bindusára, supposing the former to have commenced his reign about B. C. 315,—forty-nine years later, or B. C. 266. The duration of his reign is said to have been thirty-six years, bringing it down to B. C. 230; but, if we deduct these periods from the date assignable to Chandragupta, of B. C. 283, we shall place Aśoka's reign from B. C. 234 to 198. Now, it is certain that a number of very curious inscriptions, on columns and rocks, by a Buddhist

---

* Supárśwa, in two MSS. † Nandasára, and 25 years: *Brahmáńda-puráńa.*

‡ See note * in p. 190, *infra.*

§ The *Matsya-puráńa* gives him a reign of 70 years.

|| Aśoka is the reading of all my MSS.

¶ These are the first four of the series. ** And so the *Brahmáńda-puráńa.*

†† See note ||, above. ‡‡ I find 36.

§§ The best account, in our language, of Aśoka, is by Sir Erskine Perry, in the *Journal of the Bombay Asiatic Society*, Vol. III., Part II., pp. 149—173.

śaratha;[1] his son will be Sangata; his son will be

prince, in an ancient form of letter, and the Páli language, exist in India; and that some of them refer to Greek princes, who can be no other than members of the Seleucidan and Ptolemæan dynasties, and are, probably, Antiochus the Great* and Ptolemy Euergetes, kings of Syria and Egypt in the latter part of the third century before Christ. Journal of the Asiatic Society of Bengal, February and March, 1838. The Indian king appears always under the appellation Piyadasi (or Priyadarśin), 'the beautiful;' and is entitled Devánam piya, 'the beloved of the gods.' According to Buddhist authorities, the Rasawáhiní and Dípawaṁsa, quoted by Mr. Turnour (Journal of the Asiatic Society of Bengal, December 1837, p. 1056, and November, 1838, p. 930), Piyadasi or Piyadassano is identified, both by name and circumstances, with Aśoka; and to him, therefore, the inscriptions must be attributed. Their purport agrees well enough with his character; and their wide diffusion, with the traditionary report of the number of his monuments. His date is not exactly that of Antiochus the Great; but it is not very far different; and the corrections required to make it correspond are no more than the inexact manner in which both Brahmanical and Buddhist chronology is preserved may well be expected to render necessary.

[1] The name of Daśaratha, in a similar ancient character as that of Piyadasi's inscriptions, has been found at Gayá, amongst Buddhist remains, and, like them, deciphered by Mr. Prinsep: Journal of the Asiatic Society of Bengal, August, 1837, p. 677. A different series of names occurs in the Váyu;† or: Kuśála, 8 years; Bandhupálita, Indrapálita,‡ Daśavarman,§ 7 years; Śatadhara, 8 years; and Bṛihadaśwa,‖ 7 years.¶ The Bhágavata agrees in

* For some strictures on this position, see General Cunningham's *Bhilsa Topes*, p. 112.

† Immediately after Aśoka.

‡ I find: Bandhupálita, 8 years; Indrapálita, 10 years.

§ My MSS. yield Devavarman.

‖ So read all my MSS.; and yet, a little farther on, they agree in naming Bṛihadratha as the king put to death by Pushpamitra.

¶ The *Brahmáńda-puráńa* has, after Aśoka: Kuláта, 8 years; Bandhu-

Śáliśúka; his son will be Somaśarman; his son will be Śatadhanwan;[1]* and his successor will be Bŕihadratha. These are the ten Mauryas, who will reign over the earth for a hundred and thirty-seven years.[2]

The dynasty of the Śungas will, next, become possessed of the sovereignty; for Pushpamitra,[3] the general (of the last Maurya prince), will put his master to

---

most of the names; and its omission of Daśaratha is corrected by the commentator.

[1] Śatadhanwan, Bhágavata.

[2] The Váyu says nine Sumúrtyas† reigned 137 years.‡ The Matsya and Bhágavata have ten Mauryas, and 137 years. The detailed numbers of the Váyu and Matsya differ from their totals;§ but the copies are, manifestly, corrupt.

[3] The Bhágavata omits this name, but states that there were ten Śungas; although, without Pushpamitra, only nine are named. The Váyu and Matsya have the same account of the circumstances of his accession to the throne: the former gives him a reign of sixty, the latter, of thirty-six, years. In a play attributed to Kálidása, the Málavikágnimitra, of which Agnimitra is the hero, his father is alluded to as the Senání or general, as if he had deposed his master in favour, not of himself, but of his

---

pálita, 8 years; something unintelligible, and denoting a hiatus; Harsha, 8 years; Sammati, 9 years; Śáliśúka, 13 years; Devadharman, 7 years; Śatadhanus, 8 years; Bŕihadratha, 87 years.

* Corrected from "Śaśadharman", for which I find no warrant, Professor Wilson's Hindu-made translation excepted.

† I find only the reading Mauryas; nor is there room for a longer name:

इत्येते नव मौर्यास्तु ये भोक्ष्यन्ति वसुंधराम् ।
सप्तत्रिंशच्छतं पूर्णं तेभ्यः शुङ्गो भविष्यति ॥

‡ Nine Mauryas, and 137 years: *Brahmáńda-puráńa*. Its details, in my MS., require correction, therefore.

§ The *Matsya-puráńa* does not seem to profess to specify the period of each king's reign.

‖ And so gives the *Brahmáńda-puráńa*.

death, and ascend the throne. His son will be Agnimitra;[1][*] his son will be Sujyeshtha;[2] his son will be Vasumitra;[3] his son will be Árdraka;[4] his son will be

son. Agnimitra is termed king of Vidiśá, not of Magadha. Pushpamitra is represented as engaged in a conflict with the Yavanas on the Indus; thus continuing the political relations with the Greeks or Scythians of Bactria and Ariana. See Hindu Theatre, Vol. I., p. 347.

[1] 8 years, Váyu;† omitted, Matsya.

[2] 7 years, Váyu and Matsya.‡ But the latter places him after Vasumitra;§ and, in the drama, the son of Agnimitra is called Vasumitra.

[3] 8 years, Váyu; 10 years, Matsya.||

[4] Andraka, Váyu; Antaka, Matsya: they agree in his reign, 2 years.¶ Bhadraka, Bhágavata.

* In one MS., Animitri; in another, Amitra: readings of no value.

General Cunningham informs me that he possesses two coins of an Agnimitra, containing characters similar to those of Aśoka's inscriptions.

† The following stanza—corrupt, probably,—occurs there, not naming Agnimitra:

पुष्पमित्रसुताश्चाष्टौ भविष्यन्ति समा नृपाः ।
भविता चापि सुज्येष्ठः सप्त वर्षाणि वै ततः ॥

From this it appears that Pushpamitra had sons who ruled for eight years. And then came Sujyeshṭha, whose relationship to his predecessors is not stated.

The first half of this stanza may have been, originally, something like the following loose verse from the *Brahmáńḍa-puráńa*, which makes Agnimitra son of Pushpamitra, and assigns him a reign of 8 years:

तत्सुतोऽग्निमित्र चाष्टौ भविष्यति समा नृपः ।

‡ The *Brahmáńḍa-puráńa* has the same.

§ In the *Matsya-puráńa* I find, after Pushpamitra, Vasujyeshṭha (Vasuśreshṭha, in two MSS.), and then Vasumitra. According to the *Harsha-charita*, Agnimitra had a son Sumitra, killed by Múladeva. See my *Vásavadattá*, Preface, p. 53.

|| And so has the *Brahmáńḍa-puráńa*.

¶ My copies of the *Váyu-puráńa* give a reign of 10 years. The *Brahmáńḍa-puráńa* has Bhadra, and 2 years.

Pulindaka;[1] * his son will be Ghoshavasu;[2] his son will be Vajramitra;[3] his son will be Bhágavata;[4] his son will be Devabhúti.[5] † These are the ten Śungas, who will govern the kingdom for a hundred and twelve years.[6]

Devabhúti, the (last) Śunga prince, being addicted to immoral indulgences, his minister, the Kańwa ‡

---

[1] 3 years, Váyu § and Matsya. ‖

[2] 3 years, Váyu; ¶ omitted, Matsya; ** Ghosha, Bhágavata.

[3] 9 years, Matsya. ††

[4] Bhága. Matsya; 32 years, Váyu and Matsya. ‡‡

[5] Kshemabhúmi, Váyu; Devabhúmi, Matsya: 10 years, both. §§

[6] The Bhágavata says 'more than a hundred,' शताधिकम् । The commentator explains it 112, द्वादशाधिकम् । The Váyu and Matsya ‖‖ have the same period. ¶¶

---

* Pulinda, a shorter form, in a single copy. The same is the reading of the *Bhágavata-puráńa*.

† One MS. has Devabhúri.

‡ Corrected, here and at the beginning of the next paragraph, from "Káńwa", which I find nowhere. The *Brahmáńd́a-puráńa* first applies to Vasudeva the term Kańwa; afterwards, that of Kańwáyana.

§ So has the *Brahmáńd́a-puráńa*, also.

‖ In my MSS., Marunandana, and 3 years.

¶ And so has the *Brahmáńd́a-puráńa*.

** I find a name that looks like Megha: but all my MSS. are very doubtful here. The specification of three years is added.

†† The *Váyu-puráńa* has a name which looks, in my MSS., like Vikramitra: only this is most unlikely, as being meaningless. The reign is of 14 years, according to one MS.; 9, possibly, according to the rest. The *Brahmáńd́a-puráńa* has Vajramitra, and 14 years. The *Váyu-puráńa*, in all probability, really has the same.

‡‡ Bhágavata, and 32 years: *Brahmáńd́a-puráńa*.

§§ The *Brahmáńd́a-puráńa* has Devabhúmi, and 10 years.

‖‖ What total the *Matsya-puráńa* has is not to be made out from my MSS.: the detailed reigns occupy, however, 112 years. Though its text declares the Śungas to be ten, it names but nine.

¶¶ The *Brahmáńd́a-puráńa* has, also, 112 years:

शतं पूर्णं दश द्वे च तेभ्यः शुङ्गो भविष्यति ।

named Vasudeva, will murder him, and usurp the kingdom. His son will be Bhúmimitra;* his son will be Náráyańa; his son will be Suśarman.† These four Kańwáyanas‡ will be kings of the earth for forty-five§ years.[1]

---

[1] The names of the four princes agree in all the authorities.|| The Matsya transfers the character of Vyasanin to the minister, with the further addition of his being a Brahman,—Dwija. In the lists given by Sir William Jones and Colonel Wilford, the four Kańwas are said to have reigned 345 years; but, in seven copies of the Vishńu Puráńa, from different parts of India, the number is, as given in the text, forty-five: एते काण्वायनाश्चत्वारः पञ्चचत्वारिंशद्वर्षाणि भूपतयो भविष्यन्ति। There is, however, authority for the larger number, both in the text of the Bhágavata and the comment. The former¶ has:

काण्वायना इमे भूमिं चत्वारिंशच्च पञ्च च।
शतानि त्रीणि भोक्ष्यन्ति वर्षाणां च कलौ युगे॥

And the latter: काण्वायना वर्षाणां त्रीणि शतानि पञ्चचत्वारिंशद्वर्षाणि भूमिं भोक्ष्यन्ति। There is no doubt, therefore, of the purport of the text; and it is only surprising that such a chronology should have been inserted in the Bhágavata, not only in opposition to all probability, but to other authority. The Váyu and Matsya not only confirm the lower number, by stating it as a total, but by giving it in detail; thus:

---

* Bhúmitra: *Bhágavata-puráńa.*

† Sudharman: *Brahmáńda-puráńa.*

‡ Corrected, here and further on, from "Kańwas", for which I find no authority. And see the original as quoted in the Translator's note in this page.

§ One MS. yields "forty".

|| The *Bhágavata-puráńa* omits, in his place, Suśarman, whose name is supplied by the commentator Śrídhara. See, further, note *, above.

The *Váyu-puráńa* has, in my MSS., Bhútimitra, not Bhúmimitra; and its account of the Kańwáyanas, if decipherable, would, perhaps, prove different from that of our Puráńa.

¶ XII., I., 19.

Suśarman, the Kańwa,* will be killed by a powerful† servant, named Śipraka,‡ of the Andhra§ tribe, who will become king, (and found the Andhrabhŕitya dynasty¹).‖ He will be succeeded by his brother,

Vasudeva	will reign	9 years.
Bhúmimitra	. . . . .	14
Náráyańa	. . . . .	12
Suśarman	. . . . .	10
	Total :	45 years.

And six copies of the Matsya concur in this statement.¶

¹ The expressions Andhrajátíyas and Andhrabhŕityas have much perplexed Colonel Wilford, who makes three races out of one,—Andhras, Andhrajátíyas, and Andhrabhŕityas: Asiatic Researches, Vol. IX., p. 101. There is no warrant for three races, in the Puráńas, although the Matsya, and, perhaps, the Váyu, distinguishes two, as we shall hereafter see. Our text has but one, to which all the terms may be applied. The first of the dynasty was an Andhra by birth or caste (Játíya), and a servant (bhŕitya) of the last of the Kańwa race. So the Váyu: सिन्धुको ह्यन्ध्रजातीयः । The Matsya:

काण्वायनस्ततो भृत्यः सुशर्माणं प्रसह्य तम् ।
शिशुकोऽन्ध्रः सजातीयः प्राप्स्यतीमां वसुंधराम् ॥

And the Bhágavata:**

हत्वा काण्वं सुशर्माणं तद्भृत्यो वृषलो बली ।
गां भोक्ष्यत्यन्ध्रजातीयः कंचित्कालमसत्तमः ॥

* One MS. has Kańwáyana.

† I find बलात्, 'by violence'.

‡ Two MSS. give Kshipraka.

§ Corrected, here and elsewhere, from "Ándhra". Similarly, I have amended "Ándhrabhŕitya".

‖ These words I have enclosed in parentheses, as being additional to the Sanskrit.

¶ And so do the four to which I have access. The *Brahmáńda-puráńa* gives the same total of years for the dynasty of the Kańwas, whom it describes as Bráhmans.

** XII., I., 20.

Kŕishńa;[1] his son will be Śríśátakarńi;[2]* his son will be Púrńotsanga;[3] his son will be Śátakarńi;[4]† his son

---

The terms 'an Andhra by caste' and 'a Bhŕitya' or servant, with the addition, in the last passage, of Vŕishala, 'a Śúdra', all apply to one person and one dynasty. Wilford has made wild work with his triad. The name of the first of this race is variously read: Sindhuka, Váyu; Śiśuka, Matsya; Balin,‡ Bhágavata;§ and, according to Wilford, Chhesmaka‖ in the Brahmáńda Puráńa, and Śúdraka or Śúraka in the Kumáriká Khańda of the Skanda Puráńa: Asiatic Researches, Vol. IX., p. 107. He reigned 23 years: Váyu and Matsya.¶ If the latter form of his name be correct, he may be the king who is spoken of in the prologue to the Mŕichchhakatiká.

[1] 10 years,** Váyu; 18 years, Matsya.

[2] 56 years, Váyu; 18 years, Matsya; 10 years, Brahmáńda, Wilford;†† Simálakarńi, Matsya;‡‡ Śántakarńa,§§ Bhágavata.

[3] Omitted, Váyu; 18 years, Matsya; Paurńamása, Bhágavata.

[4] Omitted, Váyu ¶¶ and Bhágavata; 56 years, Matsya:

---

* In one MS., Śriśántakarńi. Also *vide infra*, p. 198, note §.

† The correct form, Śátakarńi, is of frequent occurrence, in various MSS. of several Puráńas accessible to me, both where this name stands by itself and where it appears as a family-designation. Also *vide infra*, p. 198, note §.

‡ Colonel Wilford strangely gives "Ballhika, or, rather, Ballhita." *Asiatic Researches*, Vol. IX., p. 107.

§ See the stanza cited just above.

‖ In the *Asiatic Researches*, Vol. IX., p. 116, Colonel Wilford has Chhismaka, and rightly, if my MS. is trustworthy.

¶ And so states the *Brahmáńda-puráńa*. The names of the Andhra-bhŕitya kings, with the duration of their reigns, I give, from that Puráńa, in a group. *Vide infra*, p. 201, note ‡‡.

** Both the name and the period are uncertain in my MSS. Colonel Wilford has Kŕishńa, and 18 years.

†† *Vide infra*, p. 201, note ‡‡, near the end.

‡‡ *Vide infra*, p. 200, note *.

§§ The reading there is Śriśántakarńa.

‖‖ In Colonel Wilford's manuscript extracts, I find Púrńotsanga, and 18 years. Also see the *Asiatic Researches*, Vol. IX., p. 116.

¶¶ Śátakarńi, and 56 years, in the collection just spoken of. Colonel

will be Lambodara;[1] his son will be Ivílaka;[2*] his son will be Meghaswáti;[3] his son will be Pafumat;[4] his

---

but the latter has, before him, a Śriváswáni,† 18 years.

[1] 18 years, Matsya.‡

[2] Apílaka, 12 years, Váyu and Matsya;§ Chivilika or Vivilika,|| Bhágavata.

[3] Omitted, Váyu and Matsya.¶

[4] Pafumávi,** 24 years, Váyu; Aṭamána,†† Bhágavata.

Wilford, in the Asiatic Researches where referred to in my last note, has the same. It is noticeable, that, at the same time, he does not state the length of Śrisátakarńi's reign,—56 years,—but leaves a blank.

* Two MSS. exhibit Divilaka. Colonel Wilford professes to have found Vivilaka.

† This strange word must, certainly, be a mistake. *Vide infra*, p. 200, note †.

‡ In Colonel Wilford's excerpts, the *Váyu-puráńa* here, again, agrees with the *Matsya-puráńa*. But I suspect interpolation. Also see the *Asiatic Researches*, Vol. IX., p. 116.

§ My MSS. of the *Matsya-puráńa* have Apitaka; and so has the Radcliffe copy, according to Professor Wilson. *Vide infra*, p. 199, note 4.

|| The name intended seems to be Vikala. At all events, it is a trisyllable; as is evident from the verse where it occurs for the second time:

मेघस्वातिश्च विवस्वाद्दृढमानस्तु तस्य च ।

Colonel Wilford has Vivilaka, which may have suggested Professor Wilson's "Vivilika".

¶ It agrees, here, according to my MSS., and according to the Radcliffe MS. as represented by Professor Wilson, with our Puráńa. *Vide infra*, p. 200, note §.

** This name looks rather doubtful. Colonel Wilford's MS. of extracts has Padurávi. The Colonel prints "Pafumáhi".

The person here intended may be the same as Puḍumáyi, or whatever his name is, mentioned in the Nasik cave-inscriptions. See the *Journal of the Bombay Asiatic Society*, Vol. VII., p. 52.

†† Corrected from "Drirhamána", which is quite indefensible, and must have been misread for something else. The "rh" is meant for 'ḍh'. See the verse quoted in note ||, above. Colonel Wilford has the name I have given, of which I find no variant.

son will be Arishtakarman;[1]* his son will be Hála;[2] his son will be Pattalaka;[3]† his son will be Pravilasena;[4]‡ his son will be Sundara (named) Śátakarńin;[5]§ his son will be Chakora Śátakarńin;[6] his son will be Śiva-

---

[1] Nemikŕishńa, 25 years, Váyu; Arishtakarńi, 25 years, Matsya.||

[2] Hála, 1 year, Váyu; 5 years, Matsya; Háleya, Bhágavata.

[3] Mańdalaka,¶ 5 years, Matsya;** omitted, Bhágavata.††

[4] Purishasena,‡‡ 21 years, Váyu; Purindrasena, 5 years, Matsya; Purishatara,§§ Bhágavata.

[5] Śátakarńi only, Váyu and Matsya: the first gives him three years;|| || the second, but one.¶¶ Sunanda,*** Bhágavata.

[6] Chakora,††† 6 months, Váyu; Vikarńi, 6 months, Matsya.

---

* Arishtakarńa is the name given by Colonel Wilford.

† Corrected from "Tálaka", which I find in no MS. of our Puráńa. Professor Wilson's Hindu-made version has Uttálaka. Colonel Wilford gives the name correctly. See, further, note ††, below.

‡ Three MSS. have, like Colonel Wilford, Pravillasena; one, Pulindasena.

§ Corrected from "Śátakarńi". In like manner, I have amended, just below, "Chakora Śátakarńi" and "Śiváśri Śátakarńi". Colonel Wilford has Sundara Śátakarńa and Chakora Śátakarńi.

|| Aniahfakarman: *Bhágavata-puráńa.*

¶ Corrected from "Mandalaka".

** The *Váyu-puráńa* here assigns a reign of 5 years to some king whose name is utterly corrupted in my MSS. Colonel Wilford has Pulaka, and 5 years: *Asiatic Researches*, Vol. IX., p. 116.

†† Not so: it has Talaka, which Colonel Wilford found, and which is in all my MSS., &c.

‡‡ I find Purikashena; and so found Colonel Wilford.

§§ I find Purishabhíru. Colonel Wilford's "Purishbhora" is impossible.

|| || In the *Váyu-puráńa*, according to my copies, Śátakarńi is made to reign but one year:

शातकर्णिर्वर्षमेकं भविष्यति नराधिपः ।

And so says Colonel Wilford.

¶¶ *Vide infra*, p. 201, note †.

*** Sunandana is the name; and Colonel Wilford so has it.

††† The *Váyu-puráńa* has Chakoraśátakarńi. Also *vide infra*, p. 201, note ‡. Chakora is the name in the *Bhágavata-puráńa*.

swáti;[1] his son will be Gomatíputra;[2]* his son will be Pulimat;[3] his son will be Śivaśrí Śátakarńin;[4]† his son will be Śivaskandha;[5]‡ his son will be Yajnaśrí;[6]§

---

[1] 28 years, Váyu || and Matsya.¶

[2] Gotamiputra,** 21 years, Váyu and Matsya.

[3] Pulomat,†† 28 years, Matsya; Purimat, Bhágavata.

[4] Omitted, Váyu; 7 years, Matsya; Medaśiras,‡‡ Bhágavata.

[5] Omitted, Váyu; 7 years, Matsya.§§

[6] 29 years, Váyu;||| 9 years, Matsya.

---

* A single MS. has Gotamiputra, which may be a restoration of the original reading of the *Vishńu-puráńa*. See note §, below. The *Bhágavata-puráńa* has Gomatiputra.

† Colonel Wilford bisects him into Sátakarńi and Śivaśri.

‡ One MS. gives Śivaskanda, the reading of Colonel Wilford, of the Translator's Bengal version, and that of the *Bhágavata-puráńa*.

§ Sátakarńi, and called king of the south,—as Professor Wilson presently states,—is referred to in an inscription at Junagur. See the *Journal of the Asiatic Society of Bengal*, for 1838, pp. 330 and 341; and the *Journal of the Bombay Asiatic Society*, Vol. VII., pp. 120 and 126. This inscription, which is in Sanskrit, shows that the name of the king in question begins with a dental sibilant.

Further, in the Nasik cave-inscriptions, names are found which are supposed to correspond to Śrísátakarńi, Gotamiputra Śrísátakarńi, and Yajnaśri Sátakarńi. *Journal of the Bombay Asiatic Society*, Vol. V., pp. 43, 47, 56.

We have, it is evident, excellent authority for accepting Gotamiputra, as against Gautamiputra and Gomatiputra.

|| According to Colonel Wilford, the *Váyu-puráńa* has Śivaswámin. I find Śivaswáti.

¶ Colonel Wilford represents the *Bhágavata-puráńa* as naming Vaťaka and Śivaswáti between Chakora and Gomatiputra. The name Vaťaka is in no MS. that I have examined; and there is no room for it in the line where it was supposed to occur.

** Gautamiputra is in both Puráńas, in my copies; and Colonel Wilford has this name. But see note §, above, *ad finem*; also, note § in p. 201, *infra*.

†† The *Váyu-puráńa* has no name here.

‡‡ Corrected from "Medhaśiras".

§§ *Vide infra*, p. 201, note ||.

||| Yajnaśri Sátakarńin, and 19 years, in all my copies of the *Váyu-puráńa* but one, which gives, like Colonel Wilford, 29 years.

his son will be Vijaya;[1] his son will be Chandraśrí;[2] his son will be Pulomárchis.[3] These[4] thirty Andhra-

---

[1] 6 years, Váyu * and Matsya.

[2] Dańdaśri,† 3 years, Váyu; Chandraśri,‡ 10 years, Matsya; Chandravijua,§ Bhágavata.

[3] Pulovápi,|| 7 years, Váyu; Pulomat, 7 years, Matsya; Salomadhi,¶ Bhágavata.

[4] The Váyu and Bhágavata state, also, 30 kings, and 456 years;** the Matsya has 29†† kings, and 460 years. The actual enumeration of the text gives but 24 names; that of the Bhágavata, but 23; that of the Váyu, but 17. The Matsya has the whole 29 names, adding several to the list of our text; and the aggregate of the reigns amounts to 435 years and 6 months.‡‡ The difference between this and the total specified arises, probably, from some inaccuracy in the MSS. As this list appears to be fuller than any other, it may be adviseable to insert it as it occurs in the Radcliffe copy of the Matsya Puráńa:§§

---

* Colonel Wilford has Sátakarńí, and 60 years. I suspect an error.

† The full name, in the *Váyu-puráńa*, is Dańdaśrí Sátakarńí.

‡ *Vide infra*, p. 201, note **. My MSS. here harmonise neither with the Radcliffe as quoted by Professor Wilson, nor with the MS. which he used for his short notes hereabouts.

§ Corrected from "Chandravijaya", the name that Colonel Wilford, also, has. The original runs:

विजयस्य सुतो भाव्यश्चन्द्रविजः पुलोमविः ।

|| Colonel Wilford seems to have found Puloman.

¶ Corrected, here and below, from "Sulomadhi" Colonel Wilford's "Lomadhi" is a mere blunder, and easily enough to be accounted for. See the verse quoted in note §, above.

** The aggregate which I find is 411 years:

समाः शतानि चत्वारि पञ्च षड् नवैव च ।

†† My MSS. of the *Matsya-puráńa* agree in saying 19; and herein, to begin with, they must, all, be corrupt

‡‡ This aggregate cannot be received with confidence, as must be clear from the details given in my numerous annotations on the list that follows.

§§ It must have been some other copy, and one abounding with omissions, that Professor Wilson followed for his last twenty-four notes pre-

bhŕitya kings will reign four hundred and fifty-six years.

---

1. Śiśuka . . . . 23 years.
2. Kŕishńa 18
3. Simalakarńi* 18
4. Púrńotsanga. 18
5. Śrívaswáni†. 18
6. Śátakarńi 56
7. Lambodara 18
8. Apítaka‡. 12
9. Sangha§ 18
10. Śátakarńi‖ 18
11. Skandhaswáti 7
12. Mrigendra¶ 3
13. Kuntalaswáti** 6
14. Swátikarńa 1
15. Pulomávit†† 36
16. Gorakshááswaśri‡‡ . . . 25

---

ceding that under annotation; else, why the numerous discrepancies that present themselves, when we look into details? My four MSS. of the *Matsya-puráńa*, while, differing considerably among themselves, differ quite as much from the Radcliffe copy as here cited. Whatever the importance of the matter before us, it being hopeless, with my materials, to make out, with certainty, the twenty-nine desired kings, and the duration of the reign of each, I shall not enter into many particulars, in dealing with the Translator's regal catalogue.

* To be corrected to Śrímallakarńi. Compare note 2 in p. 195, *supra*. And I find 10 years assigned to him, in all my MSS.

† Skandhastambhi is the reading in my copies.

‡ *Vide supra*, p. 196, notes 2 and §.

§ My MSS. have Meghaswáti.

‖ Swáti is the reading which I find.

¶ Mŕigendraswátikarńa, in my MSS.

** All my copies give Kuntalaswátikarńa.

†† Pulomávi is the name in my MSS.; and then follows Meghaswáti, with 38 years.

‡‡ My MSS. have Gaurakŕishńa, Naorikŕishńa, and Vikŕishńa. Compare note 1 in p. 197, *supra*.

After these, various races will reign; as, seven

17.	Hála	5 years.	
18.	Mantalaka*	5	
19.	Purindrasena†	5	
20.	Rajádaswáti‡	0	6 months.
21.	Śivaswáti	28	
22.	Gautamiputra§	21	
23.	Pulomat	28	
24.	Śivaśri	7	
25.	Skandhaswáti‖	7	
26.	Yajnaśri¶	9	
27.	Vijaya	6	
28.	Vadaśri**	10	
29.	Pulomat	7	

Total: 435 years, 6 months.

Several of the names vary, in this list, from those in my copy. The adjuncts Swáti and Śátikarńa†† appear to be conjoined, or not, with the other appellations, according to the convenience of the metre, and seem to be the family designations or titles. The dynasty‡‡ is of considerable chronological interest, as it ad-

* This is the name in one of my MSS.; the rest having Mańdalaka. *Vide supra*, p. 197, notes 3 and ¶.

† My copies give, after this name, Sundaraswátikarńa, and 1 year. *Vide supra*, p. 197, note 5, and the annotations thereon.

‡ Chakoraswátikarńa, in my MSS.

§ This corrects the name in note 2 in p. 198, *supra*, which see, and the annotation thereon.

‖ I find Śivaskandaśátakarńi, and 9 years.

¶ Yajnaśriśátakarńika, and 20 years, according to my MSS.

** In my copies, Chańdaśriśátakarńi. See notes 2 and ‡ in p. 199, *supra*.

†† I find Swátikarńa; also, Śátakarńin, Śátakarńi, and Śátakarńika.

‡‡ Below are the details of the Andhrabhrityas, according to the chapter of the *Brahmáńda-puráńa* copied in Colonel Wilford's volume of Pauráńik extracts:

Chhismaka	23 years.
Kŕishńa	18
Śriśátakarńi	18

Ábhíras, ten Gardabhilas,* sixteen Śakas, eight

---

mits of some plausible verifications. That a powerful race of Andhra princes ruled in India in the beginning of the Christian

---

Púrńotsanga	18 years.
Sátakarńi	56
Lambodara	18
Ápítaka	12
Sandása	18
Ávi (??)	12
Skandaswáti	7
Bhávaka	5
Pravillasena	12
Sundara Śátakarńi	1
Chakora Śátakarńi	6
Mahendra Śátakarńi	3
Kuntala Śátakarńi	8
Swátisheńa	1
Yantramáti (??)	34
Śátakarńi	29
Ávi (??)	4
Śivaskanda Śátakarńi	8
Yajnaśri Śátakarńi	19
Dańdaśri Śátakarńi	3
Puloman (*sic*)	7

The reign of Chakora is here given as of six years,—not months, as in the *Matsya-puráńa*.

The *Brahmáńda-puráńa* asserts that these kings will be thirty in number. The duration of the dynasty is given, but is expressed rather enigmatically. Apparently, it is 418 years.

Colonel Wilford, in preparing his table of the Andhrabhrityas, in the *Asiatic Researches*, Vol. IX., p. 116, could not have followed, exclusively, for the *Brahmáńda-puráńa*, the extract of his which I have been obliged to use without means of controlling it. Thus, his text must have differed from mine: or he would not have given the reign of Śrísátakarńi as of ten years. And again, he assigns 28 years to Skandaswáti; his extract assigning only 7, and most distinctly, too. Like myself, he seems to have had no other than the strange-looking readings Ávi and Yantramáti.

* Corrected from "Garddhabas", an inadvertence for "Gardabhas", which I find nowhere. Professor Wilson's Hindu-made version has Gardabhiras.

Yavanas, fourteen Tusháras,* thirteen Muńdas,

---

era, we learn from Pliny, who describes them as possessed of thirty fortified cities, with an army of 100,000 men and 2000 elephants. The Andræ† of this writer are, probably, the people of the upper part of the Peninsula; Andhra being the proper designation of Telingana. The Peutingerian tables, however, place the Andre-Indi on the banks of the Ganges; and the southern princes may have extended, or shifted, the site of their power. Towards the close of the dynasty, we find names that appear to agree with those of princes of middle India, of whom mention is made by the Chinese; as, Yue-gnai (Yajnaśrí), king of Kia-pili, A. D. 408 (Des Guignes, I., 45), and Ho-lo-mien (Pulomán‡), king of Magadha in 621 (ibid., I., 56). The Pauráńik lists place these two princes more nearly together; but we cannot rely implicitly upon their accuracy. Calculating from Chandragupta downwards, the Indian date of Yajna and the Chinese Yue-gnai corresponds; for we have:

10 Mauryas	137	years.
10 Śungas	112	
4 Kańwáyanas	45	
27 Andhras	437§	
	731	
Deduct, for Chandragupta's date,	312	B.C.
	419	A.C.,

But I suspect that Gardabhila is only a Bengal corruption of Gardabhin; and that it had its origin, in part, in the liability, in the local characters, of confusion between ल and भ. Compare Vol II., p. 100, note †.

Colonel Wilford writes "Gardabbinas", though regard for grammar would have led him to write Gardabhins. *Asiatic Researches*, Vol. IX., pp. 155 and 219.

* One MS. has Tushkaras. For the Tusháras or Tukháras, see Vol. II., p. 176, note **; and p. 186, note 5, with the annotations thereon.

† Pliny speaks of *gens Andaræ*: VI., XIX.

‡ The nominative case of Pulomat.

§ This total is exceedingly doubtful. Whence is it taken, too?

eleven Maunas, — (altogether, seventy-nine prin-

a date remarkably near that derivable from the Chinese annals. If the Indian Pulomán be the same with the Chinese Ho-lo-mien, there must be some considerable omission in the Paurāńik dynasty. There is a further identification in the case of Ho-lo-mien, which makes it certain that a prince of Magadha is intended; as the place of his residence is called, by the Chinese, Kia-so-mo-pu-lo-ching and Po-to-li-tse-ching, or, in Sanskrit, Kusumapura and Pátaliputra.* The equivalent of the latter name consists not only in the identity of the sounds Pátali and Po-to-li, but in the translation of 'putra' by 'tse'; each word meaning, in their respective languages, 'son.' No doubt can be entertained, therefore, that the city intended is the metropolis of Magadha,—Pátaliputra, or Palibothra. Wilford identifies Pulomat or Pulomán† with the Po-lo-mu-en of the Chinese; but Des Guignes interprets Po-lo-mu-en-kuē,‡ 'royaume des Brahmanes.' Buchanan (Hamilton), following the Bhágavata, as to the name of the last king, Salomadhi, would place him about A.D. 846; but his premises are far from accurate, and his deduction, in this instance at least, is of no weight: Genealogies of the Hindus, Introduction, p. 16. He supposes the Andhra kings of Magadha to have retained their power on the Ganges until the Mohammedan invasion (or the twelfth century), when they retired to the south, and reigned at Warankal, in Telingana. Inscriptions and coins, however, confirm the statement of the Puráńas, that a different dynasty succeeded to the Andhras some centuries before the Mohammedan conquests; and the Chinese, also, record, that, upon the death of the king of Magadha, Ho-lo-mien (Pulomán?), some time before A. D. 648, great troubles in India took place. Des Guignes. Some very curious and authentic testimony to the actual existence of these Andhra kings has been

* The full representation of the Chinese is "Kusumapura City" and "Pátaliputra City".

† See note ‡ in the preceding page.

‡ Equivalent to *Bráhmańa-ráshtra*.

ces),[1]* who will be sovereigns of the earth for one

---

lately afforded by the discovery of an ancient inscription in Gujerat, in which Rudra Dáman, the Kshatrapa (or Satrap) of Suráshṭra, is recorded to have repeatedly overcome Sátakarṇi,† king of the southern country (Dakshiṇápatha). The inscription is without date; but it is in an old character, and makes mention of the two Maurya princes, Chandragupta and Aśoka, as if not very long prior to its composition. Mr. J. Prinsep, to whom we are indebted for the deciphering and translating of this important document, has been, also, successful in deciphering the legends on a series of coins belonging to the princes of Suráshṭra, amongst whom the name of Rudra Dáman occurs; and he is inclined, although with hesitation, to place these princes about a century after Aśoka,—or Rudra Dáman, about 153 B. C.: Journal of the Asiatic Society of Bengal, May, 1837, and April, 1838. According to the computation hazarded above, from our text, the race of Andhra kings should not commence till about 20 years B. C., which would agree with Pliny's notice of them; but it is possible that they existed earlier in the south of India, although they established their authority in Magadha only in the first centuries of the Christian era.

[1] These parallel dynasties are thus particularized in our other authorities:

Ábhíras, 7, Matsya; 10, Váyu; kings of Avabhṛiti, 7, Bhágavata.‡

Gardabhins, 10,§ Matsya,‖ Váyu, Bhágavata.

---

* I have parenthesized this summation, as being added from the commentary.

† Corrected from "Śátakarṇi". *Vide supra*, p. 198, note §.

‡ It calls these Ábhíras by the name of Ávabhṛityas. The commentator on the *Bhágavata-puráṇa* says they were so denominated, as being kings of the city of Avabhṛiti.

§ 7, in both the Puráṇas, in all my copies of them.

‖ Gardabhilas is the name in all my MSS. of the *Matsya-puráṇa*, which recognizes only seven of them. But *vide supra*, p. 202, note *, on the probability that Gardabhila is a mere corruption.

thousand three hundred and ninety-nine* years; and,

Śakas, 18,† Matsya, Váyu; Kankas, 16, Bhágavata.

Yavanas, 8, Matsya, Váyu, Bhágavata.

Tusháras, 14, Matsya, Váyu; Tushkáras,‡ 14, Bhágavata.

Marúńdas,§ 13, Váyu; Purúńdas,|| 13, Matsya; Surúńdas,¶ 10, Bhágavata.

Maunas, 18,** Váyu; Húńas, 19, Matsya;†† Maulas,‡‡ 11, Bhágavata.§§

Total:|||| 85 kings, Váyu; 89, Matsya; 76, and 1899 years, Bhágavata.

The other two authorities give the years of each dynasty severally. The numbers are, apparently, intended to be the same; but those of the Matsya are palpable blunders, although almost all the MSS. agree in the reading. The chronology of the Váyu is: Ábhíras, 67 years; Gardabhins, 72; Śakas, 380; Yavanas, 82; Tusháras, 500 (all the copies of the Matsya have 7000); Marúńdas,

---

* Corrected, on the authority of all my MSS., from "ninety". And the commentary has एकोनचतुर्दशशतवर्षाणि ।

† 10, in the *Váyu-puráńa*, according to my MSS.

‡ I find Pushkaras.

§ One MS. yields Muruńdas, the better reading, almost certainly.

|| My oldest MS. yields Puraúdas; two, Puruńdas; the remaining, Purunjas.

¶ Guruńdas, according to my MSS., &c.

** This is to be exchanged for 11. The MSS. have 18, it is true; but, further on, they correct themselves. *Vide infra*, p. 210, note ¶.

†† The *Matsya-puráńa* has, besides, several particulars which I cannot decipher.

‡‡ This is, probably, a Bengal corruption of Maunas, the name which my MSS. &c yield. On the liability of confusion between ष and ख, *vide supra*, p. 208, note *.

The *Bhágavata-puráńa* says that the Maunas will reign for a period of 300 years

§§ The *Brahmáńda-puráńa*, in my one MS., agrees with the *Váyu-puráńa*, as known to me, a few particulars excepted. Thus: it assigns the Śakas 300 years; it has Swarańdas, not Muruńdas: and it makes the Mauna kings eleven only.

|||| These totals are supplied by the Translator.

then, eleven Pauras will be kings for three hundred

200;* and Mlechchhas † (intending, perhaps, Maunas), 300 years. Total, ‡ 1601 years; or less than 19 years to a reign. They are not, however, continuous, but nearly contemporary, dynasties; and, if they comprise, as they probably do, the Greek and Scythian princes of the west of India, the periods may not be very wide of the truth. The Matsya begins the list with one more dynasty,—another Andhra (*vide supra*, p. 194, note 1), of whom there were seven:

अन्ध्राणां संस्थिते राज्ये तेषां भृत्यान्वया नृपाः ।
सप्तैवान्ध्रा भविष्यन्ति दशाभीरास्ततो नृपाः ॥

"When the dominion of the Andhras has ceased, there shall be seven other Andhras, kings of the race of their servants; and, then, nine§ Ábhíras." The passage of the Váyu, although somewhat similar in terms, has a different purport:

अन्ध्राणां संस्थितानां च‖ तेषां वंश्याः समाः पुनः ।
सप्तैव तु भविष्यन्ति दशाभीरास्ततो नृपाः ॥

"Of these, the Andhras having passed away, there shall be seven contemporary races; as, ten Ábhíras," &c The passage is differently read in different copies; but this is the only intelligible reading. At the same time, it subsequently specifies a period for the duration of the Andhra dynasty, different from that before given, or three hundred years, as if a different race was referred to:

अन्ध्रा भोक्ष्यन्ति वसुधां शते द्वे च शतं च वै ।¶

---

* This interpretation may be doubtful. The original, as alone I find it, runs:

शतान्यर्धचतुर्थानि भवितारस्त्रयोदश ।
मुरुण्डा वृषलैः सार्धं तथान्ये म्लेच्छजातयः ॥

† *Vide infra*, p. 210, note ¶.

‡ This is the Translator's total.

§ Only one of my MSS. has a reading that yields a number; and that number is ten.

‖ The lection which I find is संस्थिताः पञ्च ।

¶ So have, to be sure, all my MSS. of the *Váyu-puráńa*; and the grammar and metre are correct Still, the verse looks unnatural. I

years.[1] When they are destroyed, the Kaila-

"The Andhras shall possess the earth two hundred years and one hundred." The Matsya has twice five hundred:

अन्ध्राः श्रीपर्वतीयाश्च ते द्वे पञ्चशतं समाः ।

"The Śriparvatíya Andhras, twice five hundred years." One MS. has, more consistently, fifty-two years: द्विपञ्चाशतं समाः. But there is, evidently, something faulty in all the MSS. The expression of the Matsya, 'Śriparvatíya Andhras,' is remarkable; Śriparvata being in Telingana. There is, probably, some confusion of the two races, the Magadha and Tailinga kings, in these passages of the Puráńas. The Bhágavata has a dynasty of seven Andhra kings, but of a different period (*vide supra*, p. 194, note 1). Colonel Wilford has attempted a verification of these dynasties; in some instances, perhaps, with success, though, certainly, not in all. The Ábhíras he calls the shepherd-kings of the north of India. They were, more probably, Greeks, or Scythians, or Parthians, along the lower Indus. Traces of the name occur, as formerly observed,* in the Abiria of Ptolemy; and the Ahira,† as a distinct race, still exist in Gujerat. Araish-i-Mahfil. The Śakas are the Sacæ; and the duration of their power is not unlikely to be near the truth. The eight Yavana kings may be, as he supposes, Greek princes of Bactria, or, rather, of Western India. The Tusháras he makes the Parthians. If the Bhágavata has the preferable reading, Tushkáras,‡ they should not be surprised if it were a corruption of the same words that we find in the *Brahmáńda-puráńa*:

अन्ध्रा भोक्ष्यन्ति वसुधां शते द्विःपञ्चाशतं च वै ।

The period here recognised is of two hundred and fifty years.

* Vol. II., p. 185, note 9. Also see the same volume, p. 133, text, and note *.

Dr. Bháu Dájí announces that he has discovered an inscription of the Ábhíras near Násik. One of their kings, he says, was Íswarasena, son of Śivadatta. *Journal of the Bombay Asiatic Society*, Vol. VIII., p. 243.

† For the tribe of Ahira, see Sir H. M. Elliot's *Supplemental Glossary*, pp. 8—9.

‡ It does not seem that it has. *Vide supra*, p. 206, note ‡.

kila* Yavanas will be kings, the chief of whom will

were the Tochari, a Scythian race. The Murúṅḍas, or, as he has it, Maurúṅḍas, he considers to be a tribe of Huns,—the Morundæ of Ptolemy. According to the Matsya, they were of Mlechchha origin (Mlechchha-sambhava). The Váyu calls them Árya-mlechchhas; quere, barbarians of Ariana. Wilford regards the Maunas as, also, a tribe of Huns; and the word is, in all the MSS. of the Matsya, Húṅas;† traces of whom may be still found in the west and south of India:‡ Inscription at Merritch, Journal of the Royal Asiatic Society, Vol. III., p. 103. The Gardabhins Wilford conjectures to be descendants of Bahram Gor, king of Persia; but this is very questionable. That they were a tribe in the west of India may be conjectured; as some strange tales prevail, there, of a Gandharva, changed to an ass, marrying the daughter of the king of Dhárá: (Asiatic Researches, Vol. VI., p. 35, and Vol. IX., p. 147; also, 'Cutch', by Mrs. Postans, p. 18); fables suggested, no doubt, by the name Gardabha, signifying 'an ass'. There is, also, evidently, some affinity between these Gardabhins and the old Gadbiyá Paisá, or 'ass-money', as vulgarly termed, found in various parts of Western India, and which is, unquestionably, of ancient date: Journal of the Asiatic Society of Bengal, December, 1835, p. 688. It may be the coinage of the Gardabha princes; Gardabha being the original of Gadhá, meaning, also, an 'ass'. I have elsewhere conjectured the possibility of their being current about a century and a half before our era: Journal of the Royal Asiatic Society, Vol. III., p. 385. Colonel Tod, quoting a parallel passage in Hindi, reads, instead of Gardabhin,§ Gor-ind, which he explains "the Indras (or lords) of Gor"; but the reading is, undoubtedly, erroneous.

¹ The copies agree in reading Pauras; but the commentator

* Almost as common as this reading is Kalilkila; and I find Kilakila and Kaichchhikila, also. See, further, p. 211, *infra*, notes 1 and ‡.

† See Vol. II., p. 134, note †.

‡ This position is open to much doubt.

§ Corrected from "Garddhabhin".

be Vindhyaśakti: his son will be Puranjaya;* his son will be Rámachandra; his son will be Dharma,† from

remarks that it is, sometimes, Maunas:‡ but they have already been specified; unless the term be repeated in order to separate the duration of this dynasty from that of the rest. Such seems to be the purport of the similar passage of the Bhágavata:§ "These kings (Andhras, &c.,) will possess the earth 1099 years, and, the eleven Maulas, 300:"

एते भोक्ष्यन्ति पृथिवीं दश वर्षशतानि च ।
नवाधिकां च नवतिं मौना ‖ एकादश क्षितिम् ॥
भोक्ष्यन्त्यब्दशतान्यङ्ग त्रीणि • • • • • ।

No such name as Pauras occurs in the other authorities. The analogy of duration identifies them with the Mlechchhas of the Váyu: "Eleven Mlechchhas will possess the earth for three centuries:"

शतानि त्रीणि भोक्ष्यन्ते म्लेच्छा एकादशैव¶ तु ।

And the Váyu may refer to the Maunas; as no other period is assigned for them. The periods of the Bhágavata—1099 and 300,—come much to the same as that of our text, 1390;** the one including the three centuries of the Maunas, the other stating it separately. The Váyu, apparently, adds it to the rest; thus making the total 1601,†† instead of 1390. It is evident that the

* Parapuranjaya, in one MS. *Vide infra*, p. 212, notes § and ‖.

† Corrected from "Adharma", for which I find no authority. The original runs: ततोऽधर्मः । Even Professor Wilson's Bengal translation has Dharma.

‡ Three of my MSS. actually have Maunas.

§ XII., I., 29, 30.

‖ I find मौना: । *Vide supra*, p. 206, note ‡‡.

¶ One of my MSS. reads मौना ह्येकादशैव । Also *vide supra*, p. 206, note **.

** Our text affords an aggregate of 1399, like the *Bhágavata-puráńa*. *Vide supra*, p. 206, note *.

†† The Translator, not the *Váyu-puráńa*, supplies this total.

whom will be Varánga,* Kŕitanandana, Sushinandi,† Nandiyaśas, Śiśuka, and Pravíra: these will rule for a hundred and six years.[1] From them will proceed

same scheme is intended by the several authorities; although some inaccuracy affects either the original statement or the existing manuscripts.

[1] Kilakila, Kolakila, Kolikila, Kilinakila, as it is variously read.‡ Sir William Jones's Pandit stated that he understood it to be a city in the Marátha country (Asiatic Researches, Vol XI., p. 142); and there has been found a confirmation of his belief, in an inscription where Kilagila,§ as it is there termed, is called the capital of Márasimha Deva, king of the Konkan: Journal of the Royal Asiatic Society, Vol. IV., p. 282. This inscription dates A. D. 1058. The Puráńas refer, probably, to a long antecedent date, when the Greek princes, or their Indo-Scythic successors, following the course of the Indus, spread to the upper part of the western coast of the Peninsula. The text calls them Yavanas; and the Váyu and Matsya say they were Yavanas in institutions, manners, and policy: धर्मतः कामतोऽर्थतः ।|| The Bhágavata¶ names five of their princes,—Bhútananda, Vangiri, Śiśunandi, Yaśonandi,** and Pravíraka,—

* Four MSS. have Vangara; one, Vyangala.

† Substituted for the "Śudhinandi" of the former edition, which I have met with nowhere. Sushinandi, the ordinary lection, is the word in Professor Wilson's Hindu-made version. One MS. has Sukhinandi; one, Śushirnandi; one, Śishyanandi.

‡ Four MSS. of the *Váyu-puráńa* have Kolikilas; one, Kilakilas. Two copies of the *Matsya-puráńa* give Kilikilas; one, Kilakilas; the fourth, Kilakalas. The reading of the *Brahmáńḍa-puráńa* is Kalakilas. The *Bhágavata-puráńa* speaks of Kilikilá, which the commentator Śrídhara says is the name of a city. The commentator on the *Vishńu-puráńa* calls the city Kolikilá.

§ It seems to be a mountain, giving name to a stronghold thereon.

|| These words I find in the *Matsya-puráńa*, but not in the *Váyu-puráńa*.

¶ XII., I., 30, 31.

** Called brother of Śiśunandi.

thirteen sons; then, three Báhlíkas; and Pushpamitra, and Paťumitra, and others, to the number of

---

who will reign 106 years; and they are, therefore, imperfect representatives of the series in our text. The Matsya has no further specific enumeration of any dynasty. The Váyu makes Pravíra the son of Vindhyaśakti;* the latter reigning 96 years, and the former, 60.† The latter is king of Kánchanapurí,‡ 'the golden city,' and is followed by four sons, whose names are not mentioned. Between Vindhyaśakti and Pravíra, however, a dynasty of kings is introduced, some of the names of which resemble those of the Kilakila princes of the text.§ They are: Bhogin (the son of Śeshanága‖), Sadáchandra, Nakhavat, Dhanadharmita,¶ Vimśaja, Bhútinanda,—at a period before the end of the Śungas? (the copies have शुङ्गानां च** कुलस्यान्ते), Madhunandi, his younger brother, Nandiyaśas;†† and, in his race, there will be

---

* Dr. Bháu Dáji has published an inscription from Ajanta, in which, he says, there is mention of a king Vindhyaśakti and his son Pravarasena. The same names of sire and son are found, he alleges, in the *Váyu-puráńa*. His MSS. must differ, then, from mine. See the *Journal of the Bombay Asiatic Society*, Vol. VII., p. 65.

† In the *Brahmáńd́a-puráńa*, it seems to be stated that Dauhitra and others—see below,—will reign for sixty years; and then follows something quite unintelligible in my MS.

‡ In the *Váyu-puráńa*, the city is called Kánchanaká.

§ The *Váyu-puráńa* is anything but clear, hereabouts, in my MSS. It speaks—see the next note,—of Parapuranjaya (or Swárapuranjaya, according to three copies out of five); and he is said to be son of Śesha, king of the Nágas. *Vide supra*, p. 210, note *.

‖ I find, in the *Váyu-puráńa*:

शेषस्य नागराजस्य पुत्रः परपुरंजयः।

The *Brahmáńd́a-puráńa* has the same verse.

¶ Three MSS. of the *Váyu-puráńa* have Dhanadharman; the remaining two, Dhanadharma.

** One MS. has तु; and so reads the *Brahmáńd́a-puráńa*. The resulting sense is "after the Śungas".

†† The *Brahmáńd́a-puráńa*, at least as known to me, has, instead of these names: Rámachandra, Nakhavat(?), Varadharmin, Vangava(?), Bhúminanda, Śiśunandi, Nandiyaśas.

thirteen, will rule over Mekalá.[1] There will be nine

---

three other Rajas,—Dauhitra,* Śiśuka, and Ripukáyán.† These are called princes of Vidiśa or Videśa,‡—the latter meaning, perhaps, 'foreign,'— and constitute the Nága dynasty. Our text calls Vindhyaśakti a Múrdhábhishikta, §—a warrior of a mixed race, sprung from a Brahman father and Kshattriya mother.||

[1] The text of this passage runs thus: तत्पुत्रास्त्रयोदशैव बाह्लीकाश्च त्रयः । ततः पुष्पमित्रपटुमित्रास्त्रयोदश¶ मेकलाश्च ।" 'Their sons,' तत्पुत्राः, the commentator explains by विन्ध्यशक्त्यादीनां यथायथं त्रयोदश पुत्राः, "thirteen sons of Vindhyaśakti and the rest." The Bhágavata has a different statement, identifying the sons of the Vindhya race with the Báhlikas, and making them thirteen:

तेषां त्रयोदश सुता भवितारश्च बाह्लिकाः ।

"The Báhlikas will be their thirteen sons." As the commentator: तेषां भूतनन्दादीनां यथायथं बाह्लिका नामानस्त्रयोदश सुता भविष्यन्ति । "There will be, severally, thirteen sons, called Báhlikas, of Bhútananda and the rest." The following verse is:

पुष्पमित्रोऽथ राजन्यो दुर्मित्रोऽस्य तथैव च ।

"Pushpamitra, a king, and, then, Durmitra." Who or what they were does not appear. The commentator says: "Pushpamitra

---

* Variants: Dauhitrya and Daihitra.

† I find nothing like this name, but, in most of my MSS., Purikaya. The rest seem to speak of a city, Purikayá. The *Brahmáńda-puráńa* gives Purikáya.

‡ All my MSS. have Vaideśa, with Vaidiśaka as its adjective. One or other must be wrong.

§ The commentator explains this term, and rightly, by *mukhya*. He adds that there is a variant, मूर्धसिक्तः, which he explains by क्षत्रिय-मुख्यः ।

|| This is the definition of what is more ordinarily written *múrdhávasikta*.

¶ Not one of my MSS. has anything but -पटुमित्रास्त्रयोदश । The Translator's reading seems to be corrupted from a fragment of the comment: पुष्पमित्रादयस्त्रयोदश ।

** See note * in p. 215, *infra*.

kings in the seven Kośalas; and there will be as

was another king; and Durmitra was his son:" तस्य पुष्पमित्रो नामाभवो राजकः । तस्य च दुर्मित्रो नाम पुत्रः । Here is, evidently, careless and inaccurate compilation. The Váyu, though not quite satisfactory, accords better with our text. "Pravira," it says, "will have four sons. When the Vindhya race is extinct, there will be three Báhlika kings,—Supratika, Nabhira, who will reign thirty years, and Śakyamánábhava* (quere this name), king of the Mahishas.† The Pushpamitras will then be, and the Paṭumitras, also, who will be seven kings of Mekalá. Such is the generation:"

तस्य (प्रवीरस्य) पुत्रास्तु चत्वारो भविष्यन्ति नराधिपाः ।
विन्ध्यकानां कुलेऽतीते नृपा वै बाह्लिकास्त्रयः ॥
सुप्रतीको नभीरश्च‡ समा भोक्ष्यन्ति त्रिंशतिः § ।
शक्यमानाभवो राजा‖ महिषीणां महीपतिः ॥
पुष्पमित्रा भविष्यन्ति पटुमित्रास्तथैव च (or पटुमित्रास्त्रयोदश ¶) ।
मेकलायां नृपाः सप्त भविष्यन्तीति संततिः ॥**

The plural verb, with only two Báhlika names, indicates some omission; unless we correct it to भोक्ष्येते 'they two will reign:' but the following name and title, "Śakyamánábhava, king of the Mahishas," seems to have little connexion with the Báhlikas. If, in a subsequent part of the citation, the reading 'trayodaśa' be correct, it must, then, be thirteen Paṭumitras; but it will be difficult to know what to do with 'sapta', 'seven.'†† If, for 'santa-

* See note ‖, below.

† The Sanskrit cited requires 'Mahishins'.

‡ One MS. has सुप्रतीकोऽथ भारश्च, which gives Bhara, instead of Nabhira.

§ One of my MSS. gives त्रिंशतिः, the reading of the *Brahmáńḍa-puráńa*.

‖ In one of my MSS., शिशुको नामाभवद्राजा; and the *Brahmáńḍa-puráńa*, in my one copy, has साको नामाभवद्राजा ।

¶ This is the only reading of my MSS.; and the *Brahmáńḍa-puráńa* has the same.

** The *Brahmáńḍa-puráńa* has the same verses, but, in my single MS., in a very corrupt form.

†† The seven kings of Mekalá are unnamed, as in our Puráńa. As to the Pushpamitras and the Paṭumitras, the import is, probably, that

many Naishadha princes.'*

tiḥ', we might read 'saptatiḥ', 'seventy', the sense might be, "these thirteen kings ruled for seventy-seven years.† However this may be, it seems most correct to separate the thirteen sons or families of the Vindhya princes from the three Báhlikas, and them from the Pushpamitras and Paṭumitras, who governed Mekalá, a country on the Narmadá (see Vol. II., p. 160, note 4‡). What the Báhlikas (or princes of Balkh,) had to do in this part of India is doubtful. The Durmitra of the Bhágavata has been conjectured, by Colonel Tod (Transactions of the Royal Asiatic Society, Vol. I., p. 325), to be intended for the Bactrian prince Demetrius: but it is not clear that even the Bhágavata considers this prince as one of the Báhlikas; and the name occurs nowhere else.

[1] For the situation of Kośalá, see Vol, II., p. 172, note 2.

there were thirteen of the latter, while the number of the former is not mentioned. See the next note, near the end.

* On referring to the beginning of note 1 in p. 213, *supra*, it will be seen that the Translator has transcribed a part of the original of this passage. I repeat a few words there given, and continue the quotation: ततः पुष्पमित्रपटुमित्रास्त्रयोदश। मेकलाश्च सप्त। कोशलायां तु नवैव भूपतयो भविष्यन्ति। नैषधास्तु तावन्त एव भूपतयो भविष्यन्ति। "Then the Pushpamitras and the Paṭumitras, thirteen, *will reign*; and the Mekalas *will be* seven; and there will be nine kings in Kośalá; and there will be just as many Naishadha kings." The comment is as follows: पुष्पमित्राद्यस्त्रयोदश। मेकला मेकलदेशजाः सप्त। कोशलायां नवैव। नैषधास्तावन्तो नवैव भूपतयो भविष्यन्ति।

Thus, it is not said where the Pushpamitras and the Paṭumitras—dynasties, probably, named from their founders, Pushpamitra and Paṭumitra,—will reign; there is no mention, as there is in the *Váyu-puráṇa* of Mekalá; we are told nothing, here, of the Kośalas, but of the city of Kośalá: and the "seven" defines the number of the Mekala kings.

If we suppose that our text—which, here, is in prose, and, therefore, comparatively liable to vitiation, should read पुष्पमित्राश्च, it will harmonize with the *Váyu-puráṇa*, in not defining the number of the Pushpamitras, and in recognizing the Paṭumitras as thirteen. *Vide supra*, p. 214, note ††.

One of my MSS. yields Mekalakas, for Mekalas.

† Such, owing to the word *iti*, could not be the sense, even if the reading were as it is suggested to alter it.

‡ The only Mekalá named there is a designation of the river Narmadá.

In Magadhá,* a sovereign† named Viśwasphatika will establish other tribes: he will extirpate the Kshattriya (or martial) race, and elevate fishermen,‡ bar-

---

The three copies of the Váyu read Komalá, and call the kings the Meghas, "more strong than sapient:"§

कोमलायां|| तु राजानो भविष्यन्ति महाबलाः ।
मेघा इति समाख्याता बुद्धिमन्तो न वै च¶ तु ॥

The Bhágavata agrees with our text.** The Váyu says, of the Naishadhas, or kings of Nishadha, that they were, all, of the race of Nala: नलवंशप्रसूताः । The Bhágavata adds two other races, seven Andhras (*vide supra*, p. 199, note 4), and kings of Vaidúra; with the remark, that these were, all, contemporaries; being, as the commentator observes, petty or provincial rulers,— खण्डमण्डलेषु भूपाः ।

In the extract from the *Váyu-puráńa* in the note under annotation, there is mention, however, of a Mekalá,—a city, in all likelihood, and the capital of the Mekala kings of our text.

* Corrected from "Magadha", the Sanskrit being मगधायाम् । A city seems to be intended.

† The original does not designate him as such.

‡ *Kaivarta*. The word is, probably, here used in the sense of the offspring of Nishádа men and Áyogaví women. See the *Laws of the Mánavas*, X., 34.

§ From the correction made in note ¶, below, it comes out that the Meghas were 'both strong and sapient.'

|| The proper and more ancient form is Kosalá,—with the dental sibilant; and, as स and श are frequently interchanged by careless scribes, there is no doubt that कोसलायां is the right word here. The *Brahmáńḍa-puráńa* has कोशलायां, yielding Kośalá.

¶ The correct reading, unquestionably, is that which I find, नवैव । The kings of Kosalá are, thus, said to be nine in number.

** Its words—XII., I., 33,—are:

एककाला इमे भूपाः सप्तान्ध्राः सप्त कौशलाः ।
विदूरपतयो भाव्या नैषधास्तत एव हि ॥

Here the kings of the Kuśalas are distinctly declared to be seven.

barians,* and Brahmans, (and other castes) to power.[1] The nine Nágas† will reign in Padmávatí, Kántipurí,‡

[1] The Váyu has Viśwasphâńi § and Viśwasphiñi; the Bhágavata, Viśwasphúrti, or, in some MSS., Viśwaphúrji.‖ The castes he establishes, or places in authority, to the exclusion of the Kshattriyas, are called, in all the copies of our text, Kaivartas, Paius,¶ Pulindas, and Brahmans. The Váyu (three MSS.) has Kaivartas, Panchakas, Pulindas, and Brahmans:

कैवर्तान्पञ्चकांश्चैव पुलिन्दान्ब्राह्मणांस्तथा ।

The Bhágavata** has Pulindas, Yadus, and Madrakas. The Váyu describes Viśwasphâńi as a great warrior, and, apparently, as a eunuch:

विश्वस्फाणिर्महासत्त्वो युद्धे विष्णुसमो बली ।
विश्वस्फाणिर्नरपतिः क्लीबाकृतिरिवोच्यते†† ॥

He worshipped the gods and manes, and, dying on the banks of the Ganges, went to the heaven of Indra:

देवान्पितॄंश्च विप्रांश्च तर्पयित्वा यथाक्रमम् ।
जाह्नवीतीरमासाद्य शरीरं त्यक्ष्यते बली ।
संन्यस्य स्वशरीरं तु शक्रलोकं गमिष्यति ॥‡‡

* The original says Yadus and Pulindas.

† Nágasena, called one of the Nágas, is mentioned in the *Harsha-charita*, and is said to have been slain at Padmávatí. See my *Vásavadattá*, Preface, p. 53. A Nágasena is named in the second inscription on the Allahabad pillar. See the *Journal of the Asiatic Society of Bengal*, 1837, p. 979; also, the *Journal of the Bombay Asiatic Society*, Vol. VIII., p. 247.

‡ Variants: Kantipurí and Kántápurí. One of the best of my MSS. names the first only of the three cities in the text.

§ This is the name that I find in the *Váyu-puráńa*. The *Brahmáńda-puráńa* has Viśwasphárńi and Viśwasphâńi.

‖ This is no reading. The more ordinary that I find is Viśwasphúrji.

¶ In only one MS. have I met with this reading. See note *, above.

** XII., 1., 34.

†† I find two better readings than this; namely, क्लीबाकृतिरिवोच्यते and क्लीबाकृतिरवोच्यते। The latter is the lection of the *Brahmáńda-puráńa*, also.

‡‡ The *Brahmáńda-puráńa* has four lines, instead of these three, and says that the king committed suicide by throwing himself into the Ganges.

and Mathurá; and the Guptas of Magadha,* along the Ganges, to Prayága.[1] † A prince named Devarakshita

[1] Such appears to be the purport of our text: नव नागाः पद्मावत्यां कान्तिपुर्यां मथुरायाम्। अनुगङ्गाप्रयागं मागधा गुप्ताश्च भोक्ष्यन्ति।‡ The nine Nágas might be thought to mean the same as the descendants of Śesha Nága; but the Váyu has another series here, analogous to that of the text: "The nine Náka kings will possess the city Champávati;§ and the seven Nágas (?)‖, the pleasant city Mathurá. Princes of the Gupta race will possess all these countries, the banks of the Ganges to Prayága, and Sáketa, and Magadhá:"¶

नव नाकास्तु भोक्ष्यन्ति पुरीं चम्पावतीं नृपाः।
मथुरां च पुरीं रम्यां नागा भोक्ष्यन्ति सप्त वै॥
अनुगङ्गाप्रयागं च साकेतं** मगधांस्तथा।
एताञ्जनपदान्सर्वान्भोक्ष्यन्ते गुप्तवंशजाः॥

This account is the most explicit, and, probably, most accurate, of all. The Nákas were Rajas of Bhagulpoor; the Nágas,†† of Mathurá; and the intermediate countries, along the Ganges,‡‡ were governed by the Guptas (or Rajas of the Vaiśya caste).

* See note ‡, below.

† For a peculiar reading of this passage, on the warrant of two MSS. consulted by the Reverend Dr. Mill, making the Magadhas and the Guptas rulers over the Mágadhas, see the *Journal of the Asiatic Society of Bengal*, 1837, p. 10.

‡ The natural sense of these last words is: "The Mágadhas and the Guptas will rule over Prayága on the Ganges." Any place at the confluence of sacred rivers may be called Prayága.

§ In Colonel Wilford's MS. excerpts, the text yields Padmávati, with which the *Brahmáńda-puráńa* agrees.

‖ Mennas, according to Colonel Wilford's extracts. And here, again, the *Brahmáńda-puráńa* has the same reading.

¶ According to the Sanskrit, "the Magadhas".

** साकेतं, in three copies of the *Váyu-puráńa*.

†† For the situation of the kingdom of the Nágas, see the *Journal of the Asiatic Society of Bengal*, 1865, Part I., pp. 116, 117.

‡‡ See note ‡, above.

will reign, in a city on the sea-shore, over the Kosalas,

The Bhágavata* seems to have taken great liberties with the account; as it makes Viśwasphúrti king over Anugangá,—the course of the Ganges from Hurdwar† (according to the commentator,) to Prayága,—residing at Padmavati:‡

वीर्यवान्क्षत्रमुत्साद्य पद्मवत्यां स वै पुरि।
अनुगंगामाप्रयागं गुप्तां भोक्ष्यति मेदिनीम् ॥§

omitting the Nágas altogether, and converting 'gupta' into an epithet of 'medini',—"the preserved (or protected) earth." Wilford‖ considers the Nágas, Nákas, and Guptas to be, all, the same. He says: "Then came a dynasty of nine kings, called the nine Nágas, or Nákas. These were an obscure tribe, called, for that reason, Guptavaṁśas. There were nine families of them, who ruled, independent of each other, over various districts in Anugangá, such as Padmávatí," &c. &c. That city he calls Patna; but, in the Málati and Mádhava,¶ Padmávatí lies amongst the Vindhya hills. Kántipurí he makes Cotwal, near Gwalior. The reading of the Váyu, Champávatí, however, obviates the necessity of all vague conjecture. According to Wilford, there is a powerful tribe, still called Nákas, between the Jumna and the Betwa.** Of the existence and power of the Guptas, however, we have recently had ample proofs, from inscriptions and coins, as in the Chandragupta and Samudragupta of the Allahabad column (Journal of the Asiatic Society of Bengal, March and June, 1834), and Kumáragupta, Chandragupta, Samudragupta, Śaśigupta, &c., on the Archer coins, found at Kanauj and elsewhere (Asiatic Re-

* XII., I., 35.

† The commentator has Gangádwára.

‡ The same as Padmávatí. This the Translator had; but I have corrected it as above.

§ For a previous translation of this stanza and its preceding context, with remarks thereon, by the Reverend Dr. Mill, see the *Journal of the Asiatic Society of Bengal*, 1837, pp. 16, 17.

‖ *Asiatic Researches*, Vol. IX., pp. 114, 116.

¶ See Professor Wilson's *Select Specimens of the Theatre of the Hindus*, Vol. II., p. 95, note †.

** Colonel Wilford's words are: "on the banks of the Jumná and the Betwá-nadí."

Oḋras,* Puńḋrakas,† and Támraliptas.[1]‡ The Guhas§ will possess Kalinga,|| Máhishaka,¶ and the

searches, Vol. XVII., pl. I., fig. 5, 7, 15, 19; and Journal of the Asiatic Society of Bengal, November 1835, pl. 38 and 39; and in other numbers of the same Journal), in all which, the character in which the legends are written is of a period prior to the use of the modern Devanágarí, and was current, in all probability, about the fifth century of our era, as conjectured by Mr. Prinsep. See his table of the modifications of the Sanskrit alphabet from 543 B. C. to 1200 A. D.: Journal of the Asiatic Society of Bengal, March, 1838.

[1] The Váyu also mentions the descendants of Devarakshita, (or Daivarakshitas), as kings of the Kośalas, Támralipta, and the sea-coast;** so far conforming with our text, as to include the

* The compound in which these names are combined allows of our reading either Oḋras or Auḋras. One MS. yields Udras.

† Some MSS. omit this people. One copy yields Pauńḋrakas.

‡ Most of my MSS. have कोशलौड्रपुण्ड्रताम्रलिप्तसमुद्रतटपुरीं च, which implies "a city on the sea-shore", in addition to the Kośalas, &c. But some copies give, instead of -पुरीं, 'city," -पर्यन्तां, which extends the dominion of Devarakshita as far as the sea-coast.

§ The only grammatical reading that I find—and it occurs in only one MSS.,—is as follows: कलिङ्गमाहिषकमाहेन्द्रभौमा गुहा भोक्ष्यन्ति; which makes the rulers Guhas of Bhauma (?). This is, however, extremely doubtful. My copies of the *Váyu-puráńa* have Guha, in the singular; as if a person were intended. In the *Mahábhárata*, *Śánti-parvan*, *ll.* 7559, we read of the Guhas, a nation in the south of India, who, possibly, took their name from Guha, prince of the Nishádas, a friend of Ráma.

I have nowhere found a lection answering to Professor Wilson's "mountains of Mahendra". The *Váyu-puráńa* has महेन्द्रनिलयान् ।

|| Corrected from "Kálinga".

¶ Corrected from "Máhibaka". Máhishmas, according to one MS. The *Váyu-puráńa* has the short form, Máhishas.

** The *Váyu-puráńa* has more, in all my copies. Its reading seems to be:

कोशलांश्चान्ध्रपौण्ड्रांश्च ताम्रलिप्तान्ससागरान् ।

We are to add, then, the Andhras and the Pauńḋras. For the Andhras,

mountains of Máhendra.[1] * The race of Mańidhána † will occupy the countries of the Naishádas,: Naimishikas, and Kálatoyas.[2] The people called Kanakas §

---

western parts of Bengal, Tumlook, Medinipoor, and Orissa. One copy reads Andhra, perhaps for Odra, Orissa; and one has Champá,|| for the capital, which is, probably, an error, although the two other MSS., being still more faulty, do not offer the means of correction.

[1] The Váyu has the same. The countries are parts of Orissa and Berar.

[2] The Váyu has sons of Mańidhánya for the ruling dynasty, but names the countries those of the Naishadhas, Yudakas,¶ Śaiśikas,** and Kálatoyakas.†† The first name applies to a tract of country near the Vindhya mountains, but the last, to a country in the north.‡‡ The west or southwest, however, is, probably, intended, in this place.

---

see Vol. II., p. 170, note ‡, and p. 184, note †; also, p. 189, note 4, and p. 205, note 1, *supra*: for the Pauńdras, Vol. II., p. 177, note ††, and p. 184, note †. Puńdra, whence the Pauńdras are supposed to have originated, is mentioned in p. 122, *supra*.

It is most probable that the people spoken of along with the Pauńdras or Pauńdrakas, in the *Laws of the Mánavas* and in the *Mahábhárata*, are the Andhras, not the Andras.

* Corrected from "Mahendra".

† Corrected from "Mańidhana". One MS. has Mańidhányaka; one, Mańidháva; several, Mańidhára, the name in Professor Wilson's Hindu-made translation. The *Brahmáńda-puráńa* has Máladhánya.

‡ Corrected from "Nishádas". § Káuas, according to one MS.

|| So read three of my MSS.; the rest having something very different, but illegible.

¶ Padukas or Pudakas, according to my MSS. The *Brahmáńda-puráńa*, in Colonel Wilford's manuscript extract from it, has Padumas.

** Agreeably to different MSS., these people are called Śalmikas, Śaliśinas, Śaliśitas, and Śausitas. See Vol. II., p. 177, text and note *.

†† After the passage, in the *Brahmáńda-puráńa*, corresponding to this, there is, evidently, a considerable hiatus in Colonel Wilford's MS. extract.

‡‡ See Vol. II., p. 165, note 5.

will possess the Amazon country* and that called Múshika.[1]† Men of the three tribes, but degraded, and Ábhíras and Śúdras, will occupy Śauráshtra, Avanti, Śúra, Arbuda, and Marubhúmi;‡ and Śúdras, outcastes, and barbarians will be masters of the banks

---

[1] The Strí Rájya is, usually, placed§ in Bhote. It may, perhaps, here designate Malabar, where polyandry equally prevails. Múshika, or the country of thieves, was the pirate-coast of the Konkan. The Váyu reads Bhokshyaka (or Bhokhyaka) for Múshika:

स्त्रीराज्यं भोक्षकांश्च भोक्ष्यन्ति जनपदांस्तथा । ||

The Bhágavata omits all these specifications subsequent to the notice of Viśwasphúrti.

---

* *Strí-rájya.* But one of my copies has Trairájya.

† According to one MS., the people here spoken of are the Bhúshikas; and so read some copies of the *Mahábhárata*, where Professor Wilson found Múshikas. See Vol. II., p. 178.

‡ I find nothing to justify this rendering. The ordinary reading, as known to me, is as follows: सौराष्ट्रावन्तिशूद्रानर्बुदमरुभूमिविषयांश्च व्रात्याद्विजाभीरशूद्राद्या भोक्ष्यन्ति । "Outcastes, unregenerate *tribes*, Ábhíras, Śúdras, and such others will govern the Sauráshtras, the Avantis, and the Śúdras, and the regions of Arbuda and Marubhúmi."

Several of my best MSS. yield, instead of Śúdras, as the name of a nation, Śúras. Both the Śúdras and the Śúras are found mentioned in association with the Ábhíras. See Vol. II., p. 133, note *; p. 184, note 1; and p. 185, notes § and *; also, p. 224, *infra*, note ‡.

After the Śúdras—the nation so called,—a single copy introduces the Ábhíras; and another copy has 'mountaineers', *adrija*, in lieu of 'unregenerate *tribes*', *adwija*.

Ábhíra, equally with Śúdra, denotes a caste, as well as a people.

Sauráshtra—for which the Translator's "Śaurashtra" must be exchanged, in order to obtain a recognized word,—cannot be substituted for Suráshtra, whence Surat.

§ By whom?

|| This verse, as thus given, is of extremely doubtful correctness, in its second half. The words in my MSS. were, apparently, corrupted from something different.

The *Váyu-puráńa* here concludes its specification of peoples and tribes.

of the Indus, Dárvika, the Chandrabhágá, and Kásmíra.[1*]

[1] From this we might infer that the Vishńu Puráńa was compiled when the Mohammedans were making their first encroachments on the west. They seem to have invaded, and to have settled, in Sindh early in the eighth century, although Indian princes continued on the Indus for a subsequent period: Scriptor. Arab. de Rebus Indicis, Gildemeister, p. 6. They were engaged in hostilities, in 698 or 700, with the prince of Kabul, in whose name, however disguised by its Mohammedan representations of Ratil, Ratbal, or Ratibal,† it is not difficult to recognize the genuine Hindu appellation of Ratanpál or Ratnapála. Their progress in this direction has not been traced; but, at the period of their invasion of Sindh, they advanced to Multan, and, probably, established themselves there, and at Lahore, within a century. Cashmere they did not occupy till a much later date; and the Rája Tarangińí takes no notice of any attacks upon it. But the Chinese have recorded an application from the king of Cashmere, Chin-tho-lo-pi-li,—evidently the Chandrápída of the Sanskrit,—for aid against the Arabs, about A. D. 713: Gildemeister, p. 13. Although, therefore, not actually settled at the Punjab so early as the beginning, they had commenced their incursions, and had,

* The ordinary reading is: सिन्धुतटदार्विकोर्वीचन्द्रभागाकाश्मीरविषयान्व्रात्या म्लेच्छादयः शूद्रा भोक्ष्यन्ति । "Unregenerate *tribes*, barbarians, and other Śúdras will rule over the banks of the Indus, and the regions of the Dárviká, of the Chandrabhágá, and of Kásmíra."

One of my MSS. has, instead of -दार्विको°, -पर्वतो°. On this reading, we must translate: "the regions of the Chandrabhágá and of Kásmíra, as far as the banks of the Indus."

My best copies of the commentary have the following: दार्विकोर्वी । देविकातटवर्त्ता भूमिः । The Dárviká river is, thus, identified with the Deviká. For the Deviká, see Vol. II., p. 144, text, and note 4; and p. 147, notes 2 and †.

The Translator's "Dárvika", so far as I know, is nothing.

† Dr. Gildemeister does not appear to have found the last two variants here given.

These will, all, be contemporary monarchs, reigning over the earth;—kings of churlish spirit, violent tem-

no doubt, made good their footing, by the end, of the eighth, or commencement of the ninth, century. This age of the Puráńa is compatible with reference to the contemporary race of Gupta kings, from the fourth or fifth to the seventh or eighth century:* or, if we are disposed to go further back, we may apply the passage to the Greek and Indo-Scythian princes. It seems more likely to be the former period; but, in all such passages, in this or other Puráńas, there is the risk that verses inspired by the presence of Mohammedan rulers may have been interpolated into the original text. Had the Mohammedans of Hindusthán, however, been intended by the latter, the indications would have been more distinct, and the localities assigned to them more central. Even the Bhágavata, the date of which we have good reason for conjecturing to be the middle of the twelfth century, and which influenced the form assumed, about that time, by the worship of Vishńu, cannot be thought to refer to the Mohammedan conquerors of Upper India. It is there stated that "rulers fallen from their castes, or Śúdras, will be the princes of Sauráshtra, Avanti, Ábhíra, Śúra, Arbuda, and Málava;† and barbarians, Śúdras, and other outcastes, not enlightened by the Vedas, will possess Kásmíra, Kaunti, and the banks of the Chandrabhágá and Indus:"

सौराष्ट्रावन्त्याभीराश्च शूराः अर्बुदमालवाः ।
व्रात्याद्विजा भविष्यन्ति शूद्रप्राया जनाधिपाः ॥
सिन्धोस्तटं चन्द्रभागां कौन्तीं काश्मीरमण्डलम् ।
भोक्ष्यन्ति शूद्रा व्रात्याद्या म्लेच्छाश्चाब्रह्मवर्चसः ॥

Now, it was not until the fourteenth and fifteenth centuries that the Mohammedans established themselves in Gujerat and Malwa; and the Bhágavata was, unquestionably, well known, in various

* This position is not yet established.

† Peoples, not countries, are intended in the original. For "Sauráshṭra", *vide supra*, p. 222, note ‡, *ad finem*.

‡ I find, now, that शूद्रा, is the more ordinary reading. See Vol. II., p. 133, note *.

per, and ever addicted to falsehood and wickedness. They will inflict death on women, children, and cows; they will seize upon the property of their subjects;* they will be of limited power, and will, for the most part, rapidly rise and fall: their lives will be short, their desires insatiable; and they will display but little piety. The people of the various countries intermingling with them will follow their example; and, the barbarians being powerful in the patronage of the princes, whilst purer tribes are neglected, the people will perish.[1] Wealth and piety will decrease day by day,

parts of India, long before that time. (Account of Hindu Sects, Asiatic Researches, Vol. XVI.†) It cannot, therefore, allude to Mohammedans. By specifying the princes as seceders from the Vedas, there is no doubt that the barbarians and outcastes intended are so only in a religious sense; and we know, from indisputable authorities, that the western countries, Gujerat, Ábu, Málava, were the chief seats, first of the Buddhists, and, then, of the Jainas, from a period commencing, perhaps, before the Christian era, and scarcely terminating with the Mohammedan conquest. Inscriptions from Ábu; Asiatic Researches, Vol. XVI.

[1] The commentator, having, no doubt, the existing state of things in view, interprets the passage somewhat differently. The original is: तैश्च विमिश्रा जनपदास्तच्छीलवर्तिनो राजाश्रयशुष्मिणो म्लेच्छाचार्याश्च‡ विपर्ययेण वर्तमानाः प्रजाः क्षपयिष्यन्ति। The comment explains शुष्मिणः 'strong' (बलिनः), and adds: 'the Mlechchhas will be in the centre, and the Áryas, at the end:' म्लेच्छा मध्ये चार्याश्चान्ते इत्येतत्सूचेय; meaning, if any thing, that

* परस्वादानरुचयः। There is a variant, परस्वदारपराः, "intent on the wives of others."

† Or Professor Wilson's collected Works, Vol. 1.

‡ Two of my MSS., unaccompanied by the commentary, have म्लेच्छाचाराश्च, and, at the end of the passage extracted, क्षयमेष्यन्ति।

until the world will be wholly depraved.* Then property alone will confer rank; wealth will be the only

---

the unbelievers are in the heart of the country, and the Hindus, on the borders;—a description, however, never correct, except as applicable to the governments, and, in that case, inconsistent with the text, which had, previously, represented the bordering countries in the hands of outcastes and heretics. All that the text intends is, to represent infidels and foreigners high in power, and the Brahmans depressed. It is not unlikely that the reading is erroneous,—notwithstanding the copies concur,—and that the passage should be, here, the same as that of the Váyu:

तैर्विमिश्रा जनपदा म्लेच्छाचाराश्च सर्वशः ।
विपर्ययेण वर्तन्ते नाशयिष्यन्ति वै प्रजाः ॥ †

"Intermixed with them, the nations, adopting, everywhere, barbaric institutions, exist in a state of disorder; and the subjects shall be destroyed;" the expression Mlechchháchárás cha‡ being used instead of Mlechchhás cháryás cha. A passage similar to that of the text—noticing the intermixture of Hindus and barbarians,—occurs in a different place (see Vol. II., p. 190, note 1§), and designates the condition of India in all ages. At no period has the whole of the population followed Brahmanical Hinduism.

---

* ततश्चानुदिनमल्पाल्पह्रासाद्व्यवच्छेदाद्धर्मार्थयोर्जगतः संक्षयो भविष्यति ।

† The *Matsya-puráńa* has:

तैर्विमिश्रा जनपदा आर्या म्लेच्छाश्च सर्वशः ।
विपर्ययेण वर्तन्ते क्षयमेष्यन्ति वै प्रजाः ॥

Herewith, as to the words आर्या म्लेच्छाः,—or आर्यम्लेच्छाः, as most MSS. of the *Matsya-puráńa* read,—agrees the *Brahmáńda-puráńa*, as known to me. One of my copies of the *Váyu-puráńa*, too, has आर्यम्लेच्छाः ।

‡ And such appears to have been the reading of our Puráńa, before its text was tampered with by the commentator. See note ‡ in the preceding page.

§ With reference to the verse there quoted, see note †, above, at the end.

source of devotion; passion will be the sole bond of union between the sexes; falsehood will be the only means of success in litigation; and women will be objects merely of sensual gratification. Earth will be venerated but for its mineral treasures;[1]* the Brahmanical thread will constitute a Brahman; external types (as the staff and red garb,†) will be the only distinctions of the several orders of life;‡ dishonesty§ will be the (universal) means of subsistence; weakness will be the cause of dependence; menace and presumption will be substituted for learning;¶ liberality will be devotion;** simple ablution will be purification;[2]†† mutual assent will be marriage; fine clothes

[1] That is, there will be no Tirthas,—places held sacred, and objects of pilgrimage; no particular spot of earth will have any especial sanctity.

[2] Gifts will be made from the impulse of ordinary feeling, not in connexion with religious rites, and as an act of devotion; and ablution will be performed for pleasure or comfort, not religiously, with prescribed ceremonies and prayers.

* रत्नाद्यभानितैव पृथिवीहेतुः। The Translator's explanation of these words is taken from the commentary.

† This explanation is supplied by the Translator.

‡ लिङ्गधारणमेवाश्रमहेतुः।

§ *Anyáya.*

|| *Avriti*, 'protection,' 'security.'

¶ भयगर्भोच्चारणमेव पाण्डित्यहेतुः।

** The original adds आढ्यतैव साधुत्वहेतुः, implying, that a man, if rich, will be reputed pure.

†† स्नानमेव प्रसाधनहेतुः। This seems to mean, that mere bathing will pass for a complete toilette.

will be dignity;[1] and water afar off will be esteemed a holy spring.* Amidst all castes, he who is the strongest will reign over a principality† thus vitiated by many faults. The people, unable to bear the heavy burthens‡ imposed upon them by their avaricious sovereigns, will take refuge amongst the valleys of the mountains, and will be glad to feed upon (wild) honey, herbs, roots, fruits, leaves, and flowers: their only covering will be the bark of trees; and they will be exposed to the cold, and wind, and sun, and rain. No man's life will exceed three and twenty years. Thus, in the Kali age, shall decay constantly proceed, until the human race approaches its annihilation.

When the practices taught by the Vedas and the institutes of law shall nearly have ceased, and the close of the Kali age shall be nigh, a portion of that divine being who exists, of his own spiritual nature, in the character of Brahma, and who is the beginning and the end, and who comprehends all things, shall descend upon earth: he will be born in the family of

---

[1] The expression Sad-veśa-dhárin (सद्वेशधारिन्) is explained to mean either one who wears fine clothes, or who assumes the exterior garb of sanctity.§ Either interpretation is equally allowable.

---

* "Holy spring" is to render *tírtha*.

† *Bhú-maṇḍala*, 'the earth.'

‡ The original has *kara-bhára*, 'load of taxes.'

§ The commentator confines himself to explaining the term by *dámbhika*, 'a hypocrite.'

Vishńuyaśas,—an eminent Brahman of Sambhala* village,—as Kalki, endowed with the eight superhuman faculties. By his irresistible might he will destroy all the Mlechchhas and thieves, and all whose minds are devoted to iniquity. He will, then, reestablish righteousness upon earth; and the minds of those who live at the end of the Kali age shall be awakened, and shall be as pellucid as crystal. The men who are, thus, changed by virtue of that peculiar time shall be as the seeds of human beings, and shall give birth to a race who shall follow the laws of the Kŕita age (or age of purity). As it is said: "When the sun and moon, and (the lunar asterism) Tishya,† and the planet Jupiter are in one mansion, the Kŕita age shall return."[1]‡

Thus, most excellent Muni, the kings who are past, who are present, and who are to be, have been enumerated. From the birth of Parikshit to the coronation of Nanda it is to be known that 1015 years have

---

[1] The Bhágavata agrees§ with the text, in these particulars. The chief star of Tishya is δ in the constellation Cancer.||

---

* Called Śambhala, in the *Bhágavata-purána*, XII., II., 18. Neither the family of Vishńuyaśas nor the village of Kalki is specified in the *Váyu-purána*, the *Matsya-purána*, and the *Brahmáńda-purána*.

† More commonly denominated Pushya.

‡ The whole of this paragraph is condensed, or loosely rendered; and the same remark holds good as to the rest of the chapter.

§ It corresponds almost literally: XII., II., 24. A similar stanza is found in the *Váyu-purána* and in the *Brahmáńda-purána*.

|| See Colebrooke's *Miscellaneous Essays*, Vol. II., table opposite p. 323.

elapsed.[1*] When the two first stars of the seven

---

[1] All the copies concur in this reading:

यावत्परिक्षितो जन्म यावन्नन्दाभिषेचनम् ।
एतद्वर्षसहस्रं तु ज्ञेयं पञ्चदशोत्तरम् ॥

Three copies of the Váyu assign to the same interval 1050 years,

---

* We read, in the *Bhágavata-puráńa*, XII., II., 26—32:

आरभ्य भवतो जन्म यावन्नन्दाभिषेचनम् ।
एतद्वर्षसहस्रं तु शतं पञ्चदशोत्तरम् ॥
सप्तर्षीणां तु यौ पूर्वौ दृश्येते उदितौ दिवि ।
तयोस्तु मध्ये नक्षत्रं दृश्यते यत्समं निशि ॥
तेनैव ऋषयो युक्तास्तिष्ठन्त्यब्दशतं नृणाम् ।
ते त्वदीये द्विजाः काल अधुना चाश्रिता मघाः ॥
विष्णोर्भगवतो भानुः कृष्णाख्योऽसौ दिवं गतः ।
तदाविशत्कलिर्लोकं पापे यद्रमते जनः ॥
यावत्स पादपद्माभ्यां स्पृशन्नास्ते रमापतिः ।
तावत्कलिर्वै पृथिवीं पराक्रान्तुं न चाशकत् ॥
यदा देवर्षयः सप्त मघासु विचरन्ति हि ।
तदा प्रवृत्तस्तु कलिर्द्वादशाब्दशतात्मकः ॥
यदा मघाभ्यो यास्यन्ति पूर्वाषाढां महर्षयः ।
तदा नन्दात्प्रभृत्येष कलिर्वृद्धिं गमिष्यति ॥

"From your birth [Parikshit is addressed by Śuka,] to the inauguration of Nanda, 1115 years will elapse.

"Of the seven Ŕishis two are first perceived rising in the sky; and the asterism which is observed to be, at night, even with the middle of those two stars is that with which the Ŕishis are united; and they remain so during a hundred years of men In your time, and at this moment, they are situated in Maghá.

"When the splendour of Vishńu, named Kŕishńa, departed for heaven, then did the Kali age, during which men delight in sin, invade the world. So long as he continued to touch the earth with his holy feet, so long the Kali age was unable to subdue the world.

"When the seven Ŕishis were in Maghá, the Kali age, comprising 1200 [divine] years [432.000 common years], began; and, when, from Maghá, they shall reach Púrváshádhá, then will this Kali age attain its growth, under Nanda and his successors."

This rendering is by Colebrooke, and will be found in his *Miscellaneous Essays*, Vol. II., pp. 356, 357; or *Asiatic Researches*, Vol. IX., p. 359.

Rishis (the great Bear) rise in the heavens, and some

पञ्चाशदुत्तरं; and of the Matsya five copies have the same, पञ्चाशदुत्तरं, or 1050 years, whilst one copy has 1500 years, पञ्चशतोत्तरम्।* The Bhágavata† has 1115 years:

एतद्वर्षसहस्रं तु शतं पञ्चदशोत्तरम्।

which the commentator explains, "a thousand years and a hundred with fifteen over": वर्षसहस्रं पञ्चदशोत्तरं शतं च। He notices, nevertheless,—although he does not attempt to account for the discrepancy,—that the total period from Parikshit to Nanda was, actually, according to the duration of the different intermediate dynasties, as enumerated by all the authorities, fifteen centuries; viz.:

Magadha kings	1000 years.
Pradyota, &c.	138
Śiśunága, &c.	362
	1500 years.

The shorter period is best proportioned to the number of kings; for, reckoning from Sahadeva, (who was contemporary with Parikshit), and taking the number of the Bárhadrathas from the Matsya,‡ we have thirty-two of them, five of the Pradyota race,§ and ten Śaiśunágas;‖ or, in all, forty-seven, which, as the divisor of 1050, gives rather more than twenty-two years to a reign. The Váyu and the Matsya further specify the interval from Nanda to Pulomat (the last of the Andhra kings), as being 836¶ years; a total that does not agree exactly with the items previously specified:

---

* In Colonel Wilford's manuscript extract from the *Brahmáńḍa-puráńa*, the reading is पञ्चदशोत्तरं, thus making the period one of 1015 years.

† See note * in the preceding page.

‡ *Vide supra*, p. 177, note 1.

§ *Vide supra*, p. 178.

‖ *Vide supra*, p. 182.

¶ The *Matsya-puráńa* and the *Brahmáńḍa-puráńa* seem to say so; but, in all my five copies of the *Váyu-puráńa*, there is the word प्रमाणं, where Professor Wilson finds mention of Pulomat.

lunar asterism is seen at night at an equal distance between them, then the seven Rishis continue station-

9	Nandas	100 years.
10	Mauryas	137
10	Śungas	112
4	Kańwas	45
29	Andhras	460
62		854 years.

In either case, the average duration of reign is not improbable; as the highest number gives less than fourteen years to each prince. It is important to remember that the reign of Parikshit is, according to Hindu chronology, coeval with the commencement of the Kali age; and, even, therefore, taking the longest Pauráńik interval, we have but sixteen centuries between Chandragupta,—or, considering him as the same with Sandrocoptos, nineteen centuries B. C.,—for the beginning of the Kali age. According to the chronology of our text, however, it would be but B. C. 1415; to that of the Váyu and Matsya, B. C. 1450; and to that of the Bhágavata, 1515. According to Colonel Wilford's computations (Asiatic Researches, Vol. IX., Chronological Table, p. 116), the conclusion of the Great War took place B. C. 1370. Buchanan conjectures it to have occurred in the thirteenth century B. C. Vyása was the putative father of Páńdu and Dhritarásht́ra,* and, consequently, was contemporary with the heroes of the Great War. Mr. Colebrooke† infers, from astronomical data, that the arrangement of the Vedas, attributed to Vyása, took place in the fourteenth century B. C. Mr. Bentley brings the date of Yudhisht́hira, the chief of the Páńdavas, to 575 B. C. (Historical View of the Hindu Astronomy, p. 67); but the weight of authority is in favour of the thirteenth or fourteenth century

* *Vide supra*, p. 158.

† *Miscellaneous Essays*, Vol. I., pp. 109, 110, and pp. 200—202. Also see an extract from a searching and critical article by Professor Whitney, quoted in the present work, Vol. II., pp. 273—275.

ary, in that conjunction, for a hundred years of men.[1] At the birth of Parikshit, they were in Maghá; and the Kali age then commenced, which consists of 1200 (divine) years. When the portion of Vishńu (that had been born from Vasudeva) returned to heaven, then

B. C., for the war of the Mahábhárata, and the reputed commencement of the Kali age.

[1] A similar explanation is given in the Bhágavata,* Váyu, and Matsya Puráńas; and like accounts, from astronomical writers, are cited by Mr. Colebrooke (Asiatic Researches, Vol. IX., p. 358). † The commentator on the Bhágavata thus explains the notion: "The two stars (Pulaha and Kratu,) must rise or be visible before the rest; and whichever asterism is in a line south from the middle of those stars is that with which the seven stars are united; and so they continue for one hundred years."‡ Colonel Wilford has, also, given a like explanation of the revolution of the Ṛishis (Asiatic Researches, Vol. IX., p. 83). According to Bentley, the notion originated in a contrivance of the astronomers to show the quantity of the precession of the equinoxes: "This was by assuming an imaginary line, or great circle, passing through the poles of the ecliptic and the beginning of the fixed Maghá, which circle was supposed to cut some of the stars in the Great Bear. * * * *. The seven stars in the Great Bear being called the Ṛishis, the circle so assumed was called the line of the Ṛishis; and, being invariably fixed to the beginning of the lunar asterism Maghá, the precession would be noted by stating the degree &c. of any moveable lunar mansion cut by that fixed line or circle, as an index." Historical View of the Hindu Astronomy, p. 65.

* *Vide supra*, p. 230, note *.

† Or *Miscellaneous Essays*, Vol. II., p. 355.

‡ These are, mostly, Colebrooke's own words, a little altered. The Sanskrit is very much fuller. See the *Asiatic Researches*, Vol. IX., p. 360; or *Miscellaneous Essays*, Vol. II., p. 357.

the Kali age commenced. As long as the earth was touched by his sacred feet, the Kali age could not affect it. As soon as the incarnation* of the eternal Vishńu had departed, the son of Dharma,—Yudhishṭhira,†—with his brethren,‡ abdicated the sovereignty. Observing unpropitious portents, consequent upon Kŕishńa's disappearance, he placed Parikshit upon the throne. When the seven Rishis are in Púrváshádhá, then Nanda will begin to reign;[1] and thenceforward the influence of the Kali will augment.§

---

[1] The Bhágavata has the same; and this agrees with the period assigned for the interval between Parikshit and Nanda, of 1050 years; as, including Maghá, we have ten asterisms to Púrváshádhá, or 1000 years. The Váyu and Matsya are so very inaccurate, in all the copies consulted, that it is not safe to affirm what they mean to describe.‖ Apparently, they state, that, at the end of the Andhra dynasty, the Ŕishis will be in Kŕittiká, which furnishes other ten asterisms; the whole being nearly in accordance with the chronology of the text; as the total interval from Parikshit to the last of the Andhras is 1050 + 836 = 1886; and the entire century of each asterism, at the beginning and end of the series, need not be taken into account. The copies of the Matsya read:

---

* *Amśa.*

† *Vide supra*, pp. 102 and 159.

‡ Read "younger brethren", the original being अनुजैः ।

§ प्रयास्यन्ति यदा चैते पूर्वाषाढां महर्षयः ।
तदा नन्दात्प्रभृत्येष कलिर्वृद्धिं गमिष्यति ॥

‖ The interesting passages thus referred to, consisting of some ten stanzas in each Puráńa, and of about as many in the *Brahmáńḍa-puráńa*, are so extremely corrupt, in all my MSS., that I am unable to cite them. Specimens of what I find in my copies will be seen in notes in the two following pages.

The day that Kṛishṅa shall have departed from the earth will be the first of the Kali age, the duration of

---

सप्तर्षयस्तदा प्राहुः प्रदीप्तेनाग्निना * समम् ।

"The seven Ṛishis are on a line with the brilliant Agoi;" that is, with Kṛittiká, of which Agni is the presiding deity.† The Váyu intends, in all probability, the same phrase; but the three copies have प्रतीपे राज्ञि,‡ a very unintelligible clause. Again, it seems as if they intended to designate the end of the Andhra race as the period of a complete revolution, or 2700 years; for the Váyu has:

सप्तविंशैः शते भविष्या अन्ध्राणान्तेऽन्वया पुनः ।§

"The races at the end of the Andhras will be after 2700 years." The Matsya has:

सप्तविंशतिः भाव्येन अन्ध्राणान्तेऽन्वयात् (?) पुनः ।||

---

* Corrected, on the authority of all my MSS., from प्रदीप्ताग्निना, which breaks the metre.

† Whence Kṛittiká has Ágneya as a synonym. See Vol. II., p. 277, *ad calcem*.

‡ The text of the *Váyu-puráńa* is, evidently, somewhat corrupt hereabouts; but, in the context of the passage from which these words are taken, the computations are retrograde. Thus, we read:

महापद्माभिषेकात्तु जन्म यावत्परिक्षितः ।
एतद्वर्षसहस्रं तु ज्ञेयं पञ्चाशदुत्तरम् ॥

All my MSS. have, to be sure, at the beginning of this stanza, महा-देवाभिषेकात् । But the *Matsya-puráńa* and the *Brahmáńḍa-puráńa* furnish the restoration of what is, without question, the true lection.

§ This line is immetrical and ungrammatical, and says nothing of "the end of the Andhras". My best MSS. have:

सप्तविंशैः शतैर्भाव्या अन्ध्राणां तेऽन्वयाः पुनः ।

The corresponding verse of the *Brahmáńḍa-puráńa* is, in my sole copy, crowded with mistakes of transcription

|| I can but partially amend this incorrect verse by the aid of my MSS. One of them ends it with अन्ध्राणां त्वन्वयः पुनः । The *Brahmáńḍa-puráńa* gives, at its close: तेऽन्वयः पुनः । Compare the reading in the note immediately preceding.

which you shall hear: it will continue for 360.000 years of mortals. After twelve hundred divine years shall have elapsed, the Kŕita age shall be renewed.

Thus, age after age, Brahmans, Kshattriyas, Vaiśyas, and Śúdras, excellent Brahman, men of great souls, have passed away by thousands, whose names, and

---

And, at the close of the passage, after specifying, as usual, that "the seven Ŕishis were in Maghá, in the time of Parikshit":

सप्तर्षयो मघायुक्ताः काले परीक्षिते शते * ।

the Váyu adds:

अन्ध्रान्ते स चतुर्विंशे भविष्यन्ति च ते मताः † ।

a passage which, though repeated in the MSS., is, obviously, most inaccurate; although it might, perhaps, be understood to intimate that the Ŕishis will be in the twenty-fourth asterism after the Andhra race: but that would give only 1400 years from Parikshit to Pulomat; whilst, if the twenty-fourth from Maghá was intended, it would give 2400 years; both periods being incompatible with previous specifications. The Matsya has a different reading of the second line, but one not much more satisfactory:

ब्राह्मणास्तु चतुर्विंशे भविष्यन्ति शतं समाः ।

"A hundred years of Brahmá will be in the twenty-fourth (asterism?)." In neither of these authorities, however, is it proposed, by the last-cited passages, to illustrate the chronology of princes or dynasties. The specification of the period, whatever it may be, is that of the era at which the evil influence of the Kali age is to become most active and irresistible.

---

* All my MSS. have पारिक्षिते; and शतं ends the verse, in one of them. So, perhaps, the *Matsya-puráńa* is intended to read; and so the *Váyu-puráńa* and the *Brahmáńda-puráńa* actually do read, according to my copies.

† शतं समाः is, probably, the correct reading of the end of this verse. My best MSS. give, at its beginning, अन्ध्रांशे ।

tribes, and families I have not enumerated to you, from their great number, and the repetition of appellations it would involve.* Two persons,—Devápi, of the race of Púru,† and Maru,‡ of the family of Ikshwáku,—through the force of devotion,§ continue alive throughout the whole four ages, residing at the village of Kalápa.|| They will return hither, in the beginning¶ of the Kŕita age, and, becoming members of the family of the Manu, give origin to the Kshattriya dynasties.[1] In this manner, the earth is possessed, through every series of the three first ages,—the Kŕita, Tretá, and Dwápara,—by the sons of the Manu; and some remain in the Kali age, to serve as the rudiments of renewed generations, in the same way as Devápi and Maru are still in existence.**

I have now given you a summary account of the sovereigns of the earth: to recapitulate the whole would be impossible even in a hundred lives. These

---

[1] The Bhágavata has the same; Devápi, as the commentator observes, being the restorer of the Lunar, and Maru, of the Solar, race.

---

* बहुत्वान्नामधेयानां परिसंख्या कुले कुले ।
पुनरुक्तबहुत्वात्तु न मया परिकीर्त्तिताः ॥

† So yield all my MSS.; but we should here read Kuru. *Vide supra*, pp. 148 and 152.

‡ See Vol. III., p. 325.

§ *Yoga*.

|| See Vol. III., p. 197, text and note §.

¶ There is no word, in the Sanskrit, corresponding to this.

** See *Original Sanskrit Texts*, Part I., p. 149 (pp. 277, 278, in the 2nd ed.).

and other kings, who, with perishable frames, have possessed this ever-during world, and who, blinded with deceptive notions of individual occupation, have indulged the feeling that suggests "This earth is mine—it is my son's—it belongs to my dynasty," have, all, passed away. So, many who reigned before them, many who succeeded them, and many who are yet to come, have ceased, or will cease, to be. Earth laughs, as if smiling with autumnal flowers, to behold her kings unable to effect the subjugation of themselves.* I will repeat to you, Maitreya, the stanzas that were chanted by Earth, and which the Muni Asita† communicated to Janaka, whose banner was virtue: "How great is the folly of princes, who are endowed with the faculty of reason, to cherish the confidence of ambition, when they themselves are but foam upon the wave! Before they have subdued themselves, they seek to reduce their ministers, their servants, their subjects, under their authority; they then endeavour to overcome their foes.‡ 'Thus', say they, 'will we conquer the ocean-circled earth', and, intent upon their project, behold not death, which is not far off. But what mighty matter is the subjugation of the sea-girt earth to one who can subdue himself? Emanci-

* विलोक्यात्मजयोद्योगयात्राव्यग्रान्नराधिपान् ।
पुष्पप्रहासैः शरदि हसतीव वसुंधरा ॥

Read "harassed with the enterprise of self-conquest".

† It is not clear who he was. The best known Asita was son of Bharata: *Rámáyańa*, *Bála-káńd́a*, LXX., 27; *Ayodhyá-káńd́a*, CX., 15; &c. See Vol. III., p. 297, note ‡.

‡ पूर्वमात्मजयं कृत्वा जेतुमिच्छन्ति मन्त्रिणः ।
ततो भृत्यांश्च पौरांश्च जिगीषन्ते तथा रिपून् ॥

"They wish, after subduing themselves, to reduce," &c.

pation from existence is the fruit of self-control. It is through infatuation* that kings desire to possess me, whom their predecessors have been forced to leave, whom their fathers have not retained. Beguiled by the selfish love of sway, fathers contend with sons, and brothers with brothers, for my possession.† Foolishness has been the character of every king who has boasted 'All this earth is mine—everything is mine—it will be in my house for ever'; for he is dead. How is it possible that such vain desires should survive in the hearts of his descendants, who have seen their progenitor, absorbed by the thirst of dominion, compelled to relinquish me, whom he called his own, and tread the path of dissolution?‡ When I hear a king sending word to another, by his ambassador, 'This earth is mine; immediately resign (your pretensions to) it,' I am moved to violent laughter, (at first); but it soon subsides, in pity for the infatuated fool."

These were the verses, Maitreya, which Earth recited, and by listening to which, ambition § fades away, like snow before the sun. I have now related to you the whole (account of the) descendants of the Manu, amongst whom have flourished kings endowed with

---

* *Vimúdhatwa.*

† मत्कृते पितृपुत्राणां भ्रातृणां चापि विग्रहाः ।
जायन्तेऽत्यन्तमोहेन ममत्वायतचेतसाम् ॥

‡ दृष्ट्वा ममत्वायतचित्तमेकं
विहाय मां मृत्युपथं व्रजन्तम् ।
तस्यान्वयस्थस्य कथं ममत्वं
हृद्यास्पदं मत्प्रभवं करोति ॥

§ *Mamatwa.*

a portion* of Vishńu, engaged in the preservation of the earth. Whoever shall listen (reverently and) with faith, to this narrative, proceeding from the posterity of Manu, shall be purified entirely from all his sins, and, with the perfect possession of his faculties, shall live in unequalled affluence, plenty, and prosperity. He who has heard of the races of the Sun and Moon, of Ikshwáku, Jahnu, Mándhátŕi,† Sagara, and Raghu, who have, all, perished;‡ of Yayáti, Nahusha, and their posterity, who are no more; of kings of great might, resistless valour, and unbounded wealth, who have been overcome by still more powerful time, and are, now, only a tale; he will learn wisdom, and forbear to call either children, or wife, or house, or lands, or wealth, his own. The arduous penances that have been performed by heroic men obstructing fate for countless years, religious rites and sacrifices of great efficacy and virtue, have been made, by time, the subject only of narration.§ The valiant Pŕithu traversed the universe, everywhere triumphant over his foes; yet he was blown away, like the light down of the Simal||

---

* The original has *aṅśáṅśa*, "a portion of a portion."

† Corrected, here and below, from "Mándhátri".

‡ Read "Sagara, Ávikshita, and the Raghus". The Translator was mistaken in thinking that he found anything answering to "who have, all perished". The original runs:

इक्ष्वाकुजह्नुमान्धातृसगराविक्षितान्रघून् ।

Ávikshita, or the son of Avikshit, was Marutta. See Vol. III., p. 243, and p. 244, note §.

§ तप्तं तपो यैः पुरुषप्रवीरै-
रुद्बाहुभिर्वर्षगणाननेकान् ।
इष्टाश्च यज्ञा बलिनोऽतिवीर्याः
कृतास्तु कालेन कथावशेषाः ॥

|| *Śálmali*, in the original. *Semal* is the Hindi for it.

tree, before the blast of time. He who was Kártavírya subdued innumerable enemies, and conquered the seven zones of the earth; but now he is only the topic of a theme, a subject for affirmation and contradiction.[1] Fie upon the empire of the sons of Raghu, who triumphed over Daśánana,* and extended their sway to the ends of the earth! For was it not consumed, in an instant, by the frown of the destroyer? † Mándhátri, the emperor of the universe, is embodied only in a legend; and what pious man who hears it will ever be so unwise as to cherish the desire of possession ‡ in his soul? Bhagíratha, Sagara, Kakutstha, Daśánana, Ráma, § Lakshmańa, Yudhishthira, and others have been. Is it so? Have they ever really existed? Where are they now? We know not. ‖ The powerful kings

---

[1] To be the cause of Sankalpa, 'conviction,' 'belief,' and Vikalpa, 'doubt,' 'disbelief.' The Bhágavata indulges in a similar strain, and, often, in the same words. The whole recalls the words of the Roman satirist:

> I, demens, et saevas curre per Alpes,
> Ut pueris placeas, et declamatio fias. ¶

---

* Here, again,—see the preceding page, note ‡,—the Translator has strangely misapprehended the original, which speaks of the empire "of Daśánana, Ávikshita, and Rághava":

दशाननाविक्षितराघवाणाम् ।

All my MSS. have this reading, yielding Ávikshita, though Avikshita would equally well suit the metre.

† The original has Antaka, who is one with Yama. See Vol. I., p. 168, note 1; and Vol. II., p. 112, note.

‡ "Desire of possession" is to render *mamatwa*.

§ The Sanskrit has Rághava.

‖ सत्यं न मिथ्या क्व नु ते न विद्मः ।

¶ Juvenal, X., 166, 167.

who now are, or who will be, as I have related them to you, or any others who are unspecified,* are, all, subject to the same fate;† (and the present and the future will perish and be forgotten, like their predecessors).‡ Aware of this truth, a wise man will never be influenced by the principle of individual appropriation; and, regarding them as only transient and temporal possessions, he will not consider children and posterity, lands and property, or whatever else is personal, to be his own.§

---

* *Abhidheyáh.*

† सर्वे भविष्यन्ति यथैव पूर्वे ।

‡ There is nothing, in the Sanskrit, answering to the words which I have here marked off with parentheses.

§ एतद्विदित्वा न नरेण कार्यं
ममत्वमात्मन्यपि पण्डितेन ।
तिष्ठन्तु तावत्तनयात्मजायाः
क्षेत्रादयो ये तु शरीरतोऽन्ये ॥

VISHŃU PURÁŃA.

BOOK V.

CHAPTER I.

The death of Kaṁsa announced. Earth, oppressed by the Daityas, applies to the gods. They accompany her to Vishńu, who promises to give her relief. Kaṁsa imprisons Vasudeva and Devakí. Vishńu's instructions to Yoganidrá.

MAITREYA.[1]—You have related to me a full account of all the different dynasties of kings, and of their

[1] The whole of this Book is dedicated to the biography of Kŕishńa. Many of the Puráńas omit this subject altogether, or only allude to it occasionally. In others, it is equally prominent. The Brahma Puráńa gives the story exactly in the same words as our text. Which has the best right to them may be questioned; but, as it is usually met with, the Brahma Puráńa is a very heterogeneous compilation. The Hari Vaṁśa has a narrative more detailed than that of the text, with additions and embellishments of its own. The Brahma Vaivarta, throughout, celebrates the acts of Kŕishńa; and one portion of it, the Kŕishńa Janma Khańda, especially describes his boyhood and youth. The incidents are the same, in general, as those in the text; but they are lost amidst interminable descriptions of Kŕishńa's sports with the Gopís, and with his mistress Rádhá,—a person not noticed elsewhere: the whole is in a style indicative of a modern origin. The Agni Puráńa and Padma Puráńa (Uttara Káńda) have accounts of Kŕishńa; but they are mere summaries, compiled, evidently, from other works. The principal authority for the adventures of Kŕishńa is the Bhágavata, the tenth Book of which

successive transactions. I wish, now, to hear a more particular description, holy Ŕishi,* of the portion of Vishńu[1] that came down upon earth, and was born in

is exclusively devoted to him. It is this work which has, no doubt, mainly extended the worship of Kŕishńa; as its popularity is evinced by its having been translated into all the spoken languages of India professing to have a literature. The Premságar, its Hindí version, is well known; but there are, also, translations in Maráthí, Telugú, Támil, &c. It does not seem likely, however, that the Vishńu Puráńa has copied the Bhágavata; for, although its greater conciseness may, sometimes, look like abridgment, yet the descriptions are, generally, of a more simple and antiquated character. Here, as usual, the Mahábhárata is, no doubt, the earliest extant authority: but it is not the earliest; for, whilst it omits to narrate most of his personal adventures unconnected with his alliance with the Páńdavas, it often alludes to them, and names, repeatedly, his capital, his wives, and his progeny. It also devotes a section, the Mausala Parvan, to the destruction of the Yádavas. The story of Kŕishńa, the prince and hero, must have been complete, when the Mahábhárata was compiled. It is doubtful, however, if Kŕishńa, the boy, and his adventures at Vŕindávana, were not subsequent inventions. There are no allusions to them, in the poem, of an unsuspicious nature. The only ones that I have met with are contained in a speech by Śiśupála,†—Sabhá Parvan, Vol. I., p. 360,—in which he reviles Kŕishńa; but they may easily have been interpolated. There may be others scattered through the poem; but I have not observed them.

[1] The notices of Kŕishńa's origin and character, in various passages of the Mahábhárata, are by no means consistent, and indicate different dates, at least. In an address to him by Arjuna,—Vana Parvan, Vol. I., p. 426,—he is said to have passed thousands of years in various holy places, engaged in arduous

* *Brahmarshi.* See Vol. III., p. 68, note 1.

† On the passage referred to, see *Original Sanskrit Texts*, Part IV., pp. 170, *et seq.*, and p. 248.

the family of Yadu. Tell me, also, what actions he* performed in his descent as a part of a part of the Supreme, upon the earth.'

---

penances. He is frequently identified with the Ṙishi Náráyańa; or he and Arjuna are said to be Náráyańa and Nara:†

सं देवानां च बीजेषु नरनारायणौ ऋषी ।‡

In the Dána-dharma, he is represented as a worshipper of Śiva, and propitiating him and his wife Umá, and receiving, as boons, from them, wives and children.§ As a warrior and prince, he is always on the scene; but he is, repeatedly, called an Aḿśa (or portion) of Vishńu; whilst, in a great number of places, he is identified with Vishńu or Náráyańa, and is, consequently, 'all things.' This latter is his character, of course, amongst the Vaishńavas, agreeably to the text of the Bhágavata: कृष्णस्तु भगवान्स्वयं, "Kŕishńa is the lord (Vishńu) himself."

' This is a still further diminution of Kŕishńa's dignity: he is not even a part, but 'a part of a part,' Aḿśáḿśávatára (अंशांशावतार). But this, the commentator maintains, is to be understood only of his form or condition as man, not of his power; as it suffered no diminution, either in its primary or secondary state,—as light, by suffusion, suffers no decrease; and a verse of the Veda is cited to this effect: "Though that which is full be taken from what is full, yet the remainder is undiminished:"

पूर्णस्य पूर्णमादाय पूर्णमेवावशिष्यते ।

"Kŕishńa is, nevertheless, the very supreme Brahma; though it be a mystery how the Supreme should assume the form of a man:"

परं ब्रह्म नराकृति परं गूढं परं ब्रह्म ।
मनुष्याकृतिं कृष्णस्तु भगवान्स्वयं . . . ॥¶

* In the original, भगवान्पुरुषोत्तमः, 'the divine Purushottama.'

† See Vol. I., p. 111, note 1; and Vol. III., p. 68, note 1; also, *Original Sanskrit Texts*, Part IV., pp. 192—208.

‡ *Mahábhárata*, *Śánti-parvan*, *sl.* 13165.

§ See *Original Sanskrit Texts*, Part IV., pp. 103, *et seq.*

The first verse of the quotation, as given by the commentator, runs:

पूर्णमदः पूर्णमिदं पूर्णात्पूर्णमुदच्यते ।

This passage is from the *Śatapatha-bráhmańa*, XIV., VIII., 1.

¶ Thus cited by the commentator.

PARÁŚARA.—I will relate to you, Maitreya, the account which you have requested;—the birth of a part of a part of Vishńu, and the benefits which his actions conferred upon the world.*

Vasudeva formerly married the daughter of Devaka, the illustrious Devakí,† a maiden of celestial beauty.‡ After their nuptials, Kaḿsa, the increaser of the race of Bhoja, drove their car, as their charioteer. As they were going along, a voice in the sky, sounding aloud, and deep as thunder, addressed Kaḿsa, and said: "Fool that you are, the eighth child of the damsel whom you are driving in the car shall take away your life."[1]§ On hearing this, Kaḿsa drew his sword, and was about to put Devakí to death; but Vasudeva interposed, saying: "Kill not Devakí, great warrior. Spare her life;

So the Bhágavata,|| in one passage, predicts that the Para-purusha (Purushottama, or Vishńu,) will be born, visibly, in the dwelling of Vasudeva:

वसुदेवगृहे साक्षाद्भगवान्पुरुषः परः ।
जनिष्यते तत्प्रियार्थं संभवन्तु सुरस्त्रियः ॥

[1] The Bhágavata tells the circumstance as in the text. The Hari Vaḿśa makes Nárada apprise Kaḿsa of his danger. Nárada's interposition is not mentioned until afterwards, by our authority. Devakí is the cousin of Kaḿsa. *Vide supra*, p. 98.

---

* विष्णोरंशांशसंभूतिचरितं जगतो हितम् ।

For the original and an improved translation of the present Chapter, from its beginning to this point, see *Original Sanskrit Texts*, Part IV., p. 217. A considerable extract from the commentary, with an English version, will, also, be found in the following pages.

† *Vide supra*, p. 98. ‡ *Devatopamá.*

§ यामेतां वहसे मूढ सह भार्यां रथे स्थिताम् ।
अस्यास्तवाष्टमो गर्भः प्राणानपहरिष्यति ॥

|| X., I., 23. I have completed the stanza.

and I will deliver to you every child that she may bring forth." Appeased by which promise, and relying on the character of Vasudeva, Kaṁsa desisted from the attempt.

At that time, Earth, overburthened by her load, repaired to Mount Meru, to an assembly of the gods, and, addressing the divinities, with Brahmá at their head, related, in piteous accents, all her distress. "Agni," said Earth, "is the progenitor of gold; Súrya, of rays of light.[1] The parent and guide* of me, and of all spheres, is the supreme† Náráyaṅa, who is Brahmá, the lord of the lord of patriarchs: the eldest of the eldest-born; one with minutes and hours;‡ one with time; having form, though indiscrete. This assemblage of yourselves, O gods, is but a part of him. The Suns,§ the Winds, the Saints,|| the Rudras, the Vasus, the Aświns, Fire,¶ the patriarch-creators of the universe, of whom Atri is the first, all are but forms of the mighty and inscrutable** Vishṅu. The

[1] Agni, or fire, refines gold, burns away the dross, according to the commentator. The sun is the lord of the rays of light, or, as the cause of rain and vegetation, the lord of cattle. The phrase is: गवां सूर्यः पतो गुरुः ।

* "Parent and guide" is to render *guru*. *Vandya* is a variant.

† *Guru*.

‡ कलाकाष्ठानिमेषात्मा ।

§ Corrected from "sun"; the original exhibiting the plural. For a similar passage, in which the Suns are spoken of, *vide infra*, p. 258.

|| आदित्या मरुतः साध्याः, "the Ádityas, the Maruts, and the Sádhyas." See Vol. II., pp. 27, 78, 22.

¶ *Vahnayaḥ*; i. e., the Agnis, or 'Fires'. There are forty-nine of them. See Vol. I., p. 156, note 1. Also compare note § to p. 258, *infra*.

** "Mighty and inscrutable" is intended to represent *aprameya*.

Yakshas, Rákshasas, Daityas, spirits of evil,* serpents, and children of Danu, the singers and nymphs of heaven, are forms of the great spirit, Vishńu. The heavens, painted with planets, constellations,† and stars; fire, water, wind, and myself, and every perceptible thing; the whole universe itself, consists of Vishńu. The multifarious forms of that manifold being encounter and succeed one another, night and day, like the waves of the sea.‡ At this present season, many demons, of whom Kálanemi is the chief, have overrun, and continually harass, the region of mortals. The great Asura Kálanemi,[1] that was killed by the powerful Vishńu, has revived in Kaḿsa, the son of Ugrasena; and many other mighty demons, more than I can enumerate,—as Arishta,§ Dhenuka, Keśin, Pralamba, Naraka, Sunda,¶ and the fierce Báńa,** the son of Bali,[2]—are born in the palaces of kings. Countless hosts†† of proud and powerful spirits, chiefs

[1] According to the Váyu, Kálanemi, or Káyavadha, was a son of Virochana, the grandson of Hirańyakaśipu.‡‡ His death is described in the Hari Vaḿśa.§§

[2] These appear subsequently in the narration, and are destroyed by Krishńa.

* *Piśácha.* See Vol. II., p. 74, notes 2 and 3. † *Riksha.*

‡ तथाप्यनेकरूपस्य तस्य रूपाण्यहर्निशम् ।
बाध्यबाधकतां यान्ति कल्लोला इव सागरे ॥

§ See Vol. II., p. 70, note §. ‖ See Vol. II., p. 71.

¶ See Vol. II., p. 69, note 1. ** See Vol. II., p. 69.

†† *Akshauhińí.*

‡‡ See Vol. II., pp 30 and 69.

§§ Chapter XLIX.

As we shall see, two of them, Dhenuka and Pralamba, were slain by Balaráma.

of the demon-race, assuming celestial forms, now walk the earth; and, unable to support myself beneath the incumbent load, I come to you for succour. Illustrious deities, do you so act, that I may be relieved from my burthen; lest, helpless, I sink into the nethermost abyss."*

When the gods had heard these complaints of Earth, Brahmá, at their request, explained to them how her burthen might be lightened. "Celestials," said Brahmá, "all that Earth has said is, undoubtedly, true. I, Mahádeva,† and you all, are but Náráyańa: but the impersonations of his power are for ever mutually fluctuating; and excess or diminution is indicated by the predominance of the strong and the depression of the weak.‡ Come, therefore; let us repair to the northern coast of the milky sea, and, having glorified Hari, report to him what we have heard. He, who is the spirit of all, and of whom the universe consists, constantly, for the sake of Earth, descends, in a small portion of his essence, to establish righteousness below." Accordingly, Brahmá,§ attended by the gods, went to the milky sea, and there, with minds intent upon him, praised him whose emblem is Garuda.

"O thou," said Brahmá, "who art distinct from holy writ;[1] whose double nature is twofold wis-

---

[1] Anámnáya (अनाम्नाय); not the immediate object of the

* *Rasátala.* See Vol. II., p. 209, note 1, and p. 211, note 1.

† Called, in the original, Bhava. See Vol. I., p. 116.

‡ विभूतयस्तु याश्चास्य तासामेव परस्परम् ।
आधिक्यं न्यूनता बाध्यबाधकत्वेन वर्त्तते ॥

§ Substituted, by the Translator, for Pitámaha.

dom,[1] superior and inferior, and who art the essential end of both; who, alike devoid and possessed of form, art the twofold Brahma;[2] smallest of the least, and largest of the large; all, and knowing all things; that spirit which is language; that spirit which is supreme; that which is Brahma, and of which Brahma is composed! Thou art the Ŕig-, the Yajur-, the Sáma-, and the Atharva-Vedas.* Thou art accentuation,† ritual, signification,‡ metre, and astronomy; history, tradition,§ grammar, theology, ‖ logic,¶ and law:** thou who art inscrutable. Thou art the doctrine that investigates the distinctions between soul,

---

Vedas,†† which is devotion, not abstraction; ritual or worship, not knowledge.

[1] The two kinds of knowledge (द्वे विद्ये) are termed Pará (परा), 'supreme,' and Apará (अपरा), 'other' or 'subordinate'. The first is knowledge of Param Brahma, of spirit abstractedly considered, perfect knowledge derived from abstraction; the second is knowledge of Śabda-Brahma, of spirit as described and taught in the Vedas or their supplementary branches. The identity of the Supreme with both descriptions of holy knowledge pervades the whole of the address.

[2] Param Brahma and Śabda-Brahma. See the preceding note.

* ब्रह्मोवाच ।
द्वे विद्ये त्वमनाम्नाय परा चैवापरा तथा ।
ते एव भवतो रूपे मूर्तामूर्तात्मिके प्रभो ॥
द्वे ब्रह्मणी त्वणीयोऽति स्थूलात्मन्सर्वसर्ववित् ।
शब्दब्रह्म परं चैव ब्रह्म ब्रह्ममयस्य यत् ॥

† *Śikshá.* ‡ *Nirukta.* See Vol. III., p. 67.

§ *Puráńa.*

‖ *Mímáńsá.*

¶ *Nyáyika* or *nyáyaka.*

** Here the original addresses Adhokshaja. See Vol. I., p. 28, note †.

†† This is the commentator's definition.

and life,* and body,† and matter endowed with qualities:[1] and that doctrine is nothing else but thy nature inherent in and presiding over it.[2] ‡ Thou art imperceptible, indescribable, inconceivable: without name, or colour, or hands, or feet; pure, eternal, and infinite.§ Thou hearest without ears, and seest without eyes. Thou art one and multiform. Thou movest without feet; thou seizest without hands. Thou knowest all, but art not by all to be known.[3] He who beholds

---

[1] The doctrine alluded to may be either intended generally; or, in the several instances,—the discussion of the spiritual soul and living soul, of body subtile and sensible, and of matter endowed with qualities,—reference may be purposed to the Vedánta, Yoga, and Sánkhya systems.

[2] That is, as the Śabda-Brahma, the Supreme is identical with philosophical doctrines, being the object, the instigator, and the result.

[3] This is taken from the Vedas,¶ the original of which is

---

* The *jívátman* and the *paramátman*, or individuated spirit and the supreme spirit, according to the commentator. The former, as contrasted with the latter,—pure spirit, Brahma,—is a synthesis of spirit and cognitive internal organ, which organ Brahma does not possess. See my translation of *A Rational Refutation of the Hindu Philosophical Systems*, Preface, p. ix., note ‡, *et aliter*.

† Body, says the commentator, in its gross aspect and in its tenuous.

‡ आत्मात्मदेहगुणवद्विचाराचारि यद्वचः ।
तदप्याद्यपते नान्यदध्यात्मात्मस्वरूपवत् ॥

§ परात्परम् ।

‖ शृणोष्यकर्णः परिपश्यसि त्व-
मचक्षुरेको बहुरूपरूपः ।
अपादहस्तो जवनो ग्रहीता
त्वं वेत्सि सर्वं न च सर्ववेद्यः ॥

¶ The passage is from the *Śwetáśwatara-upanishad*,—III., XIX.

thee as the most subtile of atoms, not substantially existent, puts an end to ignorance; and final emancipation is the reward of that wise man whose understanding cherishes nothing other than thee in the form of supreme delight.[1]* Thou art the common centre of all,[2] the protector of the world; and all beings exist in thee. All that has been, or will be, thou art. Thou art the atom of atoms; thou art spirit; thou only art distinct from primeval nature.[3]† Thou, as the lord of fire:‡ in

quoted and translated by Sir William Jones: see his Works, Vol. XIII., p. 368. The passage is thus cited by the commentator on our text:

अपाणिपादो जवनो ग्रहीता
पश्यत्यचक्षुः स शृणोत्यकर्णः ।
स वेत्ति वेद्यं न च तस्य वेत्ता
तमाहुरग्र्यं पुरुषं महान्तम् ॥

"Without hand, or foot, he runs, he grasps; without eyes, he sees; and, without ears, he hears. He knoweth all that may be known; and no one knoweth him. Him they call the first great spirit."

[1] Vareńya rúpa: explained by Paramánanda múrti, "he whose form (or impersonation) is supreme felicity."

[2] Literally, 'navel of all', त्वं विश्वनाभिः । The passage is also read त्वं विश्वमादिः, "Thou art all and the first;" the cause or creator.

[3] Or the passage is understood, "Thou art one subsequently to Prakřiti:" त्वमेकः प्रकृतेः परस्तात् ।§ That is, thou art Brahmá,

* अणोरणीयांसमसत्स्वरूपं
त्वां पश्यतोऽज्ञाननिवृत्तिरग्र्या ।
धीरस्य धीर्यस्य बिभर्ति नान्य-
द्वरेण्यरूपात्परतः परात्मन् ॥

† The ordinary reading is त्वमेकः परतः परस्मात् ।

‡ Literally, 'the divine Fire', भगवान्हुताशः । *Hutása* is fire, especially in its divine aspect, as Agni.

§ This is the reading of some MSS.

four manifestations,[1] givest light and fertility to Earth. Thou art the eye of all,* and wearer of many shapes, and unobstructedly traversest the three regions of the universe.† As fire, though one, is variously kindled, and, though unchangeable in its essence, is modified in many ways, so thou, lord, who art one omnipresent form, takest upon thee all modifications that exist.‡ Thou art one supreme; thou art that supreme and eternal state which the wise behold with the eye of knowledge. There is nothing else but thou, O lord: nothing else has been, or will be. Thou art both discrete and indiscrete, universal and individual,§ omniscient, all-

---

the active will of the Supreme, creating forms from rudimental matter.

[1] As the three fires || enjoined by the Vedas, and the fire (metaphorically) of devotion; or, lightning, fire generated artificially, solar heat, and the fire of digestion (or animal fire): or, Vishńu, in that character, bestows vigour,¶ beauty, power, and wealth.

---

* To the letter, 'the eye everywhere' or 'in all respects', विश्वतश्चक्षुः। The Translator renders the explanation of the commentator.

† त्रेधा पदं त्वं निदधे विधातः।

It is said, thus, that he planted his step in three places. The reference, the scholiast says, is to the three steps of Vishńu. See Vol. III., p. 18, text and note ‡.

‡ यथाग्निरेको बहुधा समिध्यते
विकारभेदैरविकाररूपः।
तथा भवान्सर्वगतैकरूपो
रूपाण्यशेषाण्यनुपुष्यतीश॥

I find no variant of the first line that regularizes the prosody.

§ समष्टिव्यष्टिरूपवान्, "collective and distributive."

|| The three principal fires, out of an aggregate of five, are here intended. See Vol. III., p. 176, note §; and p. 11, note 1, *supra*.

¶ *Varchas.*

seeing, omnipotent, possessed of (all) wisdom, and strength, and power. Thou art liable neither to diminution nor increase; thou art independent, and without beginning; thou art the subjugator (of all). Thou art unaffected by weariness, sloth, fear, anger, or desire. Thou art free from soil,* supreme, merciful,[1] uniform,† undecaying,‡ lord over all, the stay of all, the fountain of light, imperishable. To thee, uninvested by material envelopes,[2] unexposed to sensible imaginings,§ aggregate of elemental substance,[3] spirit supreme,‖ be adoration! Thou assumest a shape, O pervader of the universe, not as the consequence of virtue or vice, nor from any mixture of the two, but for the sole object of maintaining piety (in the world)."[4]

---

[1] Prita. One copy has Śánta, 'calm,' 'undisturbed.'¶

[2] Beyond the separate layers or envelopes of elementary substances (see Vol. I., p. 40); or, according to the Vedánta notions, uninvested by those grosser sheaths or coverings, derived from food and the like, by which subtile body is enclosed.

[3] Mahávibhúti saṁsthána (महाविभूतिसंस्थान). Vibhúti is explained by Prapancha,—sensible, material, or elementary substance, constituting body.

[4] The passage is somewhat obscurely expressed, and is differently interpreted. It is:

नाकारणात्कारणाद्वा कारणाकारणान्न च ।

"Not from no cause, nor from cause, nor from cause and no

---

* *Niravadya.*

† *Niranishṭha.* And several MSS. have *niradhishṭa.*

‡ *Akshara-krama*, 'of unfailing might.'

§ निरस्तकल्पनाभावन ।

‖ *Purushottama.*

¶ I find the variant *prápta.*

The unborn, universal* Hari, having heard, with his mental ear,† these eulogiums, was pleased, and thus spake to Brahmá: "Tell me, Brahmá, what you and the gods desire. Speak boldly, certain of success."‡ Brahmá, beholding the divine, universal§ form of Hari, quickly prostrated himself, and again renewed his praises: "Glory to thee, the thousand-formed, the thousand-armed, the many-visaged, many-footed; to thee, the illimitable author of creation, preservation, and destruction; most subtile of the subtile, most vast of the great;¶ to thee, who art nature, intellect, and consciousness; and who art other spirit even than the spir-

---

cause." The term 'no cause' may, the commentator says, designate fixed prescribed duties, the Nitya-karman; 'cause' may signify occasional sacrifices, the Kámya-karman: neither of these can form any necessity for Vishńu's descent, as they might of a mere mortal's being born on the earth. Or, Káraña is explained to mean 'obtaining pleasure', from Ka (क) and Arańa (अरण). 'obtaining;' obtaining happiness, or the cause of it, piety, virtue (धर्म); and, with the negative, Akárańa (अकारण), the reverse, pain, the consequence of wickedness (अधर्म). The purport is clear enough: it is merely meant to state, that Vishńu is not subject to the necessity which is the cause of human birth.

* विश्वरूपधरः ।

† Literally, 'with *his* mind,' *manasá*.

‡ तदुच्यतामशेषं वः सिद्धमेवावधार्यताम् ।

§ *Viśwarúpa*.

|| तुष्टाव भूयो देवेषु साध्वसावनतात्मसु ।

This means, that Brahmá resumed his panegyric, "the gods being prostrated in awe." There are no variants in my MSS.

¶ सूक्ष्मातिसूक्ष्मातिबृहत्प्रमाण-
गरीयसामप्यतिगौरवात्मन् ।

itual root of those principles![1] Do thou show favour upon us. Behold, lord, this earth—oppressed by mighty Asuras, and shaken to her mountain-basements,*—comes to thee, who art her invincible defender, to be relieved from her burthen. Behold me, Indra,† the Áświns,‡ Varuńa, and Yama, the Rudras, the Vasus, the Suns, the Winds, Fire,§ and all other celestials, prepared to execute whatever thou shalt will that we shall do. Do thou, in whom there is no imperfection, O sovereign of the deities, give thy orders to thy servants. Lo! we are ready."

When Brahmá had ended, the supreme lord plucked off two hairs, one white and one black, and said to the gods: "These my hairs shall descend upon earth, and shall relieve her of the burthen of her distress.[2] Let all

[1] The term Pradhána, which is repeated in this passage, is explained, in the second place, to mean Pums, 'soul' or 'spirit':

प्रधानबुद्धीन्द्रियवत्प्रधान-
मूलापरात्मन्भगवन्प्रसीद ।

[2] The same account of the origin of Kŕishńa is given in the Mahábhárata, Ádi Parvan, Vol. I., p. 266. The white hair is impersonated as Balaráma; the black, as Kŕishńa. The commentator on our text maintains that this is not to be literally understood: "Vishńu did not intend that the two hairs should become incarnate; but he meant to signify, that, should he send them, they would be more than sufficient to destroy Kamsa and

* पीडितशैलबन्धा ।

† Designated, in the original, by his epithet *Vŕitra-ripu*, 'the foe of Vŕitra.' See Vol. II., p. 79, note ‡.

‡ The Sanskrit names Násatya and Dasra. The two are often called Násatyas, as well as Aświns. *Vide supra*, p. 103.

§ *Agni*. Read 'the Fires'. *Vide supra*, p. 249, note ¶.

[2] *Śl.* 7306—7308. The passage is extracted, translated, and commented on, in *Original Sanskrit Texts*, Part IV., pp. 220—222.

the gods, also, in their own portions, go down to earth, and wage war with the haughty Asuras, who are there incorporate,* and who shall, every one of them, be destroyed. Doubt not of this. They shall perish before the (withering) glance of mine eyes. This my (black) hair shall be impersonated in the eighth conception of the wife of Vasudeva, Devakí,—who is like a goddess,—and shall slay Kaḿsa, who is the demon Kálanemi." Thus having spoken, Hari disappeared; and the gods, bowing to him, though invisible, returned to the summit of Mount Meru, from whence they descended upon earth.†

The Muni Nárada informed Kaḿsa that the supporter of the earth, Vishńu,‡ would be the eighth child of Devakí: and, his wrath being excited by this report, he placed both Vasudeva and Devakí in confinement. Agreeably to his promise, the former delivered to Kaḿsa each infant, as soon as it was born. It is said that these, to the number of six, were the children of the demon Hirańyakaśipu,§ who were introduced into the womb (of Devakí), at the command of Vishńu,

his demons. Or, the birth of Ráma and Krishńa was a double illusion, typified by the two hairs." This seems to be a refinement upon an older and somewhat undignified account of the origin of Krishńa and his brother. The commentator on the Mahábhárata argues that they are to be understood merely as the media by which Devakí and Rohińí conceived.

* *Púrvotpanna*, "who were produced aforetime," is what I find.

† For the original of this paragraph, the native comment on it, and a translation of both, see *Original Sanskrit Texts*, Part IV., pp. 218 and 220.

‡ The Translator often, as here, puts "Vishńu", where the original has Bhagavat.

§ See Vol. II., p. 30.

(during the hours of Devakí's repose), by (the goddess) Yoganidrá,[1] the great illusory energy * of Vishńu, by whom, as utter ignorance,† the whole world is beguiled. To her Vishńu said: "Go, Nidrá, to the nether regions, and, by my command, conduct, successively, six (of their princes), to be conceived of Devakí. When these shall have been put to death by Kańsa, the seventh conception shall be formed of a portion of Śesha, who is a part of me; and this you shall transfer, before the time of birth,‡ to Rohińí, another wife of Vasudeva, who resides at Gokula.§ The report shall run, that Devakí miscarries, through the anxiety of imprisonment, and dread of the Raja of the Bhojas.¶ From being extracted from his mother's womb, the child shall be known by the name of Sankarshańa; and he shall be (valiant and strong, and) like the peak of the white mountain** (in bulk and complexion). I will, myself,

[1] Yoganidrá †† (योगनिद्रा) is the sleep of devotion or abstraction, the active principle of illusion, personified, and also termed Máyá and Mahámáyá, also Avidyá (or ignorance). In the Durgá Máhátmya of the Márkańdeya Puráńa, she appears as Deví or Durgá, the Śakti or bride of Śiva, but, in our text, as Vaishńaví, or the Śakti of Vishńu.

* *Mahámáyá*, "the great illusion."

† *Avidyá*.

‡ संभूतिकाले, which, the commentator alleges, means "at the time of birth".

§ Compare p. 111, *supra*.

‖ रोधोपरोधतः, "from confinement in prison," according to the commentator.

¶ The original, *Bhojarája*, intends Kańsa. *Vide infra*, p. 271, note ‡.

** For the mountain-range here mentioned, called Śwetádri, see Vol. II., p. 102; also, *ibid.*, pp. 114, 115, and 256.

†† See *Original Sanskrit Texts*, Part IV., pp. 370, 371.

become incarnate in the (eighth) conception of Devakí; and you shall immediately take a similar character, as the embryo-offspring of Yaśodá. In the night of the eighth lunation of the dark half of the month Nabhas,* in the season of the rains, I shall be born. You shall receive birth on the ninth. Impelled and aided by my power, Vasudeva shall bear me to the bed of Yaśodá, and you, to that of Devakí. Kaṁsa shall take you, and hold you up, to dash you against a stone; but you shall escape (from his grasp,) into the sky, where the hundred-eyed† Indra: shall meet and do homage to you, through reverence for me, and shall bow before you, and acknowledge you as his sister. Having slain Śumbha, Niśumbha,§ and numerous other demons,[1] you shall sanctify the earth in many places.[2] Thou art

[1] Allusion is here made to the exploits of Durgá, as celebrated especially in the Durgá Máhátmya; and it must be posterior to the date of that or some similar composition. The passage may be an interpolation; as the Márkańdeya Puráńa, in general, has the appearance of being a more recent compilation than the Vishńu.||

[2] This refers to the Píthasthánas,¶ fifty-one places, where, according to the Tantras, the limbs of Satí** fell, when scattered

* The Sanskrit has नभसि कृष्णाष्टम्यां, "Kŕishńa's eighth of Nabhas," which denotes the eighth day of the light fortnight of Nabhas, sacred to Kŕishńa. Nabhas is the same month as Śrávańa,—July and August.

† Ordinarily, Indra is said to have a thousand eyes, as is indicated by his epithet *sahasráksha*. ; Śakra, in the Sanskrit.

§ Corrected from "Sumbha" and "Nisumbha". The two Dánavas referred to were brothers.

|| See Vol. I., Preface, p. LV., note *.

¶ See Vol. I., Preface, pp. LXXXIX. and XC.

** Corrected, here and below, from "Śatí".

wealth, progeny,* fame, patience, heaven and earth, fortitude,† modesty, nutrition,‡ dawn, and every other female (form or property).§ They who address thee. morning and afternoon, with reverence and praise, and call thee Áryá, Durgá, Vedagarbhá, Ambiká, Bhadrá, Bhadrakálí,¶ Kshemyá,** or Kshemankarí,†† shall receive, from my bounty,‡‡ whatever they desire. Propitiated with offerings of wine, and flesh, and various

by her husband, Śiva, as he bore her dead body about, and tore it to pieces, after she had put an end to her existence, at Daksha's sacrifice. This part of the legend seems to be an addition to the original fable made by the Tantras; as it is not in the Puránas (see the story of Daksha's sacrifice).§§ It bears some analogy to the Egyptian fable of Isis and Osiris. At the Píthasthánas, however, of Jwálámukhí, Vindhyavásiní,|| Kálighát,¶¶ and others, temples are erected to the different forms of Devi or Sati, not to the phallic emblem of Mahádeva, which, if present, is, there, as an accessory and embellishment, not as a principal; and the chief object of worship is a figure of the goddess,—a circumstance in which there is an essential difference between the temples of Durgá and shrines of Osiris.

* I do not find सन्तति, but सन्नति, 'humility;' and so reads the commentator, who explains the word by विनय.

† *Dhriti*. Two pages on, it is rendered by "patience"; "fortitude" being there employed to translate *dhairya*.

‡ *Pushti*.

§ Compare the list in Vol. I., p. 109

|| See Vol. I., p. 116, note 1.

¶ See Vol. I., Preface, p LXXXIX.

** Corrected from "Kshemi".

†† I find the variant Kshemakarí.

‡‡ *Prasáda*.

§§ Vol. I., pp. 120—134.

|| Near Mirzapore.

¶¶ A few miles south of Calcutta.

viands, thou shalt bestow upon mankind all their prayers. Through my favour, all men shall ever have faith in thee. Assured of this, go, goddess, and execute my commands."*

* ते सर्वे सर्वदा भद्रे मत्प्रसादादसंशयम् ।
असंदिग्धा भविष्यन्ति गच्छ देवि यथोदितम् ॥

CHAPTER II.

The conception of Devakí: her appearance: she is praised by the gods.

THE nurse of the universe, (Jagaddhátrí,) thus enjoined by the god of gods, conveyed the six several embryos (into the womb of Devakí[1]), and transferred the seventh, (after a season,) to that of Rohińí; after which, Hari, for the benefit of the three regions, became incarnate, as the conception of the former princess, and Yoganidrá, as that of Yaśodá, exactly as the supreme Vishńu* had commanded. When the portion of Vishńu had become incorporate upon earth, the planetary bodies moved in brilliant order in the heavens, and the seasons were regular and genial.† "No person could bear to gaze upon Devakí, from the light (that invested her); and those who contemplated her radiance felt their minds disturbed. The gods, invisible to mortals, celebrated her praises continually, from the time that Vishńu was contained in her person. "Thou", said the divinities, "art that Prakŕiti, infinite and subtile, which

---

[1] It is mentioned, in the preceding Chapter, that they were, all, put to death, in which the Hari Vaḿśa concurs. The Bhágavata makes Kaḿsa spare them, and restore them to their parents; as he had nothing to apprehend from their existence.

---

* *Parameshṭhin* is the term here rendered "supreme Vishńu." The commentator explains it by *parameśwara*. Parameshṭhin is the same as Brahmá, in Vol. II., p. 19, note.

† ततो ग्रहगणः सम्यक्प्रचचार दिवि द्विज ।
विष्णोरंशे महीं याते ऋतवोऽप्यभवञ्छुभाः ॥

formerly bore Brahmá in its womb. Then wast thou the goddess of speech, the energy of the creator of the universe, and the parent of the Vedas.* Thou, eternal being, comprising, in thy substance, the essence of all created things, wast identical with creation; thou wast the parent of the triform sacrifice, becoming the germ of all things.† Thou art sacrifice, whence all fruit proceeds; thou art the wood,‡ whose attrition engenders fire. As Aditi,§ thou art the parent of the gods; as Diti,|| thou art the mother of the Daityas, (their foes). Thou art light,¶ whence day is begotten; thou art humility,** the mother of (true) wisdom; thou art kingly policy,†† the parent of order;‡‡ thou art modesty, the progenitrix of affection;§§ thou art desire, of whom love is born; thou art contentment, whence resignation is derived;¶¶ thou art intelligence, the mother of knowledge;*** thou art patience,††† the parent of fortitude;‡‡‡

* There is neither this nor so much in the original:

ततो वाणी जगद्धातुर्वेदगर्भासि शोभने ।

For Vedagarbhá, *vide supra*, p. 262.

† सृज्यस्वरूपगर्भा च सृष्टिभूता सनातने ।
बीजभूता च सर्वस्य यज्ञगर्भा भवस्त्रयी ॥

‡ *Arańi*. See Vol. III., p. 330, note *.

§ See Vol. II., pp. 26, 27.

|| See Vol. II., pp. 26 and 30.

¶ *Jyotsná*, 'the morning twilight.' See Vol. I., p. 81.

** *Sannati*. See Vol. I., pp. 109 and 155.

†† *Níti* is the term rendered "kingly policy".

‡‡ *Naya*. See Vol. I., p. 110.

§§ *Praśraya*; explained by *vinaya*. See Vol. I., p. 111, note 1.

||| कामगर्भा तथेच्छा । Comment: कामः काम्योऽर्थः । गर्भे यस्या इच्छाभिलाषः ।

¶¶ तुष्टिस्तोषगर्भिणी ।

*** *Avabodha*. ††† *Dhriti*. See Vol. I., pp. 109, 110. ‡‡‡ *Dhairya*.

thou art the heavens, and thy children are the stars;* and from thee does all (that exists) proceed. Such, goddess, and thousands more, are thy mighty faculties; and now innumerable are the contents of thy womb, O mother of the universe.† The whole earth, decorated with oceans, mountains,‡ rivers, continents, forests,§ cities, villages, towns,|| and hamlets;¶ all the fires, waters, and winds; the stars, asterisms, and planets; the sky, crowded with the variegated chariots of the gods; and ether, that provides space for all substance;** the several spheres of earth, sky, and heaven, of saints, sages, ascetics, and of Brahmá;†† the whole egg of Brahmá, with all its population of gods, demons,‡‡ spirits,§§ snake-gods, fiends,|||| demons,¶¶ ghosts, and imps,*** men and animals, and whatever creatures have life, comprised in him who is their eternal lord, and the object of all apprehension; whose real form, nature, name, and dimensions are not within human ap-

---

* The original has *graha*, *ṛiksha*, and *tárakú*. Compare the Sanskrit extract of note **, below.

† *Jagaddhátrí*.

‡ I have inserted this word, for *adri*.

§ This, too, I have intercalated, for *vana*.

|| *Kharvaṭa*.

¶ *Kheṭa*.

** ग्रहर्क्षतारकाचित्रं विमानशतसंकुलम् ।
अवकाशमशेषाणां यद्ददाति नभश्च यत् ॥

†† *Maharloka*, *janaloka*, *tapoloka*, and *Brahmaloka*. They are named in the original. See Vol. I., p. 98, note 1. and Vol. II., pp. 226, *et seq.*

‡‡ *Daitya*, in the original.

§§ To represent both *gandharva* and *cháraṇa*.

|||| *Yaksha*.

¶¶ *Rákshasa*.

*** *Guhyaka*. See Vol. III., p. 116, note †.

prehension:—are, now, with that Vishńu, in thee.* Thou art Swáhá; thou art Swadhá:† thou art wisdom, ambrosia,‡ light, and heaven. Thou hast descended upon earth, for the preservation of the world. Have compassion upon us, O goddess; and do good unto the world. Be proud to bear that deity by whom the universe is upheld."§

---

* तैरनन्तैरनन्तोऽसौ सर्वेशः सर्वभावनः ।
रूपकर्मस्वरूपाणि न परिच्छेदगोचरे ।
यस्याखिलप्रमाणानि स विष्णुर्गर्भगस्तव ॥

Some MSS., as is observed by the commentator, have नाम- instead of रूप-. The Translator has taken both, and has omitted to render कर्म-, which is defined by *lílá*, while *rúpa* is defined by *tattwa*.

Some remarks on the expression *lílá* will be found in one of my annotations on Chapter XIII. of this Book.

† For Swáhá and Swadhá, see Vol. I., pp. 109, and 156, 157.

‡ *Sudhá*. See Vol. II., p. 300, note *.

§ प्रीत्या त्वं धारयेशानं धृतं येनाखिलं जगत्

Íśána, ordinarily denoting Śiva, here appears as a name of Vishńu. It is similarly applied in the *Mahábhárata*, *Ádi-parvan*, *l*. 22.

CHAPTER III.

Birth of Krishńa; conveyed, by Vasudeva, to Mathurá, and exchanged with the new-born daughter of Yaśodá. Kaḿsa attempts to destroy the latter, who becomes Yoganidrá.

THUS eulogized by the gods, Devakí bore, in her womb, the lotos-eyed (deity), the protector of the world. The sun of Achyuta rose in the dawn of Devakí, to cause the lotos-petal of the universe to expand. On the day of his birth, the quarters of the horizon were irradiate with joy, as if moonlight was diffused over the whole earth.* The virtuous experienced new delight, the strong winds were hushed, and the rivers glided tranquilly, when Janárdana was about to be born. The seas,† with their own melodious murmurings, made the music, whilst the spirits and the nymphs of heaven danced and sang; the gods, walking the sky, showered down flowers upon the earth; and the (holy) fires glowed with a mild and gentle flame. At midnight, when the supporter of all was about to be born, the clouds emitted low pleasing sounds, and poured down rain of flowers.

As soon as Anakadundubhi‡ beheld the child, of the complexion of the lotos-leaves, having four arms, and the (mystic mark) Śrívatsa on his breast, he ad-

---

* तज्जन्मदिनमत्यर्थमाह्लाद्यमलदिङ्मुखम् ।
बभूव सर्वलोकस्य कौमुदी शशिनो यथा ॥

Kaumudí, in this passage, means, according to the commentator, the full-moon of Kaumuda, a name of the month of Kárttika.

† *Sindhu.*

‡ *Vide supra*, p. 101, note 1.

dressed him in terms of love and reverence, and represented the fears he entertained of Kaṁsa. "Thou art born," said Vasudeva, "O sovereign god of gods, bearer of the shell, the mace, and the discus; but, now, in mercy, withhold this thy celestial form; for Kaṁsa will, assuredly, put me to death, when he knows that thou hast descended in my dwelling." Devakí, also, exclaimed: "God of gods, who art all things, who comprisest all the regions of the world in thy person,* and who, by thine illusion, hast assumed the condition of an infant, have compassion upon us, and forego this thy four-armed shape; nor let Kaṁsa, the impious son of Diti, know of thy descent."

To these applications Bhagavat answered, and said: "Princess, in former times, I was prayed to by thee, and adored, in the hope of progeny. Thy prayers have been granted; for I am born thy son."† So saying, he was silent. And Vasudeva, taking the babe, went out, that same night: for the guards were, all, charmed by Yoganidrá, as were the warders at the gates of Mathurá; and they obstructed not the passage of Ánakadundubhi. To protect the infant from the heavy rain that fell from the clouds of night, Śesha, (the many-headed serpent), followed Vasudeva, and spread his hoods (above their heads); and, when the prince, with the child in his arms, crossed the Yamuná river, deep as it was, and dangerous with numerous whirlpools,

* यो ऽनन्तरूपो ऽखिलविश्वरूपो
गर्भे ऽपि लोकान्वपुषा बिभर्ति ।

† स्तुतो ऽहं यत्त्वया पूर्वं पुत्रार्थिन्या तदद्य ते ।
सफलं देवि संजातं जातो ऽहं यत्तवोदरात् ॥

the waters were stilled, and rose not above his knee.* On the bank he saw Nanda and the rest, who had come thither to bring tribute due to Kaṁsa; but they beheld him not.[1] † At the same time, Yaśodá was, also, under the influence of Yoganidrá, whom she had brought forth, as her daughter, and whom (the prudent) Vasudeva took up, placing his son in her place, by the side of the mother. He then quickly returned home. When Yaśodá awoke, she found that she had been delivered of a boy, as black as the dark leaves of the lotos; and she was greatly rejoiced.

Vasudeva, bearing off the female infant (of Yaśodá), reached his mansion, (unobserved, and entered), and placed the child in the bed of Devakí. He then remained as usual. The guards were awakened by the cry of the new-born babe; and, starting up, they sent word to Kaṁsa, that Devakí had borne a child. Kaṁsa immediately repaired to the residence of Vasudeva, where he seized upon the infant. In vain Devakí convulsively entreated him to relinquish the child.‡ He

---

[1] The Bhágavata, more consistently, makes Vasudeva find Nanda and the rest fast asleep, in their houses, and subsequently describes their bringing tribute or tax (kara) to Kaṁsa.

---

* यमुनां चातिगम्भीरां नानावर्त्तशताकुलाम् ।
वसुदेवो वहन्विष्णुं जानुमात्रवहां ययौ ॥

† This last clause is supplied by the Translator. The commentator adds, that Nanda and his companions came, because beguiled by Yoganidrá; and this remark seems to have been misunderstood. The original is:

नन्दादीन्गोपवृद्धांश्च यमुनायां ददर्श सः ।

‡ मुञ्च मुञ्चेति देवक्या [illegible] निवारितः ।

threw it (ruthlessly,) against a stone; but it rose into the sky, and expanded into a gigantic figure, having eight arms, each wielding some formidable weapon.* This (terrific being) laughed aloud, and said to Kaṁsa: "What avails it thee, Kaṁsa, to have hurled me (to the ground)? He is born who shall kill thee,—the mighty one amongst the gods, who was, formerly, thy destroyer. Now quickly secure him, and provide for thine own welfare." Thus having spoken, the goddess, decorated with heavenly garlands and perfumes, and hymned by the spirits of the air,† vanished from before the eyes of Bhojarája.[1]‡

[1] Chief of the tribe of Bhoja, a branch of the Yádavas. *Vide supra*, p. 73.

* अवाप रूपं च महत्सायुधाष्टमहाभुजम् ।

† *Siddha*.

‡ Corrected from "Bhoja rájá". In another place, *Bhojarája* is rendered, and rightly, "the Raja of the Bhojas", *i. e.*, Kaṁsa. *Vide supra*, p. 260, text and note ¶.

CHAPTER IV.

Kaṁsa addresses his friends, announces their danger, and orders male children to be put to death.

KAMSA, much troubled in mind, summoned all his principal Asuras,—Pralamba, Keśin, and the rest,- and said to them: "O valiant chiefs, Pralamba, Mahábáhu,* Keśin, Dhenuka, Pútaná, Arishta, and all the rest of you, hear my words. The vile and contemptible denizens of heaven are assiduously plotting against my life;† for they dread my prowess. But, heroes, I hold them of no account. What can the impotent Indra or the ascetic‡ Hara perform? Or what can Hari accomplish, except the murder of his foes by fraud?§ What have we to fear from the Ádityas, the Vasus, the Agnis, or any others of the immortals, who have, all, been vanquished by my resistless arms? Have I not seen the king of the gods, when he had ventured into the conflict, quickly retreat from the field, receiving my shafts upon his back,—not, bravely, upon his breast? When, in resentment, he withheld the fertilizing showers from my kingdom, did not my arrows compel the clouds to part with their waters, as much as were required? Are not all the monarchs of the earth in terror

---

* I have inserted this name. The Translator seems to have taken the word for an epithet, and as not worth rendering. See an annotation near the end of Chapter XII. of this Book. Mahábáhu, a Dánava, is spoken of in the *Harivaṁśa*, *sl.* 200.

† मां हन्तुममरैर्यत्नः कृतः किल दुरात्मभिः ।

‡ *Ekachárin*; 'solitary', according to the commentator.

§ हरिणा वापि किं साध्यं छिद्रेष्वसुरघातिना ।

of my prowess, and subject to my orders, save, only, Jarásandha, my sire?[1*] Now, chiefs of the Daitya race, it is my determination to inflict still deeper degradation upon these evil-minded and unprincipled gods.† Let, therefore, every man who is notorious for liberality‡ (in gifts to gods and Brahmans), every man who is remarkable for his celebration of sacrifices, be put to death; that, thus, the gods shall be deprived of the means by which they subsist.§ The goddess who has been born as the infant child of Devakí has announced to me that he is again alive who, in a former being, was my death. Let, therefore, active search be made for whatever young children there may be upon earth; and let every boy in whom there are signs of unusual vigour be slain (without remorse)."

Having issued these commands, Kaṁsa retired into his palace, and liberated Vasudeva and Devakí from their captivity. "It is in vain," said he to them, "that

---

[1] Jarásandha, prince of Magadha, was the father-in-law of Kaṁsa.

---

* *Guru*, in the original. The commentator says that Jarásandha was his 'superior', because his father-in-law.

† अमरेषु च मेऽवज्ञा जायते दैत्यपुङ्गवाः ।
हास्यं मे जायते वीरास्तेषु यत्नपरेष्वपि ॥
तथापि खलु दुष्टानां तेषामभ्यधिकं मया ।
अपकाराय दैत्येन्द्रा यतनीयं दुरात्मनाम् ॥

‡ *Yaśasvin* is so defined by the commentator. *Tapasvin*, 'ascetic', is a variant.

§ I find no reading but

कार्यो देवापकाराय तेषां सर्वात्मना वधः ।

Kaṁsa married Rájívalochaná, daughter of Jarásandha, king of Magadha. See the *Mahábhárata*, *Sabhá-parvan*, *ll.* 610.

I have slain (all) your children; since, after all, he who is destined to kill me has escaped. It is of no use to regret the past.* The children you may hereafter have may enjoy life unto its natural close: no one shall cut it short." Having thus conciliated them, Kaṁsa, alarmed for himself, withdrew into the interior apartments of his palace.

* तदलं परितापेन ।

CHAPTER V.

Nanda returns, with the infants, Kŕishńa and Balaráma, to Gokula. Pútaná killed by the former. Prayers of Nanda and Yaśodá.

WHEN Vasudeva was set at liberty, he went to the waggon of Nanda, and found Nanda there, rejoicing that a son was born to him.[1] Vasudeva spake to him kindly, and congratulated him on having a son in his old age. "The yearly tribute," he added, "has been paid to the king; and men of property should not tarry (near the court), when the business that brought them there has been transacted.* Why do you delay, now that your affairs are settled? Up, Nanda, quickly, and set off to your own pastures;† and let this boy, the son whom Rohińí has borne me, accompany you, and be brought up, by you, as this your own son." Accordingly, Nanda and the other cowherds, their goods being placed in their waggons, and their taxes having been paid to the king, returned (to their village).

[1] It is, literally, 'went to the cart' or 'waggon,' नन्दस्य शकटं गतः; as if Nanda and his family dwelt in such a vehicle, as the Scythians are said to have done. The commentator explains Śakaṭa (शकट) "the place of loosing or unharnessing the waggon," शकटावमोचनस्थानम्। In the Bhágavata,‡ Vasudeva does not quit Mathurá, but goes to the halting-ground of Nanda, who has come to that city, to pay his taxes: ययौ तदवमोचनम्; explained by the comment यत्र वसतिस्तत्र शकटोत्तारभूमिम्।

* The commentator gives the reason: महाधनानां पुरजनसंनिधाने न युक्तम्।

† Literally, 'herd',—*gokula*.

‡ X., Prior Section, V., 20.

Some time after they were settled at Gokula, (the female fiend) Pútaná, the child-killer, came thither, by night, and, finding (the little) Kŕishńa asleep, took him up, and gave him her breast to suck.[1] Now, whatever child is suckled, in the night, by Pútaná instantly dies; but Kŕishńa, laying hold of the breast with both hands, sucked it with such violence, that he drained it of the life;* and the hideous † Pútaná, roaring aloud, and giving way in every joint,‡ fell on the ground, expiring. The inhabitants of Vraja awoke, in alarm, at the cries of the fiend, (ran to the spot, and) beheld Pútaná lying on the earth, and Kŕishńa in her arms. Yaśodá, snatching up Kŕishńa, waved over him a cow-tail brush, to guard him from harm, whilst Nanda placed (dried) cow-dung (powdered,) upon his head. He gave him, also, an amulet;[2] saying, at the same time: "May Hari,

---

[1] In the Hari Vaḿśa,§ this female fiend is described as coming in the shape of a bird.

[2] The Rakshá—the preserver, or preservative against charms,—is a piece of thread or silk, or some more costly material, bound round the wrist or arm, with an appropriate prayer, such as that in the text. Besides its application to children, to avert the effects of evil-eyes, or to protect them against Ďáens or witches, there is one day in the year, the Rákhi Púrńimá, or full moon in the month of Śrávańa (July—August), when it is bound upon the wrists of adults by friendly or kindred Brahmans, with a short prayer or benediction. The Rákhí is, also, sent, sometimes, by

---

* कृष्णस्तु तत्स्तनं गाढं कराभ्यामतिपीडितम्।
गृहीत्वा प्राणसहितं पपौ क्रोधसमन्वितः॥

† Because, says the commentator, she resumed, at the time of death, her proper form.

‡ विच्छिन्नस्नायुबन्धना।

§ Śl. 3493.

the lord of all beings (without reserve), protect you; he from the lotos of whose navel the world was developed, and on the tip of whose tusks the globe was upraised from the waters!* May that Keśava, who assumed the form of a boar, protect thee!† May that Keśava, who, as the man-lion,‡ rent, with his sharp nails, the bosom of his foe, ever protect thee! May that Keśava, who, appearing, first, as the dwarf,§ suddenly traversed, in all his might, with three paces, the three regions of the universe, constantly defend thee!¶ May Govinda guard thy head; Keśava, thy neck; Vishńu, thy belly;** Janárdana, thy legs and feet; the eternal and irresistible Náráyańa, thy face, thine arms,†† thy mind, and faculties of sense!‡‡ May all ghosts, goblins,§§ and spirits ‖ malignant and unfriendly, ever fly thee,¶¶ appalled by the bow, the discus, mace, and

persons of distinction, and, especially, by females, to members of a different family, or even race and nation, to intimate a sort of brotherly or sisterly adoption. Tod's Rajasthan. Vol. I., pp. 312, 313.

* See Vol. I., p. 61, note 2.

† येन दंष्ट्राग्रविधृता धारयत्यवनी जगत् ।

‡ Nrisimha. See Vol. II., p. 34, note 1; also, p. 106, supra.

§ See Vol. I., Preface, p. LXXV.

‖ See Vol. III., p. 18, text and note ‡.

¶ वामनो रक्षतु सदा भवन्तं यः क्षणादभूत् ।
त्रिविक्रमः क्रमाक्रान्तत्रैलोक्यः स्फुरदायुधः ॥

** गुह्यं चजठरम् ।

†† बाहू प्रबाहू च: the two divisions of the arms.

‡‡ रक्षत्वव्याहतैश्वर्यस्तव नारायणोऽव्ययः ।

§§ Kúshmáńda. See Vol. I., p. 166.

‖ Rákshasa.

¶¶ क्षयं यान्तु ।

sword of Vishńu, and the echo of his shell! May Vaikuńt́ha* guard thee in the cardinal points; and, in the intermediate ones, Madhusúdana!† May Hŕishíkeśa‡ defend thee in the sky; and Mahídhara,§ upon earth!" Having pronounced this prayer to avert all evil,|| Nanda put the child to sleep, in his bed¶ underneath the waggon. Beholding the vast carcass of Pútaná, the cowherds were filled with astonishment and terror.

* A metronym of Vishńu; one of the names of his mother being Vikuńt́há. See Vol III., text and note ††.

† "The destroyer of Madhu", a demon. See Vol. II., p. 52.

‡ Corrected from "Rishíkeśa". For Hŕishíkeśa, see Vol. I., p. 2, note 1.

§ Being interpreted, "the upholder of the earth."

|| *Swastyayana.*

¶ *Paryanńká*, 'cot', according to the commentator.

CHAPTER VI.

Krishńa overturns a waggon: casts down two trees. The Gopas depart to Vrindávana. Sports of the boys. Description of the season of the rains.

ON one occasion, whilst Madhusúdana was asleep underneath the waggon, he cried for the breast; and, kicking up his feet, he overturned the vehicle; and all the pots and pans* were upset and broken. The cowherds and their wives (hearing the noise,) came, exclaiming: "Ah! ah!" And there they found the child sleeping on his back. "Who could have upset the waggon?" said the cowherds. "This child," replied some boys, (who witnessed the circumstance). "We saw him," said they, "crying, and kicking the waggon with his feet; and so it was overturned. No one else had anything to do with it." The cowherds were exceedingly astonished at this account; and Nanda, not knowing what to think, took up the boy; whilst Yaśodá offered worship to the broken pieces of pots and to the waggon, with curds, flowers, fruit, and unbruised grain.†

The initiatory rites requisite for the two boys were performed by Garga,‡ who was sent to Gokula, by Vasudeva, for that purpose. He celebrated them without

* Some MSS have, instead of कुम्भभाण्डं, कुम्भभाजनम्। The commentator takes notice of this variant.

† यशोदा शकटारूढभग्नभाण्डकपालिकाः।
शकटं चार्चयामास दधिपुष्पफलाक्षतैः॥

‡ See Vol. II., p. 213.

the knowledge of the cowherds;[1] and the wise sage, eminent amongst the wise, named the elder of them Ráma, and the other, Kŕishńa. In a short time, they began to crawl about the ground, supporting themselves on their hands and knees, and creeping everywhere, often amidst ashes and filth. Neither Rohińí nor Yaśodá was able to prevent them from getting into the cow-pens, or amongst the calves, where they amused themselves by pulling their tails. As they disregarded the prohibitions of Yaśodá, and rambled about together constantly, she became angry, and, taking up a stick, followed them, and threatened the dark-complexioned Kŕishńa with a whipping.* Fastening a cord round his waist, she tied him to the wooden mortar;[2] and, being in a great passion, she said to him: "Now, you naughty boy, get away from hence, if you can." She then went about her domestic affairs. As soon as she

---

[1] The Bhágavata † describes Garga's interview with Nanda, and the inducements of the latter to keep the former's celebration of the Saḿskáras (or initiatory rites) of the two boys secret from the Gopas. Garga there describes himself as the Purohita ‡ (or family priest) of the Yádavas.

[2] The Ulúkhala (or mortar) is a large wooden bowl, on a solid stand of timber; both cut out of one piece. The pestle is, also, of wood; and they are used chiefly for bruising or threshing unwinnowed corn, and separating the chaff from the grain. As important agents in household economy, they are regarded as sacred, and even hymned in the Vedas. §

---

* यशोदा यष्टिमादाय कोपेनानुगता च तम् ।
कृष्णं कमलपत्राक्षं तर्जयन्ती रुषा तदा ॥

The MSS. containing the commentary omit this stanza.

† X., Prior Section, Chapter VIII.

‡ Rather, as *áchárya*.

§ As in the *Ŕigveda*, I., XXVIII., 5 and 6.

had departed, the lotos-eyed Kŕishńa, endeavouring to extricate himself, pulled the mortar after him, to the space between two Arjuna-trees that grew near together. Having dragged the mortar between these trees, it became wedged awry there; and, as Kŕishńa pulled it through, it pulled down the trunks of the trees.* Hearing the crackling noise, the people of Vraja came to see what was the matter; and there they beheld the two large trees, with shattered stems and broken branches, prostrate on the ground, with the child fixed between them, with a rope round his belly, laughing, and showing his white little teeth, just budded. It is hence that Kŕishńa is called Dámodara,—from the binding of the rope (dáman) round his belly (udara).[1]† The elders of the cowherds, with Nanda at their head, looked upon these circumstances with alarm, considering them as of evil omen.‡ "We cannot remain in this place," said they. "Let us go to some other (part of the) forest; for here many evil signs threaten us with destruction:—the death of Pútaná, the upsetting of the

[1] Our text and that of the Hari Vaḿśa take no notice of the legend§ of Nalakúbara and Mańigríva, sons of Kubera, who, according to the Bhágavata,¶ had been metamorphosed, through a curse of Ndrada, into these two trees, and for whose liberation this feat of Kŕishńa was intended.

* भग्नावुत्तुङ्गशाखाग्रौ तेन तौ यमलार्जुनौ ।

† ततश्च दामोदरतां स ययौ दामबन्धनात् ।

‡ मन्त्रयामासुरुद्विग्ना महोत्पातातिभीरवः ।

§ This legend is referred to by the commentator.

Corrected from "Nalakuvera".

¶ X., Prior Section, IX., 22, 23. Nalakúbara and Mańigríva are there called *guhyakas*.

waggon, and the fall of the trees without their being blown down by the wind. Let us depart hence, without delay, and go to Vŕindávana, where terrestrial prodigies may no more disturb us."

Having thus resolved, the inhabitants of Vraja communicated their intention to their families, and desired them to move without delay. Accordingly, they set off, with their waggons and their cattle, driving before them their bulls, and cows, and calves.* The fragments of their household stores they threw away; and, in an instant, Vraja was overspread with flights of crows. Vŕindávana was chosen by Kŕishńa,—whom acts do not affect,†—for the sake of providing for the nourishment of the kine; for there, in the hottest season, the new grass springs up as verdantly as in the rains. Having repaired, then, from Vraja to Vŕindávana, the inhabitants of the former drew up their waggons in the form of a crescent.[1]‡

---

[1] The Hari Vamśa,§ not satisfied with the prodigies which had alarmed the cowherds, adds another, not found, it is believed, anywhere else. The emigration, according to that work, originates, not with the Gopas, but the two boys, who wish to go to Vŕindávana; and, in order to compel the removal, Kŕishńa converts the hairs of his body into hundreds of wolves, who so harass and alarm the inhabitants of Vraja, that they determine to abandon their homes.

---

* ततः क्षणेन प्रययुः शकटैर्गोधनैस्तथा ।
यूथशो वत्सपालाश्च कालयन्तो व्रजौकसः ॥

† *Aklishta-karman*, "resolute in achievement," or "indefatigable."

‡ स समावासितः सर्वो व्रजो वृन्दावने ततः ।
शकटीवाटपर्यन्तचन्द्रार्धाकारसंस्थितिः ॥

§ Chapter LXV.

As the two boys, Ráma and Dámodara, grew up, they were ever together in the same place, and engaged in the same boyish sports.* They made themselves crests of the peacocks' plumes, and garlands† of forest-flowers, and musical instruments of leaves and reeds, or played upon the pipes used by the cowherds.‡ Their hair was trimmed like the wings of the crow;[1] and they resembled two young princes, portions of the deity of war.§ They were robust; and they roamed about, (always) laughing and playing, sometimes with each other, sometimes with other boys; driving, along with the young cowherds, the calves to pasture. Thus, the two guardians of the world were keepers of cattle, until they had attained seven years of age, in the cow-pens of Vrindávana.||

Then came on the season of the rains, when the atmosphere laboured with accumulated clouds, and the quarters of the horizon were blended into one by

---

[1] The Káka-paksha, or crow's wing, implies the hair left on each side of the head; the top being shaved.

---

* वत्सपालौ च संवृत्तौ रामदामोदरौ ततः।
एकस्थानस्थितौ गोष्ठे चेरतुर्बाललीलया॥

† *Avatamsaka*, a word of various meanings. According to the scholiast, it here signifies 'ear-rings'.

‡ गोपवेणुकृतातोद्यौ पत्रवाद्यकृतस्वनौ।

§ काकपक्षधरौ बालौ कुमाराविव पावकी।

Kumára, Skanda, or Kárttikeya is called Pávaki, because a son of Pávaka. The commentator says that the two parts—*ansás*—or forms of Kárttikeya, Śákha and Viśákha, are meant by "the two Pávakis".

|| महाव्रजे।

the driving showers.* The waters of the rivers rose, and overflowed their banks, and spread beyond all bounds, like the minds of the weak and wicked, transported beyond restraint by sudden prosperity.† The pure radiance of the moon was obscured by heavy vapours; as the lessons of holy writ are darkened by the arrogant scoffs of fools (and unbelievers).‡ The bow of Indra§ held its place in the heavens, all unstrung, like a worthless man elevated, by an injudicious prince, to honour.|| The white line of storks appeared upon the back of the cloud, in such contrast as the bright conduct of a man of respectability¶ opposes to the behaviour of a scoundrel.** The ever-fitful lightning, in its new alliance with the sky, was like the friendship of a profligate†† for a man of worth.‡‡ Overgrown by the spreading grain,§§ the paths were indistinctly traced, like the speech of the ignorant, that conveys no positive meaning.|||

* There is here a stanza,—and one recognized by the commentator,—which the Translator has passed by:

सद्यजातनवशष्पाढ्या शक्रगोपावृता मही ।
तदा मारकतेवासीत्पद्मरागविभूषिता ॥

"The earth, luxuriant with new-grown grass, and bestrown with *śakragopas*, then became emerald and, as it were, adorned with rubies."

The *śakragopa* or *indragopa* is a beautiful insect which no one that has seen it in India can ever forget.

† मनांसि दुर्विनीतानां प्राप्य लक्ष्मीं नवामिव ।

‡ सद्वाक्यवादो मूर्खाणां प्रगल्भाभिरिवोक्तिभिः ।

§ Śakra, in the original.

|| यथाज्ञताविवेकस्य नृपस्येव परिग्रहे ।

¶ *Kulína.* ** *Durvritta.* †† *Durjana.* ‡‡ *Pravara.*

§§ My MSS. have *śashpa*, 'young grass,'—not *sasya*.

||| शष्पासस्यसमुन्मार्गाः अव्यक्तानामिवोक्तयः ।

At this time, Kŕishńa and Ráma, accompanied by the cow-boys, traversed the forests, that echoed with the hum of bees and the peacock's cry.* Sometimes they sang in chorus, or danced together; sometimes they sought shelter from the cold, beneath the trees; sometimes they decorated themselves with flowery garlands,†—sometimes, with peacocks' feathers; sometimes they stained themselves of various hues, with the minerals of the mountain; sometimes, weary, they reposed on beds of leaves, and, sometimes, imitated, in mirth, the muttering of the thunder-cloud; sometimes they excited their juvenile associates to sing;‡ and, sometimes, they mimicked the cry of the peacock, with their pipes. In this manner, participating in various feelings and emotions, and affectionately attached to each other, they wandered, sporting and happy, through the wood. At evening-tide came Kŕishńa and Balaráma,§ like two cow-boys,|| along with the cows and the cowherds. At evening-tide, the two immortals, having come to the cow-pens, joined, heartily, in whatever sports amused the sons of the herdsmen.¶

* उन्मत्तशिखिसारङ्गे नदिन्मत्ते महावने ।

† The Sanskrit has garlands of *kadamba*-blossoms.

‡ गायतामन्यगोपानां प्रशंसापरमौ क्वचित् ।

§ Here called, in the original, Bala.

|| गोपवेषधरौ, "clad like cowherds," is one reading; गोपवेणुधरौ, "carrying cowherds' pipes," is another.

¶ विकाले च यथायोग्यं व्रजमेत्य महाबलौ ।
गोपैः समानैः सहितौ चिक्रीडातेऽमराविव ॥

CHAPTER VII.

Kríshńa combats the serpent Káliya: alarm of his parents and companions: he overcomes the serpent, and is propitiated by him: commands him to depart from the Yamuná river to the ocean.

ONE day, Kríshńa, unaccompanied by Ráma, went to Vríndávana. He was attended by (a troop of) cowherds, and gaily decorated with wild flowers. On his way, he came to the Yamuná,* which was flowing in sportive undulations, and sparkling with foam, as if with smiles, as the waves dashed against the borders. Within its bed, however, was the fearful pool of the serpent Kálíya,†—boiling with the fires of poison,—[1]: from the fumes of which, large trees upon the bank were blighted, and by whose waters, when raised, by a gale, into the air, birds were scorched. Beholding this dreadful (lake), which was like another mouth of death, Madhusúdana reflected, that the wicked and poisonous Kálíya, who had been vanquished by him-

[1] The commentator says, this means nothing more than that the waters of the pool were hot: विषाग्निना शृतं तप्तवारि यस्मिन्।§ I do not know if hot springs have been found in the bed, or on the borders, of the Jumna. The hot well of Sítá-kuńd, near Mongir, is not far from the Ganges.

* Kálindí, one of its synonyms, in the original. The Yamuná is so called from Mount Kalinda, whence it rises.

† In some MSS., he is here called Káliya; and so his name is ordinarily written in the sequel. For his origin and abode, see Vol. II., p. 74, note 1, and p. 210, note 1.

: विषाग्निशृतवारिकम्।

§ I do not find these words, but something like them, in the commentary.

self (in the person of Garuda), and had been obliged to fly from the ocean (where he had inhabited the island Ramańaka), must be lurking at its bottom, and defiling the Yamuná, the consort of the sea, so that neither men nor cattle could slake their thirst by her waters. Such being the case, he determined to dislodge the Nága, and enable the dwellers of Vraja to frequent the vicinage without fear:* for it was the especial purpose, he considered, of his descent upon earth, to reduce to subjection all such violators of law. "Here," thought he, "is a Kadamba-tree, which is sufficiently near. I can climb up it, and thence leap into the serpent's pool." Having thus resolved, he bound his clothes† tightly about him, and jumped, boldly,‡ into the lake of the serpent-king. The waters, agitated by his plunge amidst them, were scattered to a considerable distance from the bank; and, the spray falling upon the trees, they were immediately set on fire by the heat of the poisonous vapour combined with the water; and the whole horizon was in a blaze.§ Krishńa, having dived into the pool, struck his arms in defiance;[1] and the snake-

[1] Slapping the upper part of one arm with the hand of the other is a common act of defiance amongst Indian athletes.

* तदस्य नागराजस्य कर्तव्यो निग्रहो मया ।
निस्त्रासास्तु सुखं येन चरेयुर्व्रजवासिनः ॥

† *Parikara*, 'a girdle.'

‡ *Vegita*, 'expeditiously.'

§ तेनाभिपतता तत्र क्षोभितः स महाह्रदः ।
अत्यर्थं दूरजातांस्तु तांसिषेच महीरुहान् ॥
ते हि दुष्टविषज्वालातप्ताम्बुपवनोक्षिताः ।
जज्वलुः पादपाः सद्यो ज्वालाव्याप्तदिगन्तराः ॥

king, hearing the sound, quickly came forth. His eyes were coppery red; and his hoods were flaming with deadly venom. He was attended by many other (powerful and) poisonous snakes,—feeders upon air,—and by hundreds of serpent-nymphs, decorated with rich jewels, whose ear-rings glittered with trembling radiance, as the wearers moved along.* Coiling themselves around Kŕishńa, they, all, bit him with teeth from which fiery poison was emitted. Kŕishńa's companions, beholding him in the lake, encompassed by the snakes twining around him, ran off to Vraja, lamenting and bewailing aloud his fate.† "Kŕishńa," they called out, "has foolishly plunged into the serpent's pool, and is there bitten to death by the snake-king. Come and see." The cowherds, and their wives, and Yaśodá, hearing this news, which was like a thunderbolt, ran, immediately, to the pool, frightened out of their senses, and crying: "Alas! alas! where is he?" The Gopis were retarded by Yaśodá, who, in her agitation, stumbled and slipped at every step;‡ but Nanda, and the cowherds, and the invincible§ Ráma hastened to (the banks of) the Yamuná, eager to assist Kŕishńa. There they beheld him (apparently) in the power of the serpent-king, encompassed by twining snakes, and making no effort (to escape). Nanda, as soon as he set his eyes upon his

* प्रकम्पिततनूत्क्षेपचलत्कुण्डलकान्तयः ।

† तं तत्र पतितं दृष्ट्वा सर्पभोगनिपीडितम् ।
गोपा व्रजमुपागम्य चुक्रुशुः शोकलालसाः ॥

‡ हा हा क्वासाविति जनो गोपीनामतिविह्वलः ।
यशोदया समं भ्रान्तो द्रुतं प्रस्खलितं ययौ ॥

§ *Adbhuta-vikrama.*

son, became senseless; and Yaśodá, also, (when she beheld him, lost all consciousness). The Gopís, overcome with sorrow, wept, and called affectionately, and with convulsive sobs,* upon Keśava. "Let us all," said they, "plunge, with Yaśodá, into the fearful pool of the serpent-king. We cannot return to Vraja. For what is day, without the sun? What, night, without the moon? What is a herd of heifers, without its lord? What is Vraja, without Kríshńa? Deprived of him, we will go no more to Gokula. The forest will lose its delights; it will be like a lake without water.† When this dark-lotos-leaf-complexioned Hari is not present, there is no joy in the maternal dwelling. How strange is this! And, as for you, ye cowherds, how, poor beings, will you live amidst the pastures, when you no longer behold the brilliant lotos-eyes of Hari?‡ Our hearts have been wiled away by the music of his voice.§ We will not go, without Puńdaríkáksha, to the folds|| of Nanda. Even now, though held in the coils of the serpent-king, see, friends, how his face brightens with smiles, as we gaze upon him!"

When the mighty son of Rohińí,¶ (Balaráma,) heard these exclamations of the Gopís, and, with disdainful glance, beheld the cowherds overcome with terror,

* भयकातर्यगद्गदम् ।

† अरण्यं नातिसेव्यं च वारिहीनं यथा सरः ।

Some MSS. begin this line with अरण्यः;—referring to Vraja,—the reading preferred by the commentator.

‡ उत्फुल्लपङ्कजदलस्पष्टकान्तिविलोचनम् ।
अपश्यन्तो हरिं दीनाः कथं गोष्ठे भविष्यथ ॥

§ अत्यर्थमधुरालापहृताशेषमनोधनम् ।

|| Gokula.

¶ Rauhińeya, in the original.

Nanda gazing fixedly upon the countenance of his son, and Yaśodá unconscious, he spake to Kŕishńa in his own character: "What is this, O god of gods? The quality of mortal is sufficiently assumed. Dost thou not know thyself eternal? Thou art the centre of creation; as the nave is of the spokes of a wheel.* A portion of thee have I, also, been born, as thy senior.† The gods, to partake of thy pastimes as man, have, all, descended under a like disguise; and the goddesses have come down to Gokula, to join in thy sports. Thou, eternal, hast, last of all, appeared below.‡ Wherefore, Kŕishńa, dost thou disregard these divinities, who, as cowherds, are thy friends and kin? these sorrowing females, who, also, are thy relations?§ Thou hast put on the character of man; thou hast exhibited the tricks of childhood. Now let this fierce snake, though armed with venomed fangs, be subdued (by thy celestial vigour)."¶

---

* त्वमस्य जगतो नाभिरराणामिव संश्रयः ।

† Only thus much is translated of the following:

कर्तापहर्ता पाता च त्रैलोक्यं त्वं त्रयीमयः ॥
सेन्द्ररुद्राश्विवसुभिरादित्यैर्मरुदग्निभिः ।
चिन्त्यसे त्वमचिन्त्यात्मन्समस्तैश्चैव योगिभिः ॥
जगत्यर्थे जगन्नाथ भारावतरणेच्छया ।
अवतीर्णोऽसि मर्त्येषु तवांशश्चाहमग्रजः ॥

The scholiast tacitly recognizes these lines as part of the text, and comments on them.

‡ The original is, here, not very closely adhered to:

मनुष्यलीलां भगवन्भजतो भवतः सुराः ।
विडम्बयन्तस्त्वल्लीलां सर्व एव समासते ॥
अवतार्य भवान्पूर्वं गोकुलेऽत्र सुराङ्गनाः ।
क्रीडार्थमात्मनः पश्चादवतीर्णोऽसि शाश्वत ॥

§ Here, again, the rendering is very free.

Bála-chápala.

¶ तदयं दम्यतां कृष्ण दुरात्मा दशनायुधः ।

Thus reminded (of his real character, by Ráma), Kŕishńa smiled gently, and (speedily) extricated himself from the coils of the snakes. Laying hold of the middle hood of their chief with both his hands, he bent it down, and set his foot upon the hitherto unbended head, and danced upon it in triumph. Wherever the snake attempted to raise his head, it was again trodden down; and many bruises were inflicted on the hood, by the pressure of the toes of Kŕishńa.* Trampled upon by the feet of Kŕishńa, as they changed position in the dance, the snake fainted, and vomited forth much blood.[1] Beholding the head and neck of their lord thus injured, and the blood flowing (from his mouth), the females† of the snake-king implored the clemency of Madhusúdana. "Thou art recognized, O god of gods!" they exclaimed. "Thou art the sovereign of all; thou art light supreme, inscrutable; thou art the mighty lord,‡ the portion of that (supreme light). The

[1] The expressions are भग्नस्य रेचकैः and दण्डपातनिपातेन। And Rechaka and Dańdapáta are said to be different dispositions of the feet in dancing; variations of the bhrama, or pirouette: the latter is the a-plomb, or descent. It is also read Dańdapáda-nipátena,§ "the falling of the feet, like that of a club." ||

* चालनं चापि हस्ताभ्यामुभाभ्यां मध्यमं फणम् ।
पादद्वाभ्युपशिरसि भ्रमणतीर्थविक्रमः ॥
भ्रमः पदेऽभवत्तस्य ग्रावस्थित्यविघूर्णितः ।
पदोन्नतिं च कुरुते नमाभाश्च ततः शिरः ॥

† *Patni*, 'wives.'

‡ *Parameśvara.*

§ Also, दण्डपादनिपातेन।

|| The commentary quotes a considerable extract, from some unnamed metrical authority, on the steps in dancing.

gods themselves are unable worthily to praise thee, the lord self-existent.* How, then, shall females proclaim thy nature? How shall we (fully) declare him, of whom the egg of Brahmá, made up of earth, sky, water, fire, and air, is but a small portion of a part? Holy sages have in vain sought to know thy eternal essence.† We bow to that form: which is the most subtile of atoms, the largest of the large; to him whose birth is without a creator, whose end knows no destroyer, and who, alone, is the cause of duration. There is no wrath in thee; for thine is the protection of the world; and, hence, this chastisement of Káliya. Yet, hear us.§ Women are to be regarded with pity by the virtuous: animals are humanely treated, even by fools.|| Let, therefore, the author of wisdom¶ have compassion upon this poor creature. Thyself, as an oviparous, hooded snake, art the upholder of the world. Oppressed by thee, he will speedily perish.** What is this feeble serpent, compared to thee, in whom the universe re-

* न समर्थाः सुरा स्तोतुं यमनन्यभवं प्रभुम् ।

† यतयो न विदुर्नित्यं यत्स्वरूपमयोगिनः ।

‡ *Paramártha.*

§ कोपः स्वल्पोऽपि ते नास्ति स्थितिपालनमेव ते ।
कारणं कालियस्यास्य दमने श्रूयतामतः ॥

|| The only readings that I find yield a very different sense. The ordinary original is:

स्त्रियोऽनुकम्प्याः साधूनां मूढा दीनाश्च जन्तवः ।

Instead of दीनाश्च, one MS. has दीना च ।

¶ ज्ञमतां वर,—the vocative.

** समस्तजगदाधारो भवानल्पबलः फणी ।
त्वया च पीडितो जह्यान्मुहूर्तार्धेन जीवितम् ॥

Kŕishńa is not here called a snake. Some copies have, instead of अल्पबलः, चाल्पबलः ।

poses? Friendship and enmity are felt towards equals and superiors, (not for those infinitely beneath us*). Then, sovereign of the world, have mercy upon us. This (unfortunate) snake is about to expire. Give us, as a gift of charity, our husband."

When they had thus spoken, the Nága himself, almost exanimate, repeated, feebly, their solicitations for mercy. "Forgive me," he murmured, "O god of gods! How shall I address thee, who art possessed, through thine own strength and essence, of the eight great faculties,—in energy unequalled?† Thou art the Supreme, the progenitor of the supreme (Brahmá). Thou art the Supreme Spirit; and from thee the Supreme proceeds. Thou art beyond all finite objects. How can I speak thy praise?‡ How can I declare his greatness from whom come Brahmá, Rudra, Chandra, Indra, the Maruts, the Aświns, the Vasus, and Ádityas; of whom the whole world is an infinitely small portion,§ a portion destined to represent his essence; and whose nature, primitive or derived,|| Brahmá and the immortals do not comprehend? How can I approach him, to whom the gods offer incense and flowers¶ culled from the groves of Nandana; whose incarnate forms the king of

* I have parenthesized these words; there being nothing, in the original, answering to them. Even a Pauráṇik writer would not use in such a lax way a word corresponding to "infinitely".

† तवाष्टगुणमैश्वर्यं नाथ स्वाभाविकं परम् ।
निरस्तातिशयं यस्य तस्य स्तोष्यामि किं त्वहम् ॥

‡ त्वं परस्त्वं परस्याद्यः परं त्वत्तः परात्मकः ।
परस्मात्परमो यस्त्वं तस्य स्तोष्यामि किं त्वहम् ॥

§ एकावयवसूक्ष्मांशः ।

|| *Sat* and *asat*.

¶ *Pushpánulepana*, "ungents made from flowers."

the deities ever adores, unconscious of his real person; whom the sages that have withdrawn their senses from all external objects worship in thought, and, enshrining his image in the purposes of their hearts, present to it the flowers of sanctity?[1]* I am quite unable, O god of gods, to worship or to hymn thee. Thy own clemency must, alone, influence thy mind to show me compassion. It is the nature of snakes to be savage; and I am born of their kind. Hence, this is my nature, not mine offence. The world is created, as it is destroyed, by thee; and the species, form, and nature of all things in the world are thy work. Even such as thou hast created me, in kind, in form, and in nature, such I am; and such are my actions.† Should I act differently, then, indeed, should I deserve thy punishment; for so thou hast declared.[2] Yet, that I have been

---

[1] Bháva-pushpas. There are said to be eight such flowers: clemency, self-restraint, tenderness, patience, resignation, devotion, meditation, and truth.‡

[2] Both in the Vedas and in the institutes of law; where it is enjoined, that every one shall discharge the duties of his caste and condition; and any deviation from them merits punishment; as by the texts निषिद्धाचरणे दण्ड्यः, "In following prohibited observances, a person is punishable;" and स्वभावविहितं कर्म

---

* बहिःसंहृत्य यद्रूपं ध्यानेनार्चन्ति योगिनः ।
भावपुष्पादिभिर्नाथ सोऽर्च्यते मा कथं मया ॥

† यथाहं भवता सृष्टो जात्या रूपेण चेश्वर ।
स्वभावेन च संयुक्तस्तथेदं चेष्टितं मया ॥

‡ The commentator has: *ahiṅsá*, *indriya-nigraha*, *sarva-bhúta-dayá*, *kshamá*, *śama*, *tapas*, *dhyána*, *satya*.

punished by thee is, indeed, a blessing; for punishment from thee alone is a favour.* Behold, I am now without strength, without poison,—deprived of both by thee! Spare me my life. I ask no more. Command me what I shall do."†

Being thus addressed by Káliya, Kríshńa replied:‡ "You must not tarry here, (nor anywhere) in the stream of the Yamuná. Depart, (immediately), with your family and followers, to the sea, where Garuda, the foe of the serpent-race, will not harm you, when he sees the impression of my feet upon your brow."§ So saying, Hari set the snake-king at liberty, who, bowing, reverentially, to his victor,‖ departed to the ocean; abandoning, in the sight of all, the lake he had haunted, accompanied by all his females, children, and dependants. When the snake was gone, the Gopas hailed Govinda as one risen from the dead, and embraced him, and bathed his forehead with tears of joy.¶ Others, contemplating the water of the river, now freed from

---

कुर्वन्नाप्नोति किल्बिषम्.** "Who does acts unsuited to his natural disposition incurs guilt."

---

* तथापि यच्छमनत्स्वामी दण्डं पातितवान्मयि ।
स सोढोऽयं वरो दण्डस्त्वत्तो मे नान्यतो वरः ॥

† हतवीर्यो हतविषो दमितोऽहं त्वयाच्युत ।
जीवितं दीयतामेकमाज्ञापय करोमि किम् ॥

‡ This introduction is supplied by the Translator.

§ *Múrdhan*, 'head.'

‖ 'To Kríshńa', in the original.

¶ गते सर्पे परिष्वज्य मृतं पुनरिवागतम् ।
गोपा मूर्धनि गोविन्दं सिषिचुर्नेत्रजैर्जलैः ॥

** These quotations are taken from the commentary.

peril,* were filled with wonder, and sang the praise of Kŕishńa, who is unaffected by works.† Thus, eminent by his glorious exploits, and eulogized by the Gopas and Gopís, Kŕishńa returned to Vraja.‡

---

* दृष्ट्वा विपक्षवां महीम् ।

† *Aklishŕa-karman.* *Vide supra*, p. 262, note †.

‡ Instead of the reading of two verses, here rendered, the MSS. containing the commentary have three verses, naming Baladeva, Nanda and Yaśodá, as accompanying Kŕishńa on his way back to Vraja.

CHAPTER VIII.

The demon Dhenuka destroyed by Ráma.

AGAIN, tending upon the herds, Ráma and Keśava* wandered through the woods, and (on one occasion), came to a pleasing grove of palms, where dwelt the fierce demon† Dhenuka,‡ feeding upon the flesh of deer.§ Beholding the trees covered with fruit, and desirous of gathering it, the cowherds called out (to the brothers), and said: "See, Ráma; see, Kŕishńa! In this grove, belonging to the great Dhenuka, the trees are loaded with ripe fruit, the smell of which perfumes the air. We should like to eat some. Will you throw some down?"|| As soon as the boys had spoken, Sankarshańa and Kŕishńa (shook the trees, and) brought down the fruit on the ground. Hearing the noise of the falling fruit, the fierce¶ and malignant demon** (Dhenuka), in the form of an ass, hastened to the spot, in a (great) passion, and began to kick Ráma†† on the

---

* The original has Bala.

† *Dánava.*

‡ According to the *Harivańśa*, *śl.* 3114, Dhenuka was the same as Khara, for whom see Vol. III., p. 316, note ||.

§ The reading accepted by the commentator yields "flesh of men and kine."

|| हे राम हे कृष्ण सदा धेनुकेनैष रक्ष्यते ।
भूप्रदेशो यतस्तस्मात्पक्वानीमानि सन्ति वै ॥
फलानि पश्य तालानां गन्धामोदितदिंशि च ।
वयमेतान्यभीप्सामः पात्यन्तां यदि रोचते ॥

¶ *Durásada.*

** *Daitya.*

†† Substituted, by the Translator, for Bala.

breast with his hinder heels. Ráma,* however, seized him by both hind legs, and, whirling him round, until he expired, tossed his carcass to the top of a palm-tree, from the branches of which it struck down abundance of fruit, like rain-drops poured upon earth by the wind.† The animals that were of kin to Dhenuka came running to his aid; but Kŕishńa and Ráma‡ treated them in the same manner,§ until the trees were laden with dead asses,[2] and the ground was strewed with ripe fruit. Henceforward, the cattle grazed, unobstructed, in the palm-grove, and cropped the new pasturage, where they had never before ventured.[1]

---

[1] This exploit is related in the Bhágavata, Hari Vamśa, and other Vaishńava Puráńas, much in the same strain, but not always in the same place. It more commonly precedes the legend of the discomfiture of Káliya.

---

* Elsewhere it is said that Kŕishńa slew Dhenuka. See, for instance, the *Mahábhárata*, *Udyoga-parvan*, *ll.* 4410.

† ततः फलान्यनेकानि तालाग्रान्निपतन्खरः ।
पृथिव्यां पातयामास महावातोऽम्बुदानिव ॥

‡ Balabhadra, in the original. See the next note.

§ अन्यानप्यस्य वै ज्ञातीनागतान्दैत्यगर्दभान् ।
कृष्णश्चिक्षेप तालाग्रे बलभद्रश्च लीलया ॥

[2] *Daitya-gardabha.* This term is applied, throughout the chapter, to Dhenuka and his kindred. Their proper form, then, was the asinine, though they were of demonic extraction.

CHAPTER IX.

Sports of the boys in the forest. Pralamba, the Asura, comes amongst them: is destroyed by Ráma, at the command of Kŕishńa.

WHEN the demon in the form of an ass, and all his tribe,* had been destroyed, the grove of palms became the favourite resort of the Gopas and their wives;† and the sons of Vasudeva, greatly pleased, repaired to the Bháńdíra fig-tree.‡ They continued to wander about, shouting, and singing, and gathering fruits and flowers from the trees; now driving the cows afar to pasture; now calling them by their names; now carrying the foot-ropes of the kine upon their shoulders; now ornamenting themselves with garlands of forest-flowers. They looked like two young bulls, when the horns first appear.§ Attired, the one in yellow, and the other, in sable garments, they looked like two clouds, one white, and one black, surmounted by the bow of Indra.‖ Sporting, mutually, with frolics beneficial to the world, they roamed about, like two monarchs over all the collected

---

* *Anuga.*

† "Of the kine", likewise, and first of all: गोगोपगोपीनाम् ।

‡ भाण्डीरवटं is the reading here followed; but that accepted by the commentator is भाण्डीरवनं, his explanation of which is: भद्रीरत्वाद्वटस्तत्संबन्धि वनम् । The tree referred to is, therefore, called Bhaddíra. In other works, however, it is called Bháńdíra, also.

§ The allusion here, the commentator says, is to their hair, as being tonsured in a peculiar fashion. *Vide supra*, p. 263, note 1.

‖ सुवर्णाञ्जनचूर्णाभ्यां तौ तदा रूषिताम्बरौ ।
महेन्द्रायुधसंयुक्तौ श्वेतकृष्णाविवाम्बुदौ ॥

sovereigns of the earth. Assuming human duties, and maintaining the human character, they strayed through the thickets, amusing themselves with sports suited to their mortal species and condition, in swinging on the boughs of trees,* or in boxing, and wrestling,† and hurling stones.

Having observed the two lads thus playing about, the Asura Pralamba, seeking (to devour) them, came amongst the cowherd boys, in the shape of one of themselves, and mixed, without being suspected, in their pastimes;‡ for he thought, that, thus disguised, it would not be difficult to find an opportunity to kill, first, Kŕishńa, and, afterwards, the son of Rohińí.§ The boys commenced playing at the game of leaping like deer, two and two together.[1]|| Govinda was matched with Śrídáman,¶ and Balaráma,** with Pralamba:

[1] Jumping with both feet at once,—as deer bound,—two boys together. The one that holds out longest, or comes to a given point first, is the victor; and the vanquished is then bound to carry him to the goal, if not already attained, and back again to the starting-post, on his shoulders. The Bhágavata does not specify the game, but mentions that the vanquished carry the victors on their backs.

* स्कन्दोलिकाभिः । Comment: मनुष्यवल्कलमयदोलादिभिः ।

† *Vyáyáma.*

‡ सोऽवगाहत निःशङ्कस्तेषां मध्यममानुषः ।
मानुषं वपुरास्थाय प्रलम्बो दानवोत्तमः ॥

§ Rauhińeya, in the original.

|| हरिणाक्रीडनं नाम बालक्रीडनकं ततः ।
प्रक्रीडिता हि ते सर्वे द्वौ द्वौ युगपदुत्पतन् ॥

¶ A friend of Kŕishńa.

** Bala, in the Sanskrit.

the other boys were coupled with one another, and went leaping away. Govinda* beat his companion, and Balaráma,† his; and the boys who were on Kríshńa's side were, also, victorious. Carrying one another, they reached the Bhánďíra-fig; and from thence those who were victors were conveyed back to the starting-ground by those who were vanquished.‡ It being Pralamba's duty to carry Sankarsháńa, the latter mounted upon his shoulders, like the moon riding above a dark cloud; and the demon ran off with him, but did not stop.§ Finding himself, however, unable to bear the weight of Balaráma,‖ he enlarged his bulk, (and looked) like a black cloud in the rainy season. Balaráma,¶ beholding him like a scorched mountain,—his head crowned with a diadem, and his neck hung round with garlands, having eyes as large as cart-wheels, a fearful form, and shaking the earth with his tread,—called out, as he was carried away, to his brother: "Kríshńa, Kríshńa, I am carried off by some demon, disguised as a cowherd, and huge as a mountain.** What shall I do? Tell me, Madhusúdana.†† The villain runs away with speed." Kríshńa‡‡ opened his mouth, smiling,—for he well knew

* Substituted, by the Translator, for Kríshńa.

† "The son of Rohińí, in the original."

‡ पुनर्ववृतिरे सर्वे ये ये तत्र पराजिताः ।

§ संकर्षणं तु स्कन्धेन शीघ्रमुत्क्षिप्य दानवः ।
न तस्थौ प्रजगामैव सचन्द्र इव वारिदः ॥

‖ Rauhińeya, in the Sanskrit.

¶ In the Sanskrit, Sankarshańa.

** This sentence is rendered very freely.

†† The original has Madhunishúdana.

‡‡ The Sanskrit has Govinda.

the might of the son of Rohińí,*—and replied: "Why this subtle pretext of merely mortal nature,† thou who art the soul of all the most subtile of subtile things? Remember yourself, the radical cause of the whole world,—born before all cause, and all that is alone, when the world is destroyed.‡ Dost thou not know that you and I are, alike, the origin of the world, who have come down to lighten its load? The heavens are thy head; the waters are thy body;§ earth is thy feet; thy mouth|| is eternal fire; the moon is thy mind;¶ the wind, thy breath; thy arms and hands are the four regions of space.** Thou hast, O mighty lord, a thousand heads,†† a thousand hands, and feet, and bodies. A thousand Brahmás spring from thee, who art before all, and whom the sages praise in myriads of forms.‡‡ No one (but I) knoweth thy divine person. Thy incarnate person is glorified by all the gods. Knowest thou not, that, at the end of all, the universe disappears in thee; that, upheld by thee, this earth sustains living and inanimate things;§§ and that, in the character of uncreated time, with its divisions of ages, developed

---

* Rauhíneya, in the original.

† किमयं मानुषो भावो व्यक्तमेवावलम्ब्यते।

‡ Here, again, the translation is far from literal.

§ *Múrti.*

|| *Vaktra.*

¶ *Manas.*

** दिशश्चतस्रोऽव्यय बाहवस्ते।

†† *Vaktra.*

‡‡ सहस्रपद्मोद्भवयोनिराद्यः
सहस्रशस्त्वां मुनयो गृणन्ति।

§§ *Charáchara.*

from an instant, thou devourest the world?* As the waters of the sea, when swallowed up by submarine flame, are recovered by the winds, and thrown, in the form of snow, upon the Himáchala, where, coming into contact with the rays of the sun, they reassume their watery nature;[1] so, the world, being devoured by thee,

---

[1] This passage is read and explained differently in different copies.† In some it is:

यत्तं यथा वाडववह्निनाम्बु:
हिमस्वरूपं परिगृह्य कस्तम् ।
हिमाचले भानुमतोंऽशुसंगा-
ज्जलत्वमुपैति पुनस्तदेव ॥

And this is explained: सामुद्रमम्बु वाडवाख्येन वह्निना यत्तं भक्षितं घनीभूय हिमस्वरूपं कस्तकसंज्ञेन वायुना वाडवापिगतेन सूर्यरश्मिनाडीमयेन परिगृह्य गृहीत्वा खमाकाशमारूढं सत् हिमाचले भवतीति शेषः ॥ "The water of the ocean, devoured by the fire called Vádava, becoming condensed, or in the form of dew or snow, is seized by the wind called Kastaka,§ from which the Vádava fire has departed, consisting of a pipe of the solar rays, and, being placed in the air, lies or is on the Himáchala," &c. This is rather an awkward and confused representation of the notion; and the other reading is somewhat preferable. It consists simply in sub-

---

* युगादिभेदैरणुकालरूपो
निमेषपूर्वो जगदेतदत्सि ।

The "instant", or 'twinkling', is here intended as the smallest division of time, extending to *yugas* or ages.

† The various readings of the passage are, according to my copies of the text, few and unimportant; and my several MSS. of the commentary all agree together. The Translator transcribes but a small portion of the scholiast's remarks.

‡ I have displaced the immetrical reading वाडवापिगताम्बु, in favour of the only one that I find in MSS., including those accompanied by the commentary.

§ According to some copies of the commentary, the wind here spoken of is called Karshaka. This name, at all events, is intelligible, which the other is not.

at the period of dissolution, becomes, of necessity, at the end of every Kalpa, the world again, through thy creative efforts.* Thou and I, soul of the universe, are but one and the same cause of the creation of the earth, although, for its protection, we exist in distinct individuals. Calling to memory who thou art, O being of illimitable might,† destroy, of thyself, the demon. Suspending awhile your mortal character, do what is right."

Thus reminded by the magnanimous Kŕishńa, the powerful Baladeva‡ laughed, and squeezed Pralamba

stituting कार्ष्णं for वर्षं; that is, according to the commentary, अम्बु वाडवाग्निना भक्षं कार्ष्णं केन वायुना वाडवाग्निजतेनार्करश्मिना-दीनयेन वर्षं हिमाचले पिण्डं हिमरूपं परिगृह्य क्षिप्तं सत्।§ "The water devoured by the fire is thrown, by the wind Ka,|| made of a solar ray &c., on the Himáchala, where it assumes the form of snow;" and so on. However disfigured by inaccurate views of some of the instruments in operation, the physiology is, in the main very correct, and indicates accurate observation of natural phenomena. The waters of the ocean, converted into vapour by solar heat, are raised, by the same influence, into the air, and thence borne, by the winds, to the summits of lofty mountain-

* एवं त्वया संहृतेऽस्मिन्-
जगत्समस्तं पुनरप्यवश्यम्।
तथैव सर्गाय समुद्यतस्त्व
जगत्त्वमभ्येत्युपकल्पनीय॥

† *Ameyátman.*

‡ Bala, in the original.

§ I do not find this; and it seems to have been put together, with additions, from the words of the scholiast. Perhaps the Translator here transcribes some marginal gloss on the latter part of the scholiast's explanation; for the first quotation contains only a part of it.

|| Nowhere do I meet with the कारकं of the Translator, from which he has extracted "Ka". The only variant of वर्षं, in my MSS., is कार्ष्णं, the वर्षं of which, the commentator explains, signifies हिमाचले पिण्डम्।

with his knees,* striking him, at the same time, on the head (and face), with his fists, so as to beat out both his eyes. The demon, vomiting blood from his mouth, and having his brain forced through the skull,† fell upon the ground, and expired. The Gopas, beholding Pralamba slain, were astonished, and rejoiced, and cried out "Well done", and praised Balaráma.‡ And, thus commended by his play-fellows, and accompanied by Kŕishńa, Bala,§ after the death of the Daitya Pralamba, returned to Gokula.[1]

---

ranges, where they are arrested by a diminished temperature, descend in the form of snow, and again supply the streams that perpetually restore to the sea the treasures of which it is as perpetually plundered.

[1] According to the Hari Vaḿśa,|| the gods, themselves, praised this proof of Ráma's strength (bala), and hence he derived the name of Balaráma.

---

* The Sanskrit has nothing corresponding to the words "with his knees".

† निष्कासितमस्तिष्कः ।

‡ Substituted, by the Translator, for Bala.

§ The original has Ráma.

|| *Śl.* 3786.

CHAPTER X.

Description of autumn. Kríshńa dissuades Nanda from worshipping Indra: recommends him and the Gopas to worship cattle and the mountains.

WHILST Ráma and Keśava were sporting, thus, in Vraja, the rainy season ended, and was succeeded by the season of autumn, when the lotos is full-blown. The (small) Śapharí fish, in their watery burrows,* were oppressed by the heat, like a man by selfish desires, who is devoted to his family.† The peacocks, no longer animated by passion, were silent amidst the woods, like holy saints‡ who have come to know the unreality of the world. The clouds, of shining whiteness, exhausted of their watery wealth, deserted the atmosphere, like those who have acquired wisdom, and depart from their homes.§ Evaporated by the rays of the autumnal sun, the lakes were dried up, like the hearts of men, when withered by the contact of selfishness.‖ The (pellucid) waters of the season were suitably embellished by white water-lilies; as are the minds of the pure, by the apprehension of truth. Brightly, in the starry sky, shone the moon, with undiminished orb, like the saintly being who has reached the last stage of

* पल्वलोदके ।

† पुत्रक्षेत्रादिसक्तेन ममत्वेन यथा गृही ।

‡ *Yogis.*

§ उत्सृज्य जलसर्वस्वं विमलाः सितमूर्त्तयः ।
तत्यजुश्चाम्बरं मेघा गृहं विज्ञानिनो यथा ॥

‖ बह्वालम्बममत्वेन हृदयानीव देहिनाम् ।

bodily existence, in the company of the pious.* The rivers and lakes† slowly retired from their banks; as the wise, by degrees, shrink from the selfish attachment that connects them with wife and child.‡ First abandoned by the waters of the lake, the swans§ again began to congregate, like false ascetics whose devotions are interrupted, and they are again assailed by innumerable afflictions.|| The ocean was still and calm, and exhibited no undulations, like the perfect sage who has completed his course of restraint, and has acquired undisturbed tranquillity of spirit.¶ Everywhere the waters were as clear and pure** as the minds of the wise who behold Vishńu in all things. The autumnal sky was wholly free from clouds, like the heart of the ascetic†† whose cares have been consumed by the fire of devotion. The moon allayed the fervours of the sun; as discrimination alleviates the pain to which egotism gives birth. The clouds of the atmosphere, the muddiness of the earth, the discoloration‡‡ of the waters, were, all, removed by autumn; as abstraction§§ detaches the senses from the objects of perception. The exercise of inspiring, suppressing, and expiring the vital

* चरमदेहात्मा योगी साधुकुले यथा ।

† "Rivers and lakes" is for *jaláśaya*.

‡ ममत्वं क्षेत्रपुत्रादिरूढं शनैर्यथा बुधाः ।

§ *Haṁsa*.

|| क्लेशैः कुयोगिनोऽशेषैरन्तरायहता इव ।

¶ समवाप्तमहायोगो निश्चलात्मा यथा यतिः ।

** "Clear and pure" is to render *ati-prasanna*.

†† *Yogin*.

‡‡ *Kálushya*, 'foulness.'

§§ *Pratyáhára*, 'restraint of the senses.'

air was as if performed, daily, by the waters of the lakes, (as they were full, and stationary, and, then, again declined).[1] *

At this season, when the skies were bright with stars,† Kŕishńa, repairing to Vraja, found all the cowherds busily engaged in preparing for a sacrifice‡ to be offered to Indra;[2] and, going to the elders, he asked

---

[1] A set of very poor quibbles upon the terms§ of the Práńáyáma: or, Púraka,|| drawing in the breath through one nostril; literally, 'filling;' Kumbhaka, closing the nostrils, and suppressing the breath,—keeping it stationary or confined, as it were in a Kumbha or water-pot; and Rechaka, opening the other nostril, and emitting the breath,—literally, 'purging' or 'depletion.' The waters of the reservoirs, replenished, in the beginning of the autumnal season, by the previous rains, remain, for a while, full, until they are drawn off for irrigation, or reduced by evaporation; thus representing the three operations of Púraka, Kumbhaka, and Rechaka.

[2] No public worship is offered to Indra, at present; and the only festival in the Hindu kalendar, the Śakradhwajotthána,¶—the erection of a flag in honour of Śakra or Indra,—should be held on the twelfth or thirteenth of Bhádra,** (which is in the

---

* प्राणायाम इवाम्भोभिः सरसां कृतपूरकैः ।
अभ्यस्तेऽनुदिवसं रेचकैः कुम्भकादिभिः ॥

† *Nakshatra.*

‡ *Makha.*

§ The commentator gives a quotation, apparently from some Yoga treatise, elucidating them.

|| The Translator had, here, and near the end of the note, "Púrańa", which occurs in the commentator's explanation of the technicality *púraka*: पूरकः । पूरणं वायोः ।

¶ The names of the festival which I find are Śakrotthána, Śakrotthánadhwajotsava, Indradhwajasamutthána, &c.

** Light fortnight. The month of Bhádra includes part of August and part of September.

them, as if out of curiosity, what festival* of Indra it was in which they took so much pleasure.† Nanda replied to his question, and said: "Satakratu‡ (or Indra) is the sovereign of the clouds and of the waters. Sent by him, the former bestow moisture upon the earth, whence springs the grain by which we and all embodied beings subsist; with which, also, and with water, we please the gods.§ Hence, too, these cows bear calves, and yield milk, and are happy, and well-nourished,‖ So, when the clouds are seen distended with rain, the earth is neither barren of corn, nor bare of verdure; nor is man distressed by hunger. Indra,¶ the giver of water, having drunk the milk of earth by the solar rays, sheds it, again, upon the earth, for the sustenance of all the world. On this account, all sovereign princes offer, with pleasure, sacrifices to Indra,** at the end

---

very middle of the rainy season), according to the Tithi Tattwa,†† following the authority of the Káliká and Bhavishyottara Puráńas. The Śakradhwajotthána is, also, a rite to be performed by kings and princes. It may be doubted, therefore, if the text intends any particular or appointed celebration.

---

* *Maha.*

† This sentence is much more compressed than the original.

‡ See Vol. I., p. 150.

§ उपभुञ्जानास्तर्पयामश्च देवताः।

‖ क्षीरवत्य इमा गावो वत्सवत्यश्च निर्वृताः।
तेन संवर्धिताः सस्यैः पुष्टास्तुष्टा भवन्ति वै॥

¶ Parjanya, in the original.

** The original has Śakra.

†† See Raghunandana's *Institutes of the Hindoo Religion*, Vol. I., pp. 73—75. Also see the *Śabdakalpadruma*, *sub voce* शक्रध्वज।

of the rains;* and so, also, do we, and so do other people."

When Kŕishńa† heard this speech from Nanda, in regard to the worship of Indra,‡ he determined to put the king of the celestials into a passion, and replied: We, father, are neither cultivators of the soil, nor dealers in merchandise: cows are our divinities;§ and we are sojourners in forests. There are four branches of knowledge,—logical, scriptural, practical, and political.[1] Hear me describe what practical science is. Agriculture, commerce, and tending of cattle,—the knowledge of these three professions constitutes practical science.‖ Agriculture is the subsistence of farmers; buying and selling, of traders. Kine are our support. Thus, the knowledge of means of support¶ is threefold. The object that is cultivated by any one should be, to him,

---

[1] Or, Ánvíkshikí (आन्वीक्षिकी), the science of inquiring by reasoning, Tarka (तर्क), or logic; Trayí (त्रयी), the three Vedas collectively, or the doctrines they teach: Vártá (वार्त्ता), rendered 'practical,' is the knowledge of the means of acquiring subsistence (वृत्ति): the fourth is Dańdaníti (दण्डनीति), the science of government, both domestic and foreign.**

---

* प्रावृषि, "during the rainy season," literally. But the Translator has the authority of the comment: प्रावृषि। मतार्थमिति शेषः। शरत्-कालप्रवर्तनात् ।

† In the original, Dámodara.

‡ Śakra, in the Sanskrit.

§ The original has the singular.

‖ विद्या ह्येका महाभाग वार्त्ता वृत्तित्रयाश्रया ।

¶ "The knowledge of means of support" is to render *vártá*.

** This note is taken, as to its substance, from the commentary. Compare Vol. I., p. 85, note 1; and p. 86, note *.

as his chief divinity:* that should be venerated and worshipped, as it is his benefactor. He who worships the deity of another, and diverts from him the reward that is his due,† obtains not a prosperous station,‡ either in this world or in the next. Where the land ceases to be cultivated, there are bounds assigned, beyond which commences the forest: the forests are bounded by the hills; and so far do our limits extend. We are not shut in with doors, nor confined within walls; we have neither fields nor houses; we wander about, happily, wherever we list, travelling in our waggons.[1] The spirits of these mountains,§ it is said, walk the woods in whatever forms they will, or, in their proper persons, sport upon their own precipices.|| If they should be displeased with those who inhabit the forests, then, transformed to lions and beasts of prey, they will kill the offenders. We, then, are bound to worship the mountains, to offer sacrifices to cattle.¶ What have we to do with Indra?** Cattle and moun-

[1] These nomadic habits are entirely lost sight of in the parallel passages of those Purāṇas in which the juvenile life of Kṛishṇa is narrated. The text of the Hari Vaṁśa is, in most of the other verses, precisely the same as that of the Vishṇu Purāṇa; putting, however, into the mouth of Kṛishṇa a long additional eulogium on the season of autumn.

* विद्यया यो यया युक्तस्तस्य सा दैवतं महत् ।

† योऽन्यस्याः फलमश्नन्वै पूजयत्यपरां नरः ।

‡ "A prosperous station" is for *śobhana*.

§ Literally, "these mountains."

|| *Sānu*.

¶ गिरियज्ञस्त्वयं तस्माद्गोयज्ञश्च प्रवर्त्यताम् ।

** Mahendra, in the original.

tains are (our) gods. Brahmans offer worship with prayer; cultivators of the earth adore their landmarks;* but we, who tend our herds in the forests and mountains,† should worship them and our kine. Let prayer and offerings, then, be addressed to the mountain Govardhana; and kill a victim in due form.‡ Let the whole station collect their milk,§ without delay, and feed, with it, the Brahmans, and all who may desire to partake of it. When the oblations|| have been presented, and the Brahmans have been fed, let the Gopas circumambulate the cows, decorated with garlands¶ of autumnal flowers. If the cowherds will attend to these suggestions, they will secure the favour of the mountain, of the cattle, and, also, mine."

When Nanda and the other Gopas heard these words of Kŕishńa, their faces expanded with delight, and they said that he had spoken well. "You have judged rightly, child," exclaimed they. "We will do exactly as you have proposed, and offer adoration to the mountain." Accordingly, the inhabitants of Vraja worshipped the mountain, presenting to it curds, and milk, and flesh; and they fed hundreds and thousands of Brahmans, and many other guests who came (to the ceremony),

* *Sítá.* But there is a variant,—the reading of the commentator,—*síra*, 'the plough.'

† अद्रिवनाश्रयाः। Some MSS. have अद्रिवनौकसः।

‡ तस्माद्गोवर्धनः शैलो भवद्भिर्विविधार्हणैः।
अर्च्यतां पूज्यतां मेध्यं पशुं हत्वा विधानतः॥

§ The Translator has taken this meaning of *sandoha* from the comment: सर्वगृहोद्भवक्षीरादिः।

|| *Homa.*

¶ *Ápída*, 'chaplet.'

even as Kŕishńa had enjoined: and, when they had made their offerings, they circumambulated the cows and the bulls, that bellowed as loud as roaring clouds.* Upon the summit of Govardhana, Kŕishńa presented himself, saying "I am the mountain," and partook of much food presented by the Gopas; whilst, in his own form as Kŕishńa, he ascended the hill, along with the cowherds, and worshipped his other self.[1] Having promised them many blessings,† the mountain-person of Kŕishńa vanished; and, the ceremony being completed, the cowherds returned to their station.

---

[1] The Hari Vaḿśa says:‡ "An illusory Kŕishńa, having become the mountain, ate the flesh that was offered:"

मांसं च मायया कृष्णो गिरिर्भुत्वा समश्नुते ।

Of course, the 'personified' mountain is intended, as appears from several of the ensuing passages; as 'for instance', he says,§ presently: "I am satisfied; and then, in his divine form, he smiled:"

संतृप्तोऽस्मीति दिव्येन रूपेण प्रजहास वै ।

The Hari Vaḿśa affords, here, as in so many other places, proofs of its Dakhini origin. It is very copious upon the homage paid to the cattle, and their decoration with garlands and plumes of peacocks' feathers, of which our text takes no notice. But, in the south of India, there is a very popular festival, that of the Punjal, scarcely known in the north, when cattle are decorated and worshipped; a celebration which has, no doubt, suggested to the compiler of the Hari Vaḿśa the details which he describes.

---

* गावः शैलं ततश्चक्रुरर्चितास्ताः प्रदक्षिणम् ।
वृषभाश्चापि नर्दन्तः सतोया जलदा इव ॥

† गोपा लब्ध्वा ततो वरान् ।

‡ Śl. 3874.

§ Śl. 3876.

CHAPTER XI.

Indra, offended by the loss of his offerings, causes heavy rain to deluge Gokula. Kṛishṅa holds up the mountain Govardhana, to shelter the cowherds and their cattle.

INDRA,* being thus disappointed of his offerings, was exceedingly angry, and thus addressed a cohort of his attendant clouds, called Saṁvartaka. "Ho! clouds," he said, "hear my words, and, without delay, execute what I command. The insensate cowherd Nanda, assisted by his fellows, has withheld the usual offerings to us, relying upon† the protection of Kṛishṅa. Now, therefore, afflict the cattle, that are their sustenance, and whence their occupation‡ is derived, with rain and wind. Mounted upon my elephant, as vast as a mountain-peak, I will give you aid, in strengthening the tempest." When Indra§ ceased, the clouds, obedient to his commands, came down, in a fearful storm of rain and wind, to destroy the cattle. In an instant, the earth, the points of the horizon, and the sky were, all, blended into one by the heavy and incessant shower. The clouds roared aloud, as if in terror of the lightning's scourge, and poured down uninterrupted torrents.|| The whole earth was enveloped in (impenetrable) darkness by the thick and volumed clouds;

* Śakra, in the Sanskrit.

† *Ádhmáta*, 'Inflated by.'

‡ *Gopatya*.

§ The original has Surendra.

|| विद्युल्लताकशाघातत्रस्तैरिव घनैर्घनम् ।
नादापूरितदिक्चक्रैर्धारासारमपात्यत ॥

and above, below, and on every side, the world was water. The cattle, pelted by the storm, shrunk, cowering, into the smallest size, or gave up their breath:* some covered their calves with their flanks; and some beheld their young ones carried away by the flood. The calves, trembling in the wind, looked piteously at their mothers, or implored, in low moans, as it were, the succour of Kŕishńa.† Hari, beholding all Gokula agitated with alarm,—cowherds, cowherdesses, and cattle;‡ all in a state of consternation,—thus reflected: "This is the work of Mahendra, in resentment of the prevention of his sacrifice; and it is incumbent on me to defend this station of herdsmen. I will lift up this spacious mountain from its stony base, and hold it up, as a large umbrella, over the cow-pens." § Having thus determined, Kŕishńa immediately plucked up the mountain Govardhana, and held it (aloft), with one hand, in sport, saying|| to the herdsmen: "Lo! the mountain is on high. Enter beneath it, quickly; and it will shelter you from the storm. Here you will be secure, and at your ease, in places defended from the wind. Enter, (without delay); and fear not that the mountain will

---

* गावस्तु तेन पतता वर्षवातेन वेगिना ।
धूताः प्राणाञ्जहुः सन्नत्रिकसक्थिशिरोधराः ॥

† The Sanskrit says nothing of the calves looking piteously at their mothers:

वत्साश्च दीनवदनाः पवनाकम्पितकन्धराः ।
त्राहि त्राहीत्यल्पशब्दाः कृष्णमूचुरिवार्त्तकाः ॥

‡ In the original, the cows are named before their keepers.

§ इममद्रिमहं धैर्यादुत्पाट्योरुशिलातलम् ।
धारयिष्यामि गोष्ठस्य पृथुच्छत्रमिवोपरि ॥

|| Here the Sanskrit gives Kŕishńa the title of Jagannátha.

fall." Upon this, all the people, with their herds, and their waggons and goods, and the Gopís, distressed by the rain, repaired to the shelter of the mountain, which Kŕishńa held, steadily, (over their heads). And Kŕishńa, as he supported the mountain, was contemplated, by the dwellers of Vraja, with joy and wonder; and, as their eyes opened wide with astonishment and pleasure, the Gopas and Gopís sang his praise.* For seven days and nights did the vast clouds, sent by Indra, rain upon the Gokula of Nanda, to destroy its inhabitants; but they were protected by the elevation of the mountain: and the slayer of Bala, Indra, being foiled in his purpose, commanded the clouds to cease.† The threats of Indra‡ having been fruitless, and the heavens clear, all Gokula came forth (from its shelter), and returned to its own abode. Then, Kŕishńa, in the sight of the surprised inhabitants of the forests, restored the great mountain Govardhana to its original site.[1]

[1] It seems not unlikely that this legend has some reference to the caves or cavern-temples in various parts of India. A remarkable representation of it occurs upon the sculptured rocks of Mahabalipoor. It is related, much to the same purport, in the Bhágavata, &c. Śiśupála, ridiculing the exploit, asserts that Govardhana was nothing more than an ant-hill.

* This sentence is rendered very freely.

† This sense is not conveyed by the original:

मिथ्याप्रतिज्ञो बलभिद्वारयामास तान्घनान् ।

Indra, not named, is here referred to as Balabhid. For Bala, an enemy of the celestials, see the *Ŕigveda, passim.*

‡ Devendra, in the Sanskrit.

CHAPTER XII.

Indra comes to Gokula; praises Kŕishńa, and makes him prince over the cattle. Kŕishńa promises to befriend Arjuna.

AFTER Gokula had been saved by the elevation of the mountain, Indra* became desirous of beholding Kŕishńa. The conqueror of his foes, accordingly, mounted his vast elephant, Airávata,† and came to Govardhana, where the king of the gods beheld the mighty Dámodara‡ tending cattle, and assuming the person of a cow-boy, and, although the preserver of the whole world, surrounded by the sons of the herdsmen.§ Above his head he saw Garuda, the king of birds,‖ invisible to mortals,¶ spreading out his wings, to shade the head of Hari. Alighting from his elephant, and addressing him apart, Śakra, his eyes expanding with pleasure, thus spake to Madhusúdana: "Hear, Kŕishńa, the reason why I have come hither,—why I have approached thee; for thou couldest not, otherwise, conceive it. Thou, who art the supporter of all,** hast descended upon earth, to relieve her of her burthen. In resentment of my obstructed rites, I sent the clouds, to deluge Gokula; and they have done this evil deed.††

* Designated, in the original, by his epithet Pákaśásana, 'the chastiser of Páka', a Daitya slain by Indra.

† See Vol. I., p. 146, note 1.

‡ The Sanskrit has Kŕishńa.

§ The translation is, here, compressed.

‖ पक्षिपुङ्गव ।

¶ अन्तर्धानगतम् । There is a variant, अन्तर्हितगतम् ।

** The original adds *Parameśwara*.

†† *Kadana*. The commentator explains it by *vimarda*.

Thou, by raising up the mountain, hast preserved the cattle; and, of a verity, I am much pleased, O hero, with thy wondrous deed. The object of the gods is, now, methinks, accomplished; since, with thy single hand, thou hast raised aloft this chief of mountains. I have now come, by desire of the cattle,[1] grateful for their preservation, in order to install you as Upendra; and, as the Indra of the cows, thou shalt be called Govinda."[2]* Having thus said, Mahendra took a ewer†

[1] Gobhiś cha choditah (गोभिश्च चोदितः); that is, 'delegated,' says the commentator, 'by the cow of plenty, Kámadhenu, and other celestial kine, inhabitants of Goloka, the heaven of cows.' But this is, evidently, unauthorized by the text; as celestial cattle could not be grateful for preservation upon earth: and the notion of Goloka, a heaven of cows and Krishńa, is a modern piece of mysticism, drawn from such sectarial works as the Brahma Vaivarta Puráńa and Hari Vamśa.

[2] The purport of Indra's speech is to explain the meaning of two of Krishńa's names, Upendra and Govinda. The commentators on the Amara Kośa agree in explaining the first, the younger brother of Indra, इन्द्रानुजत्वादुपेन्द्रः, conformably to the synonym that immediately follows, in the text of Amara,‡ Indrávaraja (इन्द्रावरज), a name that occurs also in the Mahábhárata; Krishńa, as the son of Devakí, who is an incarnation of Aditi, being born of the latter, subsequently, to Indra. Govinda is he who knows, finds, or tends, cattle; Gáḿ vindati (गां विन्दति). The Pauráńik etymology makes the latter the Indra (इन्द्र, quasi इन्द्र) of cows; and, in this capacity, he may well be considered as a minor or

* गोभिश्च चोदितः कृष्ण त्वत्सकाशमिहागतः ।
त्वया त्राताभिरत्यर्थं युष्मत्सत्कारकारणात् ॥
स त्वां कृष्णाभिषेक्ष्यामि गवां वाक्यप्रचोदितः ।
उपेन्द्रत्वे गवामिन्द्रो गोविन्दस्त्वं भविष्यसि ॥

† *Ghaṅṭá.*

‡ I., I., I., 16.

from his elephant,* Airávata, and, with the holy water

---

inferior Indra; such being the proper sense of the term Upendra (Upa in composition); as, Upa-puráńa, 'a minor Puráńa,' &c. The proper import of the word Upendra has, however, been anxiously distorted by the sectarian followers of Kŕishńa. Thus, the commentator on our text asserts that Upa is, here, synonymous with Upari (उपरि), and that Upendratwa, 'the station of Upendra,' means 'rule in the heaven of heavens, Goloka;' a new creation of this sect, above Satya-loka, which, in the uncorrupt Pauráńik system, is the highest of the seven Lokas: see Vol. II., p. 227. So the Hari Vaṁśa† makes Indra say:

ममोपरि यथेन्द्रस्त्वं स्थापितो गोभिरीश्वरः ।
उपेन्द्र इति कृष्ण त्वां गास्यन्ति दिवि देवताः ॥

"As thou, Kŕishńa, art appointed, by the cows, Indra superior to me, therefore the deities in heaven shall call thee Upendra." The Bhágavata does not introduce the name, though it, no doubt, alludes to it, in making the divine cow Surabhi, who is said to have come from Goloka with Indra, address Kŕishńa, and say:

इन्द्रं नस्त्वाभिषेक्ष्यामो ब्रह्मणा चोदिता वयम् ।

"We, instructed by Brahmá, will crown you as our Indra." Accordingly, Kŕishńa has the water of the Ganges thrown over him by the elephant of Indra; and Indra, the gods, and sages praise him, and salute him by the appellation of Govinda. The Hari Vaṁśa§ assigns this to Indra alone, who says: "I am only the Indra of the gods: thou hast attained the rank of Indra of the kine; and they shall, for ever, celebrate thee, on earth, as Govinda:"

अहं किलेन्द्रो देवानां त्वं गवामिन्द्रतां गतः ।
गोविन्द इति लोकास्त्वां‡ स्तोष्यन्ति भुवि शाश्वतम् ॥

All this is very different from the sober account of our text, and is, undoubtedly, of comparatively recent origin.

---

* *Upendra.*

† *Śl.* 4005, 4006.

‡ लोके is the reading in the passage as cited by the commentator.

§ *Śl.* 4004, 4005.

it contained, performed (the regal ceremony of) aspersion. The cattle, as the rite was celebrating, deluged the earth with their milk.

When Indra* had, by direction of the kine, inaugurated Kŕishńa,† the husband of Śachí‡ said to him, affectionately: "I have, thus, performed what the cows enjoined me. Now, illustrious being, hear what further I propose, with a view to facilitate your task.§ A portion of me has been born as Arjuna,|| the son of Pŕithá.¶ Let him ever be defended by thee, and he will assist thee in bearing thy burthen.** He is to be cherished by thee, Madhusúdana, like another self." To this, Kŕishńa†† replied: "I know thy son,‡‡ who has been born in the race of Bharata; and I will befriend him as long as I continue upon earth. As long as I am present, invincible§§ Śakra, no one shall be able to subdue Arjuna in fight. When the great demon|||| Kaḿsa has been slain, and Arishńa, Keśin, Kuvalayápíd́a, Naraka,¶¶ and other fierce Daityas shall have been put to death,

---

* Devendra, in the original.

† The Sanskrit has Janárdana.

‡ Śachipati, a title of Indra. See Vol. II., p. 72, note 2.

§ भारावतरणेच्छया ।

|| *Vide supra*, pp. 101, 102, and pp. 158, 159

¶ In the original, Kŕishńa is here addressed as *purusha-vyághra*, "tiger of a man." See Vol. III., p. 118, note §; also, *supra*, p. 1, note *.

** भारावतरणे साह्यं स ते वीरः करिष्यति ।

†† Bhagavat, in the Sanskrit.

‡‡ The original has Pártha, a metronym of Arjuna. *Vide supra*, pp. 101, 102.

§§ *Arindama.*

|||| One of the Daityas, Mahábáhu, is intended by the term translated "the great demon". *Vide supra*, p. 272, note *.

¶¶ These Daityas, Kuvalayápíd́a excepted, are named in p. 260, *supra.*

there will take place a great war,* in which the burthen of the earth will be removed.† Now, therefore, depart; and be not anxious on account of thy son: for no foe shall triumph over Arjuna, whilst I am present. For his sake, I will restore to Kuntí‡ all her sons, with Yudhishṫhira at their head, unharmed, when the Bhárata war is at an end."

Upon Kṛishńa's § ceasing to speak, he and Indra|| mutually embraced; and the latter, mounting his elephant, Airávata, returned to heaven. Kṛishńa, with the cattle and the herdsmen, went his way to Vraja, where the wives of the Gopas watched for his approach.¶

---

* *Mádhava.*

† In the original, Indra is here addressed as Sahasráksha, 'thousand-eyed.' *Vide supra*, p. 261, text and note †.

‡ Kuntí, so called from her father, Kunti or Kuntibhoja, is the same person as Pṛithá. *Vide supra*, pp. 101, 102, and 158, 159.

§ Janárdana's, according to the Sanskrit.

|| Substituted, by the Translator, for Devarája.

¶ कृष्णोऽपि सहितो गोभिर्गोपालैश्च पुनर्व्रजम् ।
आजगामाथ गोपीनां दृष्टिपूतेन वर्त्मना ॥

There is a variant, ending the second verse with the words दृष्टिपातैकभाजनम् ।

CHAPTER XIII.

Kríshńa praised by the cowherds: his sports with the Gopís: their imitation and love of him. The Rása-dance.

AFTER Śakra had departed, the cowherds said to Kríshńa,* whom they had seen holding up Govardhana: "We have been preserved, together with our cattle, from a great peril, by your supporting the mountain (above us). But this is very astonishing child's play, unsuitable to the condition of a herdsman; and all thy actions are those of a god. Tell us what is the meaning of all this.† Káliya has been conquered in the lake;‡ Pralamba has been killed; Govardhana has been lifted up: our minds are filled with amazement. Assuredly, we repose at the feet of Hari, O thou of unbounded might.§ For, having witnessed thy power, we cannot believe thee to be a man. Thy affection, Keśava, for our women and children, and for Vraja; the deeds that thou hast wrought, which all the gods would have attempted in vain; thy boyhood, and thy

---

* The original gives him the epithet *aklishńa-kárin*, the same as *aklishńa-karman*, for which *vide supra*, p. 282, note †.

† बालक्रीडेयमतुला गोपालत्वं जुगुप्सितम् ।
दिव्यं च कर्म भवतः किमेतत्तात कथ्यताम् ॥

‡ *Toya*. The scene of Káliya's defeat was the Yamuná. *Vide supra*, p. 288.

§ सत्यं सत्यं हरेः पादौ शपामोऽमितविक्रम ।

The cowherds adjure Kríshńa by the feet of Hari. And the commentators repeat the leading words of the text, of which I find no variants: पादौ पादाभ्यां शपामः । The original has nothing about sleeping.

prowess; thy humiliating* birth amongst us,—are contradictions that fill us with doubt, whenever we think of them. Yet, reverence be to thee, whether thou be a god, or a demon,† or a Yaksha, or a Gandharva, or whatever we may deem thee; for thou art our friend." When they had ended, Kŕishńa remained silent, for some time,‡ as if hurt and offended,§ and then replied to them: "Herdsmen, if you are not ashamed of my relationship; if I have merited your praise; what occasion is there for you to engage in any discussion (concerning me)? If you have (any) regard for me: if I have deserved your praise; then be satisfied to know that I am your kinsman.|| I am neither god nor Yaksha, nor Gandharva, nor Dánava. I have been born your relative; and you must not think differently of me." Upon receiving this answer, the Gopas held their peace, and went into the woods,¶ leaving Kŕishńa apparently displeased.**

But Kŕishńa, observing the clear sky bright with the autumnal moon, and the air perfumed with the fragrance of the wild water-lily,†† in whose buds the clustering bees were murmuring their songs,‡‡ felt inclined to join with the Gopís in sport. Accordingly, he§§ and Ráma commenced singing sweet low strains,

* Aśobhana. † Dánava.

‡ "For a moment," according to the original, kshańam.

§ Prańaya-kopavat, "affectionately vexed."

|| तदात्मबन्धुसदृशी बुद्धिर्वः क्रियतां मयि ।

¶ Variant: Vraja, instead of vana.

** Prańaya-kopin; the same as prańaya-kopavat. See note §, above.

†† तथा कुमुदिनीं फुल्लामामोदितदिगन्तराम् ।

‡‡ वनराजिं तथा कूजद्भृङ्गमालामनोरमाम् ।

§§ Called, in the original, Śauri.

in various measures,* such as the women loved; and they, as soon as they heard the melody, quitted their homes, and hastened to meet the foe of Madhu.† One damsel gently sang an accompaniment to his song; another attentively listened to his melody. One, calling out upon his name, then shrunk abashed; whilst another, more bold, and instigated by affection, pressed close to his side.‡ One, as she sallied forth, beheld some of the seniors (of the family), and dared not venture, contenting herself with meditating on Kŕishńa,§ with closed eyes, and entire devotion, by which, immediately, all acts of merit were effaced by rapture, and all sin was expiated by regret at not beholding him;|| and others, again, reflecting upon the cause of the world, in the form of the supreme Brahma, obtained, by their sighing, final emancipation. Thus surrounded by the Gopís, Kŕishńa¶ thought the lovely moonlight night of autumn propitious to the Rása-dance.[1] Many

---

[1] The Rása-dance is danced by men and women, holding each others' hands, and going round in a circle, singing the airs to which they dance. According to Bharata, the airs are various, both in melody and time; and the number of persons should not exceed sixty-four:

अनेकनर्तकीयोज्यं चित्रतालजयान्वितम् ।
आचतुःषष्टियुग्मत्वाद्रासकं मसृणोद्धतम् ॥**

---

* There are four readings here, all containing unintelligible technicalities. The commentators dwell on this passage at length.

† Madhusúdana.

‡ ययौ च काचित्प्रेमान्धा तत्पार्श्वमविलम्बिता ।

§ Govinda, in the original.

|| This is a very free rendering.

¶ For Govinda, again.

** Quoted by the commentators.

of the Gopís imitated the different actions of Kríshńa, and, in his absence, wandered through Vríndávana, (representing his person). "I am Kríshńa," cries one. "Behold the elegance of my movements." "I am Kríshńa," exclaims another. "Listen to my song."* "Vile Káliya, stay! For I am Kríshńa," is repeated by a third, slapping her arms in defiance. A fourth calls out: "Herdsmen, fear nothing; be steady: the danger of the storm is over. For, lo! I lift up Govardhana, for your shelter."† And a fifth proclaims: "Now let the herds graze where they will: for I have destroyed Dhenuka." Thus, in various actions of Kríshńa, the Gopís imitated him, whilst away, and beguiled their sorrow by mimicking his sports.‡ Looking down upon the ground, one damsel calls to her friend, as the light down upon her body stands erect (with joy), and the lotoses of her eyes expand: "See, here are the marks of Kríshńa's feet, as he has gone along sportively, and left the impressions of the banner, the thunderbolt, and the goad.[1]§ What lovely maiden has been his compan-

[1] The soles of the feet of a deity are, usually, marked by a variety of emblematical figures. This is carried to the greatest extravagance by the Buddhists; the marks on the feet of Gautama

* कृष्णोऽहमेतल्ललितं व्रजाम्यालोक्यतां गतिः।
अन्या ब्रवीति कृष्णस्य मम गीतिर्निशाम्यताम्॥

† अलं वृष्टिभयेनात्र धृतो गोवर्धनो मया।

‡ एवं नानाप्रकारासु कृष्णचेष्टासु तास्तदा।
गोप्यो व्यग्राः समं चेरू रम्यं वृन्दावनं वनम्॥

§ ध्वजवज्राङ्कुशाब्जाङ्करेखावन्त्यालि पश्यत।
पदान्येतानि कृष्णस्य लीलालंकृतगामिनः॥

According to the Pauráńik writers, "the acts of the divinity are his, *lílá*, or sport"; and even "his appearances are regarded as his *lílá*, or

ion, inebriate with passion, as her irregular footmarks testify?* Here Dámodara has gathered flowers from on high; for we see alone the impressions of the tips of his feet. Here a nymph has sat down with him, ornamented with flowers, fortunate in having propitiated Vishńu in a prior existence.† Having left her in an arrogant mood, because he had offered her flowers, the son of Nanda has gone by this road; for, see, unable to follow him with equal steps, his associate has here tripped along upon her toes, and, holding his hand, the damsel has passed, as is evident from the uneven and intermingled footsteps.‡ But the rogue has merely

---

being 130. See Transactions of the Royal Asiatic Society, Vol. III., p. 70. It is a decoration very moderately employed by the Hindus.

---

pastime". Professor Wilson's collected works, Vol. I., p. 194; Vol. III., p. 147.

A similar phraseology, as if with design to convey an impressive idea of the divine nature,—absolute inertness and aternity being the sublimest attributes of the Supreme,—has been employed elsewhere than in India. "Every providential energy of deity, about a sensible nature, was said, by ancient theologists and philosophers, to be the *sport* of divinity." Thomas Taylor, *Metamorphosis, &c. of Apuleius*, p. 43, note 1.

For the scholastic Supreme of the Hindus,—which, only that it has neither mate nor emanations, may be compared with the *Βυθός* of Gnosticism,—see note * to p. 253, *supra*. Brahma, the sole existence,—all else being sheer phantasm,—is pure spirit, and, therefore, incognitive. In short, it is not to be construed to the imagination, and is indistinguishable, save to the eye of faith, from a nonentity.

The Puráńas generally modify this view, which is that of the Vedánta philosophy. See Vol. I., p. 41, note 2; and p. 172, notes 1 and *.

For extracts from Dr. South and Erigena, see the supplement to this note, at the end of the volume.

* कापि तेन समं याता कृतपुण्या मदालसा ।
पदानि तस्याश्चैतानि घनान्यल्पतनूनि च ॥

† अन्यजन्मनि सर्वात्मा विष्णुरभ्यर्चितो यया ।

‡ This sentence, in its latter portion, is freely translated.

taken her hand, and left her neglected; for here the paces indicate the path of a person in despair. Undoubtedly, he promised that he would quickly come again; for here are his own footsteps returning with speed. Here he has entered the thick forest, impervious to the rays of the moon; and his steps can be traced no further."* Hopeless, then, of beholding Kŕishńa, the Gopís returned, and repaired to the banks of the Yamuná, where they sang his songs;† and presently they beheld the preserver of the three worlds,‡ with a smiling aspect, hastening towards them. On which, one exclaimed "Kŕishńa! Kŕishńa!" unable to articulate anything else; another affected to contract her forehead with frowns, as drinking, with the bees of her eyes, the lotos of the face of Hari; another, closing her eyelids, contemplated, internally, his form, as if engaged in an act of devotion. Then Mádhava, coming amongst them, conciliated some with soft speeches, some, with gentle looks;§ and some he took by the hand: and the illustrious deity sported with them in the stations of the dance. As each of the Gopís, however, attempted to keep in one place, close to the side of Kŕishńa, the circle of the dance could not be constructed; and he, therefore, took each by the hand, and,

* प्रविष्टो गहनं कृष्णः पदमत्र न लक्ष्यते ।
निवर्तध्वं शशाङ्कस्य नैतद्दीधितिगोचरे ॥

† *Charita*, 'achievements.'

‡ Also here called *akĺishía-chesht́ita*, "unwearied in exploits." Compare *akĺishía-karman*, in note † to p. 262, *supra*.

§ भ्रूभङ्गुरीक्षितैः, "with frowning looks."
ताभिः प्रसन्नचित्ताभिर्गोपीभिः सह सादरम् ।
रराम रासगोष्ठीभिरुदारचरितो हरिः ॥

when their eyelids were shut by the effects of such touch, the circle was formed.[1] Then proceeded the

[1] This is a rather inexplicit statement;* but the comment makes it clear. Kŕishńa, it is said, in order to form the circle, takes each damsel by the hand, and leads her to her place. There he quits her; but the effect of the contact is such, that it deprives her of the power of perception; and she contentedly takes the hand of her female neighbour, thinking it to be Kŕishńa's. The Bhágavata† is bolder, and asserts that Kŕishńa multiplied himself, and actually stood between each two damsels:

रासोत्सवः संप्रवृत्तो गोपीमण्डलमण्डितः ।
योगेश्वरेण कृष्णेन तासां मध्ये द्वयोर्द्वयोः ।‡
प्रविष्टेन गृहीतानां कण्ठे स्वनिकटं स्त्रियः ॥
यं मन्येरन् . . . . ।§

The Rása-dance, formed of a circle graced by the Gopís, was, then, led off by the lord of magic, Kŕishńa having placed himself in the midst of every two of the nymphs."|| The Hari Vaḿśa¶ intimates the same, though not very fully:

ताश्च पङ्क्तीकृताः सर्वा रमयन्ति मनोरमम् ।
गायन्त्यः कृष्णचरितं द्वन्द्वशो गोपकन्यकाः ॥

"Then all the nymphs of the cowherds, placing themselves in couples in a row, engaged in pleasant diversion, singing the deeds of Kŕishńa." The Pankti, or row, is said, by the commentator,**

* And the rendering is very far from being literal.

† X., Prior Section, XXIII., 3.

‡ The commentator Ratnagarbha, who quotes the first two verses of this stanza, gives the second thus:

योगेश्वरेण तन्मध्ये प्रविष्टेन द्वयोर्द्वयोः ।

§ I have completed Professor Wilson's partial citation of this passage.

|| M. Hauvette-Besnault's translation of the entire passage quoted above is as follows: "La fête du rása, embellie par le cercle des Gopís, était menée par Crichńa, qui, usant de sa puissance magique et se plaçant entre elles, deux à deux, les tenait embrassées par le cou; et chaque femme croyait qu'il était auprès d'elle."

Vide infra, p. 331, note **.

¶ Śl. 4088.

** Nílakańťha.

dance, to the music of their clashing bracelets, and songs that celebrated, in suitable strain, the charms of

to mean, here, the Mańdala, or ring; and the 'couples', to imply that Kríshńa was between every two. He quotes a verse* to this effect, from some other Vaishńava work: अङ्गनामङ्गनामन्तरे माधवो माधवं चान्तरे चाङ्गना: • • • • संजगौ वेणुना देवकीनन्दन: । "Between each two damsels was Mádhava; and between each two Mádhavas was a nymph; and the son of Devakí played on the flute". For, in fact, Kríshńa is not only dancing with each, but also, by himself, in the centre. For this the commentator on the Hari Vaḿśa cites a passage from the Vedas:

वस्ते पुरुरूपो वपूंषि ऊर्ध्वा तस्थौ त्र्यविं रेरिहाण: ।†

Literally, "The many-formed (being) assumes (various) bodies. One form stood apart, occupying triple observance."‡ Now, if the verse be genuine, it probably refers to something that has little to do with Kríshńa; but it is explained to apply to the Rása; the form of Kríshńa being supposed to be meant, as wholly distinct from the Gopís, and yet being beheld, by every one of them, on each side and in front of her. In the meditation upon Kríshńa which is enjoined in the Brahma Vaivarta, he is to be contemplated in the centre of the Rása Mańdala, in association with his favourite Rádhá. But the Mańdala described in that work is not a ring of dancers, but a circle of definite space at Vŕindávana, within which Kríshńa, Rádhá, and the Gopís divert them-

* The quotation seems to be prose.

† Rightly, and as quoted by the commentator:

पदा वस्ते पुरुरूपा वपूंष्यूर्ध्वा तस्थौ त्र्यविं रेरिहाणा ।

This is the first verse of *Rigveda*, III., LV., 14. Professor Wilson, in his translation of the *Rigveda*, Vol. III., p. 98, renders it thus: "The earth wears bodies of many *forms*: she abides on high, cherishing her year and a half old (calf)."

‡ This interpretation does not represent accurately the meaning of the verse as explained by the commentator on the *Harivaḿśa*. But the commentator's explanation is not worth stopping to set forth.

the autumnal season.* Kŕishńa sang the moon of autumn,—a mine of gentle radiance; but the nymphs repeated the praises of Kŕishńa alone.† At times, one of them, wearied by the revolving dance, threw her arms, ornamented with tinkling bracelets, round the neck‡ of the destroyer of Madhu;§ another, skilled in the

selves, not very decorously. This work has, probably, given the tone to the style in which the annual festival, the Rása Yátrá, is celebrated, in various parts of India, in the month of Kárttika, upon the sun's entrance into Libra, by nocturnal dances, and representations of the sports of Kŕishńa. A circular dance of men and women, however, does not form any prominent feature at these entertainments; and it may be doubted if it is ever performed. Some of the earliest labourers in the field of Hindu mythology have thought this circular dance to typify the dance of the planets round the sun (Maurice, Ancient History of Hindus, Vol. I., p. 108; Vol. II., p. 356); but there is no particular number assigned to the performers, by any of the Hindu authorities, beyond its limitation to sixty-four. At the Rása Mańdala of the Brahma Vaivarta, Rádhá is accompanied by thirty-six of her most particular friends amongst the Gopís; but they are, each, attended by thousands of inferior personages; and none of the crowd are left without male multiples of Kŕishńa. The only mysticism hinted at, in that Puráńa, is, that these are, all, one with Kŕishńa; the varied vital conditions of one spirit being represented by the Gopís and the illusory manifestations of Kŕishńa; he himself being supreme, unmodified soul.

* ततः प्रववृते रासश्चलद्वलयनिःस्वनः ।
अनुयातशरत्काव्यगेयगीतिरनुक्रमात् ॥

† कृष्णः शरच्चन्द्रमसं कौमुदीं कुमुदाकरम् ।
जगौ गोपीजनस्त्वेकं कृष्णनाम पुनः पुनः ॥

‡ दत्तौ • स्कन्धे, "placed on the shoulder."

§ *Madhu-nighátin.*

art of singing his praises, embraced him.* The drops of perspiration from the arms of Hari were like fertilizing rain, which produced a crop of down upon the temples† of the Gopís. Kŕishńa sang the strain that was appropriate to the dance. The Gopís repeatedly exclaimed "Bravo, Kŕishńa!" to his song. When leading, they followed him; when returning,‡ they encountered him; and, whether he went forwards or backwards, they ever attended on his steps. Whilst frolicking thus with the Gopís, they considered every instant, without him, a myriad§ of years; and, prohibited (in vain) by husbands, fathers, brothers, they went forth, at night, to sport with Kŕishńa, the object of their affection.|| Thus, the illimitable being, the benevolent remover of all imperfections, assumed the character of a youth amongst the females of the herdsmen of Vraja;¶ pervading their natures, and that of their lords, by his own essence, all-diffusive like the wind. For, even as, in all creatures, the elements of ether, fire, earth, water, and air are comprehended, so, also, is he everywhere present, and in all.**

---

* काचित्प्रविलसद्बाहुः परिरभ्य चुचुम्ब तम् ।
गोपी गीतस्तुतिव्याजनिपुणा मधुसूदनम् ॥

The damsel not only embraced but kissed him.

† The original, *kapola*, yields 'cheeks.'

‡ *Valane*, "In turning."

§ *Koṭi*, 'ten millions.'

|| कृष्णं गोपाङ्गना रात्रौ रमयन्ति रतिप्रियाः ।

¶ सोऽपि कैशोरकवयो मानयन्मधुसूदनः ।
रेमे ताभिरमेयात्मा क्षपासु क्षपिताहितः ॥

** In the *Journal Asiatique* for 1865, pp. 373—445 (Series VI., Vol. V.), M. Hauvette-Besnault has published the text, accompanied by an exact and elegant translation, of the *Panchádhyáyí*, *i. e.*, Chapters XXIX.—XXXIII. of the *Bhágavata-puráńa*, Book X., Prior Section, on the frolics of Kŕishńa with the *gopís*. In his introductory remarks, M. Hauvette-Besnault has pertinently quoted, in the original, nearly the whole of the present Chapter of the *Vishńu-puráńa*.

This careful scholar would render a real service to literature by completing the edition of the *Bhágavata-puráńa* which was left unfinished by the lamented Burnouf. The concluding Books of the *Bhágavata*, as may be inferred even from the notes of the present volume, are well worthy of translation in detail.

CHAPTER XIV.

Kríshńa kills the demon Arishía, in the form of a bull.

ONE evening, whilst Kríshńa* and the Gopís were amusing themselves in the dance, the demon Arishía, disguised as a savage bull,† came to the spot, after having spread alarm through the station. His colour was that of a cloud charged with rain; he had vast‡ horns; and his eyes were like two (fiery) suns. As he moved, he ploughed up the ground with his hoofs; his tongue was repeatedly licking his lips; his tail was erect; the sinews of his shoulders were firm, and, between them, rose a hump of enormous dimensions; his haunches were soiled with ordure, and he was a terror to the herds; his dewlap hung low; and his face was marked with scars, from butting against the trees.§ Terrifying all the kine, the demon who perpetually haunts the forests in the shape of a bull, destroying hermits and ascetics, advanced.‖ Beholding an animal of such a formidable aspect, the herdsmen and their women were exceedingly frightened, and called aloud on Kríshńa, who came to their succour, shouting, and slapping his arms in defiance.¶ When the Daitya heard the noise, he turned upon his challenger; and, fixing

---

* Janárdana, in the original.

† The Sanskrit simply calls Arishía *samada*, 'furious.'

‡ *Tíkshńa*, 'sharp.'

§ The description of Arishía is not rendered to the letter.

‖ पातयन्स गवां गर्भान्दैत्यो वृषभरूपधृक् ।
सूदयंस्तापसानुग्रो वनान्यटति यः सदा ॥

¶ सिंहनादं ततश्चक्रे तलशब्दं च केशवः ।

his eyes and pointing his horns at the belly of Keśava, he ran furiously upon the youth. Kŕishńa stirred not from his post, but, smiling in sport and derision, awaited the near approach of the bull, when he seized him, as an alligator* would have done, and held him, firmly, by the horns, whilst he pressed his sides with his knees. Having thus humbled his pride, and held him captive by his horns,† he wrung his throat, as if it had been a piece of wet cloth, and, then, tearing off one of the horns, he beat the fierce demon with it, until he died, vomiting blood from his mouth. Seeing him slain, the herdsmen glorified Kŕishńa,‡ as the companies of the celestials of old praised Indra,§ when he triumphed over (the Asura) Jambha.[1]‖

---

[1] This exploit is related a little more in detail in the Bhágavata and Hari Vaḿśa.

---

* *Gráha.*

† तस्य दर्पबलं भङ्क्त्वा गृहीतस्य विषाणयोः।

‡ The original has Janárdana.

§ Substituted, by the Translator, for Sahasráksha. *Vide supra*, p. 331, note †.

‖ There is mention of Jambha and Kujambha in p. 3, *supra*. In the *Mahábhárata*, *Śánti-parvan*, *śl.* 3660, Jambha, Bala, and Páka are named together.

CHAPTER XV.

Kaṁsa informed, by Nárada, of the existence of Kṛishṅa and Balaráma: he sends Keśin to destroy them, and Akrúra, to bring them to Mathurá.

AFTER (these things had come to pass,) Arishṭa the bull-demon,* and Dhenuka, and Pralamba had been slain, Govardhana had been lifted up, the serpent Káliya had been subdued, the two trees had been broken, the female fiend Pútaná had been killed, and the waggon had been overturned, Nárada went to Kaṁsa, and related to him the whole, beginning with the transference of the child from Devakí to Yaśodá. Hearing this from Nárada, Kaṁsa was highly incensed with Vasudeva, and bitterly reproached him, and all the Yádavas, in an assembly of the tribe. Then, reflecting what was to be done, he determined to destroy both Ráma and Kṛishṅa, whilst they were yet young, and before they had attained to manly vigour; for which purpose he resolved to invite them from Vraja, under pretext of the solemn rite of the lustration of arms,† when he would engage them in a trial of strength with his chief boxers, Cháṅúra and Mushṭika, by whom they would, assuredly, be killed.‡ "I will send," he said, "the noble Yadu,§ Akrúra, the son of Swaphalka,|| to Gokula, to bring them hither. I will order the fierce Keśin, who haunts the woods of Vṛindávana, to attack

---

* *Kakudmin.* † *Dhanur-maha.*

‡ There is much freedom in the rendering of this sentence.

§ *Yadu-pungava.*

|| *Vide supra*, p. 94.

them; and he is of unequalled might, and will surely kill them.* Or, if they arrive here, my elephant, Kuvalayápíd́a, shall trample to death these two cow-boy sons of Vasudeva." Having thus laid his plans to destroy Ráma and Janárdana, the impious Kaḿsa sent for the heroic Akrúra, and said to him: "Lord of liberal gifts,[1] attend to my words, and, out of friendship for me, perform my orders. Ascend your chariot, and go hence to the station of the herdsman Nanda.† Two vile boys,‡ portions of Vishńu, have been born there, for the express object of effecting my destruction. On the fourteenth lunation I have to celebrate the festival of arms;[2] and I wish them to be brought here, by you,

---

[1] Dána-pati. The epithet refers to Akrúra's possession of the Syamantaka gem (*vide supra*, p. 91), although, as here used by Kaḿsa, it is an anachronism; the gem not becoming his until after Kŕishńa's maturity.

[2] Dhanur-maha (धनुर्मह). The same phrase occurs in the different authorities. In its ordinary acceptation, it would imply any military festival. There is one of great celebrity, which, in the south of India, closes the Daśahará, or festival of Durgá, when military exercises are performed, and a field is ravaged, as typical of the opening of a campaign. Worship is paid to military implements. The proper day for this is the Vijaya daśamí, or tenth of the light half of Áświna, falling about the end of September or beginning of October. Transactions of the Bombay Society, Vol. III., p. 73; also, Amara Kośa,§ under the word लोहाभिसार|| (Lohábhisára). Both our text and that of the Bhá-

---

* वृन्दावनचरं घोरमादेक्ष्यामि च केशिनम् ।
तत्रैवासावतिबलस्तावुभौ घातयिष्यति ॥

† *Nanda-gokula.*

‡ The original has "sons of Vasudeva", वसुदेवसुतौ ।

§ II., VIII., II., 69.

|| More usually read लोहाभिहार.

to take part in the games, and that the people may see them engage in a boxing-match with my two dexterous athletæ,* Cháńúra and Mushťika; or, haply, my elephant, Kuvalayápíďa, driven against them by his rider,† shall kill these two iniquitous youngsters, sons of Vasudeva. When they are out of the way, I will put to death Vasudeva himself, the cowherd Nanda, and my foolish father, Ugrasena; and I will seize upon the herds and flocks,‡ and all the possessions, of the rebellious Gopas, who have ever been my foes. Except thou, lord of liberality,§ all the Yádavas are hostile to me: but I will devise schemes for their extirpation; and I shall, then, reign over my kingdom,|| in concert with thee, without any annoyance. Through regard for me, therefore, do thou go, as I direct thee; and thou shalt command the cowherds to bring in, with speed, their supplies of milk, and butter, and curds."¶

---

gavata, however, intimate the celebration of the feast in question on the fourteenth day of the fortnight (in what month, is not specified); and an occasional 'passage of arms,' therefore, is all that is intended. The fourteenth day of the light lunation of any month is, commonly, held appropriate for a holyday or religious rite. It will be seen, in the sequel,** that the leading feature of

---

* 'Pancratiasts,' more nearly; *malla*, in the Sanskrit. For the import of this term, see an annotation near the end of Chapter XX. of the present Book.

† *Mahá-mátra.*

‡ *Go-dhanáni.*

§ *Dána-pati.*

|| अयादवं, says the original,—"freed from Yádavas."

¶ यथा च माहिषं सर्पिर्दधि चाप्युपहार्य वै ।
गोपाः समानयन्त्वाशु त्वया वाच्यास्तथा तथा ॥

** See Chapter XX. of this Book.

Being thus instructed, the illustrious Akrúra readily undertook to visit Kŕishńa;* and, ascending his stately chariot, he† went forth from the city of Mathurá.

---

the ceremonial was intended to have been a trial of archery,—spoiled by Kŕishńa's breaking the bow that was to have been used on the occasion.

* इत्याज्ञप्तस्तथाक्रूरो महाभागवतो द्विज ।
प्रीतिमानभवत्कृष्णं श्वो द्रक्ष्यामीति सत्वरः ॥

† *Madhu-priya* is the epithet which the original here gives him. It means, literally, "dear to the Madhus;" *i. e.*, the commentators say, "to the family of Madhu."

CHAPTER XVI.

Keśin, in the form of a horse, slain by Kŕishńa: he is praised by Nárada.

KEŚIN, confiding in his prowess, having received the commands of Kamsa, set off to (the woods of) Vŕindávana, with the intention of destroying Kŕishńa. He came (in the shape of a steed), spurning the earth with his hoofs, scattering the clouds with his mane, and springing, in his paces, beyond the orbits of the sun and moon. The cowherds and their females, hearing his neighings, were struck with terror, and fled to Govinda for protection, calling upon him to save them. In a voice deep as the roaring of the thunder-cloud, Kŕishńa replied to them: "Away with these fears of Keśin! Is the valour of a hero annihilated by your alarms? What is there to apprehend from one of such little might, whose neighings are his only terrors; a galloping and vicious steed, who is ridden by the strength of the Daityas?* Come on, wretch! I am Kŕishńa: and I will knock all thy teeth down thy throat, as the wielder of the trident† did to Púshan.[1]:

---

[1] As Vírabhadra did to Púshá§ or Púshan,—a form of Súrya,—at the sacrifice of Daksha. See Vol. I., p. 131, note‖.

---

* किमनेनाल्पसारेण हेषिताटोपकारिणा ।
दैतेयबलवाह्येन वल्गता दुष्टवाजिना ॥

† *Pinákadhŕik.* The *pináka* is, here, a club.

: एह्येहि दुष्ट कृष्णोऽहं पूष्णोरिव पिनाकधृक् ।
पातयिष्यामि दशनान्वदनादखिलांस्तव ॥

§ Nominative case of, not an optional substitute for, Púshan.

‖ Also see *Original Sanskrit Texts*, Vol. IV., pp. 168 and 332.

Thus defying him to combat, Govinda went to encounter Keśin. The demon ran upon him, with his mouth opened wide; but Kŕishńa,* enlarging the bulk of his arm, thrust it into his mouth, and wrenched out the teeth, which fell from his jaws like fragments of white clouds.† Still, the arm of Kŕishńa, in the throat of the demon, continued to enlarge, like a malady increasing, from its commencement, till it ends in dissolution.‡ From his torn lips the demon vomited foam and blood; his eyes rolled in agony; his joints gave way; he beat the earth with his feet;§ his body was covered with perspiration; he became incapable of any effort. The formidable demon,|| having his mouth rent open by the arm of Kŕishńa, fell down, torn asunder, like a tree struck by lightning. He lay separated into two portions, each having two legs, half a back, half a tail, one ear, one eye, and one nostril. Kŕishńa stood,¶ unharmed and smiling, after the destruction of the demon, surrounded by the cowherds, who, together with their women, were filled with astonishment at the death of Keśin, and glorified the amiable god with the lotos-eyes.** Nárada, the Brahman,†† invisible, seated

---

* Janárdana, in the original.

† केशिनो वदनं तेन विशता कृष्णबाहुना ।
शातिता दशनाः पेतुः सिताभ्रावयवा इव ॥

‡ The only reading that I find is यथा व्याधिरासंभूतेरुपेक्षितः । Ratnagarbha's interpretation is: "like a disease neglected from its beginning": उत्पत्तिमारभ्य उपेक्षितः अचिकित्सितः । Śrídhara's comment is briefer.

§ Here follow the untranslated words शकृन्मूत्रं समुत्सृजन् ।

|| *Asura.*

¶ Insert 'unwearied', अनायस्ततनुः । ** *Puńdaríkáksha.*

†† *Vipra.* Nárada is commonly considered to be a Devarshi. See Vol. III., p. 68, l. 1; but also see Vol. I., p. 100, note 2.

in a cloud, beheld the fall of Keśin, and delightedly exclaimed: "Well done! lord of the universe,* who, in thy sports,† hast destroyed Keśin, the oppressor of the denizens of heaven!‡ Curious to behold this great combat between a man and a horse,—such a one as was never before heard of,—I have come from heaven. Wonderful are the works that thou hast done, in thy descent (upon the earth). They have excited my astonishment; but this, (above all), has given me pleasure. Indra§ and the gods lived in dread of this horse, who tossed his mane, and neighed, and looked down upon the clouds. For this, that thou hast slain the impious Keśin, thou shalt be known, in the world, by the name of Keśava.[1] || Farewell!¶ I will now depart. I shall meet thee again, conqueror of Keśin, in two days more, in conflict with Kaṁsa."** When the son of Ugra-

[1] Or Keśi and va 'who kills,'—from vadh or badh, 'to kill.' But this is a Paurāṅik etymology, and less satisfactory than the usual grammatical one of Keśa, 'hair,' and 'va' possessive affix; Kṛishṅa corresponding, in this respect, to the Apollo Crinitus. It is, also, derived from the legend of his origin from 'a hair' (*vide supra*, p. 258, note 2). And, again, Keśa is said to purport 'radiance' or 'rays', whether of the sun, or moon, or fire,—all which are the light of Kṛishṅa,—whence he is called Keśava, 'the rayed' or 'radiant'. Mahābhārata, Moksha Dharma.

* *Jagannātha.*

† *Vide supra*, p. 325, note §.

‡ *Tridivaukas.*

§ Substituted, by the Translator, for Śakra.

|| Compare the *Harivaṁśa*, *śl.* 4337:

यस्मात्त्वया हतः केशी तस्मान्मच्छासनं शृणु ।
केशवो नाम नाम्ना त्वं ख्यातो लोके भविष्यसि ॥

¶ स्वस्त्यस्तु ते ।

** See Chapter XX. of this Book.

sena, with his followers, shall have been slain, then, upholder of the earth, will earth's burthens have been lightened by thee.* Many are the battles of the kings that I have to see, in which thou shalt be renowned. I will now depart, Govinda. A great deed, and acceptable to the gods, has been done by thee. I have been much delighted with thee, and now take my leave."† When Nárada had gone, Kŕishńa, not in any way surprised, returned, with the Gopas, to Gokula,— the sole object of the eyes of the women of Vraja.[1]

---

[1] The legend is told by all the other narrators of Kŕishńa's juvenile exploits.

---

* भारावतारकर्त्ता त्वं पृथिव्याः पृथिवीधर ।

† सोऽहं यास्यामि गोविन्द देवकार्यं महत्कृतम् ।
त्वया सभाजितश्चाहं स्वस्ति तेऽस्तु व्रजाम्यहम् ॥

CORRIGENDA, &c.

P. 2, note ‡. Also see Vol. I., p. 200, supplement to p. 152.

P. 11, note *. Purúravas and Urvaśí are, both, named in the *Ŕigveda*, X., XCV. For other references touching them, see *Original Sanskrit Texts*, Part I., p. 226, *et aliter* (2nd ed.).

P. 14, note **. In *śl.* 1761 of the *Harivanśa*, we find its second mention of Jahnu and his wife Káverí. Probably it was in note 2 to p. 136 that Professor Wilson entertained the intention, which he pretermitted to fulfil, of recurring to Káverí.

P. 15, l. 1. *Read* Kuśa.

P. 15, notes, l. 14. For Girivraja, see p. 180, note 1.

P. 17, l. 3 *ab infra*. For the original, from this point of Chapter VII. to its end, and an improved translation, see *Original Sanskrit Texts*, Part I., pp. 349—351 (2nd ed.).

P. 20, notes, l. 4 *ab infra*. *Read* पितरं.

P. 26, notes, ll. 9 and 12. For अक्लिष्टकर्मन्, here rendered "remorseless", see p. 362, note †.

P. 26, notes, l. 2. *Read* Devaráta.

P. 26, notes, l. 5. *Read* वसुस्त्वामन्वयो.

P. 30, note *. I am indebted to Dr. Muir for calling my attention to the Asura Swarbhánu of the *Ŕigveda*, V., XL. See *Original Sanskrit Texts*, Part I., pp. 469, 470 (2nd ed.).

P. 31, notes, last line. That is to say, the *Bhágavata-puráńa* has Kuśa, where the *Vishńu-puráńa* has Leśa.

P. 32, l. 2. *For* Káśirája, *read* king of the Káśis. Compare supplementary note, a little below, on p. 57, notes 4 and §§. Also see my *Benares, Ancient and Mediæval*, p. 7, notes 2 and 7.

P. 32, note 2. *Read* Káśiya.

P. 32, note ||. My MSS. of the *Váyu-puráńa* are rather doubtful as to the reading Ráshtra.

P. 33, l. 5. For another Divodása, see p. 146, l. 1. Regarding the Káśis and the two Pauráńik Divodásas, I have elsewhere written as follows: "The *Ŕigveda* affords no warrant for connecting with the Káśis any person whom it mentions. It speaks of Divodása, and it speaks of Pratardana; but only in later literature are they called father and son, and rulers of the Káśis; and, where Kátyáyana, in his *Ŕigvedánukramańiká*, characterizes the latter as *Káśirája*, he may have expressed himself metachronically, under the influence of a modern tradition which he and his contemporaries accepted. As to the former, we find, indeed, in post-vaidik books, two Divodásas; into whom a single personage seems to have been parted. One of them is son of Bhadryaśwa, as in the *Ŕigveda*; but it is the other, the son of Bhimaratha, and father of Pratardana, that is called king of the Káśis. It may be added, that there is no ground for considering Badhryaśwa and Bhimaratha to be two names of one and the same person." *Benares*, &c., p. 9, note 1.

P. 36, l. 1. *Read* Ŕitadhwaja.

P. 39, notes, l. 9 *ab infra*. See, for *Kásirája*, supplementary note, a little above, on p. 32, l. 2.

P. 40, notes, l. 2. *Read* Śánti Parvan.

P. 40, note *. Káśi, too, is a patronym of Káśa.

P. 43, notes, l. 3 *ab infra*. *Read* Sṛinjaya.

P. 44, note ‡‡. *For* Kshattravṛiddha, *read* Leśa. See p. 31, note ‡.

P. 47, notes, l. 7 *ab infra*. *Read* कुरुं चापुं च पूर्वं.

P. 47, note ||. Substitute, for the whole: *Ádi-parvan*, *ll.* 3762.

P. 55, notes, l. 3 *ab infra*. Instead of नमु, some copies of the commentary read नख.

P. 67, notes ‡ and §§. We should translate: "king of the Ávantyas", to render *Ávantya*. In many such cases, the subjects of a ruler, not his territory, must be understood. Compare *Kásirája*, &c. &c.

P. 69, notes, l. 21. The "Gehlots" or Gahlots are referred to Guhila or Gobhila, as their eponymist. See the *Journal of the American Oriental Society*, Vol. VI., pp. 500, 510, and p. 518, note n.

P. 73, notes, l. 12. *Read* चट्.

P. 73, note ‡. In one copy of the commentary, I find, as the reading, Mṛittikávata,—the true name, in all probability. As to Mṛittikávatí,—by which appellation the same place seems to be designated,—it is represented as having been on the Narmadá. See the *Harivaṃśa*, *ll.* 1963.

P. 74, notes, l. 13. *Read* चलमित्रं.

P. 84, notes † and §. It should have been added, that the capital of Videha is Mithilá. This is not the name of a country, as Professor Wilson—in Vol. III., p. 330, note 1, and elsewhere,—supposes it to be.

P. 87, ll. 12, 14, and 18. The term "Káśirája", it is most likely, is no proper name here, but simply descriptive,—"king of the Káśis." See supplementary note on p. 32, l. 2, of this volume.

P. 103, note **. *For* of Avanti, the country, *read* Ávantyas.

P. 106, note †. The reading should be, undoubtedly: पुरुषंसोऽवेति.

P. 109, note ‖. Púru must be right. See the preceding note.

P. 110, l. 4. *Read* Kaṃsa.

P. 111, notes, l. 3 *ab infra*. *Read* Suvaṃśa.

P. 126, note †. Also *vide supra*, p. 101, note ***.

P. 146, note ‡‡. See supplementary note on p. 33, l. 5.

P. 148, notes, l. 7. *Read* Hari Vaṃśa.

P. 150, ll. 6 and 7. For an account, from the *Mahábhárata*, of the birth of Jarásandha, see *Original Sanskrit Texts*, Part IV., pp. 247, 248. It is, in substance, as follows. Jarásandha's father, King Bṛihadratha, had two wives. After having long been barren, each of them bore him half of a son. These moieties, contemplated with horror, were cast away. Jará, a female ghoul, that she may carry off the pieces the more readily, lays them together. The halves coalesce, and become endowed with life. The boy thus patched up wails out; whereupon the servants sally forth from Bṛihadratha's palace, and the king and queen with them. The ghouless assumes a human form, and makes over the infant to its father. She discloses that she has been worshipped, in ignorance of her real character, as the king's house-goddess, and adds, that, in gratitude for the homage done her, she has restored the monarch his son, the halves of whom, she alleges, were united into an animated whole quite independently of her will or power.

Brihadratha subsequently directs his subjects, the inhabitants of Magadha, to celebrate a great festival in Jará's honour.

Herein, as Dr Muir repeats after Professor Lassen, we are furnished with "an instance of the local adoration of particular deities in ancient India."

P. 151, notes, l. 2 *ab infra*. *For* seventh, *read* ninth.

P. 158, note 1. See Colebrooke's *Digest of Hindu Law*, Vol. II., pp. 466—476.

P. 158, note ‡. For the probably correct interpretation of the original, *Kásirája*, see supplementary note on p. 37, l. 2.

P. 159, notes, l. 4. *For* by, *read* by.

P. 169, note ††. In the *Mahábhárata*, *Ádi-parvan*, 3829, we read, that Bhimasena married काश्यां बलन्धरां, "Balandhará, daughter of the king of the Kásis." M. Fauche, mistaking an accusative for a locative, has translated: "Bhimaséna épousa dans Kâçi Balandharà." I doubt whether Kásí or Kási, as the name of a city or kingdom, is anywhere to be met with in ancient Sanskrit literature.

P. 164, note †. For Hastinapura, compare p. 133, note *.

P. 166, notes, l. 3. *Read* verse is.

P. 170, notes, l. 10. *Read* Mahâwamso.

P. 171, notes, l. 16. *Read* Rájagriha.

P. 173, notes, last line. *Read* बर्हिद्युम्नजा.

P. 180, note 1; and p. 181, note *. We here have traces of a second dynasty of Kási kings. For the first, see pp. 30-40.

P. 186, note *. The king named between Nanda and Chandragupta I have conjectured, very hesitatingly, may have borne the appellation of Bríhanmanas. See my *Benares*, &c., p. 12, note 2.

P. 189, notes, l. 8. *Read* Priyadarśin.

P. 196, note §. For further mention of Śrisátakarni, see General Cunningham's *Bhilsa Topes*, pp. 264 and 272.

P. 200, notes, l. 19. *Read* while differing.

P. 203, notes, last line. *Read* is it.

P. 212, l. 1. Here and elsewhere, the most carefully written MSS. yield Báhlikas. Váhlika, Váhlíka, &c., I am, therefore, disposed to account erroneous.

P. 231, l. 1; p. 232, l. 2; and p. 234, l. 6. *Read* Ítihás.

P. 235, notes, l. 1. *Read* महीमितापिता.

P. 237, l. 3. Regarding Devápi, see p. 153, note ††.

P. 240, notes, l. 4. A comma has disappeared from the end of the line.

P. 247, note ‖. The passage here referred to occurs, likewise, in the *Brihad-áranyaka Upanishad*, as V., 1: see Messrs. Boehtlingk and Roth's *Sanskrit-Wörterbuch*, Vol. I., under अच्. In Vol. V., again under सिच्, the same learned and most meritorious lexicographers indicate the following similar stanza from the *Atharva-veda*,—X., VIII., 29:

पूर्णात्पूर्णमुदचति पूर्णं पूर्णेन सिच्यते ।
उतो तदद्य विद्याम यतस्तत्परिषिच्यते ॥

The commentator whom I intend, in my note under remark, is Ratnagarbha. See, a little below, supplementary annotation on p. 303, note 1, &c.

P. 250, note ††. For an explanation of the term *akshauhiṇî*, see a note on Book V., Chapter XXII.

P. 252, note †. Read *Śikshá*.

P. 259, note †. *For* the native, *read* Śridhara's.

P. 261, notes, l. 7. *Read* places where.

P. 261, note *. The mistake of the Translator is borrowed from his Bengal version.

P. 262, notes, l. 4. *Read* fable, made.

P. 262, note †. *Read* Three pages.

P. 267, note *. See Vol. II., p. 337, supplementary note on p. 59, l. 8. On *adman*, as alleged to signify 'essence', see Burnouf's *Introduction à l'Histoire du Buddhisme Indien*, Vol. I., p. 502, note 2, by Dr Theodor Goldstücker. Burnouf appends to the note these words: "Je n'ai pu jusqu'ici justifier cette interprétation par les textes."

P. 280, note *. The stanza occurs in the MSS. accompanied by Śridhara's commentary.

P. 284, note *. *Read* commentators.

P. 286, note §. The words quoted by the Translator are Śridhara's.

P. 290, note †. Both the scholiasts expound the stanzas here transcribed.

P. 291, note ‖. Śridhara, who, equally with Ratnagarbha, cites the verses on dancing, attributes them to Bharata.

P. 293, l. 12. Inadvertently, I have not corrected the Translator's "Brahmá" into Brahma. But see the next note.

P. 293, note ‡. As Dr. Muir suggests to me, I should have added, that परस्राच: means 'preceding the Supreme,' not "the progenitor of the supreme (Brahma)", and परस्मात्परम: means 'supreme beyond the Supreme', not "beyond all finite objects." These hyperboles, it scarcely need be observed, are designed to express incomprehensibilities.

P. 295, notes, l. 1. I have to thank Dr Muir for calling my attention to the fact, that the adage adduced should be rendered: "He who does an act suited to his natural disposition incurs no guilt."

P. 296, note ‡. The Translator has followed the text as accepted by Śridhara.

P. 297, note §. The reading which Professor Wilson prefers is Śridhara's.

P. 297, notes, l. 8. *Read* भूमदेशो यत°.

P. 299, note ‡. आस्रोरपदं is the lection of Śridhara.

P. 303, note ‖; and p. 304, notes § and ‖. Of the two commentaries on Book V., Ratnagarbha's and Śridhara's, the Translator has relied on the former, most generally, and, in speaking of "the commentator", refers thereto, except in those scattered cases where I have noted to the contrary. These two commentaries—the latter of which was inaccessible to me, when preparing my annotations on the first twelve Chapters of Book V.,—coincide, in a noticeable degree, not only in the authorities which they adduce, but in their elucidations,—as to their general drift, and, sometimes, as to the very words in which they are delivered. Ratnagarbha's, it seems from internal evidence, is the more recent composition.

In the Translator's note to which this annotation is appended, two explanations are cited, as if occurring "in different copies". They are, in fact, from different commentaries,—Ratnagarbha's and Śridhara's, respectively. The words of Śrídhara, as professedly copied by Professor Wilson, deviate somewhat, as usual, from a punctual representation.

कार्श्यं is the lection which Śrídhara prefers to the more ordinary कृशत्वम्.

P. 304, notes, l. 2. *Read* -ब्रतेनार्के.

P. 304, note *. In commenting on this stanza, Śrídhara quotes from Daṇḍin, to whom, therefore, he must have been posterior.

P. 308, note §. The quotation is given by Śrídhara, also, who claims to take it from the *Yoga-śástra*.

P. 308, note ||. *For* commentator's, &c., *read* commentators' quotation explanatory of the technicalities *púraka*, &c.

P. 312, note *. It is Śrídhara's reading to which the Translator here accords the preference.

P. 316, note †. See, further, for Bala, p. 334, note ¶.

P. 317, note *. See, for Páka, note || in p. 334.

P. 318, note †. Read *Ghaṇṭá*

P. 326, notes, l. 6 *ab infra*. In a sermon by Dr. South, preached at Westminster Abbey, Feb. 22, 1684—5, is the following passage: "'Tis, as it were, *the sport of the Almighty*, thus to baffle and confound the sons of men by such events as both cross the methods of their actings and surpass the measure of their expectations."

With the *Βυθός* of the Gnostics compare "the superessential one of Plotinus, to whom neither Intelligence, nor Self-consciousness, nor Life, nor even *Being* can be attributed." Coleridge's *Aids to Reflection*, p. 158, (ed. of 1836).

Erigena sublimates deity into something well-nigh as shadowy: "Deus itaque nescit se quid est, quia non est quid; incomprehensibilis quippe in aliquo, et sibi ipsi et omni intellectui." *De Divisione Naturae*, II., 28 (ed. Migne, col. 589).

It seems, that, in the sphere of the profundities, the election lies, to most minds, between something like this and the popular theologies which offer, as their first principle, a Supreme constituted in the image of man.

P. 329, note *. The quotation referred to, when read unmangled, turns out to be half of a Jánakí stanza:

अङ्गनामङ्गनामन्तरे माधवो माधवं माधवं चान्तरे चाङ्गना ।
इत्थमाकल्पिते मण्डले मध्यगः संजगौ वेणुना देवकीनन्दनः ॥

P. 331, notes, l. 3 *ab infra*. *Read* चपिताहितः.

Printed by Unger Brothers (Th. Grimm), Berlin, Friedrichsstrasse 24.

www.ingramcontent.com/pod-product-compliance
Lightning Source LLC
Chambersburg PA
CBHW021113270326
41929CB00009B/860
* 9 7 8 3 7 4 1 1 5 1 7 5 0 *